THE CONTRIBUTION OF ANCIENT GREECE

Western Man
An Interdisciplinary Introduction to the History of Western Civilization

THE CONTRIBUTION OF ANCIENT GREECE

Edited by

Jacqueline Strain
Hutchins School of Liberal Studies,
Sonoma State College

HOLT, RINEHART AND WINSTON, INC.
New York   Chicago   San Francisco   Atlanta   Dallas   Montreal   Toronto

Cover illustration: Athena, patron goddess of ancient Athens, ca. 350 B.C. Head of a colossal, bronze statue discovered in the Aegean Sea near Piraeus, Greece in 1959. (Boudot-Lamotte)

Art research editor: Enid Klass

Preface

"What is history for?" [History is] "for" human self-knowledge, . . . [and knowing] yourself means knowing, first, what it is to be a man; secondly, knowing what it is to be the kind of man you are; and thirdly, knowing what it is to be the man *you* are and nobody else is. Knowing yourself means knowing what you can do; and since nobody knows what he can do until he tries, the only clue to what man can do is what man has done. The value of history, then, is that it teaches us what man has done and thus what man is.

R. G. Collingwood, The Idea of History *(New York: Oxford University Press, 1957), p. 10*

For more than a decade there has been a great deal of discussion about the relation between history and the social sciences. Many historians have wanted to make use of those disciplines which are chiefly concerned with man's psychological makeup and with his physical and social environments. To date, however, there has been a wide gap between this wish and visible accomplishments, especially in the content of university and college courses. The series "Western Man" is the product of several years of experimentation with a number of ways of organizing such an interdisciplinary course in the history of Western civilization. We had tried various combinations of texts, books of readings, paperbacks, and offprints in an attempt to reach this goal, but each combination created as many pedagogical problems as it solved. What we seemed to need in order to present exciting material in manageable and teachable form was a carefully edited integration of primary historical materials, interpretative works, and the analytical tools of sociologists, anthropologists, psychologists, and other social scientists. The result—after several years of selecting, editing, and trial in the classroom—is this series of volumes.

We have constructed these volumes in the belief that the study of one's personal and cultural history is an indispensable means by which experience is organized. We considered it desirable, therefore, that students know something about the historical development of the concept of the psyche, soul, personality, or self so that they might understand the relationship between the accomplishments made by Western man and the view of the self at a given moment in history. Likewise it is important to understand the unique historical circumstances which were the source of, and gave a particular stamp to, the institutions which comprise Western society and the values which in large part structure our individual and collective behavior. The goal of this series, then, is to give the student some insight into the concept of self, social institutions, and values as they have developed in the West from ancient to modern times.

This particular purpose has made it necessary to treat the various stages in the history of Western civilization selectively. In *The Contribution of Ancient Greece,* for example, the focus is on the emergence of self-awareness and the concomitant development of natural philosophy, abstract mathematics, rhetoric, moral philosophy, epistemology, metaphysics, political theory, formal logic, and the concept of natural law. In *The Judeo-Christian Heritage,* on the other hand, emphasis is placed primarily on the development of the religious concepts and moral values of Western society. *The Imprint of Roman Institutions* provides the student with an understanding of the early stages in the evolution of Western political and legal institutions, and the transformation of classical culture in that institutional matrix. Each period in Western history emerges as one in which a lasting dimension was given to the concept of self, social institutions, or values or to any combination of these three.

We have attempted to create a series of volumes which, with the addition of a few readily available paperbacks, can be used as the full reading assignment in a course in the history of Western civilization. Individual volumes can of course be used separately and in upper level courses. It is hoped that instructors and students will find that conceptual materials introduced in each volume will be useful in considering other historical problems.

We would like to express our deep appreciation to the students, friends, editors, and spouses who gave either support or active assistance while we were at work on this project. We would also like to thank those colleagues in the Western civilization program at Stanford University who tested our materials in the classroom and gave us both criticism and suggestions.

Donald E. Buck
Cupertino, Calif.

William J. Courtenay
Madison, Wis.

David W. Savage
Worcester, Mass.

Jacqueline Strain
Rohnert Park, Calif.

Fall 1970

Contents

Maps

Introduction

This survey of the cultural development of ancient Greece begins with an analysis of the major factors which govern all human behavior. Accompanying this account are two anthropological models which provide descriptions of the world view and social organization of the pre-Homeric Greeks (those who occupied the peninsula from around 2000 B.C. until the early eighth century B.C.). Homer's *Iliad,* written in a language made possible when the phonetic alphabet was taken over from the Phoenicians, subsequently gives the first genuinely historical insight into early Greek culture. Especially important is his depiction of the religion and values of the warrior society about which he wrote. In addition, an analysis of his vocabulary reveals how the Greeks viewed the structure of the human personality at the time.

After Homer the narrative moves into a discussion of the very complex interaction between economic growth, legal and political reform, the gradual dissolution of a family- (or tribal-) based society, and the rise of a complex, individual-oriented city-state (a *polis*) during the Archaic Age (approximately 750–500 B.C.). Throughout these years of very rapid social change, self-awareness among the Greeks grew and, in part because of it, the first lyric poetry was composed. An increasing curiosity about the nature of the world in which they lived was also stimulated once the distinction had been drawn between the self and the external world and also after many supernatural explanations of natural phenomena had been discarded. Out of this curiosity sprang science (or natural philosophy) and abstract mathematics.

By the early fifth century B.C., after warding off the threat posed by the Persians, the Athenians had built a democracy, a formidable fleet, and an empire. Sparta, in the meantime, had become a militarized city-state governed by an oligarchy. Hostility between these two city-states and their allies increased throughout the fifth century B.C. In spite of this, intellectual life in Athens reached its high point. Science and abstract mathematics had been born in the sixth century B.C., and during the fifth century a rudimentary educational system was established, rhetoric was invented, the concept of human nature evolved, and creativity in the arts (architecture, sculpture, and drama) reached its peak. There can be little doubt that expansion abroad, increased prosperity, and changes in political life were largely responsible for this second stage in the evolution of Greek intellectual life.[1]

By the close of the fifth century, Athens and Sparta were at war and a general cultural crisis ensued. This is best depicted in the historical study written by the first rationalist historian, Thucydides. In the middle of this crisis Socrates began his quest for the meaning of human life in opposition to those who had sought to under-

---

[1] As in most histories of ancient Greece, the focus is fixed on Athens during the fifth century B.C. because of the magnitude of its achievements and because so little is known about internal developments in the other city-states.

stand the physical world. Like many of his contemporaries, he realized that traditional social
values no longer were adequate guides of behavior and that natural philosophy was in a blind
alley. From his despair—and hope—an intellectual revolution was begun, and it did not end
until Plato, Aristotle, the Epicureans, Stoics, and
Skeptics had developed a variety of moral philosophies, theories of knowledge, metaphysical
systems, political theories, and the concept of
natural law. The view of the human personality
structure grew ever more sophisticated, the belief in the immortality of the soul became common, and for the first time an understanding of
the mechanism of rational thought—abstraction
and proof—was reached. Science, meanwhile,
struggled out of the doldrums and again became
a creative field of endeavor (especially during
the Hellenistic Age). Unlike science, progress in
mathematics was uninterrupted until the genius
of the Greeks was almost totally exhausted in
the third century B.C. By that point in their history they had developed the first psychological
theories,

> created a literature which is still living, still
> read: laid the basis, through Pythagoras,
> Euclid, Archimedes and others, of nearly
> 2000 years of geometry: commenced, with
> Herodotus and Thucydides, history as we
> both know and practise it: created diverse
> schools of philosophy which still exercise the
> minds of men: invented political science: laid
> the foundations of biology: created geography
> and extended cosmology: developed medicine
> far beyond anything previously known to the
> ancient world. And these were but a few of
> their achievements which can be rivalled in
> this period of human history by none.[2]

[2] J. H. Plumb, "Introduction" to *The Greeks* by
Antony Andrewes (New York: Alfred A. Knopf, Inc.,
1967), p. xxi.

CHAPTER 1

THE NATURE OF MAN AND THE CHARACTER
OF THE PRIMITIVE WORLD VIEW

The natural processes of biological evolution brought into existence in man, and man alone, a new and distinctive ability: the ability to use symbols. The most important form of symbolic expression is articulate speech. Articulate speech means communication of ideas; communication means preservation—tradition—and preservation means accumulation and progress. The emergence of the faculty of symbolling has resulted in the genesis of a new order of phenomena: an extra-somatic, cultural, order. All civilizations are born of, and are perpetuated by, the use of symbols. . . .

Leslie A. White, The Science of Culture: A Study of Man and Civilization

. . . The power of seeing one thing in another, which begets our metaphors and conceptual models (the oldest of which are *myths* of nature and human life), leads also to a characteristically human thought process known as abstraction. By logical intuition we see not only what is "the same" in two widely different things, as for instance a burning candle consumed by its flame and a living body consumed by its life, but also what makes them different. As soon as the differences are clearly recognized, the common element stands out against them, and can be conceived alone as that which both of these different things exhibit. In this way the *concept*, e.g., "matter being consumed by its own activity," is abstracted; and a mind which can make such an abstraction realizes that life is not literally a burning candle but is reasonably symbolized by one.

Susanne K. Langer, Philosophical Sketches

The most fundamental feature of myth is not a special direction of thought or a special direction of human imagination. Myth is an offspring of emotion. . . . Primitive man by no means lacks the ability to grasp the empirical differences of things. But in his conception of nature and life all these differences are obliterated by a stronger feeling: the deep conviction of a fundamental and indelible *solidarity of life* that bridges over the multiplicity and variety of its single forms. He does not ascribe to himself a unique and privileged place in the scale of nature. The consanguinity of all forms of life seems to be a general presupposition of mythical thought. . . .

Ernst Cassirer, An Essay on Man

1

Though this first chapter is intended to focus specifically on the world view of primitive man, it seems necessary first to acquire some understanding of man in general—his biological uniqueness and the factors which shape his behavior. The following selections discuss the evolution of those characteristics which are unique to man, which have made man the social animal which he has always been, and which have made culture the unique possession of the species *Homo sapiens*. This and the following chapter provide basic concepts which will be useful in analyzing the materials presented throughout the book.

HOMO LOQUENS
Macdonald Critchley[1]

Among the prerogatives of *Homo sapiens* the faculty of speech is the most obvious. Other members of the animal kingdom, not excluding the higher primates, are not so endowed, however vocal may be the individuals. By contrast, it can be asserted that no race of mankind is known, however lowly, which does not possess the power of speech. Nay more, the linguistic attainments may be subtle, complex, flexible, and eloquent—even though the cultural level be primitive in the extreme. It is indeed difficult to identify among the races of man anything which can be justly termed a "primitive" tongue.

At the very outset it is important to be clear in what way the cries, utterances, calls, and song of birds and subhuman mammals can so readily be deemed as lying outside the category of language attainment. On enquiry, it is found that no one touchstone of distinction is entailed, but rather a co-ordination of factors, some

[1] Reprinted from "Man's Capacity for Language" by Macdonald Critchley in *Evolution After Darwin*, Sol Tax, ed., Vol. II: *The Evolution of Man* by permission of The University of Chicago Press. Copyright © 1960 by The University of Chicago Press.

of which may be present in this or that animal, but which do not come together in integration until the stage of *Homo sapiens* is achieved.

Doubtless the most weighty single criterion of human speech is the use of symbols. Animals betray abrupt fluctuations in their emotional state by making sounds. To this extent they may be said to utilise signs. Whether the sign be perceived and identified as such by other members of the same species is arguable. An alarm-call may act as a signal of danger, and others within earshot may take flight. This effect may be an instance of direct signaling between one bird or mammal and another. . . . [T]he animal's cry cannot strictly be looked upon either as language or as speech. At most, it is communication. . . .

[The essence of animal communication] can be said to comprise a series of signs which refer to ideas or feelings within immediate awareness. They do not and cannot apply to circumstances within past or future time. Herein lies an all-important distinction. Man's utterances entail the use of symbols or signs of signs and consequently possess the superlative advantage of applying to events in time past, present, and future and to objects *in absentia*. This endowment has been called the "time-binding" property of human language. It also possesses the merit of beginning the process of storage of experience, a process which eventually reaches fruition with the subsequent introduction of writing. . . .

One of the principal functions of speech is to co-ordinate the behaviour of the individual members of a group. [Some have] stressed the progressively elaborate communal life which synchronizes with the development of speech. Planned hunting forays, the need for securing safety by night, the indoctrination of the young—all these are among the activities of early *Homo sapiens,* and they must have been considerably assisted by the faculty of speech. The power of speech thus confers an important survival value upon its owner.

. . . Allied to this notion is the role of an increasing utilization of tools, as an immediate precursor of speech. *Homo sapiens* has often been identified not only with *Homo loquens* but also with *Homo faber.* An animal achieves its purposes by modifying its own bodily structure, that is, by making a tool out of some part of itself. Man ventures further by making use of instruments outside his own body. . . . [M]an also began to employ a "sound tool"; that is to say, he made use of differentiated sounds as an instrument of precision, in order to indicate not only emotions but also specific objects, qualities, actions, and judgments. Both language and tools are instruments which humans alone employ to achieve definite and concrete actions. "Language, like the tool, and unlike the limb, is something objective to, and independent of, the individual who uses it." . . .

We now approach a critical point in the argument. The term *Homo faber* is ambiguous, for it can be interpreted in two very different ways. It can be read as meaning either the "tool-maker" or the "tool-user." This distinction is important and is not to be glossed over. Mere tool-taking or tool-utilizing is quite consistent with anthropoid behaviour; tool-making is not. The higher apes are not infrequently to be seen making use of a convenient stick as an implement with which to draw a delicacy within reach. But deliberately to choose and to set it carefully aside, against the contingency of finding at some possible future date an edible morsel just in-

accessible, is outside the capacity of the anthropoid. To select an instrument and keep it for future use can be reckoned as analogous to fashioning a tool out of sticks or stones to attain an immediate need or desire.

When the species can do these latter things, it steps over the frontier and qualifies as *Homo sapiens.* Similarly, in the most primitive communal groups of man's ancestors, a piece of sharp stone, a stick, a shell might have been picked up and used straightway as a weapon to fell an object of prey, as a weapon of self-defence, or as a tool for decorticating a tree-trunk or skinning a beast. This sort of activity is consistent with primate behaviour, and speech acquisition is unnecessary. But when the apelike creature breaks a stick in two or pulls its out of a bush or if he puts it aside for another occasion, it is beginning this apprenticeship for qualifying as *Homo sapiens,* and here the first beginnings of speech may be detected.

With the art of knapping of flint core-tools or flake-tools or by shaving down a stake, we have the unmistakable marks of attainment of man's stature, and speech can doubtless be assumed as a concomitant. For here we have the earliest mastery over purely perceptual thinking, the dawn of conceptual thought, and release from the shackles of time-present.

. . . Closely linked with an elaborate communal life and the construction of tools, delegation of labour can also be reckoned as a factor in the ancestry of speech. Greater efficiency in hunting and in the acquisition and preparation of food for the group follows upon the use of speech and leads to the beginnings of a simple form of specialization. . . . Human labour is a new form of social activity and gives rise to a new phenomenon, articulate speech, and to a new characteristic of the mind, the conscious reflection of objective reality. . . .

[One] way of looking upon the development of human speech out of animal vocalizations is to regard speech as the utilization of symbols. The sounds emitted by animals are in the nature of signs, while man's speech is made up of symbols. Signs *indicate* things, while symbols *represent* them. Signs are announcers of events; symbols are reminders. In other words, symbols are not restricted to the confines of immediate time and place. As "substitute" signs, symbols can refer to things out of sight and outside present experience. When an ape utters a cry of hunger, it can be looked upon as perhaps making a declaration, perhaps an impera-

Wounded Bison, c. 15,000–10,000 B.C., Altamira, Spain. "The earliest unequivocal proof of the capacity of Homo sapiens for extrinsic symbolization in a visual mode is found in the cave art of the Upper Paleolithic. Here we find the graphic representation of such animals as mammoth, rhinoceros, bison, wild horse, reindeer, etc., which could not have been present in the perceptual field of the artist when the drawings were made. The location of them in most caves excludes this possibility. . . . There also seems to be evidence in the cave art of a related human capacity, that is, the ability to project graphically synthetic images of fabulous creatures, animal-like or human-like, which were not objects of ordinary perceptual experience. These belong, rather, to the world of creative imagination. . . ."—Irving Hallowell, "Personality, Culture and Society in Behavioral Evolution," in Sigmund Koch, ed., *Psychology of a Science,* Vol. 6: *Investigations of Man as Socius: Their Place in Psychology and the Social Sciences* (New York: McGraw-Hill, 1963), p. 485. (Giraudon)

tive utterance, or even an exclamation of discomfort. No ape, however, has ever uttered the word "banana," for such a word is a concrete symbol, a tool of thought which only man can employ, and he can do so in a variety of ways, irrespective of the barriers of time and space. Man can refer to a banana in past or future tense, as well as the present. Man can talk about a banana *in absentia*. No animal can do these things, the task being far beyond its system of thought and therefore of expression. Likewise no monkey can emit a word meaning "hunger," for this term would constitute, or refer to, an abstract or universal idea.

Man's unique capacity for language and other forms of symbol-making becomes significant for the historian when it is realized that man's symbolic behavior is in large part determined by his immediate social and physical environments, his personal history, and the history of his culture. The following selection is a suggestive discussion of the process by which man acquires knowledge of the world which he inhabits and how the symbolic world created from this knowledge affects his behavior. Kenneth Boulding refers to this symbolic structure as "the image," a concept similar to what some social scientists call "world view" and a few designate as "the mazeway."

THE IMAGE
Kenneth E. Boulding[2]

As I sit at my desk, I know where I am. I see before me a window; beyond that some trees; beyond that the red roofs of the campus of Stanford University; beyond

[2] Kenneth E. Boulding, *The Image* (Ann Arbor, Mich.: University of Michigan Press, 1956), pp. 3–18. Copyright 1956 by The University of Michigan Press and reprinted with their permission.

them the trees and the roof tops which mark the town of Palo Alto; beyond them the bare golden hills of the Hamilton Range. I know, however, more than I see. Behind me, although I am not looking in that direction, I know there is a window, and beyond that the little campus of the Center for the Advanced Study in the Behavioral Sciences; beyond that the Coast Range; beyond that the Pacific Ocean. Looking ahead of me again, I know that beyond the mountains that close my present horizon, there is a broad valley; beyond that a still higher range of mountains; beyond that other mountains, range upon range, until we come to the Rockies; beyond that the Great Plains and the Mississippi; beyond that the Alleghenies; beyond that the eastern seaboard; beyond that the Atlantic Ocean; beyond that is Europe; beyond that is Asia. I know, furthermore, that if I go far enough I will come back to where I am now. In other words, I have a picture of the earth as round. I visualize it as a globe. I am a little hazy on some of the details. I am not quite sure, for instance, whether Tanganyika is north or south of Nyasaland. I probably could not draw a very good map of Indonesia, but I have a fair idea where everything is located on the face of this globe. Looking further, I visualize the globe as a small speck circling around a bright star which is the sun, in the company of many other similar specks, the planets. Looking still further, I see our star the sun as a member of millions upon millions of others in the Galaxy. Looking still further, I visualize the Galaxy as one of millions upon millions of others in the universe.

I am not only located in space, I am located in time. I know that I came to California about a year ago, and I am leaving it in about three weeks. I know that I have lived in a number of different places at different times. I know that about ten years ago a great war came to an end, that about forty years ago another great war came to an end. Certain dates are meaningful: 1776, 1620, 1066. I have a picture in my mind of the formation of the earth, of the long history of geological time, of the brief history of man. The great civilizations pass before my mental screen. Many of the images are vague, but Greece follows Crete, Rome follows Assyria.

I am not only located in space and time, I am located in a field of personal relations. I not only know where and when I am, I know to some extent who I am. I am a professor at a great state university. This means that in September I shall go into a classroom and expect to find some students in it and begin to talk to them, and nobody will be surprised. I expect, what is perhaps even more agreeable, that regular salary checks will arrive from the university. I expect that when I open my mouth on certain occasions people will listen. I know, furthermore, that I am a husband and a father, that there are people who will respond to me affectionately and to whom I will respond in like manner. I know, also, that I have friends, that there are houses here, there, and everywhere into which I may go and I will be welcomed and recognized and received as a guest. I belong to many societies. There are places into which I go, and it will be recognized that I am expected to behave in a certain manner. I may sit down to worship, I may make a speech, I may listen to a concert, I may do all sorts of things.

I am not only located in space and in time and in personal relationships, I am also located in the world of nature, in a world of how things operate. I know that when I get into my car there are some things I must do to start it; some things I must do to back out of the parking lot; some things I must do to drive home. I know that if I jump off a high place I will probably hurt myself. I know that there are some things that would probably not be good for me to eat or to drink. I know certain precautions that are advisable to take to maintain good health. I know that if I lean too far backward in my chair as I sit here at my desk, I will probably fall over. I live, in other words, in a world of reasonably stable relationships, a world of "ifs" and "thens," of "if I do this, then that will happen."

Finally, I am located in the midst of a world of subtle intimations and emotions. I am sometimes elated, sometimes a little depressed, sometimes happy, sometimes sad, sometimes inspired, sometimes pedantic. I am open to subtle intimations of a presence beyond the world of space and time and sense.

What I have been talking about is knowledge. Knowledge, perhaps, is not a good word for this. Perhaps one would rather say my *Image of the world.* Knowledge has an implication of validity, of truth. What I am talking about is what I believe to be true; my subjective knowledge. It is this Image that largely governs my behavior. In about an hour I shall rise, leave my office, go to a car, drive down to my home, play with the children, have supper, perhaps read a book, go to bed. I can predict this behavior with a fair degree of accuracy because of the knowledge which I have: the knowledge that I have a home not far away, to which I am accustomed to go. The prediction, of course, may not be fulfilled. There may be an earthquake, I may have an accident with the car on the way home, I may get home to find that my family has been suddenly called away. A hundred and one things may happen. As each event occurs, however, it alters my knowledge structure or my image. And as it alters my image, I behave accordingly. *The first proposition of this work, therefore, is that behavior depends on the image.*

What, however, determines the image? This is the central question of this work. It is not a question which can be answered by it. Nevertheless, such answers as I shall give will be quite fundamental to the understanding of how both life and society really operate. One thing is clear. The image is built up as a result of all past experience of the possessor of the image. Part of the image is the history of the image itself. At one stage the image, I suppose, consists of little else than an undifferentiated blur and movement. From the moment of birth if not before, there is a constant stream of messages entering the organism from the senses. At first, these may merely be undifferentiated lights and noises. As the child grows, however, they gradually become distinguished into people and objects. He begins to perceive himself as an object in the midst of a world of objects. The conscious image has begun. In infancy the world is a house and, perhaps, a few streets or a park. As the child grows his image of the world expands. He sees himself in a town, a country, or a planet. He finds himself in an increasingly complex web of personal relationships. Every time a message reaches him his image is likely to be changed in some degree by it, and as his image is changed his behavior patterns will be changed likewise.

We must distinguish carefully between the image and the messages that reach it. The messages consist of *information* in the sense that they are structured experiences.

The meaning of a message is the change which it produces in the image.

When a message hits an image one of three things can happen. In the first place, the image may remain unaffected. If we think of the image as a rather loose structure, something like a molecule, we may imagine that the message is going straight through without hitting it. The great majority of messages is of this kind. I am receiving messages all the time, for instance, from my eyes and my ears as I sit at my desk, but these messages are ignored by me. There is, for instance, a noise of carpenters working. I know, however, that a building is being built nearby and the fact that I now hear this noise does not add to this image. Indeed, I do not hear the noise at all if I am not listening for it, as I have become so accustomed to it. If the noise stops, however, I notice it. This information changes my image of the universe. I realize that it is now five o'clock, and it is time for me to go home. The message has called my attention, as it were, to my position in time, and I have reevaluated this position. This is the second possible effect or impact of a message on an image. It may change the image in some rather regular and well-defined way that might be described as simple addition. Suppose, for instance, to revert to an earlier illustration, I look at an atlas and find out exactly the relation of Nyasaland to Tanganyika, I will have added to my knowledge, or my image; I will not, however, have very fundamentally revised it. I still picture the world much as I had pictured it before. Something that was a little vague before is now clearer.

There is, however, a third type of change of the image which might be described as a revolutionary change. Sometimes a message hits some sort of nucleus or supporting structure in the image, and the whole thing changes in a quite radical way. A spectacular instance of such a change is conversion. A man, for instance, may think himself a pretty good fellow and then may hear a preacher who convinces him that, in fact, his life is worthless and shallow, as he is at present living it. The words of the preacher cause a radical reformulation of the man's image of himself in the world, and his behavior changes accordingly. The psychologist may say, of course, that these changes are smaller than they appear, that there is a great mass of the unconscious which does not change, and that the relatively small change in behavior which so often follows intellectual conversion is a testimony to this fact. Nevertheless, the phenomenon of reorganization of the image is an important one, and it occurs to all of us and in ways that are much less spectacular than conversion.

The sudden and dramatic nature of these reorganizations is perhaps a result of the fact that our image is in itself resistant to change. When it receives messages which conflict with it, its first impulse is to reject them as in some sense untrue. Suppose, for instance, that somebody tells us something which is inconsistent with our picture of a certain person. Our first impulse is to reject the proffered information as false. As we continue to receive messages which contradict our image, however, we begin to have doubts, and then one day we receive a message which overthrows our previous image and we revise it completely. The person, for instance, whom we saw as a trusted friend is now seen to be a hypocrite and a deceiver.

Occasionally, things that we see, or read, or hear, revise our conceptions of space and time, or of relationships. I have recently read, for instance, Vasiliev's *History of the Byzantine Empire*. As a result of reading this book I have considerably revised my image of at least a thousand years of history. I had not given the matter a great deal of thought before, but I suppose if I had been questioned on my view of the period, I would have said that Rome fell in the fifth century and that it was succeeded by a little-known empire centering in Constantinople and a confused medley of tribes, invasions, and successor states. I now see that Rome did not fall, that in a sense it merely faded away, that the history of the Roman Empire and of Byzantium is continuous, and that from the time of its greatest extent the Roman Empire lost one piece after another until only Constantinople was left; and then in 1453 that went. There are books, some of them rather bad books, after which the world is never quite the same again. Veblen, for instance, was not, I think, a great social scientist, and yet he invented an undying phrase: "conspicuous consumption." After reading Veblen, one can never quite see a university campus or an elaborate house in just the same light as before. In a similar vein, David Riesman's division of humanity into inner-directed and other-directed people is no doubt open to serious criticism by the methodologists. Nevertheless, after reading Riesman one has a rather new view of the universe and one looks in one's friends and acquaintances for signs of inner-direction or other-direction.

One should perhaps add a fourth possible impact of the messages on the image. The image has a certain dimension, or quality, of certainty of uncertainty, probability or improbability, clarity or vagueness. Our image of the world is not uniformly certain, uniformly probable, or uniformly clear. Messages, therefore, may have the effect not only of adding to or of reorganizing the image. They may also have the effect of clarifying it, that is, of making something which previously was regarded as less certain more certain, or something which was previously seen in a vague way, clearer.

Messages may also have the contrary effect. They may introduce doubt or uncertainty into the image. For instance, the noise of carpenters has just stopped, but my watch tells me it is about four-thirty. This has thrown a certain amount of confusion into my mental image. I was under the impression that the carpenters stopped work at five o'clock. Here is a message which contradicts that impression. What am I to believe? Unfortunately, there are two possible ways of integrating the message into my image. I can believe that I was mistaken in thinking that the carpenters left work at five o'clock and that in fact their day ends at four-thirty. Or, I can believe that my watch is wrong. Either of these two modifications of my image gives meaning to the message. I shall not know for certain which is the right one, however, until I have an opportunity of comparing my watch with a timepiece or with some other source of time which I regard as being more reliable.

The impact of messages on the certainty of the image is of great importance in the interpretation of human behavior. Images of the future must be held with a degree of uncertainty, and as time passes and as the images become closer to the present, the messages that we receive inevitably modify them, both as to content and as to certainty.

The subjective knowledge structure or image of any individual or organization consists not only of images of "fact" but also images of "value." We shall subject the concept of a "fact" to severe scrutiny in the course of the discussion. In the meantime, however, it is clear that there is a certain difference between the image which I have of physical objects in space and time and the valuations which I put on these objects or on the events which concern them. It is clear that there is a certain difference between, shall we say, my image of Stanford University existing at a certain point in space and time, and my image of the value of Stanford University. If I say "Stanford University is in California," this is rather different from the statement "Stanford University is a good university, or is a better university than X, or a worse university than Y." The latter statements concern my image of values, and although I shall argue that the process by which we obtain an image of values is not very different from the process whereby we obtain an image of fact, there is clearly a certain difference between them.

The image of value is concerned with the *rating* of the various parts of our image of the world, according to some scale of betterness or worseness. We, all of us, possess one or more of these scales. It is what the economists call a welfare function. It does not extend over the whole universe. We do not now, for instance, generally regard Jupiter as a better planet than Saturn. Over that part of the universe which is closest to ourselves, however, we all erect these scales of valuation. Moreover, we change these scales of valuation in response to messages received much as we change our image of the world around us. It is almost certain that most people possess not merely one scale of valuation but many scales for different purposes.

For instance, we may say A is better than B for me but worse for the country, or it is better for the country but worse for the world at large. The notion of a hierarchy of scales is very important in determining the effect of messages on the scales themselves.

One of the most important propositions of this theory is that the value scales of any individual or organization are perhaps the most important single element determining the effect of the messages it receives on its image of the world. If a message is perceived that is neither good nor bad it may have little or no effect on the image. If it is perceived as bad or hostile to the image which is held, there will be resistance to accepting it. This resistance is not usually infinite. An often repeated message or a message which comes with unusual force or authority is able to penetrate the resistance and will be able to alter the image. A devout Moslem, for instance, whose whole life has been built around the observance of the precepts of the Koran will resist vigorously any message which tends to throw doubt on the authority of his sacred work. The resistance may take the form of simply ignoring the message, or it may take the form of emotive response: anger, hostility, indignation. In the same way, a "devout" psychologist will resist strongly any evidence presented in favor of extrasensory perception, because to accept it would overthrow his whole image of the universe. If the resistances are very strong, it may take very strong, or often repeated messages to penetrate them, and when they are penetrated, the effect is a realignment or reorganization of the whole knowledge structure.

On the other hand, messages which are favorable to the existing image of the world are received easily and even though they may make minor modifications of the knowledge structure, there will not be any fundamental reorganization. Such messages either will make no impact on the knowledge structure or their impact will be one of rather simple addition or accretion. Such messages may also have the effect of increasing the stability, that is to say, the resistance to unfavorable messages, which the knowledge structure or image possesses.

The stability or resistance to change of a knowledge structure also depends on its internal consistency and arrangement. There seems to be some kind of principle of minimization of internal strain at work which makes some images stable and others unstable for purely internal reasons. In the same way, some crystals or molecules are more stable than others because of the minimization of internal strain. It must be emphasized that it is not merely logical consistency which gives rise to internal cohesiveness of a knowledge structure, although this is an important element. There are important qualities of a nonlogical nature which also give rise to stability. The structure may, for instance, have certain aesthetic relationships among the parts. It may represent or justify a way of life or have certain consequences which are highly regarded in the value system, and so on. Even in mathematics, which is of all knowledge structures the one whose internal consistency is most due to logic, is not devoid of these nonlogical elements. In the acceptance of mathematical arguments by mathematicians there are important criteria of elegance, beauty, and simplicity which contribute toward the stability of these structures.

Even at the level of simple or supposedly simple sense perception we are increasingly discovering that the message which comes through the senses is itself mediated through a value system. We do not perceive our sense data raw; they are mediated through a highly learned process of interpretation and acceptance. When an object apparently increases in size on the retina of the eye, we interpret this not as an increase in size but as movement. Indeed, we only get along in the world because we consistently and persistently disbelieve the plain evidence of our senses. The stick in water is not bent; the movie is not a succession of still pictures; and so on.

What this means is that for any individual organism or organization, there are no such things as "facts." There are only messages filtered through a changeable value system. This statement may sound rather startling. It is inherent, however, in the view which I have been propounding. This does not mean, however, that the image of the world possessed by an individual is a purely private matter or that all knowledge is simply subjective knowledge, in the sense in which I have used the word. Part of our image of the world is the belief that this image is shared by other people like ourselves who also are part of our image of the world. In common daily intercourse we all behave as if we possess roughly the same image of the world. If a group of people are in a room together, their behavior clearly shows that they all think they are in the same room. It is this shared image which is "public" knowledge as opposed to "private" knowledge. It follows, however, from the argument above that if a group of people are to share the same image of the world, or to put it more exactly, if the various images of the world which they have are to be roughly identical, and if this group of

people are exposed to much the same set of messages in building up images of the world, the value systems of all individuals must be approximately the same.

The problem is made still more complicated by the fact that a group of individuals does not merely share messages which come to them from "nature." They also initiate and receive messages themselves. This is the characteristic which distinguishes man from the lower organisms—the art of conversation or discourse. The human organism is capable not only of having an image of the world, but of talking about it. This is the extraordinary gift of language. A group of dogs in a pack pursuing a stray cat clearly share an image of the world in the sense that each is aware to some degree of the situation which they are all in, and is likewise aware of his neighbors. When the chase is over, however, they do not, as far as we know, sit around and talk about it and say, "Wasn't that a fine chase?" or, "Isn't it too bad the cat got away?" or even, "Next time you ought to go that way and I'll go this way and we can corner it." It is discourse or conversation which makes the human image public in a way that the image of no lower animal can possibly be. The term "universe of discourse" has been used to describe the growth and development of common images in conversation and linguistic intercourse. There are, of course, many such universes of discourse, and although it is a little awkward to speak of many universes, the term is well enough accepted so that we may let it stay.

Where there is no universe of discourse, where the image possessed by the organism is purely private and cannot be communicated to anyone else, we say that the person is mad (to use a somewhat old-fashioned term). It must not be forgotten, however, that the discourse must be received as well as given, and that whether it is received or not depends upon the value system of the recipient. This means that insanity is defined differently from one culture to another because of these differences in value systems and that the schizophrenic of one culture may well be the shaman or the prophet of another.

Up to now I have sidestepped and I will continue to sidestep the great philosophical arguments of epistemology.[3] I have talked about the image. I have maintained that images can be public as well as private, but I have not discussed the question as to whether images are *true* and how we know whether they are true. Most epistemological systems seek some philosopher's stone by which statements may be tested in order to determine their "truth," that is, their correspondence to outside reality. I do not claim to have any such philosopher's stone, not even the touchstone of science. I have, of course, a great respect for science and scientific method—for careful observation, for planned experience, for the testing of hypotheses and for as much objectivity as semirational beings like ourselves can hope to achieve. In my theoretical system, however, the scientific method merely stands as one among many of the methods whereby images change and develop. The development of images is part of the culture or the subculture in which they are developed, and it depends upon all the elements of that culture or subculture. Science is a subculture among subcultures. It can claim to be useful. It may claim rather more dubiously to be good. It cannot claim to give validity.

In summation, then, my theory might well be called an organic theory of knowledge. Its most fundamental proposition is that knowledge is what somebody or something knows, and that without a knower, knowledge is an absurdity. Moreover, I argue that the growth of knowledge is the growth of an "organic" structure. I am not suggesting here that knowledge is simply an arrangement of neuronal circuits or brain cells, or something of that kind. On the question of the relation between the physical and chemical structure of an organism and its knowledge structure, I am quite prepared to be agnostic. It is, of course, an article of faith among physical scientists that there must be somewhere a one-to-one correspondence between the structures of the physical body and the structures of knowledge. Up to now, there is nothing like empirical proof or even very good evidence for this hypothesis. Indeed, what we know about the brain suggests that it is an extraordinarily unspecialized and, in a sense, unstructured object; and that if there is a physical and chemical structure corresponding to the knowledge structure, it must be of a kind which at present we do not understand. It may be, indeed, that the correspondence between physical structure and mental structure is something that we will never be able to determine because of a sort of "Heisenberg principle"[4] in the investigation of these matters. If the act of observation destroys the thing observed, it is

[3] Epistemology refers to theories of the nature and origin of knowledge. [Ed.]

[4] The "Heisenberg principle" or "principle of uncertainty" states that "when any measurement is made on a very small particle, the act of measuring it with instruments, which must have some size however small, disturbs the very quantity which is being measured." (Mary B. Hesse, *Science and the Human Imagination: Aspects of the History and Logic of Physical Science* (London: SCM Press Ltd., 1954), p. 75.) [Ed.]

clear that there is a fundamental obstacle to the growth of knowledge in that direction.

All these considerations, however, are not fundamental to my position. We do not have to conceive of the knowledge structure as a physico-chemical structure in order to use it in our theoretical construct. It can be inferred from the behavior of the organism just as we constantly infer the images of the world which are possessed by those around us from the messages which they transmit to us. When I say that knowledge is an organic structure, I mean that it follows principles of growth and development similar to those with which we are familiar in complex organizations and organisms. In every organism or organization there are both internal and external factors affecting growth. Growth takes place through a kind of metabolism. Even in the case of knowledge structures, we have a certain intake and output of messages. In the knowledge structure, however, there are important violations of the laws of conservation.[5] The accumulation of knowledge is not merely the difference between messages taken in and messages given out. It is not like a reservoir; it is rather an organization which grows through an active internal organizing principle much as the gene is a principle or entity organizing the growth of bodily structures. The gene, even in the physico-chemical sense, may be thought of as an inward teacher imposing its own form and "will" on the less formed matter around it. In the growth of images, also, we may suppose similar models. Knowledge grows also because of inward teachers

as well as outward messages. As every good teacher knows, the business of teaching is not that of penetrating the student's defenses with the violence or loudness of the teacher's messages. It is, rather, that of co-operating with the student's own inward teacher whereby the student's image may grow in conformity with that of his outward teacher. The existence of public knowledge depends, therefore, on certain basic similarities among men. It is literally because we are of one "blood," that is, genetic constitution, that we are able to communicate with each other. . . .

Two mental acts which Boulding described are of special importance for an understanding of human behavior—the acts of perception and conception. His discussion of what he could see outside his study window was an analysis of an act of *perception*.

The term "perception" may be used generally for mental apprehension, but in philosophy it is now normally restricted to sense perception—to the discovery, by means of the senses, of the existence and properties of the external world. Philosophers have been concerned with the analysis of perception—that is, the study of its nature and of the processes involved in it—and with its epistemological value—that is, how far, if at all, it can be regarded as a source of knowledge about the world.

As percipients we are all familiar with perception, and so the first evidence should come from reflection on our own experience. The following points may thus be made about perception.

First, it is awareness of the external world —of material objects, to use a technical term for physical objects in general, animals, plants, and human beings insofar as they are perceptible (their bodies, in fact). The main characteristics of such objects are that they are external, independent of the percipient,

<hr>

[5] These principles state that both energy and mass (or matter) in closed systems remain constant regardless of changes in form. [Ed.]

and public, meaning that many people can perceive them at once. Perception, in being the awareness of such objects, may be contrasted with imagery, bodily sensations, or having dreams.

Second, perception is, or seems to be, intuitive—immediate and normally undoubting, a direct face-to-face confrontation with the object in sight or a direct contact in touch. Nor are we normally conscious of any processes of reasoning or interpretation in it. On the rare occasions when we reason or we have doubts about what an object is, the reasoning or doubts are about the identity or character of something already perceived—for instance, a rectangular red object or something white on the hillside.

Third, perception is variable in quality and accuracy; we may fail to notice something, to see clearly, to hear distinctly, and so forth. Three types of variation may be involved: variations in attention, in what we notice or discriminate; variations in quality or distinctness (for instance, where there is nearsightedness or fog); and variations in liability to err—we may misidentify what we perceive or mistake its qualities.

Fourth, perception nevertheless normally gives us knowledge of material objects and properties. With a few fairly obvious tests, like touching and looking closely, or using the evidence of other percipients, we can establish certainty or else correct the first sight or hearing.

Fifth, perception often issues in some judgment or assertion (to others or perhaps only to oneself)—for example, "There is a green fly on the roses" or "Here's the milkman"—but it may not.[6]

[6] Reprinted with permission of the publisher from R. J. Hirst, "Perception," in *Encyclopedia of Philosophy,* Paul Edwards, editor, Volume 6, p. 79. Copyright © U.S.A. 1967 by Crowell Collier and Macmillan, Inc. Copyright © in Great Britain and under International Copyright Union 1967 by Crowell Collier and Macmillan, Inc.

Though all human beings take in their environment through the mechanism of perception, the nature of what is perceived varies greatly from one individual to the next within a culture as well as from one culture to another.

Most people presume that their way of perceiving the world is *the* way of perceiving the world. If they hang around with people like themselves, their mode of perception may never be challenged. It is at the poles (literally and figuratively) that the violent contrasts illumine our own unarticulated perceptual prejudices. Toward the North Pole, for example, live Eskimos. A typical Eskimo family consists of a father, a mother, two children, and an anthropologist. When the anthropologist goes into the igloo to study Eskimos, he learns a lot about himself. Eskimos see pictures and maps equally well from all angles. They can draw equally well on top of a table or underneath it. They have phenomenal memories. They travel without visual bearings in their white-on-white world and can sketch cartographically accurate maps of shifting shorelines. They have forty or fifty words for what we call "snow." They live in a world without linearity, a world of acoustic space. They are Eskimos. Their natural way of perceiving the world is different from our natural way of perceiving the world.

Each culture develops its own balance of the senses in response to the demands of its environment. The most generalized formulation of the theory would maintain that the individual's modes of cognition and perception are influenced by the culture he is in, the language he speaks, and the [communication] media to which he is exposed. Each culture, as it were, provides its constituents with a custom-made set of goggles. The differences in perception are a question of degree. Some cultures are close enough to each other in perceptual patterns so that the differences pass unnoticed. Other cultural groups, such as the Eskimo and the American teen-ager, are far enough away from us to provide esthetic distance.[7]

Boulding did not stop with a description of his first mental act, that of perception. He went on to analyze this process and then constructed a theory of perception ("the image"). He thus exercised a unique human ability—the capacity to form concepts.

. . . The mind forms concepts by taking a certain number of objects which have common properties, i.e., coincide in certain respects, together in thought and abstracting from their differences, so that only the similarities are retained and reflected upon, and in this way a general idea of such-and-such a class of objects is formed in consciousness. Thus the concept . . . is that idea which represents the totality of *essential* properties, i.e., the *essence* of the objects in question. . . .[8]

All human beings have the potential for thinking conceptually, but this particular mental capacity is developed only gradually during the early years of childhood. By the age of two the child learns that things have names. When he has grasped this, he has begun to generalize, to think conceptually.

Perhaps the most important and certainly one of the most distinctive effects of concepts in human behavior is their categorizing effect in relation to those objects, situations or relations to which they refer. When objects or persons, situations, etc., are subsumed under a common name, perception of and response to the various stimuli tends to be similar as determined by the meaning, i.e., by the generalization, crystallized in the name. The name functions as a category to which stimuli either belong or do not belong. Response to

stimuli in the same category tends to be similar. . . .[9]

In short, the ability to generalize telescopes the learning process. It should be clear, too, that the character of the concepts acquired by the child is, like perception, influenced by cultural values. At the same time, these concepts act as one of the determinants of personality development and personality structure.

. . . The child's concepts of objects, persons, relationships in the social world are frequently attained more by the dictums of adults than by contact with the actual stimulus situations. For example, young children, even though they have had no contact with Hindus or Turks, acquire concepts of Hindus and Turks with appropriate accompanying attitudes. The mere fact that a particular person or object is placed in one category rather than another has unmistakable psychological consequences. But as in the case of most social stimuli, the consequences are more far-reaching, because their conceptual categorization establishes the social world as the child comes to see it.

It is this acquisition of concepts which makes possible the formation of attitudes toward the many objects, persons, and situations in the child's world. Through the formation of such attitudes, the child is eventually enabled to relate himself psychologically to his environment. In early infancy the child does not clearly distinguish between his own body and its desires and the external world. This distinction cannot be made accurately until crystallized in the concepts of "me," "mine," and "I." A host of distinctions must be made—for example, the ability

[7] John M. Culkin, "A Schoolman's Guide to Marshall McLuhan," *Saturday Review*, March 18, 1967, p. 53. Reprinted by permission of *Saturday Review* and John M. Culkin.

[8] Ernst Cassirer, *Language and Myth*, trans. by Susanne K. Langer (New York: Harper & Brothers, 1946), p. 24.

[9] Muzafer Sherif, "Some Social Psychological Aspects of Conceptual Functioning," in *The Nature of Concepts, Their Inter-relation and Role in Social Structure*, Proceedings of the Stillwater Conference on the Nature of Concepts (Stillwater, Oklahoma: Oklahoma A. & M. Press, 1950), p. 65. Reprinted by permission of the College of Arts and Sciences, Oklahoma State University.

to locate events accurately in the past, present, or future—an achievement which occurs very gradually. Further conceptualization of persons and objects with the accompanying formation of appropriate attitudes leads to the formation of a personal identity having definite psychological relationships with other persons and groups. These attitudes determine the personal identity of the individual as he experiences it and constitute his ego or self. Until such conceptual distinctions are made, the child cannot begin to set up future standards or goals for his own behavior. . . . The setting of goals for the future does not begin until around the age of seventy-two months, that is, after a considerable degree of development of conceptual functioning.

This ego development—the acquisition of concepts pertaining to objects, persons and relationships in the social world and the formation of attitudes psychologically relating the individual to these stimuli—constitutes the main core of human socialization. The work of ethnologists convincingly shows that the individual becomes altruistic, individualistic, competitive, favorably inclined toward this group of people, antagonistic toward that group, as determined by the norms or concepts existing in the society of which he is a member.[10]

While all normal human beings are capable of thinking conceptually and have, since the invention of speech, engaged to some degree in abstract thought, it was the Greeks who first recognized and defined this mental process. They were able to do so because, for a number of reasons to be discussed later, they developed the kind of detachment and self-awareness needed for an examination of the mind of man and its relationship to reality. Man in the early stages of his development lacked this knowledge of the human mind, and therefore the abstractions inherent in his language were bound closely to his immediate perceptions.

Archaeologists and anthropologists now assume that the species Homo sapiens, as it exists in its present form, evolved about 35,000 B.C. From then until sometime around 8000 B.C., human life was sustained by hunting, fishing, and the gathering of wild fruits and vegetables. This means of subsistence was revolutionized, probably first in the Near East, when man began to grow grain and domesticate animals. As a result, a settled existence became possible. Between 8000 and 5500 B.C., the village-farming community came to typify the Near East; and beginning about 4000 B.C., this new way of life spread northwest to the Aegean lands, the Balkans, and then to the western fringes of Europe. As perceiving human beings, the men of this so-called Neolithic Age possessed an "image" or world view; but unfortunately it is impossible to reconstruct it because the sources on which the historian depends do not exist. The historian must therefore turn to studies done in the nineteenth and twentieth centuries of peoples in a similar stage of psychological, social, and economic development for clues as to what the world view of Neolithic men must have been. The following description of primitive man by the anthropologist Robert Redfield is based upon that kind of evidence. It begins with a discussion of the meaning of "world view."

THE PRIMITIVE WORLD VIEW
Robert Redfield[11]

. . . The "world view" of a people . . . is the way a people characteristically look outward upon the universe. . . . "World view" suggests how everything looks to a people, "the designation of the existent as a whole." . . . Included in "world view"

[10] Sherif, "Some Social Psychological Aspects of Conceptual Functioning," pp. 67–68. Reprinted by permission of the College of Arts and Sciences, Oklahoma State University.

[11] Robert Redfield, The Primitive World and Its Transformations, pp. 85–87 and 103–108. Copyright © 1953 by Cornell University. Used by permission of Cornell University Press.

may be the conceptions of what ought to be as well as of what is; and included may be the characteristic ways in which experiences are kept together or apart—the patterns of thought—and the affective [i.e., emotional] as well as the cognitive [i.e., thinking or reflective] aspect of these things also. "World view" may be used to include the forms of thought and the most comprehensive attitudes toward life. A world view can hardly be conceived without some dimension in time, some idea of past and of future; and the phrase is large enough and loose enough to evoke also the emotional "set" of a people, their disposition to be active, or contemplative, or resigned, to feel themselves distinct from what is "out there," or to identify themselves closely with the rest of the cosmos.

But if there is an emphasized meaning in the phrase "world view," I think it is in the suggestion it carries of the structure of things as man is aware of them. It is in the way we see ourselves in relation to all else. Every world view is a stage set. On that stage myself is an important character; in every world view there is an "I" from which the view is taken. On the stage are other people, toward whom the view is directed. And man, as a collective character, is upon the stage; he may speak his lines very loudly, or he may be seen as having but a minor part among other parts. On the stage also are things seen as not the same as man, though they may be seen more or less like him. To speak yet more concretely about the nature of world view is to use words and conceptions which may be appropriate to the world view that you and I know, and not to all world views; but this is a familiar kind of difficulty in the face of which we must proceed. In our own world view nature is pretty clearly seen as something different from man and as

something toward which man takes a characteristic attitude. Unseen things are there too: beings, principles, trends, and destinies. History, with nature, is part of world view. All of this has a structure, an arrangement that the world view recognizes to persist and to have consequences for man. The thing about world view that is different from culture, ethos, or national character, is that it is an arrangement of things looked out upon, things in first instance conceived of as existing. It is the way the limits or "illimits," the things to be lived with, in, or on, are characteristically known. . . .

To the attempt to conceive the kind of world view which prevailed before the rise of cities, archaeology can provide the merest hints. . . . World view, of some sort, is as old as the other things that are equally human and that developed along with world view: culture, human nature, and personality. The archaeological evidences for a confrontation of the universe in religious or magical attitudes is, of course, far richer for the food-producing peoples of the Neolithic and Bronze Ages [ca. 8000–1200 B.C.]. . . . Before there were cities, there was a view of God and nature and man himself, and an attitude of responsibility to that which man confronted.

But it is through a consideration of the world views of the primitive peoples of present times that we may venture to characterize the generic content of the precivilized world view. . . . Three things may now be said about the world view of precivilized man, and from these things something about the great transformations that have occurred in it.

In the primary condition of humanity man looked out upon a cosmos partaking at once the qualities of man, nature, and

God. That which man confronted was not three separate things but rather one thing with aspects which, in the light of distinctions that have become much sharper since, we call by these three terms. If later world views might be compared with reference to a triangle of these three conceptions—Man, Nature, God—the primary world view was one in which the triangle itself was not very apparent. This unitary character of the cosmos in the case of the folk peoples is recognized on the one hand when it is said that the world of the folk is personal. The two ideas, put together, refer to the hardly separable interpenetration of man, Nature, and God in that which the precivilized man confronted.

. . . No more need be said here of this aspect of the primary unity. It is the involvement of man and nature that calls for emphasis now. Yet this, too, is an old story in anthropological literature. [One anthropologist] saw that primitive people commonly thought of nature as indwelling spirit, "animistically." . . . [Other anthropologists] wrote of the treatment of nature as person rather than as thing. Looking at the same facts again, but now with the ancient civilizations also in mind, [certain anthropologists] chose a somewhat different formula: "For modern scientific man the phenomenal world is primarily an 'It'; for ancient—and also for primitive—man it is a 'Thou.'" [These anthropologists] want us to understand that in this primitive world view the thing confronted is unique; that it is known directly and inarticulately and without detachment; that "it is experienced as life confronting life." . . . In the primitive world view man is *in* nature already, and we cannot speak properly of man *and* nature." In this world view there can be no mysticism, because mysticism implies a prior separation of man and nature and an effort to overcome the separation. This primary indistinction of personal, natural, and sacred qualities is the first characteristic to be asserted of the world view of precivilized man.

The second assertion to be made follows from the first. It involves a reconsideration if not actually a recall of that word "confrontation." Perhaps we should substitute the word "orientation." For in the primary world view, as nature is not sharply set off as something different from man, the verb "confront" suggests too much a separation that did not so much exist. Being already in nature, man cannot exactly confront it. Primitive man does not, and precivilized man did not, so much set out to "control, or master or exploit." The attitude with which primitive people confront the Not-Man [both the physical world and invisible powers] is commonly described as one of placation or appeal or coercion. Others have recognized that this is an inadequate statement of that attitude. The rites of preliterate peoples are also "a formal period of concentrated, enjoyable association." . . . So may we not say that in the primary world view the quality of the attitude toward the Not-Man is one of mutuality? The obligation felt is to do what falls to one in maintaining a whole of which man is part.

The third assertion as to the primary world view here to be made brings us back to a conception introduced [earlier], the moral order. In the primary world view Man and Not-Man are bound together in one moral order. The universe is morally significant. It cares. What man sees out there, that which is not himself and yet in which he somehow participates, is a great drama of conduct. Whether it be the spirit-inhabited water hole and the still more important powerful sexuality of his own being, as in the case of the Arapesh, or the rain-gods and maize plants of the Zuni, or the divine authorities of the Mesopotamian invisible state, these entities and dispositions are part of a man-including moral system. The universe is spun of duty and ethical judgment. Even where the Not-Man acts not as man should act, where the supernaturals are unjust or indecent, the conduct of these gods is thought about according to the morality that prevails on earth. The universe is not an indifferent system. It is a system of moral consequence.

So we find that everywhere in the uncivilized societies—and may therefore attribute the characteristic to the precivilized societies also—when man acts practically toward nature, his actions are limited by moral considerations. The attitude of primitive man is mixed, uncertain, to our viewpoint, accustomed as we are to separate purely physical nature toward which we act as expedience suggests. Primitive man is, as I have said, at once in nature and yet acting on it, getting his living, taking from it food and shelter. But as that nature is part of the same moral system in which man and the affairs between men also find themselves, man's actions with regard to nature are limited by notions of inherent, not expediential rightness. Even the practical, little-animistic Eskimo obey many exacting food taboos. Such taboos, religious restrictions on practical activity, rituals of propitiation or personal adjustments to field or forest, abound in ethnological literature. "All economic activities, such as hunting, gathering fuel, cultivating the land, storing food, assume a relatedness to the encompassing universe." And the relatedness is moral or religious.

The difference between the world view of primitive peoples, in which the universe is seen as morally significant, and that of civilized Western peoples, in which that significance is doubted or is not conceived at all, is well brought out in some investigations that have been made as to the concept of immanent justice in the cases of American Indian children on the one hand and Swiss children on the other. "Immanent justice" is that retribution for my faults which I believe will fall upon me out of the universe, apart from the policeman or a parental spanking. If I do what I know I should not do, will I, crossing the brook, perhaps slip and fall into the water? If I believe this will happen, I live in no indifferent universe; the Not-Man cares about my moral career. Now, when significantly large samples of children were asked questions about this, the results provide some comparisons of interest to us in considering the difference between primitive and modern world view. Of the Swiss children from six to seven years of age, 86 per cent believed in immanent justice. But the older Swiss children began to cease to believe in it; of those from twelve to eighteen years of age only 39 per cent believed. With the Indian children the development was just the other way; of the younger Hopi children 71 per cent, and of the younger Navaho children, 37 per cent believed in immanent justice. Among the older children of both Indian groups (from twelve to eighteen years of age), practically all (87 per cent and 97 per cent) believed in immanent justice. The modern European child begins with a more primitive world view which he corrects to conform to the prevailing adult view. The Indian child begins with a primitive world view which grows stronger with age. Moreover, in the more isolated Navaho community, the belief in immanent justice is stronger than it is in Navaho communities closer to white influence.

If we compare the primary world view that has been sketched in these pages with that which comes to prevail in modern times, especially in the West, where science has been so influential, we may recognize one of the great transformations of the human mind. It is that transformation by which the primitive world view has been overturned. The three characteristics of that view which have been stressed in these pages have weakened or disappeared. Man comes out from the unity of the universe within which he is orientated now as something separate from nature and comes to confront nature as something with physical qualities only, upon which he may work his will. As this happens, the universe loses its moral character and becomes to him indifferent, a system uncaring of man. The existence today of ethical systems and of religions only qualifies this statement; ethics and religion struggle in one way or another to take account of a physical universe indifferent to man.

The primitive world view is given expression in myth. In other words, the thought of primitive man is essentially in the mythic mode; that of modern Western man, on the other hand, is in the scientific mode. These modes are categories of symbolic behavior devised by Ernst Cassirer (1874–1945), one of the great philosophers of the twentieth century. According to Cassirer there are two types or modes of symbolic behavior: discursive and nondiscursive. Discursive symbolism includes language and mathematics, both of which convey facts. Nondiscursive symbolism takes form in myth, ritual, religion, and customs and conveys values which are emotionally experienced. In other words,

the symbolic forms comprise not only those of "reason," that is, everyday and scientific

cognition, but all activities characteristic of the human mind and culture, including language, myth, art, and so on. They are not simply "given" and committal for every human mind or mind in general, but develop in close interaction with the several fields of cultural activity. Cassirer's work therefore is a grand panorama, a brilliant analysis of how categories of space, time, number, ego, existence, and so on, slowly emerge in interdependence with language, myth, and science.[12]

The following selection is one of Cassirer's more elaborate discussions of myth.

THE MEANING OF MYTH
Ernst Cassirer[13]

. . . Myth has, as it were, a double face. On the one hand it shows us a conceptual, on the other hand a perceptual structure. It is not a mere mass of unorganized and confused ideas; it depends upon a definite mode of perception. If myth did not *perceive* the world in a different way it could not judge or interpret it in its specific manner. We must go back to this deeper stratum of perception in order to understand the character of mythical thought. What interests us in empirical thought are the constant features of our sense experience. Here we always make a distinction between what is substantial or accidental, necessary or contingent, invariable or transient. By this discrimination we are led on to the concept of a world of physical objects endowed with fixed and determinate qualities. But all this involves

[12] Ludwig von Bertalanffy, "On the Definition of the Symbol," in *Psychology and the Symbol,* Joseph R. Royce, ed. (New York: Random House, 1965), p. 42.

[13] Ernst Cassirer, *An Essay on Man* (New Haven: Yale University Press, 1944), pp. 76–77, 79, 81–86. Reprinted by permission of Yale University Press.

an analytical process that is opposed to the fundamental structure of mythical perception and thought. The mythical world is, as it were, at a much more fluid and fluctuating stage than our theoretical world of things and properties, of substances and accidents. . . . Nature, in its empirical or scientific sense, may be defined as "the existence of things as far as it is determined by general laws." Such a "nature" does not exist for myths. The world of myth is a dramatic world—a world of actions, of forces, of conflicting powers. In every phenomenon of nature it sees the collision of these powers. Mythical perception is always impregnated with these emotional qualities. Whatever is seen or felt is surrounded by a special atmosphere —an atmosphere of joy or grief, of anguish, of excitement, of exultation or depression. Here we cannot speak of "things" as a dead or indifferent stuff. All objects are benignant or malignant, friendly or inimical, familiar or uncanny, alluring and fascinating or repellent and threatening. We can easily reconstruct this elementary form of human experience, for even in the life of the civilized man it has by no means lost its original power. If we are under the strain of a violent emotion we have still this dramatic conception of all things. They no longer wear their usual faces; they abruptly change their physiognomy; they are tinged with the specific color of our passions, of love or hate, of fear or hope. There can scarcely be a greater contrast than between this original direction of our experience and the ideal of truth that is introduced by science. . . .

Hence if we wish to account for the world of mythical perception and mythical imagination we must not begin with a criticism of both of them from the point of view of our theoretical ideals of knowledge and truth. We must take the qualities of mythical experience on their "immediate qualitativeness." For what we need here is not an explanation of mere thoughts or beliefs but an interpretation of mythical life. Myth is not a system of dogmatic creeds. It consists much more in actions than in mere images or representations. . . . Primitive man expresses his feelings and emotions not in mere abstract symbols but in a concrete and immediate way; and we must study the whole of this expression in order to become aware of the structure of myth and primitive religion. . . .

. . . The real substratum of myth is not a substratum of thought but of feeling. Myth and primitive religion are by no means entirely incoherent, they are not bereft of sense or reason. But their coherence depends much more upon unity of feeling than upon logical rules. This unity is one of the strongest and most profound impulses of primitive thought. If scientific thought wishes to describe and explain reality it is bound to use its general method, which is that of classification and systematization. Life is divided into separate provinces that are sharply distinguished from each other. The boundaries between the kingdoms of plants, of animals, of man—the differences between species, families, genera—are fundamental and ineffaceable. But the primitive mind ignores and rejects them all. Its view of life is a synthetic, not an analytical one. Life is not divided into classes and subclasses. It is felt as an unbroken continuous whole which does not admit of any clean-cut and trenchant distinctions. The limits between the different spheres are not insurmountable barriers; they are fluent and fluctuating. There is no specific difference between the various realms of life. Nothing has a definite, invariable, static shape. By a sudden metamorphosis everything may be turned into everything.

If there is any characteristic and outstanding feature of the mythical world, any law by which it is governed—it is this law of metamorphosis. Even so we can scarcely explain the instability of the mythical world by the incapacity of primitive man to grasp the empirical differences of things. In this regard the savage very often proves his superiority to the civilized man. He is susceptible to many distinctive features that escape our attention. The animal drawings and paintings that we find in the lowest stages of human culture, in paleolithic art, have often been admired for their naturalistic character. They show an astounding knowledge of all sorts of animal forms. The whole existence of primitive man depends in great part upon his gifts of observation and discrimination. If he is a hunter he must be familiar with the smallest details of animal life; he must be able to distinguish the traces of various animals. All this is scarcely in keeping with the assumption that the primitive mind, by its very nature and essence, is undifferentiated or confused, a prelogical or mystical mind.

What is characteristic of primitive mentality is not its logic but its general sentiment of life. Primitive man does not look at nature with the eyes of a naturalist who wishes to classify things in order to satisfy an intellectual curiosity. He does not approach it with merely pragmatic or technical interest. It is for him neither a mere object of knowledge nor the field of his immediate practical needs. We are in the habit of dividing our life into the two spheres of practical and theoretical activity. In this division we are prone to forget that there is a lower stratum beneath them both. Primitive man is not liable to such forgetfulness. All his thoughts and his feelings are still embedded in this lower

original stratum. His view of nature is neither merely theoretical nor merely practical; it is *sympathetic*. If we miss this point we cannot find the approach to the mythical world. The most fundamental feature of myth is not a special direction of thought or a special direction of human imagination. Myth is an offspring of emotion and its emotional background imbues all its productions with its own specific color. Primitive man by no means lacks the ability to grasp the empirical differences of things. But in his conception of nature and life all these differences are obliterated by a stronger feeling: the deep conviction of a fundamental and indelible *solidarity of life* that bridges over the multiplicity and variety of its single forms. He does not ascribe to himself a unique and privileged place in the scale of nature. The consanguinity of all forms of life seems to be a general presupposition of mythical thought. Totemistic creeds are among the most characteristic features of primitive culture.[14] The whole religious and special life of the most primitive tribes . . . is governed by totemistic con-

[14] Among many primitive peoples certain animals or plants are treated as sacred. Such an animal or plant is a totem and is believed by totemic peoples to be the carrier of the spirits of ancestors of a given kinship group (such as clan, tribe). The totem tends to enhance group solidarity and emphasize differences between various groups within a primitive society. Totemism is another manifestation of that unity of man, nature, and the supernatural which characterizes the primitive world view.

It is widely, though not universally, held that this ancestor worship underwent a transformation. The ancestral female assumed the form of a fertility goddess while the ancestral male took the form of a god who was projected into the cosmos. The cult of the hero likewise sprang from ancestor worship. The hero cult was an outgrowth of the belief that an especially powerful figure in a kinship group continued to exist after death and continued to exert his power. [Ed.]

ceptions. And even in a much more advanced stage, in the religion of highly cultivated nations, we find a very complex and elaborate system of animal worship. In totemism man does not merely regard himself as a descendant of certain animal species. A bond that is present and actual as well as genetic connects his whole physical and social existence with his totemistic ancestors. In many cases this connection is felt and expressed as identity. . . .

. . . The firm belief in the unity of life eclipses all those differences that, from our own point of view, seem to be unmistakable and ineffaceable. We need by no means assume that these differences are completely overlooked. They are not denied in an empirical sense but they are declared to be irrelevant in a religious sense. To mythical and religious feeling nature becomes one great society, the *society of life*. Man is not endowed with outstanding rank in this society. He is a part of it but he is in no respect higher than any other member. Life possesses the same religious dignity in its humblest and in its highest forms. Men and animals, animals and plants are all on the same level. In totemistic societies we find totem-plants side by side with totem-animals. And we find the same principle—that of the solidarity and unbroken unity of life—if we pass from space to time. It holds not only in the order of simultaneity but also in the order of succession. The generations of men form a unique and uninterrupted chain. The former stages of life are preserved by reincarnation. The soul of the grandparent appears in a newborn child in a rejuvenated state. Present, past, and future blend into each other without any sharp line of demarcation; the limits between the generations of man became uncertain.

The feeling of the indestructible unity of life is so strong and unshakable as to deny and to defy the fact of death. In primitive thought death is never regarded as a natural phenomenon that obeys general laws. Its occurrence is not necessary but accidental. It always depends upon individuals and fortuitous causes. It is the work of witchcraft or magic or some other personal inimical influence. . . . Death has not always been; it came into being by a particular event, by a failure of man or some accident. Many mythical tales are concerned with the origin of death. The conception that man is mortal, by his nature and essence, seems to be entirely alien to mythical and primitive religious thought. In this regard there is a striking difference between the mythical belief in immortality and all the later forms of a pure philosophical belief. If we read Plato's *Phaedo* we feel the whole effort of philosophical thought to give clear and irrefutable proof of the immortality of the human soul. In mythical thought the case is quite different. Here the burden of proof always lies on the opposite side. If anything is in need of proof it is not the fact of immortality but the fact of death. And myth and primitive religion never admit these proofs. They emphatically deny the very possibility of death. In a certain sense the whole mythical thought may be interpreted as a constant and obstinate negation of the phenomenon of death. By virtue of this conviction of the unbroken unity and continuity of life myth has to clear away this phenomenon. Primitive religion is perhaps the strongest and most energetic affirmation of life that we find in human culture. . . .

In his individual and social feeling primitive man is filled with this assurance. The life of man has no definite limits in space or time. It extends over the whole realm of nature and over the whole of man's history. . . . [One writer] has propounded the thesis that ancestor worship is to be regarded as the first source and the origin of religion. At any rate it is one of the most general religious motives. There seem to be few races in the world which do not practice, in one or another form, a sort of death cult. It is one of the highest religious duties of the survivor, after the death of a parent, to provide him with food and other necessaries needed to maintain him in the new state on which he has entered. In many cases ancestor worship appears as the all-pervading trait that characterizes and determines the whole religious and social life. . . .

. . . [T]he general religious motives that lie at the bottom of the cult of the ancestors do not depend on particular cultural or social conditions. We find them in entirely different cultural environments. If we look at classical antiquity we meet with the same motives in Roman religion —and there, too, they have marked the whole character of Roman life. . . . All this shows in a clear and unmistakable manner that we have here come to a really universal, an irreducible and essential characteristic of primitive religion. And it is impossible to understand this element in its true sense so long as we start from the presupposition that all religion originates in fear. We must seek for another and deeper source if we wish to understand the common bond that unites the phenomenon of totemism with the phenomenon of ancestor worship. It is true that the Holy, the Sacred, the Divine, always contains an element of fear: it is, at the same time, a *mysterium fascinosum* and a *mysterium tremendum*. But if we follow our general device—if we judge the mentality of primitive man by his actions as well as by his representations or creeds —we find that these actions imply a different and stronger motive. From all sides and at every moment the life of primitive man is threatened by unknown dangers. . . . But it seems as if even in the earliest and lowest stages of civilization man had found a new force by which he could resist and banish the fear of death. What he opposed to the fact of death was his confidence in the solidarity, the unbroken and indestructible unity of life. . . .

CHAPTER 2

THE BIOLOGICAL AND PSYCHOLOGICAL BASIS OF HUMAN SOCIETY AND THE NATURE OF THE PRIMITIVE COMMUNITY

. . . The characteristics of the human animal which make culture possible are the ability to learn, to communicate by a system of learned symbols, and to transmit learned behavior from generation to generation.

Clyde Kluckhohn, Mirror for Man: The Relation of Anthropology to Modern Life

. . . It is evident that the state [the socio-political community][1] is a creation of nature, and that man is by nature a political [social] animal. And he who by nature and not by mere accident is without a state, is either a bad man or above humanity. . . . The proof that the state is a creation of nature and prior to the individual is that the individual, when isolated, is not self-sufficing; and therefore he is like a part in relation to the whole. But he who is unable to live in society, or who has no need because he is sufficient for himself, must be either a beast or a god: he is no part of a state.

Aristotle, Politics

Human nature is revealed to us by immediate knowledge of our own consciousness and by mediate knowledge of the consciousness of others. This twofold method of obtaining information attests to the presence in all men of certain fundamental traits that are more or less accentuated but never absent, that give rise to true *interactions* between men, which integrate the elements which they affect into very diverse complexes. We know, in the first place, that all members of the human species live in space and time. The sense of time, cemented by memory, integrates the infinite diversity of human experiences into the unity of the person. The sense of space puts the persons so formed into a common framework of reference where, despite the total separateness of their respective *personal* lives, they can coordinate their actions and even exchange the expression of their ideas.

It is impossible to enumerate . . . all the faculties which, when combined, constitute

[1] Aristotle, more precisely, here refers to the *polis*, a community which was both a society and a political unit. It is for this reason that *polis* is rendered as sociopolitical community. For the Greeks during much of their history the social and political, or the public and the private, were not felt to be separate. Aristotle refers to man as a *zoon politikon*, an animal who lives in a polis. Man, therefore, is a social or, perhaps more accurately translated, a sociopolitical animal. [Ed.]

the human person. We can do no more than point out that the most important and effective of these on the social plane is undoubtedly the faculty of love. Sexual love, maternal love, filial love, love for one's ancestors, divine love, the generators of a basic and universal religiosity, are, in varying degree, omnipresent characteristics of human nature. Since the dawn of history, they associated men in family groups. It is difficult to say whether sexual love or maternal love—as strong among the higher animals as among men—are physical drives or moral aspirations. But they are unquestionably products of human nature.

Jacques Rueff, "Order in Nature," Diogenes, *Vol. X*

As was pointed out in Chapter 1, all men have an "image" or world view which guides their behavior. This, however, is not the only attribute they share. It has long been assumed, for example, that certain biological needs must be satisfied; and these, combined with the long period in which the human infant is helpless, make it necessary for men to live in groups. Recently it has been suggested that the need for safety—especially as it is expressed in an infant's attachment to its mother—has necessitated group-living not only for man but also for his close relatives in the animal kingdom.

THE BIOLOGICAL ROOTS OF
SOCIAL INTERDEPENDENCE
John Bowlby[2]

. . . It is not only human infants who make a strong attachment to a mother-figure. Many species of bird make it, probably all mammals, and certainly all of man's nearest relatives, the monkeys and apes. When we look at the problem in this broader perspective we get an altogether different picture of it. It was the famous Austrian observer of animal behavior, Konrad Lorenz, who gave the lead.

[2] John Bowlby, "Security and Anxiety," *The Listener,* a publication of the British Broadcasting Corporation, March 17, 1966, pp. 384–85. Reprinted by permission of John Bowlby.

Through his work with young goslings and ducklings he demonstrated that these young creatures have a strong tendency to follow a mother-figure in spite of the fact that she does not feed them. He also demonstrated that they will follow a man. Then he and others found that they would even follow a cardboard box. In fact, goslings and ducklings have an extremely strong propensity to follow the first moving thing they meet, irrespective of getting any reward.

But what about monkeys and apes, which are so much more closely related to us biologically than birds? The first thing we discover about young monkeys and apes is that they spend the whole of their infancy very close to their mothers, and for much of the time actually clinging to her. They rarely get far from mother, and when they do she pulls them back—often by catching hold of their tails. When she moves off, either she scoops the infant up to help him cling to her or else he springs to catch hold of her. Either way the two stick together, and any attempt at a forcible separation is met with violent resistance from both parties.

This clinging by young monkeys and apes has its parallel in human young. It has been known for a long time that human infants at birth are able to support their own weight by clinging and that if they are given a rod to hang on to they will cling to that. In the ordinary course of events a human baby is happy to be held and does not cling, but if you start putting him down or even if you move suddenly he at once grabs hold of you. A baby of a few months old often clings pretty hard, and he does so particularly when he is scared. So it is a mistake to suppose that clinging is absent in humans. At one time it was imagined that this clinging of newborn babies is a relic of a time when we inhabited the trees, but a far more probable explanation is that it represents the human version of the clinging to mother that is seen in every one of the other 600 primate species. And this suggests that much of what we can discover about monkey clinging is likely to be relevant to man.

In recent years there has been a good deal of research into the behaviour of young monkeys. This has shown without the least doubt that a young monkey's strong propensity to cling is there right from the start; it does not develop because he learns that if he does so he will be fed. Actually what happens is just the opposite. A newborn monkey first clings to his mother's belly; he then discovers that there is something in the vicinity of his mouth which can be sucked, and, finally, that when he sucks he comes by food. He discovers the food because he clings to his mother.

Professor Harry Harlow of Wisconsin University has carried this story some way further. First, he showed in a series of experiments that a young monkey will cling to any object, provided it is soft. It does not need to be a real monkey mother —it can be just a dummy—and it does not

need to provide food. Secondly, he showed that as he grows older the young monkey uses whatever dummy object he is familiar with as a base from which to explore the world, and as a refuge to run to when he is frightened. Here are two of Harlow's ingenious experiments.

Imagine a large, empty packing-case some six feet on each dimension. Then put in it a few things a young monkey likes to play with. Next bring a young monkey from his familiar cage and put him in the strange box. How does he behave? All he does is lie on the floor and scream, or else curl up and suck his toes. He does not explore and he does not play, and he looks a very miserable little monkey. Yet his whole behaviour is transformed if you do just one thing—put into the box the dummy to which he has been accustomed in his own cage. The dummy is simply a roll of wire with some towelling wound round it. Yet the young monkey's behaviour is transformed. First he clings to the dummy. Then he makes a brief excursion from it and quickly returns. Then he makes a longer excursion and plays with a bit of paper, and so on. So long as the dummy is there he is an active, happy-looking little monkey; once it is removed he reverts to lying curled up on the floor.

In another of Harlow's experiments the young monkey is in his cage with his familiar dummy. Then the experimenter opens the cage and puts into it a little toy animal that moves—say a toy dog that wags its head and its tail. As soon as the little monkey sees this strange object he takes fright and rushes to cling to his familiar dummy. Once there he becomes more relaxed, looks about him and begins to take an interest in the toy dog that had alarmed him so much. After a time he even ventures away from his familiar dummy to investigate the alarming object. But if his familiar dummy is not there he remains in a state of alarm and anxiety until the toy is removed.

In both these experiments the dummy seems to provide the young monkey with a sense of security. Yet the dummy provides no real protection—any more than the toy dog threatens any real danger. I expect you will see the scientific problem this poses. To have a sense of security is one thing; to be safe may be quite another. Similarly, to be frightened is one thing and to be in real danger quite another. Yet a sense of security and being safe are obviously related in some way—just as fright and being in danger are related.

I believe the solution to this problem is not too difficult—but to see it we need to get away from the artificial surroundings of western civilization. We need to think instead of the conditions in which monkeys still live in the wild—and in which humans also lived until not so very long ago. On the one hand, the creatures must obtain sufficient food—which entails moving around to explore—and, on the other hand, they must avoid becoming the prey of animals of other species. The constant presence of predators—wolves and jackals, lions and tigers, eagles and hawks—is one of the great facts of life in the wild, but it is all too easily forgotten in a laboratory or in a modern city. It almost certainly explains much that is otherwise puzzling about the social behaviour of both monkeys and men.

During the last ten years a number of studies have been made of monkeys and apes in the wild. Whatever the species, these animals always live in groups. Some are in small family parties, but the majority live in troops which have a stable

membership—usually of from a dozen to fifty animals—and a good deal of social structure. Apart from a few well-grown males of big species, the isolated monkey or ape is absolutely unknown in the wild. DeVore, a student of baboons, points out that every baboon spends the whole of his life within a few feet of another baboon. This means that the bond that ties infant monkey to mother monkey is only one element of a general tendency for monkeys always to remain close to their kin. It is clear that this behaviour has great survival value. So long as the troop sticks together, the prospects of a predator getting a meal are slim. But once an animal becomes isolated, the predator pounces. And a young animal would have no hope of escape. This means that animals who do not develop attachment behaviour are unlikely to leave any offspring while those who do develop it live to breed. In fact there is a strong selection pressure in favour of animals who show a propensity for "togetherness."

If this analysis is right, we see the behaviour of human children in a new light. Any form of behaviour that tends to develop in all members of a species and that can be shown to have survival value has traditionally been described as instinctive. The behaviour of a young human child by which he constantly maintains proximity to familiar figures I believe is of this kind. It develops just as surely (or unsurely) as eating behaviour and sexual behaviour, and it has been, until very recent times, just as important for our survival. In fact it is as natural for a child to maintain an attachment to a mother figure as it is for a young man to maintain an attachment to a young woman. Both forms of behaviour have survival value for the species—though in neither case is the individual the least interested in what its survival value may be. What each does is what it is in his nature to do. If successful he feels good; if unsuccessful, frustrated and unhappy.

Near his mother—or at least accessible to her—a child feels secure and has confidence to explore the world and its dangers. Separated from her he feels anxious —he has no familiar base to which to retreat. (And the same is true of grown-ups: at an anxious moment we all feel better for the presence of our relatives or friends.) . . . Any move that separates young children from their mothers needs scrutiny, for we are dealing here with a deep and ancient part of human nature.

Man, then, for a number or reasons is a *social* animal, and life begins for him in a social group— the family. Here he undergoes the initial stage of the socialization process—that prolonged experience in which he develops habits of conformity to social norms. Socialization begins when the human infant first experiences parental injunctions. Throughout the first years of life the child's behavior is controlled by his parents, who keep him under constant surveillance, rewarding him when he responds as directed and punishing him when he does not. Not yet capable of learning consciously, the child acquires knowledge through trial and error, errors always being the cause of punishment or the withholding of rewards.

By the time the child is about one and a half years old, parents no longer find it necessary— and usually not even possible—to have the child constantly within purview, because he can by this time move around with ease and because he has begun to learn to control himself. Self-control at this age is based on the conscious fear of punishment or hope of reward which has been learned during the period in which parental control was being exercised without his being conscious of it.

Beginning in the second year, learning takes a different form. By this time the child becomes increasingly aware of himself as distinct from others and is therefore able to put himself in the place of others. As a result of this, children continue to learn by playing roles. Quite logically one of the first roles which is imitated is that of the parents. The child not only does this in the games he plays, but he also does it both consciously and unconsciously when he adopts his parents' standards as his own. When he violates these standards, he punishes himself just as his parents would have punished him earlier. The punishment in this case, however, is guilt. Subsequently the child learns to anticipate this guilt, and the fear of its painfulness prevents transgressions. It is this process of inner control, of the interaction between internalized parental values, guilt, and anxiety, that is called conscience or the superego. As conscience is strengthened within the individual, the need for direct control by the parents diminishes. It is important to note, however, that the degree to which this inner control is developed has varied greatly throughout the history of Western man.

By the conclusion of the initial stage of the socialization process, the child has learned a number of those habits, values, and attitudes which together comprise the culture which each generation in every human society passes on to the next.

CULTURE AND VALUES
Shepard B. Clough[3]

. . . As man has striven to know himself and the world around him, he has developed two concepts to facilitate his work. One of these concepts is that people on this earth can be grouped according to their "cultures." The other is that in every culture the way of life of people is deter-

[3] Shepard B. Clough, *Basic Values of Western Civilization* (New York: Columbia University Press, 1960), pp. 1-2, 4-5, 7-8. Reprinted by permission of Columbia University Press.

mined most basically by a set of values concerning goals to be attained. . . .

. . . This concept [of culture], which comes from the field of anthropology but which has status in all the social sciences, provides a formula for dividing mankind according to patterns of behavior, encourages refinements in the analysis of group behavior, aids in the explanation of the creation, perpetuation, and change in behavioral patterns, and helps to focus attention upon dynamic factors in group behavior.

A culture may be defined succinctly as a way of life shared by members of a human society or group of societies. Within a culture people act according to recognizable patterns, that is, they have distinctive ways of responding in feeling and thought to different types of stimuli, as for example, feeling and thinking about hunger, about other people, about sex, and about nearly all other human problems.

Cultures have symbols of their beliefs, like totem poles and national flags. They have characteristic ways of communicating their ideas and learnable knowledge. They have special techniques for accomplishing such tasks as making clothing, getting and preparing food, transporting people and their belongings, and building places in which to dwell. They have distinctive ways of organizing people for living together. They have recognizable styles of architecture, music, drawing, painting, carving, and storytelling. Most characteristic of all, however, they have basic values regarding what people want to get in life, such as entry into heaven, freedom from want, the achieving of some masterpiece, control over their physical environment, and harmony in their relations with their fellow beings.

A pattern of culture is learned by individuals who compose the culture and is transmitted from generation to generation. Consequently these patterns have a high degree of continuity, but they do fluctuate in response to population changes, famines and pestilences, inventions, and borrowing from others. . . .

. . . The basic values of a culture do not refer to the biological or psychological urges of man, like hunger and sex, but to socially created, that is, man-made, desiderata. All people must eat and drink in order to sustain life and must have sexual relations to procreate life. How people eat and drink, how they produce what they eat and drink, and how much importance they give to foods and beverages in comparison with the importance they attach to such things as paintings and religion are culturally determined. We are to a very large extent the creatures of our culture. We are "culture bound" to a degree that few of us realize and most of us hesitate to admit.

Basic values reflect in essence the choices which men have made out of a wide range of possibilities as to the way they live, the wants and desires which they try to satisfy, and the ardor with which they strive to achieve recognized goals. Values may be classified according to the aspect of human activity to which they apply. Thus there are values regarding "purpose of life" and whether this purpose revolves around the individual, some social institution such as the national state, some religion, or some divinity connected with a religion. There are values which have to do with the uses of human energy and physical resources for meeting material wants and needs (economic and material values). There are values pertaining to relations among human beings (social values). There are values which have to do with organizing men for action to accomplish some goal (political values).

There are values regarding systems of knowledge which consider some types as more valid than others (epistemological values). There are values which apply to aesthetics and the achievement of things of beauty (aesthetic values). And there are values relative to making progress toward a fuller attainment of these basic values (action values).

The total galaxy of ways of doing things and looking at things, weighted according to their respective standing in a culture, constitute the value pattern of the culture. . . .

The values which the child acquires from his parents make it possible for him to interact with others in society,[4] and in this more complex environment the development of his personality is continued.

THE RELATIONSHIP BETWEEN THE INDIVIDUAL AND SOCIETY
Robert M. MacIver and Charles H. Page[5]

The emergence of the capacity for social life is an aspect of the growth of selfhood, of personality. The child does not merely imitate the social usages of adults, as a

[4] A society is any relatively permanent group of people who either work or live together and who have organized interrelationships among themselves. A social system, then, refers to interaction among individuals and groups. It should be remembered that culture, by way of contrast, is the "transmitted and created content and patterns of values, ideas, and other symbolic-meaningful systems [which act] as factors in the shaping of human behavior and the artifacts produced through behavior." (A. L. Kroeber and Talcott Parsons, "The Concepts of Culture and of Social System," *American Sociological Review*, Vol. XXIII [1958], p. 583.)

[5] Robert M. MacIver and Charles H. Page, *Society: An Introductory Analysis* (New York: Holt, Rinehart and Winston, Inc., 1949), pp. 46–49. Reprinted by permission of Holt, Rinehart and Winston, Inc.)

parrot might pick up a language. He is certainly imitative, but in the process of imitation his own social nature is gradually revealed. . . . In the earliest stages the child makes no distinction between persons and things—the mother's breast and the nipple of the bottle are equally and solely means of organic satisfaction. Similarly his first conversations are monologues in which the child talks aloud to himself, but these gradually pass into conversations in which *inter*-change of thought takes place. . . . As the child becomes a self he discovers thereby that others too are selves. As he advances toward individual autonomy he becomes truly capable of social relations. His first play seems mere imitation and he plays to and for himself, but as he gradually learns to play with others the rules of the game cease to be external restraints imposed by others and become rules for the maintenance of which he feels himself responsible.

Several American sociologists and social psychologists have for many years studied the growth of self. Selfhood develops . . . as the child in his daydreams and in his play with dolls and with other children assumes the roles of others—of parents or other heroes in his life. More than this, the process of self-emergence involves the child's continual adjustment to the behavior of other persons, a factor considered of central significance in personality formation by some sociologists. . . . The fact that the self can come to being only in society—only within the give-and-take of group life—has again been clearly established by more recent investigators.

. . . Every individual is the offspring of a social relationship, itself determined by pre-established mores. Further, every person, as man or woman, is essentially a term in a relationship. The individual is neither beginning nor end, but a link in the succession of life. This is sociological as well as biological truth. But it does not yet express the depth of our dependence as individuals on society.

For society is more than a necessary environment, more than the soil in which we are nurtured. Our relation to the social heritage is more intimate than that of the seed to the earth in which it grows. We are born to a society the processes of which determine our heredity, and parts of which become in time our internal mental equipment—not merely an external possession. The social heritage, continuously changing because of our social experiences, evokes and directs our personality. Society both liberates and limits our potentialities as individuals, not only by affording definite opportunities and stimulations, not only by placing upon us definite restraints and interferences, but also, subtly and imperceptibly, by moulding our attitudes, our beliefs, our morals, and our ideals.

Comprehension of this fundamental and dynamic interdependence of individual and social heritage permits us to appreciate the truth of Aristotle's famous phrase, that man is a social animal. . . . Without the support of the social heritage, the individual personality does not and cannot come into being. . . .

There are . . . significant resemblances between a social and an organic structure, but there also are very significant differences. Herbert Spencer,[6] though he considered society as an organism, pointed out one great difference when he said that society has no "common sensorium," no central organ of perception or of thought. For it is only *individuals* who think and

feel. We can communicate our feelings or thoughts so that others may sympathize with us or understand us. But in fact others cannot *share* our feelings or thoughts. In this sense every self is, as it were, insulated. For feelings and thoughts are *like,* not *common*; they are experienced by individuals *as individuals.* Mind communicates with mind, but they do not form a single mind. The same influences often stir a people or a crowd, but only as they pulsate in its several members. If we speak of the "mind of a group" we have no evidence and therefore no right to conceive of it as anything but the minds of its members thinking or feeling in like ways, making like responses, and being moved by *like or common* interests.

Individuals do not belong to society as the cells "belong" to the organism. The only centers of activity, of feeling, of function, of purpose that we know are individual selves. The only society we know is one in which these selves are bound together, through time and space, by the relations of each to each which they themselves create or inherit. The only experience we know is the experience of individuals. It is only in the light of their struggles, their interests, their aspirations, their hopes and their fears, that we can assign any function and any goal to society. And conversely, it is only because they are a part of society that individuals are endowed with interests, with aspirations, with goals. It is only in society that human nature can thrive. The relationship between individual and society is not one-sided: both are essential for the comprehension of either.

The failure to recognize this interdependency characterizes the writings of the individualists of past and present. Thomas Hobbes in the seventeenth century and

---

[6] Herbert Spencer (1820–1903) was a British social philosopher. [Ed.]

even John Stuart Mill[7] in the nineteenth wrote as though society were in its very nature inimical to the expression and development of individuality. And today, on the basis of the same misunderstanding of the interrelationship, we hear loud echoes of this "threat" of the social order to the individual in our legislative assemblies or read them in the polemics of those who regard every new measure of social security as a "blow" to liberty.

The same misunderstanding, though from the opposite direction, marks the views of those thinkers who . . . declare that the individual *should* be subordinated to society; or who . . . suggest that society itself has a value beyond the service which it renders to its members. Such views imply that in some mysterious way society exists in its own right and that its welfare can be realized apart from or even at the cost of the welfare of its individuals. It is sometimes assumed that it is possible, and even desirable, to sacrifice the welfare of "the individual" (not, observe, of some individuals) to that of society. When the official "philosophers" of Mussolini and Hitler spelled out Fascist and Nazi "theory"—elaborate rationalizations purporting to explain the fact and the social worth of dictatorship—it is not surprising that they found certain . . . similar doctrines congenial to their task.

Our essential theoretical understanding of individual and society, then, is the understanding of a *relationship*—a relationship involving those processes that operate between man and man and between man and group in the constantly changing pattern of social life. Society with all the traditions, the institutions, the equipment it provides is a great changeful order of social life, arising from the psychical as well as the physical needs of the individual, an order wherein human beings are born and fulfill themselves, with whatever limitations, and wherein they transmit to coming generations the requirements of living. . . .

Other social scientists have attempted to define in more detail the nature of the psychical needs of man which, as has been suggested, can only be satisfied in a social context. One anthropologist asserts that these are sociability, security, and status.

Status gives the individual his sense of importance among his fellow men in all or most situations which concern him. It is the evaluation of the individual vis-à-vis the group or groups of which he is a part. To state it differently, status is the rank or position occupied by an individual in his group or groups, with specific attitudes, duties, and privileges between him and his fellow men who acknowledge his rank or position. . . .

Security means the individual's certainty of his bonds with his fellow men. It is provided by the circle or circles of human beings to which the individual belongs. To put it in another way, security refers to a condition of the individual in which he can with certainty and without fear of repudiation claim that a number of his fellow human beings belong to him, are of the same kind as he, share with him certain aims, thought or action patterns. In time of need he can count on their moral or material support just as they can count on his. . . .

Sociability signifies the individual's enjoyment of being with his fellow men. It means the desire on the part of the individual to maintain friendliness, affability, and companionship with his fellow human beings. It

---

[7] Thomas Hobbes (1588–1679) was an outstanding political theorist. John Stuart Mill (1806–1873), one of the most talented British intellectuals of the nineteenth century, made significant contributions to logic, ethics, economics, and politics. [Ed.]

includes the individual's desire to seek contact with fellow human beings, to promote group relations, or to enter into sexuality, aggression, submission, intrigue, etc., in a social context. . . .[8]

These needs have been satisfied in many different ways throughout history. In the ancient Near East, as we have seen, the earliest societies were comprised of village-farming communities. After 4000 B.C. this type of community began to spread to the Balkans and Western Europe. This, too, came to be the way of life of the Indo-Europeans,[9] the people from whom the first Greeks descended. Only the scantiest information about the Indo-Europeans is available.

It is plausibly suggested because of their domestication of the horse that they came from the grassy plains and steppe lands between the lower Danube and the Volga rivers. By the third millenium B.C. they had some skill in agriculture and herding, worked copper and bronze, and were organized in a strongly patriarchal society. . . .[10]

Since so little is known about these people, we must, as in Chapter 1, seek further information in the anthropologist's model of a primitive or folk society—a model derived from the study of primitive peoples in the nineteenth and twentieth centuries. The following description begins with a discussion of the methods employed in the construction of such a model or, as it is also called, an ideal type.

[8] F. L. K. Hsu, *Clan, Caste and Club* (Princeton, N.J.: Van Nostrand, 1963), p. 152.

[9] Indo-European refers to a language family. The Celtic, Romance, Teutonic, and Greek languages comprise the West Indo-European family; the Baltic, Slavonic, Iranic, and Indic the East Indo-European. Indo-European was probably spoken late in the fourth millennium B.C. The first written documents in daughter languages date from the second millennium B.C. in Asia Minor and India.

[10] Carl Roebuck, *The World of Ancient Times* (New York: Charles Scribner's Sons, 1966), pp. 75–76.

THE FOLK SOCIETY
Robert Redfield[11]

. . . All societies are alike in some respects, and each differs from the others in other respects; the further assumption made here is that folk [or primitive] societies have certain features in common which enable us to think of them as a type —a type which contrasts with the society of the modern city.

This type is ideal, a mental construction. No known society precisely corresponds with it, but the societies which have been the chief interest of the anthropologist most closely approximate it. The construction of the type depends, indeed, upon special knowledge of tribal and peasant groups. The ideal folk society could be defined through assembling, in the imagination, the characters which are logically opposite those which are to be found in the modern city, only if we had first some knowledge of non-urban peoples to permit us to determine what, indeed, are the characteristic features of modern city living. The complete procedure requires us to gain acquaintance with many folk societies in many parts of the world and to set down in words general enough to describe most of them those characteristics which they have in common with each other and which the modern city does not have.

In short, we move from folk society to folk society, asking ourselves what it is about them that makes them like each other and different from the modern city. So we assemble the elements of the ideal

[11] Reprinted from "The Folk Society" by Robert Redfield in *American Journal of Sociology*, LII (1947), pp. 293–306, by permission of The University of Chicago Press.

type. The more elements we add, the less will any one real society correspond to it. As the type is constructed, real societies may be arranged in an order of degree of resemblance to it. The conception develops that any one real society is more or less "folk." But the more elements we add, the less possible it becomes to arrange real societies in a single order of degree of resemblance to the type, because one of two societies will be found to resemble the ideal type strongly in one character and weakly in another, while in the next society strong resemblance will lie in the latter character and not in the former. This situation, however, is an advantage, for it enables us to ask and perhaps answer questions, first, as to whether certain characters tend to be found together in most societies, and then, if certain of them do, why.

Anyone attempting to describe the ideal folk society must take account of and in large degree include certain characterizations which have been made of many students, each of whom has been attentive to some but not to all aspects of the contrast between folk and modern urban society. Certain students have derived the characterization from examination of a number of folk societies and have generalized upon them in the light of contrast provided by modern urban society; the procedure defined above and followed by the writer. . . .

In the work of still other students there is apparent no detailed comparison of folk with urbanized societies or of early society with later; rather, by inspection of our own society in general, contrasting aspects of all society are recognized and named. This procedure is perhaps never followed in the unqualified manner just described, for in the instances about to be mentioned there is evidence that folk or ancient so-

ciety has been compared with modern urbanized society. Nevertheless, the emphasis placed by men of this group is upon characteristics which, contrasting logically, in real fact coexist in every society and help to make it up. Here belongs [the] contrast between *Gemeinschaft* and *Gesellschaft*,[12] or that aspect of society which appears in the relations that develop without the deliberate intention of anyone out of the mere fact that men live together, as contrasted with that aspect of society which appears in the relations entered into deliberately by independent individuals through agreement to achieve certain recognized ends. . . .

It may be asked how closely the constructed type arrived at by any one investigator who follows the procedure sketched above will resemble that reached by another doing the same. It may be supposed that to the extent to which the real societies examined by the one investigator constitute a sample of the range and variety of societies similar to the sample constituted by the societies examined by the other, and to the extent that the general conceptions tentatively held by the one are similar to those held by the other, the results will be (except as modified by other factors) the same. For the purposes of understanding which are served by the method of the constructed type, however, it is not necessary to consider the question. The type is an imagined entity, created only because through it we may hope to understand reality. Its function is to suggest aspects of real societies which deserve study, and especially to suggest hy-

[12] *Gemeinschaft* refers to a type of society which is communal, corporate, and traditional in nature. *Gesellschaft* designates a type of society that is characterized by a high degree of individualism, impersonalism, and contractual relationships. [Ed.]

potheses as to what, under certain defined conditions, may be generally true about society. Any ideal type will do, although it is safe to assert that that ideal construction has most heuristic value which depends on close and considered knowledge of real folk societies and which is guided by an effective scientific imagination— whatever that may be. . . .

The folk society is an isolated society. Probably there is no real society whose members are in complete ignorance of the existence of people other than themselves . . . Nevertheless, the folk societies we know are made up of people who have little communication with outsiders, and we may conceive of the ideal folk society as composed of persons having communication with no outsider.

This isolation is one half of a whole of which the other half is intimate communication among the members of the society. A group of recent castaways is a small and isolated society, but it is not a folk society; and if the castaways have come from different ships and different societies, there will have been no previous intimate communication among them, and the society will not be composed of people who are much alike.

May the isolation of the folk society be identified with the physical immobility of its members? In building this ideal type, we may conceive of the members of the society as remaining always within the small territory they occupy. There are some primitive peoples who have dwelt from time immemorial in the same small valley, and who rarely leave it. . . .

It is possible to conceive of the members of such a society as moving about physically without communicating with members of other groups than their own. . . . This does not result, however, in much

intimate communication between those traveling villagers and other peoples. The gypsies have moved about among the various peoples of the earth for generations, and yet they retain many of the characteristics of a folk society.

Through books the civilized people communicate with the minds of other people and other times, and an aspect of the isolation of the folk society is the absence of books. The folk communicate only by word of mouth; therefore the communication upon which understanding is built is only that which takes place among neighbors, within the little society itself. The folk has no access to the thought and experience of the past, whether of other peoples or of their own ancestors, such as books provide. Therefore, oral tradition has no check or competitor. Knowledge of what has gone before reaches no further back than memory and speech between old and young can make it go; behind "the time of our grandfathers" all is legendary and vague. With no form of belief established by written record, there can be no historical sense, such as civilized people have, no theology, and no basis for science in recorded experiment. The only form of accumulation of experience, except the tools and other enduring articles of manufacture, is the increase of wisdom which comes as the individual lives longer; therefore the old, knowing more than the young can know until they too have lived that long, have prestige and authority.

The people who make up a folk society are much alike. Having lived in long intimacy with one another, and with no others, they have come to form a single biological type. The somatic homogeneity of local, inbred populations has been noted and studied. Since the people communicate with one another and with no others, one man's learned ways of doing and thinking are the same as another's. Another way of putting this is to say that in the ideal folk society, what one man knows and believes is the same as what all men know and believe. Habits are the same as customs. In real fact, of course, the differences among individuals in a primitive group and the different chances of experience prevent this ideal state of things from coming about. Nevertheless, it is near enough to the truth for the student of a real folk society to report it fairly well by learning what goes on in the minds of a few of its members, and a primitive group has been presented, although sketchily, as learned about from a single member. The similarity among the members is found also as one generation is compared with its successor. Old people find young people doing, as they grow up, what the old people did at the same age, and what they have come to think right and proper. This is another way of saying that in such a society there is little change.

The members of the folk society have a strong sense of belonging together. The group which an outsider might recognize as composed of similar persons different from members of other groups is also the group of people who see their own resemblances and feel correspondingly united. Communicating intimately with each other, each has a strong claim on the sympathies of the others. Moreover, against such knowledge as they have of societies other than their own, they emphasize their own mutual likeness and value themselves as compared with others. They say of themselves "we" as against all others, who are "they."

Thus we may characterize the folk society as small, isolated, nonliterate, and homogeneous, with a strong sense of group solidarity. Are we not soon to acknowledge the simplicity of the technology of the ideal folk society? Something should certainly be said about the tools and toolmaking of this generalized primitive group, but it is not easy to assign a meaning to "simple," in connection with technology which will do justice to the facts as known from the real folk societies. . . . Some negative statements appear to be safe: secondary and tertiary tools—tools to make tools—are relatively few as compared with primary tools; there is no making of artifacts by multiple, rapid, machine manufacture; there is little or no use of natural power.

There is not much division of labor in the folk society: what one person does is what another does. In the ideal folk society all the tools and ways of production are shared by everybody. The "everybody" must mean "every adult man" or "every adult woman," for the obvious exception of the homogeneity of the folk society lies in the differences between what men do and know and what women do and know. These differences are clear and unexceptional (as compared with our modern urban society where they are less so). . . . All men share the same interests and have, in general, the same experience of life.

We may conceive, also, of the ideal folk society as a group economically independent of all others: the people produce what they consume and consume what they produce. Few, if any, real societies are completely in this situation. . . .

The foregoing characterizations amount, roughly, to saying that the folk society is a little world off by itself, a world in which the recurrent problems of life are met by all its members in much the same way.

This statement, while correct enough, fails to emphasize an important, perhaps the important, aspect of the folk society. The ways in which the members of the society meet the recurrent problems of life are conventionalized ways; they are the results of long intercommunication within the group in the face of these problems; and these conventionalized ways have become interrelated within one another so that they constitute a coherent and self-consistent system. Such a system is what we mean in saying that the folk society is characterized by "a culture." A culture is an organization or integration of conventional understandings. It is, as well, the acts and the objects, in so far as they represent the type characteristic of that society, which express and maintain these understandings. In the folk society this integrated whole, this system, provides for all the recurrent needs of the individual from birth to death and of the society through the seasons and the years. The society is to be described, and distinguished from others, largely by presenting this system.

This is not the same as saying, as was said early in this paper, that in the folk society what one man does is the same as what another man does. What one man does in a mob is the same as what another man does, but a mob is not a folk society. It is, so far as culture is concerned, its very antithesis. The members of a mob (which is a kind of "mass") each do the same thing, it is true, but it is a very immediate and particular thing, and it is done without much reference to tradition. It does not depend upon and express a great many conventional understandings related to one another. A mob has no culture. The folk society exhibits culture to the greatest conceivable degree. A mob is an aggregation of people doing the same

simple thing simultaneously. A folk society is an organization of people doing many different things successively as well as simultaneously. The members of a mob act with reference to the same object of attention. The members of a folk society are guided in acting by previously established comprehensive and interdependent conventional understandings; at any one time they do many different things, which are complexly related to one another to express collective sentiments and conceptions. When the turn comes for the boy to do what a man does, he does what a man does; thus, though in the end the experiences of all individuals of the same sex are alike, the activities of the society, seen at a moment of time, are diverse, while interdependent and consistent. . . .

We may say, then, that in the folk society conventional behavior is strongly patterned: it tends to conform to a type or a norm. These patterns are interrelated in thought and in action with one another, so that one tends to evoke others and to be consistent with the others. . . . We may still further say that the patterns of what people think should be done are closely consistent with what they believe is done, and that there is one way, or a very few conventional ways, in which everybody has some understanding and some share, of meeting each need that arises. The culture of a folk society is, therefore, one of those wholes which is greater than its parts. Gaining a livelihood takes support from religion, and the relations of men to men are justified in the conceptions held of the supernatural world or in some other aspect of the culture. Life, for the member of the folk society, is not one activity and then another and different one; it is one large activity out of which one part may not be separated without affecting the rest.

. . . The folk society exists not so much in the exchange of useful functions as in common understandings as to the ends given. The ends are not stated as matters of doctrine, but are implied by the many acts which make up the living that goes on in the society. Therefore, the morale of a folk society—its power to act consistently over periods of time and to meet crises effectively—is not dependent upon discipline exerted by force or upon devotion to some single principle of action but to the concurrence and consistency of many or all of the actions and conceptions which make up the whole round of life. In the trite phrase, the folk society is a "design for living."

What is done in the ideal folk society is done not because somebody or some people decided, at once, that it should be done, but because it seems "necessarily" to flow from the very nature of things. There is, moreover, no disposition to reflect upon traditional acts and consider them objectively and critically. In short, behavior in the folk society is traditional, spontaneous, and uncritical. In any real folk society, of course, many things are done as a result of decision as to that particular action, but as to that class of actions tradition is the sufficient authority. . . .

The folkways are the ways that grow up out of long and intimate association of men with each other; in the society of our conception all the ways are folkways. Men act with reference to each other by understandings which are tacit and traditional. There are no formal contracts or other agreements. The rights and obligations of the individual come about not by special arrangement; they are, chiefly, aspects of the position of the individual as a person of one sex or the other, one age-group or another, one occupational group or another, and as one occupying just that position in a system of relationships which are traditional in the society. The individual's status is thus in large part fixed at birth; it changes as he lives, but it changes in ways which were "foreordained" by the nature of his particular society. The institutions of the folk society are . . . not of the sort that is created deliberately for special purposes. . . . So, too, law is made up of the traditional conceptions of rights and obligations and the customary procedures whereby these rights and obligations are assured; legislation has no part in it.

If legislation has no part in the law of the ideal folk society, neither has codification, still less jurisprudence. . . . In the ideal folk society there is no objectivity and no systematization of knowledge as guided by what seems to be its "internal" order. The member of this mentally constructed society does not stand off from his customary conduct and subject it to scrutiny apart from its meaning for him as that meaning is defined in culture. Nor is there any habitual exercise of classification, experiment, and abstraction for its own sake, least of all for the sake of intellectual ends. There is common practical knowledge, but there is no science.

Behavior in the folk society is highly conventional, custom fixes the rights and duties of individuals, and knowledge is not critically examined or objectively and systematically formulated; but it must not be supposed that primitive man is a sort of automaton in which custom is the mainspring. It would be as mistaken to think of primitive man as strongly aware that he is constrained by custom. Within the limits set by custom there is invitation to excel in performance. There is lively competition, a sense of opportunity, and a feeling that what the culture moves one to do is well worth doing. "There is no drabness in such a life. It has about it all the allurements of personal experience, very much one's own, of competitive skill, of things well done." The interrelations and high degree of consistency among the elements of custom which are presented to the individual declare to him the importance of making his endeavors in the directions indicated by tradition. The culture sets goals which stimulate action by giving great meaning to it.

It has been said that the folk society is small and that its members have lived in long and intimate association with one another. It has also been said that in such societies there is little critical or abstract thinking. These characteristics are related to yet another characteristic of the folk society: behavior is personal, not impersonal. A "person" may be defined as that social object which I feel to respond to situations as I do, with all the sentiments and interests which I feel to be my own; a person is myself in another form, his qualities and values are inherent within him, and his significance for me is not merely one of utility. A "thing," on the other hand, is a social object which has no claim upon my sympathies, which responds to me, as I conceive it, mechanically; its value for me exists in so far as it serves my end. In the folk society all human beings admitted to the society are treated as persons; one does not deal impersonally ("thing-fashion") with any other participant in the little world of that society. Moreover, in the folk society much besides human beings is treated personally. The pattern of behavior which is first suggested by the inner experience of the individual—his wishes, fears, sensitivenesses, and interests of all sorts—is projected into all objects with which he comes into contact. Thus nature, too, is treated personally: the ele-

ments, the features of the landscape, the animals, and especially anything in the environment which by its appearance or behavior suggests that it has the attributes of mankind—to all these are attributed qualities of the human person.

In short, the personal and intimate life of the child in the family is extended, in the folk society, into the social world of the adult and even into inanimate objects. It is not merely that relations in such a society are personal; it is also that they are familial. The first contacts made as the infant becomes a person are with other persons; moreover, each of these first persons, he comes to learn, has a particular kind of relation to him which is associated with that one's genealogical position. The individual finds himself fixed within a constellation of familial relationships. The kinship connections provide a pattern in terms of which, in the ideal folk society, all personal relations are conventionalized and categorized. All relations are personal. But relations are not, in content of specific behavior, the same for everyone. As a mother is different from a father, and a grandson from a nephew, so are these classes of personal relationship, originating in genealogical connection, extended outward into all relationships, whatever. In this sense, the folk society is a familial society. . . . It is true that the fact that men are neighbors contributes to their sense of belonging together. But the point to be emphasized in understanding the folk society is that whether mere contiguity or relationship as brother or as son is the circumstance uniting men into the society, the result is a group of people among whom prevail the personal and categorized relationships that characterize families as we know them, and in which the patterns of kinship tend to be extended outward from the group of genealogically connected individuals into the whole society. The kin are the type persons for all experience.

This general conception may be resolved into component or related conceptions. In the folk society family relationships are clearly distinguished from one another. Very special sorts of behavior may be expected by a mother's brother of his sister's son, and this behavior will be different from that expected by a father's brother of his brother's son. . . . The tendency to extend kinship outward takes many special forms. In many primitive societies kinship terms and kinship behavior (in reduced degree) are extended to persons not known to be genealogically related at all, but who are nevertheless regarded as kin. . . . In the folk society groupings which do not arise out of genealogical connection are few, and those that do exist tend to take on the attributes of kinship. Ritual kinship is common in primitive and peasant societies in the forms of blood brotherhood, godparental relationships, and other ceremonial sponsorships. These multiply kinship connections; in these cases the particular individuals to be united depend upon choice. Furthermore, there is frequently a recognizedly fictitious or metaphorical use of kinship terms to designate more casual relationships, as between host and guest or between worshipper and deity.

The real primitive and peasant societies differ very greatly as to the forms assumed by kinship. Nevertheless, it is possible to recognize two main types. In one of these the connection between husband and wife is emphasized, while neither one of the lineages, matrilineal or patrilineal, is singled out as contrasted with the other. In such a folk society the individual parental family is the social unit, and connections with relatives outside this family are of

secondary importance. Such family organization is common where the population is small, the means of livelihood are by precarious collection of wild food, and larger units cannot permanently remain together because the natural resources will not allow it. But where a somewhat larger population remains together, either in a village or in a migratory band, there often, although by no means always, is found an emphasis upon one line of consanguine connection rather than the other with subordination of the conjugal connection. There results a segmentation of the society into equivalent kinship units. These may take the form of extended domestic groups or joint families (as in China) or may include many households of persons related in part through recognized genealogical connection and in part through the sharing of the same name or other symbolic designation, in the latter case we speak of the groups as clans. Even in societies where the individual parental family is an independent economic unit, as in the case of the eastern Eskimo, husband and wife never become a new social and economic unit with the completeness that is characteristic of our own society. When a marriage in primitive society comes to an end, the kinsmen of the dead spouse assert upon his property a claim they have never given up. On the whole, we may think of the family among folk peoples as made up of persons consanguinely connected. Marriage is, in comparison with what we in our society directly experience, an incident in the life of the individual who is born, brought up, and dies with his blood kinsmen. In such a society romantic love can hardly be elevated to a major principle.

In so far as the consanguine lines are well defined (and in some cases both lines may be of importance to the individual) the folk society may be thought of as composed of families rather than of individuals. It is the familial groups that act and are acted upon. There is strong solidarity within the kinship group, and the individual is responsible to all his kin as they are responsible to him. "The clan is a natural mutual aid society. . . . A member belongs to the clan, he is not his own; if he is wrong, they will right him; if he does wrong, the responsibility is shared by them." Thus, in folk societies wherein the tendency to maintain consanguine connection has resulted in joint families or clans, it is usual to find that injuries done by an individual are regarded as injuries against his kinship group, and the group takes the steps to right the wrong. The step may be revenge regulated by custom or a property settlement. A considerable part of primitive law exists in the regulation of claims by one body of kin against another. The fact that the folk society is an organization of families rather than an aggregation of individuals is further expressed in many of those forms of marriage in which a certain kind of relative is the approved spouse. The customs by which in many primitive societies a man is expected to marry his deceased brother's widow or a woman to marry her deceased sister's husband express the view of marriage as an undertaking between kinship groups. One of the spouses having failed by death, the undertaking is to be carried on by some other representative of the family group. Indeed, in the arrangements for marriage—the selection of spouses by their relatives, in brideprice, dowry, and in many forms of familial negotiations leading to a marriage—the nature of marriage as a connubial form of social relations between kindreds finds expression.

It has been said in foregoing paragraphs that behavior in the folk society is traditional, spontaneous, and uncritical, that what one man does is much the same as what another man does, and that the patterns of conduct are clear and remain constant throughout the generations. It has also been suggested that the congruence of all parts of conventional behavior and social institutions with each other contributes to the sense of rightness which the member of the folk society feels to inhere in his traditional ways of action. . . . The ways of life are folkways; furthermore, the folkways tend to be also mores— ways of doing or thinking to which attach notions of moral worth. The value of every traditional act or object or institution is, thus, something which the members of the society are not disposed to call into question; and should the value be called into question, the doing so is resented. This characteristic of the folk society may be briefly referred to by saying that it is a sacred society. In the folk society one may not, without calling into effect negative social sanctions, challenge as valueless what has come to be traditional in that society.

Presumably, the sacredness of social objects has its source, in part, at least, in the mere fact of habituation; probably the individual organism becomes early adjusted to certain habits, motor and mental, and to certain associations between one activity and another or between certain sense experiences and certain activities, and it is almost physiologically uncomfortable to change or even to entertain the idea of change. There arises "a feeling of impropriety of certain forms, of a particular social or religious value, or a superstitious fear of change." Probably the sacredness of social objects in the folk is related also to the fact that in such well-organized cultures acts and objects suggest the traditions, beliefs, and conceptions which all share. There is reason to suppose that when what is traditionally done becomes less meaningful because people no longer know what the acts stand for, life becomes more secular. In the repetitious character of conventional action (aside from technical action) we have ritual; in its expressive character we have ceremony; in the folk society ritual tends also to be ceremonious, and ritual-ceremony tends to be sacred, not secular.

The sacredness of social objects is apparent in the ways in which, in the folk society, such an object is hedged around with restraints and protections that keep it away from the commonplace and the matter-of-fact. In the sacred there is alternatively, or in combination, holiness and dangerousness. . . .

In the folk society this disposition to regard objects as sacred extends, characteristically, even into the subsistence activities and into the foodstuffs of the people. Often the foodstuffs are personified as well as sacred. . . . In the folk society, ideally conceived, nothing is solely a means to an immediate practical end. All activities, even the means of production, are ends in themselves, activities expressive of the ultimate values of the society.

This characterization of the ideal folk society could be greatly extended. Various of the elements that make up the conception could be differently combined with one another, and this point or that could be developed or further emphasized and its relations shown to other aspects of the conception. For example, it might be pointed out that where there is little or no systematic reflective thinking the customary solutions to problems of practical action only imperfectly take the form of really effective and understood control of the means appropriate to accomplish the desired end, and that, instead, they tend to express the states of mind of the individuals who want the end brought about and fear that it may not be. We say this briefly in declaring that the folk society is characterized by much magic, for we may understand "magic" to refer to action with regard to an end—to instrumental action—but only to such instrumental action as does not effectively bring about that end, or is not really understood in so far as it does, and which is expressive of the way the doer thinks and feels rather than adapted to accomplishing the end. "Magic is based on specific experience of emotional states . . . in which the truth is revealed not by reason but by the play of emotions upon the human organism. . . . [M]agic is founded on the belief that hope cannot fail nor desire deceive." In the folk society effective technical action is much mixed with magical activity. What is done tends to take the form of a little drama; it is a picture of what is desired.

The nature of the folk society could, indeed, be restated in the form of a description of the folk mind. This description would be largely a repetition of what has been written in foregoing pages, except that now the emphasis would be upon the characteristic mental activity of members of the folk society, rather than upon customs and institutions. The man of the folk society tends to make mental associations which are personal and emotional, rather than abstractly categoric or defined in terms of cause and effect. ". . . Primitive man views every action not only as adapted to its main object, every thought related to its main end, as we should perceive them, but . . . he associates them with other ideas, often of a religious or at least a symbolic nature. Thus he gives to them a higher significance than they seem to us to deserve." A very similar statement of this kind of thinking has been expressed in connection with the thinking of medieval man; the description would apply as well to man in the folk society:

> From the causal point of view, symbolism appears as a sort of shortcut of thought. Instead of looking for the relation between two things by following the hidden detours of their causal connections, thought makes a leap and discovers their relation, not in a connection of cause or effects, but in a connection of signification or finality. Such a connection will at once appear convincing, provided only that the two things have an essential quality in common which can be referred to a general value. . . . Symbolic assimilation founded on common properties presupposes the idea that these properties are essential to things. The vision of white and red roses blooming among thorns at once calls up a symbolic association in the medieval mind: for example, that of virgins and martyrs, shining with glory, in the midst of their persecutors. The assimilation is produced because the attributes are the same: the beauty, the tenderness, the purity, the colours of the roses are also those of the virgins, their red color that of the blood of the martyrs. But this similarity will only have a mystic meaning if the middle-term connecting the two terms of the symbolic concept expresses an essentiality common to both; in other words, if redness and whiteness are something more than names for physical differences based on quantity, if they are conceived of as essences, as realities. The mind of the savage, of the child, and of the poet never sees them otherwise.[13]

[13] J. Huizinga, *The Waning of the Middle Ages* (London: Arnold & Co., 1924), pp. 184–185.

The tendency to treat nature personally has recognition in the literature as the "animistic" or "anthropomorphic" quality of primitive thinking, and the contrast between the means-ends pattern of thought more characteristic of modern urban man and the personal thought of primitive man has been specially investigated.

In the foregoing account no mention has been made of the absence of economic behavior characteristic of the market in the folk society. Within the ideal folk society members are bound by religious and kinship ties, and there is no place for the motive of commercial gain. There is no money and nothing is measured by any such common denominator of value. The distribution of goods and services tends to be an aspect of the conventional and personal relationships of status which make up the structure of the society: goods are exchanged as expressions of good will and, in large part, as incidents of ceremonial and ritual activities. "On the whole, then, the compulsion to work, to save, and to expend is given not so much by a rational appreciation of the [material] benefits to be received as by the desire for social recognition, through such behavior."

The conception sketched here takes on meaning if the folk society is seen in contrast to the modern city. The vast, complicated, and rapidly changing world in which the urbanite and even the urbanized country-dweller live today is enormously different from the small, inward-facing folk society, with its well-integrated and little-changing moral and religious conceptions. At one time all men lived in these little folk societies. For many thousands of years men must have lived so; urbanized life began only very recently, as the long history of man on earth is considered, and the extreme development of a secularized and swift-changing world society is only a few generations old.

Indo-European society, of which the above must be considered but an approximate description, more than likely began to lose its primitive character when climate, overpopulation, or a food shortage forced migration to the south and east in the third millennium B.C. The first Greek-speaking Indo-Europeans invaded the Greek peninsula around 2000 B.C. By the time of their arrival numerous changes had taken place in the lands bordering the Mediterranean. For a number of reasons, about which there is little agreement among scholars, some of the farm villages, a few of which had been established as early as 8000 B.C., began to expand into cities in the fourth millennium B.C. These cities, unlike villages, had a heterogeneous population. Perhaps more importantly, they included a group of inhabitants who did not gain their livelihood directly from farming. This group had the ability to read and write and was supplied goods and services by merchants, artisans, and servants, all of whom together made up the population of a city. The process of urbanization, which spread from Mesopotamia to Egypt and the islands of the Aegean, was of the utmost importance for the future development of Western civilization. As one scholar has put it:

Civilization, as the word implies, comes with the rise of cities. It is essentially a product of city life, and spreads from urban centers to the country. As long as a population lives directly on the land, each family finds or raises its own food, builds its own domicile, and perhaps hands it on from one generation to another; public decisions are made by direct discussion, vote, declaration, command, or whatever the practice; goods are exchanged directly between interested parties. Custom usually suffices to determine people's duties and rights, and judges rely on it in deciding cases of wrong-doing or conflicts of interest. But when people cluster together in cities this ancient pattern breaks down. They can no longer hunt or raise their own food; the countryside has to supply it, day by day. They cannot offer goods in exchange for it, because they have nothing to offer that the food raisers or gatherers require day by day, so a medium of exchange becomes necessary —money. With money, commerce becomes too complicated to be conducted on a basis of customary practices; besides, people in cities are often gathered from different communities, with various customs. This makes statute law necessary. An important *cultural* contribution of civic life is the close contact of people with each other, which steps up the exchange of ideas, the chance for each individual to learn things beyond his experience and ancestral background, the ferment of novelty contrasting with the quiet repetitiousness of country life. There is a change in mentality. Also, the city provides a goal of travel; communication and movement assume a new importance. Everything tends toward the historic phenomenon we call "civilization"—the practical organization of life, public and private.[14]

As life became more complex in Egypt and the Near East, distinct social classes emerged and forms of government closely interwoven with religion were developed. The Near East for more than two millennia witnessed the establishment and destruction of a series of empires. Egypt was early unified under the kingship of the Pharaohs, and the kingdom which they governed proved to be far more stable than the empires of the Near East.

Meanwhile Crete and the Greek mainland had been invaded and settled around 3000 B.C. by peoples from Asia Minor. Before their arrival the mainland had been inhabited by people known to later Greeks and to scholars today as

[14] Susanne K. Langer, *Philosophical Sketches* (Baltimore, Md.: The Johns Hopkins Press, 1962), p. 89.

Pelasgians. By the middle of the third millennium B.C. cities had been established and Crete had become the hub of a flourishing commercial civilization usually referred to as Minoan. About 2000 B.C. the Greek-speaking Indo-Europeans invaded the mainland from the north.

. . . Neither the Greeks nor the natives into whose world they came were likely to have any idea that something big and historic was taking place. Instead they saw individual occurrences, sometimes peaceable and in no way noteworthy, sometimes troublesome and even violently destructive of lives and ways of life. Biologically and culturally these were centuries of thorough intermixture. . . . Skeletal remains show the biological fusion; language and religion provide the chief evidence with respect to culture. The end product, after a thousand years or so, was the historical people we call the Greeks. In a significant sense, the original migrants were not Greeks, but people who spoke proto-Greek and who became one element in a later composite which could lay proper claim to the name. The Angles and Saxons in Britain offer a convenient analogy: they were not Englishmen, but they were to become Englishmen one day.

It was to take the Greeks more than a thousand years to acquire a name of their own—and today they have two. In their own language they are Hellenes, and their country is Hellas. *Graeci* is the name given to them by the Romans and later adopted generally in Europe. In antiquity, furthermore, their eastern neighbors used still a third name for them—Ionians, the "men of Iavan" of the Bible. And all three are late, for we find none of them in Homer. He called his people Argives, Danaans, and, most frequently,

Cycladic Idol, Third Millennium B.C. One of a large number of standing nude, female figures produced in the islands of Cyclades during the early Bronze Age. (Albright-Knox Art Gallery, Buffalo, New York)

Achaeans. Now Achaeans, it so happens, appear quite early in non-Greek sources. . . .

It is idle to speculate when the word Achaean came to be applied to all Greeks, or why. In 1350 B.C. it was surely not. . . . When the local name "Achaean" became the word for all the Greeks, even if not the exclusive word and even if only for a brief period before it was replaced by "Hellene," the formative period may be considered ended: the common name is a symbol that Greek history proper had been launched. For us, that means with the *Iliad*.[15]

[15] From *The World of Odysseus* by M. I. Finley, pp. 5–7. Copyright 1954 by M. I. Finley, revised edition © 1965 by M. I. Finley. All rights reserved. Reprinted by permission of The Viking Press, Inc.

CHAPTER 3

THE TRANSFORMATION OF THE PRIMITIVE MIND:
Gods and Men in Homer's *Iliad*

What is peculiar to the Greeks is, even at this stage, the lucidity of their mythic categories, the order and beauty of the world as they portrayed it. Was it the small scale of their islandgirt world that inspired this self-reliant humanity, or did memories of Knossos and Mycenae spur them, like parentless children, to recover a lost patrimony, or did they grow with their position at the cross-roads open to the constant influence of neighbors? But whatever the cause, the mystery remains of a gaze which, from when we first know it in Homer, looks outward toward the world with alertest curiosity, sorts what it sees into stable orders of existence, and seeks a rationally comprehensible reality. Homer's lucidity leads straight to Aristotle, and if the early time speaks through myth and shape, the later through concept and inference, both equally constate order.

John H. Finley, Jr., Frontiers of Modern Scientific Philosophy and Humanism

In Hebrew mythology—or theology—God created Heaven and Earth, but in Greek mythology Heaven and Earth created the gods. But if the gods are not eternal, what is? The idea of Order. . . . Here is the ultimate, the eternal reality; and it is one which could be thought of as a power superior to the gods, or it could be identified with the gods.

Now, early Greek thought attributes different natural phenomena to different gods —a way of thought which of course is common enough. As for these powers of nature, we can see for ourselves that they fight with each other; we can still speak of the wind vexing the sea. But it is just as evident that these conflicts are subordinated to a larger unity; in the long run, Nature is regular. The mythical expression of this is that there are certain limits which the individual god cannot transgress. These limits can be thought of either as some shadowy power superior to the gods—*moira* [fate] or *ananke* [necessity]—or as a supreme god who, perhaps with difficulty, controls others, or as the collective will of the gods.

H. D. F. Kitto, Entretiens sur l'antiquité classique, *Vol. I*

The intellect was just not considered by Homer to be something of particular importance, or even something possessing demarcated functions. Important matters were just not consciously referred to anything like mind or a reason, and the mind was not conceded to have any legislative or judicial functions in and for itself. The *noös,* the vaguely articulated organ of recognition, or noticing things, and therefore, at most, perhaps somehow connected with memory storage rather than of knowledge *per se*, was at most for Homer one among many natural functions, each on occasion useful, but identifying itself only with its immediate object or particular end, a purely *tactical* function, and meant to be retired and rested, like the feet or the hands, when not in use. Nor is the *noös* or anything else charged with the function of judging the rightness or wrongness of a course of action, the better or worse shape of an argument, or the better or worse way of solving a problem. . . .

But of course, whether they knew it or not, even in Homer people think. True, but that is not what they thought they were doing, and they send the inquiring reader in every other direction but (perhaps) the right one. Experience, divine visitations, special birth and position—these are the credentials which supply Homeric man with what supposedly is supplied by reason and intelligence for modern man; these are the only bases upon which he can establish his right to give advice, for instance, and this advice must repose for confirmation upon these things rather than upon sheer probability and worthiness of the particular suggestions themselves, since there is no court of appeals to which the *intrinsic* worthiness of an idea can be referred, and thus the only available guarantees are extrinsic. . . .

Douglas J. Stewart, "Hesiod and the Birth of Reason,"
The Antioch Review, *Vol. XXVI*

The infiltration of the mainland by Greek-speaking Indo-Europeans at the beginning of the second millennium B.C. inaugurated what is now referred to as the Mycenaean Era. By the middle of the sixteenth century B.C. the Mycenaean Greeks (or, as they were also called, Achaeans were established on the peninsula, and during the following century their culture was much influenced by the more advanced Minoan culture which flourished on the adjacent island of Crete.

MINOANS AND MYCENAEANS
Tom B. Jones[1]

In the second millennium B.C. it was not only in the continental areas of the Near East that civilizations grew up outside the great river valleys, but also on the large islands of the Eastern Mediterranean and

[1] Reprinted with permission from Tom B. Jones, *From the Tigris to the Tiber: An Introduction to Ancient History* (Homewood, Ill.: The Dorsey Press, 1969), pp. 64–68.

in mainland Greece. As early as 6000–5000 B.C. villages had begun to appear; several sites are known in northern Greece and Cyprus with aceramic levels. After 3000 B.C., Crete had intermittent trade with Egypt, while from the islands of the Aegean traders in longboats visited the shores of Greece and western Asia Minor. As far as the Near East was concerned, continuous and important trade relations with the Aegean world did not develop until after 2000.

The Greeks of the historic period believed that long ago a great king named Minos had ruled at Knossos in north-central Crete. At the beginning of our century a British archeologist, Sir Arthur Evans, found Knossos and excavated it. He discovered that the site had been occupied by a series of peasant villages, but in the stratified layers above the village levels Sir Arthur found a succession of palaces dating roughly from 1800–1450 B.C. The final palace was so grand that Evans called it the Palace of Minos, and, as similar palaces were discovered elsewhere in Crete, along with many other evidences of civilization, the name Minoan was applied to the culture and the people. We still do not know what the inhabitants called themselves.

It seems likely that Minoan civilization was in large part brought to and developed in Crete by migrants who came from southern Asia Minor in the 19th century B.C. The imported culture contained elements borrowed from Egypt and Mesopotamia, but the system of writing, the style of architecture, and much of the technology were probably developed by the immigrants themselves before they came to Crete.

In its material aspects, Minoan civilization deserves the adjective brilliant. The palaces were all built on the same general plan: a complex of rooms and corridors at least two stories in height built around a huge central court. The principal building materials were stone, wood, and mud brick; roofs were flat. Rooms and corridors were decorated with fresco paintings in bright colors; Egyptian influence is evident in the style of painting, but the Minoans were not rigidly bound by convention so that their compositions were naturalistic and much freer than the Egyptian. Animals, human beings, flowers, outdoor scenes, religious processions and ceremonials were among the subjects portrayed. The Minoans had a handsome painted pottery that employed floral and marine motifs; fine metal work in gold, silver, and bronze; terra cotta, ivory, and faience figurines; and stone vases carved in high relief from a soft stone called steatite which had probably been covered with gold leaf.

The Minoans were engaged in agriculture and stock raising. They exported pottery, wine, olive oil, and metal work. From the finds of Minoan pottery in Egypt, Syria, Palestine, the Aegean islands, and Greece, it would appear that the Minoans dominated the carrying trade of the eastern Mediterranean to about the middle of the 16th century. They also colonized certain islands in the Aegean, probably for the purpose of trade; a Minoan palace was found on the Island of Melos.

The absence of temples in Crete along with the existence of rooms devoted to cult ceremonies in the palaces leads us to infer that Minoan rulers were priest-kings. Any guesses about Minoan religion have to be based on the frescoes, cult objects, and symbols. We can safely assume that there was a fertility cult, and the ubiquity of the double axe symbol makes it probable that the sky god of southwestern Asia Minor was worshipped. There was a stone and pillar cult; birds, snakes, and butterflies appear often in Minoan art and were probably symbolic of certain deities. The bucranium, a bull's head with horns, is also common, and reminds us of the Minotaur story which the Greeks connected with Minos and Knossos. The labyrinth in which the Minotaur was supposed to have been confined makes for interesting speculation, too. To us, the world "labyrinth" means a maze, but its original meaning was "place of the labrys," and labrys is the word for "double axe." One of the great Minoan ceremonies was bull leaping, a rite in which young men and young women, either captives of war or specially trained athletes, attempted to grasp the horns of a wild bull and do a somersault over his back; it is believed that the performance was staged in the great central court of the palace with the populus watching from the windows and galleries of the surrounding rooms.

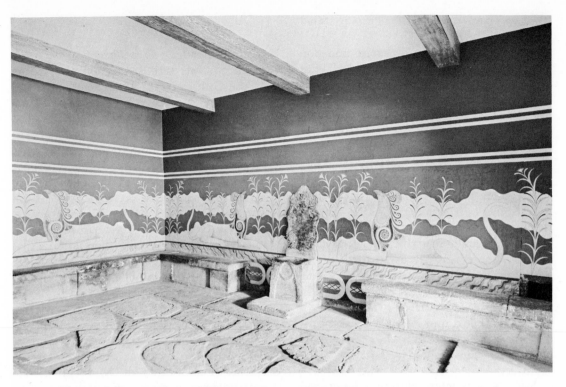

Throne Room, Palace of Minos at Knossos, c. 2000 B.C. Mycenaean murals depict man and the natural world from the perspective of Minoan culture. (Hirmer)

Detail of Throne Rome, Palace of Minos at Knossos. This griffin is illustrative of the creativity and imagination of the Minoan artist. (Consulate General of Greece)

The Minoans wrote on stone and pottery but mostly on flat clay tablets. The few texts inscribed on stone or pottery are probably dedications, but the clay tablets are accounts relating to (probably) the receipt of commodities and animals. Only a few hundred texts have been found. Minoan writing, clearly related to similar scripts of Anatolia, came in its final form to use three kinds of characters: (1) signs for numbers, (2) pictographs for objects or things (cattle, grain, vases, and the like), and (3) characters which had syllabic values. There was an early form of the script, called Hieroglyphic, and a later development which we call Linear A. The latter has been deciphered—we know most of the phonetic and other values of the signs—but the texts cannot be read because the underlying language has not been identified.

Now, a still later, closely related and derivative script called Linear B was found by Evans at Knossos, but the great proportion of the clay tablets we now possess were excavated at Greek sites in the Peloponnesus. Linear B, it now appears, was a late form developed in Greece and brought by invaders and conquerors to Crete. The script was deciphered by Michael Ventris in 1952. Moreover, the tablets can be read because the underlying language is an early dialect of Greek, related in grammar and vocabulary to the language of the Homeric poems, the *Iliad* and the *Odyssey*. The great importance of the Ventris decipherment will emerge from the following discussion.

Before 750 B.C. civilization in Greece was confined in time to the period 1550–1200 B.C. and in space to the east central part of Greece and the Peloponnesus, the southern peninsula. Village life had begun fairly early; after 2500 B.C. there was con-

siderable trade, and bronze had been introduced, but, with the exception of Lerna on the Gulf of Argos where a palace structure has been discovered, life had not gone beyond the peasant village stage. In the 19th century B.C., as the founders of Minoan civilization arrived in Crete, Greece was invaded, and many of the older towns were sacked and burned. The invaders, who seem to have come from northwestern Asia Minor, were probably the first Greek-speaking people to arrive in Greece. In actual fact, the matter is disputed, and the Greeks may not have come until 1600, but it is not possible to decide the question at the moment.

At any rate, by 1550 B.C. these early Greeks constituted the ruling class in the civilization that had grown up in Greece. One of the most spectacular centers of this culture was located at Mycenae in the northeastern part of the Peloponnesus. Mycenae was traditionally the home of Agamemnon, the legendary king who commanded the besieging force at the equally legendary siege of Troy, and thus we call this early Greek civilization Mycenaean. We also call the people of the period Mycenaeans as well as applying the term Mycenaean to the Linear B script which they used for writing.

Borrowing from the Minoans, but adapting Minoan culture to the different environment of Greece, the Mycenaeans evolved a civilization of their own which flourished in the period 1550–1200 B.C. By 1550, the Mycenaeans had replaced the Minoans in the carrying trade of the eastern Mediterranean; later, they conquered the Minoans and ruled in Crete, and they also colonized Cyprus in large numbers. The extent of Mycenaean trade can be comprehended from the fact that Mycenaean pottery has been found in western and southern Asia Minor, Syria, Palestine, Egypt, and on or just off the coasts of Sicily and Italy.

Combining the evidence of the archeological finds and the Mycenaean tablets, it is possible to reconstruct many features of Mycenaean culture. The Mycenaean realm was divided into a number of independent kingdoms. The kings lived in great fortified palaces built on hilltops. The citadel walls were constructed of huge stones, and they resembled in outward appearance the fortified towns of the contemporary Hittites. Within the fortress was a palace consisting of complexes of rooms surrounding pillared halls (megarons) equipped with huge central hearths. The principal megaron was the throne room where royal audiences were held and possibly religious ceremonies also. The throne room was decorated with fresco painting; sometimes in the Minoan style, but more frequently in a distinctive mainland style. The palaces also included quarters for the women (harems), workshops, and storerooms. It is interesting that at the Mycenaean palace at Pylos in the southwestern Peloponnesus, the throne room had frescoes representing griffins, while in the so-called Queen's Megaron in

The Octopus Vase, from Palaikastro, Crete, c. 1500 B.C. This is an example of naturalistic Minoan vase painting illustrating marine life. (Hirmer)

the women's quarters dolphins were represented; the same thing was true of the palace of Minos in Crete except that the throne room was very small and must have been used for religious ceremonies rather than royal audiences.

The Mycenaean king was called the *wanax,* a term that reeks of theocracy. Social classes included nobles (or warriors), artisans, farmers, herdsmen, slaves, and religious functionaries. The king's estates were large as were those of the religious establishments. The absence of temples, with the exception of a sanctuary found on the Island of Keos, again suggests the priest-king syndrome. Royal families were laid to rest in great "beehive" tombs of stone, built into hillsides and covered with earth. Although most of the royal tombs, like the pyramids and rock-cut tombs of Egypt, were robbed in ancient times, enough of the grave furniture survives to tell us that the tombs were well worth robbing.

Basically, the Mycenaean economy was not much different from that of Crete. Pottery, metal work, ivories, olive oil, wine, turpentine, and possibly textiles were exported. The numerous words for artisans of various kinds—weavers, carders, workers in bronze, carpenters, goldsmiths, and the like—indicate a great specialization of activity. There is much about chariots, for the Mycenaean nobles were chariot warriors.

Dimly reflected in the Homeric poems, this was the heroic age of Greece. Whether there was an Agamemnon or a Nestor, whether the Mycenaeans captured Troy, we cannot know. We do not even know whether the Mycenaeans had direct contact with the Hittites, a people who were in many ways very similar and certainly contemporary.

About 1200 B.C. Mycenaean palaces began to be attacked and destroyed. By whom? New Greek invaders? Sea raiders? We do not know. . . .

We do know, however, that the cultures of both the Mycenaeans and the Minoans were very much a part of a general eastern Mediterranean culture which included such peoples as the Hebrews, Egyptians, and Mesopotamians. The Greek or Olympian religion, which plays such a significant role in Homer's *Iliad,* is an example of the kind of cultural exchange which took place in this area.

THE ORIGINS OF GREEK RELIGION
H. J. Rose[2]

[The] Greek instinct for systematization brought the chief gods and some who are of less importance into one great family. In point of fact, their origin is extremely varied. The only one whom we can be certain the Achaians brought into Greece with them was Zeus himself, whose name, as has long been recognized, is etymologically the same as the Sanskrit Dyaus and the first syllable of the Latin Iup-piter and therefore belongs to the original language, Indo-Germanic or Wiro, spoken before the users of it broke up into separate groups and carried varieties of their tongue into new areas. Hades is traditionally "the Unseen One," *A-(w)ides,* which I still think the correct etymology, though another, which would connect it with *aia,* one of the forms of the word for "earth," is now popular. Poseidon's name is of doubtful origin. Its oldest known form is

[2] H. J. Rose, *Gods and Heroes of the Greeks: An Introduction to Greek Mythology* (London: Methuen & Co. Ltd., 1958), pp. 17–24. Reprinted by permission of Associated Book Publishers (International) Ltd.

Poseidaon, which has been ingeniously explained as "oh husband of Da," Da being, it is suggested, an old name of the pre-Greek earth-goddess. Certainly this accords with his oldest known functions and his very ancient title Gaiaochos, "holder (embracer) of Earth." The Achaians to all appearance came from some inland region and did not know the sea till they arrived in Greece; and it is quite conceivable that they evolved an earth-god mated with a native goddess of the earth and its fertility. But the derivation is neither certain nor the only one that has been put forward. Demeter or Damater, according to dialect (classical Greek split into some ten dialects in all) is perhaps again a compound of the supposed name of the local earth-goddess with the the pure Greek title Mater or Meter, "mother," which would be appropriate for a deity whose chief functions are connected with the soil and the corncrop. Her daughter seems a combination of two different goddesses, Kore, "the Maiden," that is the young corn of the new harvest, and Persephone (or Persephassa, with yet other variants of the plainly foreign name), queen of the underworld. Deities of the earth, generally known as chthonians, from *chthon,* an old name for earth, are really of two kinds, those who have to do with the surface of the ground and its fruits and those who govern the depths of the earth, where the dead go when their remains, burned or not, are buried; but the two classes tend to be confused in popular Greek thought. This is why Persephone's husband, HADES, is also called Pluton, which means "wealthy," that is to say owner and presumably giver of the chief source of wealth to a people mainly agricultural, the fruits of the earth. He, like her, is a blend of two distinct deities. The real name of HERA, if she had a name, is unknown, for Hera seems to be the feminine of *heros,* the original meaning of which is a gentleman, a man of good family, and so signifies no more than "lady." She had a very ancient cult at Argos and elsewhere, and the Achaians, who like all polytheists were very tolerant of and respectful towards new deities, adopted her cult and thought of her as the consort of their own chief god, thus displacing Dione except at what is perhaps the oldest centre in Greece of the worship of Zeus, Dodona. ATHENA (ATHANA, ATHENE) undoubtedly is a native goddess of the pre-Achaian population. Her name has the suffix characteristic of the pre-Greek language, *-na-,* and means nothing in Greek. Her worship is associated with hills, and so she easily became the protectress of the strongholds of Mycenaean lords, and when their power had ceased to be, her temple replaced the old castle, as was assuredly the case at her most famous centre of cult, Athens (*Athenai*). ARTEMIS may also be a survival from pre-Achaian days and is quite likely to have been originally not the virgin she consistently is in classical tradition but a goddess of more maternal type. It has repeatedly been pointed out that nymphs associated with her are often said to have become mothers, and there is room for the supposition that at least some of them are no more than titles of the goddess made independent; for instance, Kallisto has a name suspiciously like Artemis' title Kalliste (fairest). As to her name, a by-form of it in Doric is Artamis, and that suggests the noun *artamos,* a slaughterer, which agrees fairly well with her activity as a huntress, though to kill a beast with arrows and to butcher it are not the same thing. But whatever her origin, she was widely popular and worshipped under a variety of titles, though she was not, it would seem, originally a deity to whom the upper classes paid much attention. She is the goddess especially of the wilds, of country outside the limits of cultivation, and of all that live in it, and a patroness of hunters, which is why she is shown as a huntress herself; a bringer of sudden death to women yet at the same time their helper in childbirth and the protectress not of their offspring only but of all young things. In any case, she has no original connexion with the very different APOLLO, and why he is said to be her twin is a puzzle, unless the fact that both are archers has something to do with it. His name yields no convincing Greek etymology, though many attempts have been made to find one, and many indications, not wholly convincing yet not to be neglected, connect him with the Near East, where he may have originated. Many of his functions can be plausibly explained by supposing that he was originally what his title Nomios (He of the pastures) implies, a god of herdsmen. Anyone having charge of beasts in their summer pastures especially, that is to say on high ground where the grass stays green and edible far longer than on the plains, would need to be able to protect them against wolves and robbers, and his natural weapon would be the bow, such as Apollo regularly carries. He must also know something of the cure of hurts, theirs and his own and those of his companions, which might account for the god's medical activities. Further, it has been for many centuries a herdsman's custom to use a musical instrument both to call the cattle, who get to know a particular strain of music belonging to their own herd, and for his own amusement. This might well connect with the musical activities of Apollo, one of whose titles is

Musagetes (Leader of the Muses), were it not that he is constantly shown as a lyre-player, while the pastoral instrument is the pipe. But none of these considerations tell us how he became a prophetic deity, inspiring his priestess at Delphoi by possession not unlike that of a Siberian shaman, nor how he developed into a specialist in purifications and the great authority on ritual law, constantly consulted as to the best method of conducting the worship of a State or the correct procedure for avoiding the evil consequences of some event supposedly portentous or getting rid of some visitation such as a plague. Perhaps his most outstanding feature is that whatever his origin he developed into the most characteristically Greek of all the gods, thought of as embodying in his person the highest type of manly beauty in young maturity and author of traditional maxims recommending typically Greek moderation and sobriety. It may be mentioned in passing that he has no solar features whatever, his identification with the Sun, Helios, who has no worship in Greece proper, being a theory which gained popularity from the fifth century B.C. onwards but is patently false.

Of the rest of Zeus' near kin, his sister Hestia has a good claim to have been originally an Achaian deity, though this is not certain. At all events, a goddess of the hearth is a highly probable object of the worship of any people which can build houses with fireplaces in them, and the similarity in sound between her name and that of the Roman Vesta may not be an accident. But she is quite unimportant for mythology, for she has practically no myths. Zeus' son HERMES, or HERMEIAS, is certainly an old god, worshipped originally, it would seem, in Arkadia, his traditional birthplace being Mt. Kyllene.

His name may be connected with *herma*, that is to say stone, with reference to the stone-heaps or cairns which in Greece as in many countries served to mark out tracks or primitive roads, perhaps also to indicate spots felt to be uncanny for some reason. It would be quite natural for "him of the cairn" to emerge from such a custom, and be accordingly honoured by the users of roads, namely merchants travelling to buy or sell, heralds going with messages from one community to another, and robbers who preyed on travellers, all of whom are under Hermes' protection. We do not know by what means he became also patron of young men and their activities, especially athletic, and so the patron of their *palaestrae* or wrestling-schools, and by a further development of their cultural studies, especially rhetoric and poetry. It is at all events in this connexion that he acquires his common symbol, the cock, which cannot have originally been his, for domestic poultry were not imported into Greece till comparatively late. The allusion is to the popular sport of cock-fighting. He is himself shown in art as a handsome young man, perhaps some nineteen or twenty years old, wearing the *petasos* or broad-brimmed hat favoured by travellers and carrying a herald's staff, *kerykeion*, in Latin *caduceus*. He also on occasion carries a conjuror's wand, being one of the few Greek deities who have anything to do with magic.

With one exception, it is not clear if the Titans were ever gods of cult; the exception is KRONOS himself, whose name set ancient etymologists guessing, their most popular suggestion being that it is another form of Chronos, Time. This is doubly impossible, for formally, the aspirated palatal which we transliterate by *ch* does not lose its aspirate, and materially, Time is far too abstract a conception to be an object of really ancient cult, as apparently Kronos is. In Hekatombaion, the first month of the Attic year (roughly equivalent to July), came the Kronia, or festival of Kronos, one of those merry-makings which are perhaps especially characteristic of harvest-time (a season of course considerably earlier in a Mediterranean climate than in Great Britain and the rest of northern Europe). There was feasting, and during it masters and servants ate together. It is not uncommon to find seasonal feasts in various parts of the world at which ordinary social rules are set aside for the time being; the Romans noted with interest that the proceedings resembled their own Saturnalia, or festival of Saturnus, although this came in December, not in late summer. This is probably one of the reasons why they identified Saturnus with Kronos and thus gave rise to the story that the exiled god found a new home in Italy. Loosely connected with the Titanic family as children either of Earth herself or of some of her numerous offspring are a few figures of some importance in mythology or in cult. Pontos for instance had a son Nereus, probably an ancient sea-god displaced by Poseidon, who had a reputation for wisdom and truthfulness and became by his wife Doris the father of the Nereids, the mermaids of Greek tradition. Okeanos had a daughter Elektra (Shining one) who married Thaumas and bore him Iris, the personified rainbow, and the Harpies (*Harpyiai*), apparently wind-spirits, for their chief business in myth is to carry someone or something away, but in later tradition, from Alexandrian times down, we find them represented as bird-like creatures with the faces of women, insatiably greedy and exceedingly filthy and repulsive.

Their name means "snatchers." Keto, another child of Pontos, had monstrous offspring, appropriately (*ketos* is a sea-monster), the Graiai, who are personified old age—the name means approximately "old women" . . . and the Gorgons, Sthenno, Euryale and Medusa, i.e., Strong One, Wide-leaping and Queen, of whom the last was mortal. . . .

Finally, DIONYSOS according to nearly all our evidence was a late-comer into Greece and HEPHAISTOS, though somewhat earlier (for Homer is quite familiar with him and mentions Dionysos very little) is manifestly so. The former god seems to have become fully established in Greek cult hardly earlier than about the seventh century B.C. He apparently originated in Thrace, and was a god of the fertility and energy of nature. That he tended to specialize as a wine-god in Greece is probably due to the existence of older deities who were concerned with fertility, but if he had originally been such, his festivals would occur at times important for viticulture and wine-making, which they do not. His characteristic worship was wild, orgiastic dancing and running in the open air, on hilltops, not infrequently in winter, the result of which was so to excite the participants that they seemed to lose their own personality and be merged in that of their god, which is why they and he alike bear the title Bakchos (Bakchoi, Bakchai), whatever it may mean, and the female votaries are often called Mainades (Maenads), that is to say madwomen. This was all so unlike the normal, orderly Greek worship that we may suppose some of the stories of the god's arrival to reflect actual opposition to him and his cult. Hephaistos' progress can be traced by simply plotting on a map the position of his known shrines. They come thickest as we approach the volcanic region of Asia Minor, making it very probable that he was to begin with a deity of volcanic fires. The Greeks soon specialized him into a god of those who use fire, especially smiths, and he largely displaced Prometheus in this capacity. Hence in Greece the evidence for his cult is most abundant in comparatively industrialized districts, such as Attica, and rare or absent in more backward places.

It would seem that the Greeks from about Homer's time onward, and probably from much earlier, had lost all clear consciousness of the very mixed origin of their deities, remembering only that Dionysos came from abroad or that Aphrodite was especially associated with Cyprus and not with the mainland. They were all members of one great family, the head of which, *patér* (a word which does not imply begetting but natural authority), was Zeus. . . .

Homer, the literary figure who has left us the earliest depiction of the Olympians, was a native of Ionia, an area comprising the west coast of Asia Minor and the adjacent islands. This was one of the most important of the Greek colonies founded by migrants who had fled after a new series of invasions in the thirteenth century B.C. again created chaos in the eastern Mediterranean.

THE DARK AGES
Tom B. Jones[3]

. . . Comparatively little of Minoan and Mycenaean material culture remained following the devastating attacks of the late

[3] Reprinted with permission from Tom B. Jones, *From the Tigris to the Tiber: An Introduction to Ancient History* (Homewood, Ill.: The Dorsey Press, 1969), pp. 87–90.

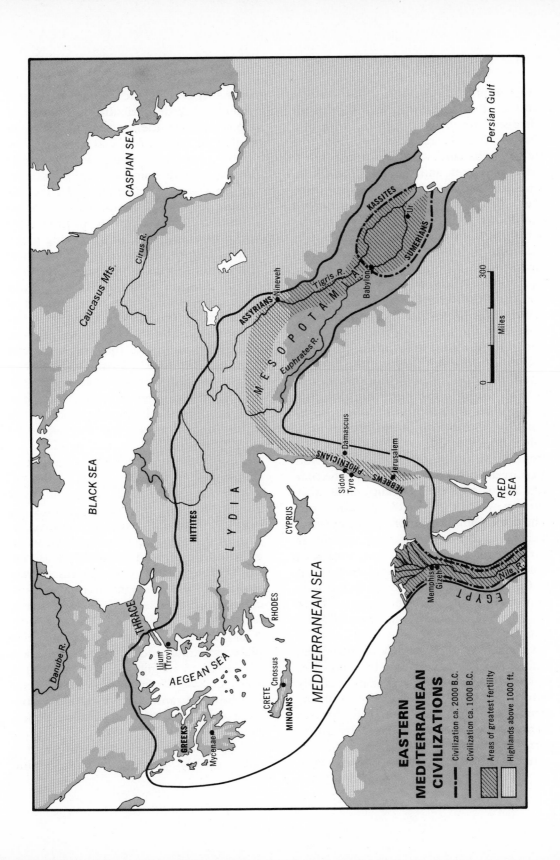

EASTERN MEDITERRANEAN CIVILIZATIONS

Civilization ca. 2000 B.C.
Civilization ca. 1000 B.C.
Areas of greatest fertility
Highlands above 1000 ft.

CASPIAN SEA

Persian Gulf

KASSITES

Ur

Cirus R.

Caucasus Mts.

ASSYRIANS
Nineveh

Tigris R.

Babylon

SUMERIANS

M E S O P O T A M I A

Euphrates R.

BLACK SEA

Damascus

PHOENICIANS

Jerusalem

Sidon
Tyre

HEBREWS

RED
SEA

HITTITES

L Y D I A

CYPRUS

300

Miles

Memphis
Gizeh

Nile R.

EGYPT

THRACE

RHODES

MEDITERRANEAN SEA

Danube R.

Ilium
(Troy)

AEGEAN SEA

Cnossus

CRETE

MINOANS

GREEKS
Mycenae

13th century B.C. It used to be thought that the destruction of the Mycenaean fortresses and villages was the work of a new wave of Greek invaders from the north, barbarians who spoke the Doric dialect of Greek and the so-called northwest Greek dialects. The Dorians came after 1200, it is true, but they may well have followed in the wake of the devastation to take advantage of the prostration of Greece which had been caused not by invasion and conquest but rather by the hit and run attacks of the same sea raiders who crippled the Near East.

While the Near East struggled to rebuild after the raids, Greece was isolated from the civilized area for many centuries, and the slow evolution of culture that occurred in Greece was largely conditioned by the Greek environment. The new Greeks who settled in Greece were iron-using herdsmen and part-time farmers. They imposed themselves as a ruling group upon assorted peoples, Greeks and pre-Greeks, whom they found in the new land and spread out to occupy unfamiliar territory which they would soon call home. The culture and institutions of the invaders had served them well enough in another environment, but adjustments would be necessary if they were to make a go of it in Greece. Thus, between 1200–750 B.C., in what we may call the Greek "Dark Ages," a new culture was gradually developed.

Greece was never a rich country even before its over-exploitation by man. The soil was thin; in some places there was only bare rock. A few fertile plains could be found in Laconia, Messenia, Boeotia, Euboea, and to a lesser extent in Attica. On the west coast where there was considerable rainfall, the forest cover was so dense that even in the classical period the region had little agriculture and a small population. On the eastern side with less rainfall the forest cover was not heavy, but as the forests were cut down to increase the arable land, there came to be a shortage of wood for building and fuel, and erosion set in. Furthermore, as the agricultural area was expanded to grow more wheat and barley for an increasing population, pasture lands were diminished so that horses and cattle became scarce. Beef almost disappeared from the Greek diet as the Greeks were forced to depend upon sheep and goats that could graze on the rocky hillsides and forage for themselves. The more inadequate the land became as a provider of food, the more the Greeks sought to feed themselves from the sea. "Landlubbers" originally, they learned to sail, to fish, and ultimately to explore the north Mediterranean and Aegean coasts for copper, iron, silver, and gold.

The rough topography of Greece naturally divides the land into small compartments, valleys and plains. In these geographic units tiny independent states began to form. Even though the invaders had arrived in large tribal groups, whatever feeling of identity with these "nations" people had once possessed was weakened by the fragmentation that occurred when they settled down to live in one little valley or plain. They began to think of themselves as natives of such a place, separate and distinct from those who lived in neighboring compartments. Outsiders were regarded with suspicion and hostility, and this "in-group" sentiment combined with the minute dimensions of the natural geographic divisions brought political unification within them rather swiftly. Centers of political life, "capitals," appeared; usually these were natural rallying points, a defensible hilltop or a likely market place.

The Greeks brought to Greece a form of political organization which we shall encounter again in Italy; we may call it the primitive Indo-European monarchy. There was a king (*basileus*), an hereditary monarch who had some religious functions and might arbitrate disputes if asked to do so, although he was primarily a war-leader who had few powers or duties in peacetime. The king was advised and assisted by a council of elders (*gerousia*) which represented the clans (groups of families), the principal social divisions of the populace. All adult males capable of bearing arms and having the means to provide themselves with weapons and armor could participate in an assembly of the people (*ecclesia*). The king convened and presided over the assembly. It, in turn, elected the new king and alone could confer upon him the power to rule. The assembly could discuss, approve, or reject proposals laid before it by the king. Only the assembly could issue a declaration of war, since in wartime the king was invested with special and extended powers which the people had the sole right to bestow upon him.

In accordance with ancestral custom, the invaders had divided up the conquered land. Equal sized plots of farm land were assigned to each family. This family land could not be bought or sold; it was administered by the patriarch, the head of the family, who directed the labors of his sons and the family servants and slaves. The sons shared equally in the division of the family lands when the patriarch died, and each son became the head of a new family. Such progressive divisions of property soon brought problems for large families since the inherited plots would become too small to support a man and his wife and children. The result was that such an unfortunate might try to bring new land under cultivation, or abandon his farmstead and move to another place, or become a worker or tenant on a larger estate. Moreover, the family plots (*kleroi*), though originally of equal size, had not been of equal fertility. Some farms were ruined by over-cropping; others located on the hillsides were damaged by erosion. Big families, poor soil, erosion—it all came to the same thing: before the Greek Dark Ages ended in 750 B.C., a few persons had most of the land, and many families had very little or none at all. Since land was wealth and wealth led to political power, the unequal division of wealth soon brought political inequality. As the poorer citizens were unable to equip themselves for military service, they lost their right to participate in the assembly. The large landholders took over the council of the elders and then began to contest with the king for authority. By progressive steps they stripped the king of his functions and at last abolished the monarchy. At the same time, as the poorer citizens were forced out of the assembly, the landholders and the tenants who were their political satellites came to have a majority in the ecclesia.

Purely economic and environmental factors thus altered governmental form as the monarchy was exchanged for a new kind of government dominated by the great landholders who now constituted a nobility. They called themselves *aristoi*, the best people, and we call this form of government aristocracy. The powers of the king were subdivided and exercised by short-term magistrates chosen from the ranks of the landed aristocrats. One official would be commander-in-chief; another would hold the principal religious authority. Still others would act as judges in cases of dispute over land ownership and similar matters; one is not surprised to learn that the common people complained that the judgments of the aristocratic officials tended to favor the landed class. As for the council, also monopolized by the *aristoi*, its functions and authority were greatly enlarged as it supervised the officials and decided what matters should be laid before the assembly for consideration.

During the Dark Ages the Greek colonists in Ionia had created a flourishing center of trade, and by the end of the period (sometime between 800 and 750 B.C.) there began to appear in this area a number of extremely creative artists, philosophers, scientists, and historians. The first of these was the poet Homer, generally regarded as the author of the *Iliad and the Odyssey*. These epic poems comprise the first major historical documents written in the Greek language.

Writing in the Greek language had again become possible when the phonetic alphabet was adopted. Though there is much dispute about the exact date, the Greeks apparently took over the phonetic alphabet from the Phoenicians some time in the eighth century B.C. After radically modifying this alphabet, they were in possession of an instrument which was to play an important role in the development of intellectual techniques that became permanent characteristics of Western thought.

    . . . Phonetic writing, by imitating human discourse, is in fact symbolising, not the objects of the social and natural order, but the very process of human interaction in speech: the verb is as easy to express as the noun; and the written vocabulary can be easily and un-

ambiguously expanded. Phonetic systems are therefore adapted to expressing every nuance of individual thought, to recording personal reactions as well as items of major social importance. Non-phonetic writing, on the other hand, tends rather to record and reify only those items in the cultural repertoire which the literate specialists have selected for written expression; and it tends to express the collective attitude towards them.[4]

Within a generation of the introduction of the phonetic alphabet, artists had evidently grasped the significance of writing as a means of preserving literary works, but this by no means signalled the end of the oral tradition. Both of Homer's epics, as well as the poetry of his successors, were composed for oral delivery. For generations

no one ever read a poem or had in fact learned anything by reading; in everyone's mind, singer and listener alike, lay the words of the poetic tradition that he had known since childhood and that alone lifted above the small present its arc of completer relevance and meaning. If everyone in a part of his being thought in this greater language and even Achilles in the *Iliad* is pictured as solacing himself by singing, some people by special gifts lived themselves more fully into it, each necessarily in his own way, since, though the language was traditional, it was not fixed in books but had to be recreated by each man, inevitably with the changes that time and temperament dictated. How the Homeric poems came to be written down when the very nature of the art implies the lack of writing is another kind of question, fixed in circumstance and doubtless lost beyond recall. Homer lived in Ionia—so much ancient tradition and his language make clear—in the late eighth century, it is thought, when writing

[4] Jack Goody and Ian Watt, "The Consequences of Literacy," *Comparative Studies in Society and History,* Vol. V (1962–1963), p. 315.

was first emerging beside the oral art. Was he recognized as so great that professional singers, perhaps of his own family, wanted his songs as heirloom of their guild, and did some clever young man—a grandson, one would like to think—see how writing could serve the purpose? If one can only guess in such matters, the oral character of the poems is beyond guess. . . .[5]

Oral-auditory cultures such as that of the early Greeks differ markedly from the literate-visual culture in which Western man has lived for the last few centuries. Nonliterate peoples live

largely in a world of sound, in contrast to western Europeans who live largely in a world of vision. Sounds are in a sense dynamic things, or at least are always indicators of dynamic things—of movements, events, activities, for which man, when largely unprotected from the hazards of life . . . , must be ever on the alert. Whatever form they take—thunder, the burble of running water, the snapping of twigs, the cries of animals, the beating of drums, the voice or music of man—they are usually of direct significance, and often even of peril, for the hearer. Sounds lose much of this significance in western Europe, where man often develops, and must develop, a remarkable ability to disregard them. . . .[6]

Another of the basic differences between these two types of culture is the means by which each maintains the continuity of its ethos.

[5] Reprinted from *Four Stages of Greek Thought* by John H. Finley, Jr., pp. 6–7, with the permission of the publishers, Stanford University Press. © 1966 by the Board of Trustees of the Leland Stanford Junior University.
[6] J. C. Carothers, "Culture, Psychiatry, and the Written Word," *Psychiatry,* Vol. XXII (1959), p. 310.

THE PRESERVATION OF TRADITION IN AN ORAL CULTURE
Eric A. Havelock[7]

. . . The "tradition," to use a convenient term, at least in a culture which deserves the name civilised, always requires embodiment in some verbal archetype. It requires some kind of linguistic statement, a performative utterance on an ambitious scale which both describes and enforces the overall habit pattern, political and private, of the group. This pattern supplies the nexus of the group. It has to become standardised in order to allow the group to function as a group and to enjoy what we might call a common consciousness and a common set of values. To become and remain standardised it has to achieve preservation outside of the daily whim of men. And the preservation will take linguistic form; it will include repeated examples of correct procedure and also rough definitions of standard technical practices which are followed by the group in question, as for example the method of building a house or sailing a ship or cooking food. Furthermore, we suggest, this linguistic statement or paradigm, telling us what we are and how we should behave, is not developed by happy chance, but as a statement which is formed to be drilled into the successive generations as they grow up within the family or clan system. It provides the content of the educational apparatus of the group. This is as true today of literate societies in which the necessary conditioning is acquired through

[7] Reprinted by permission of the publishers from Eric A. Havelock, *Preface to Plato,* pp. 41–46, Cambridge, Mass.: Harvard University Press. Copyright 1963 by the President and Fellows of Harvard College.

books or controlled by written documents as it was in preliterate society which lacked documents.

In a preliterate society, how is this statement preserved? The answer inescapably is: in the living memories of successive living people who are young and then old and then die. Somehow, a collective social memory, tenacious and reliable, is an absolute social prerequisite for maintaining the apparatus of any civilisation. But how can the living memory retain such an elaborate linguistic statement without suffering it to change in transmission from man to man and from generation to generation and so to lose all fixity and authority? One need only experiment today with the transmission of a single prosaic directive passed down by word of mouth from person to person in order to conclude that preservation in prose was impossible. The only possible verbal technology available to guarantee the preservation and fixity of transmission was that of the rhythmic word organised cunningly in verbal and metrical patterns which were unique enough to retain their shape. This is the historical genesis, . . . the moving cause of that phenomenon we still call "poetry. . . ."

. . . There remains to consider the personal situation of an individual boy or man who is urgently required to memorise and to keep green in his memory the verbal tradition on which his culture depends. He originally listens and then repeats and goes on repeating, adding to his repertoire to the limits of his mental capacity which naturally will vary from boy to boy and man to man. How is such a feat of memory to be placed within the reach not only of the gifted but of the average member of the group, for all have to retain a minimal grasp of the tradition? Only, we suggest, by exploiting psychological resources latent and available in the consciousness of every individual, but which today are no longer necessary. The pattern of this psychological mechanism . . . can be summed up if we describe it as a state of total personal involvement an therefore of emotional identification with the substance of the poetised statement that you are required to retain. A modern student thinks he does well if he diverts a tiny fraction of his psychic powers to memorise a single sonnet of Shakespeare. He is not more lazy than his Greek counterpart. He simply pours his energy into book reading and book learning through the use of his eyes instead of his ears. His Greek counterpart had to mobilise the psychic resources necessary to memorise Homer and the poets, or enough of them to achieve the necessary educational effect. To identify with the performance as an actor does with his lines was the only way it could be done. You threw yourself into the situation of Achilles, you identified with his grief or his anger. You yourself became Achilles and so did the reciter to whom you listened. Thirty years later you could automatically quote what Achilles had said or what the poet had said about him. Such enormous powers of poetic memorisation could be purchased only at the cost of total loss of objectivity. . . .

In conclusion, if one applies these findings to the history of Greek literature before Plato, one is caught up by the proposition that to call it literature in our sense is a misnomer. Homer roughly represents the terminus of a long period of non-literacy in which Greek oral poetry was nursed to maturity and in which only oral methods were available to educate the young and to transmit the group mores. Alphabetic skill was available to a few not later than 700 B.C. Precisely who these few were is a matter of dispute. The circle of alphabet-users became wider as time passed, but what more natural than that previous habits of instruction and of communication along with the corresponding states of mind should persist long after the alphabet had theoretically made a reading culture possible? This leads to the conclusion that all Greek poetry roughly down to the death of Euripides [in 406 B.C.] not only enjoyed an almost unchallenged monopoly of preserved communication but also that it was composed under conditions which have never since been duplicated in Europe and which hold some of the secret of its peculiar power. Homer may, for convenience, be taken as the last representative of the purely oral composition. Even this is dubious; it seems improbable that his poems have not benefited from some reorganisation made possible by alphabetic transcription. But this is a controversial point which does not affect the main perspective. It is certain that all his poet successors were writers. But it is equally certain that they always wrote for recitation and for listeners. They composed it can be said under audience control. The advantages of literacy were private to themselves and their peers. The words and sentences they shaped had to be such as were repeatable. They had to be "musical" in a functional sense. . . . And the content had still to be traditional. Bold invention is the prerogative of writers, in a book culture.

In short, Homer's successors still assumed that their works would be repeated and memorised. On this depended their fame and their hope of immortality. And

so they also assumed, though in the main unconsciously, that what they should say would be appropriate for preservation in the living memory of audiences. This both restricted their range to the main stream of the Greek tradition and immensely strengthened what might be called the high seriousness of their compositions. . . .

To aid their audiences in memorizing the catalogue of mores incorporated in their work, Homer and his successors not only used the literary medium of poetry but also strove to create visual images of actions or persons performing them.

Actions and their agents are in fact always easy to visualise. What you cannot visualise is a cause, a principle, a category, a relationship or the like. The abstract can be defined in many ways and at varying degrees of linguistic sophistication. Is the goddess Memory an abstraction? Is the wrath of Achilles an abstraction? In the terms in which we have defined the characteristics of preserved communication they are not. To be effectively part of the record, they have to be represented as agents or as doings particular to their context and sharply visualised. As long as oral discourse retains the need of visualisation it could not properly be said to indulge in abstraction. As long as its content remained a series of doings or of events none of these could properly be regarded as universals, which emerge only through the effort of re-arranging the panorama of events under topics, and of reinterpreting it as chains of relation and cause. The era of the abstract and the conceptual is yet to come.[8]

The Greeks of the eighth century B.C. not only had habits of mind and a communication me-

[8] Havelock, *Preface to Plato*, p. 188. Reprinted by permission of Harvard University Press. Copyright 1963 by the President and Fellows of Harvard College.

dium which differed radically from ours; they also had a vastly different view of the structure and functioning of the human personality. Twentieth-century anthropologists have demonstrated that when the highest of the primates developed the ability to think symbolically, he acquired consciousness also. It has been suggested that consciousness has the biological function of calling "directly on all the reserves of experience; it is a signal echoing through all the available associations of memory."[9] Consciousness of one's own person, of one's self as an experiencing subject, is also possible and can, in fact, be considered a unique feature of man.

> Man is a self-reflecting animal in that he alone has the ability to objectify himself, stand apart from himself, as it were, and to consider the kind of being he is and what it is that he wants to do and to become. Other animals may be conscious of their affects and the objects they perceive; man alone is capable of reflection, of self-consciousness, of thinking of himself as an object.[10]

In other words, man is the only primate which can look into a mirror and say: "That is me." Only a human being can think of "himself"; can distinguish "himself" from other objects; can create attitudes toward "himself." It is important to remember this point about consciousness as well as consciousness of self, for it was as much characteristic of primitive man as of modern man.

However, the individual's "capacity for self-objectification does not imply his objective knowledge of the psychodynamics of his total personality."[11] Neither primitive man nor Homeric man possessed this kind of knowledge. Neither realized that the human psyche or self comprised the interrelated processes of thinking (perception and conceptualization), feeling (emotion), and motivation (conation). In other words, neither understood that every individual has a united and unique inner life. Homeric language reflects this incomplete understanding of the human personality. There are, for example, no exact, single-word equivalents for "to see," "to think," "intellect," or "character" as we understand them. The reason for this deficiency is that "abstraction is undeveloped: Homeric man is too closely concerned with all the detail of his experience to stand back from it and indulge in abstraction and synthesis. . . ."[12]

The lack of words for the concepts of "soul," "spirit," "mind," or "body" is most striking. Homer's use of the word *soma* illustrates this deficiency. *Soma* is usually translated as "body," but in Homer's time the human organism was considered an aggregate of independent parts; arms and legs performed their given functions but they, with other parts of the body, did not comprise an integrated whole. Only much later in Greek history did *soma* come to represent the body as a single unit of integrated parts. This early perception of the body as an aggregate of parts can be graphically seen in Greek vase painting of the eighth century B.C.

In a similar fashion the Homeric epics reveal that the poet believed that man's psychological makeup included five separate organs—*psyche, thymos, noos* (later *nous*), *kradie*, and *phrenes*. These five organs were not neatly separated into compartments; they overlapped and sometimes were interchanged.

[9] Lancelot Law Whyte, *The Unconscious before Freud* (New York: Basic Books, Inc., 1960), p. 24.

[10] David Bidney, *Theoretical Anthropology* (New York: Columbia University Press, 1953), p. 3.

[11] A. Irving Hallowell, "Self, Society and Culture in Phylogenetic Perspective," in *Evolution after Darwin*, Sol Tax, ed., Vol. II: *The Evolution of Man* (Chicago: University of Chicago Press, 1960), p. 350.

[12] E. L. Harrison, "Notes on Homeric Psychology," *Phoenix*, Vol. XIV (1960), p. 63.

HOMERIC PSYCHOLOGY
T. B. L. Webster [13]

. . . In Homer [*psyche*] is the breath blown out in a swoon and the breath blown out in death, and is the only part of man that survives after death; it can therefore mean "ghost" but its development to mean "soul" in the modern sense is post-Homeric. The other four words have a common physical location in the upper part of the body, but *noos* unlike the other three has no demonstrable physical existence. *Kradie* means . . . the heart, *phrenes* the diaphragm, and *thymos* the breath. The beating of the heart is obviously affected by emotion; so is the pace of breathing, and this is visible in the diaphragm which appears as a dark shadow at moments of great exertion and excitement. Such phrases as "the god breathed courage into him" or "he breathed wrath" belong to the same circle of ideas. As we are accustomed now to the range of meanings which Greek words may have and to the Greek tendency to personify, it is not surprising to find that *kradie, phrenes,* and *thymos* can be used for the receptacle of ideas, or that they can be described as agents: "the *phren* of Zeus is turned," "the *kradie* and *thymos* rejoice," or even . . . that the *thymos* gives orders and talks and the heart barks and is chidden. . . . "These things are not merely matter, not even living matter; they are dynamic."

But, although it is not difficult to see that living matter which shows changes

[13] T. B. L. Webster, "Language and Thought in Early Greece," *Memoirs and Proceedings of the Manchester Literary and Philosophical Society,* Vol. XCIV (1952–1953), pp. 31–34. Reprinted by permission of T. B. L. Webster.

when psychological disturbance occurs can be regarded as an agent which displays emotion, it is not clear why these things should have anything to do with what we call intellectual activity: yet *phrenes* are the normal place in which calculations are made, the heart ponders things which in fact are carried out, and the *thymos* debates. The answer seems to be that intellectual activity and emotional activity are not clearly distinguished in Homer; thus the verbs which are used for intellectual activity—knowing, remembering, and forgetting—are also used of emotional activity. But although *phrenes, thymos* and *kradie* to a large extent overlap, certain distinctions can be drawn. *Phrenes* is more often used in intellectual contexts than *thymos* (or *kradie*). When a man has his *phrenes* taken away or harmed, he loses his understanding; when a man has his *thymos* taken away, he swoons or dies. The *phrenes,* unlike *thymos* and *kradie,* are never personified and opposed to the ego.

The other interesting word, *noos,* cannot be identified with anything physical, although it may be localised in the chest or in the diaphragm. It is an abstract noun derived from a lost verb, which possibly meant "to sniff." Its derivative verb *noein* means in Homer something like "to appreciate the situation" in the military sense, in which appreciate involves also making a plan. In many passages in Homer *noos* means the process of "appreciating the situation," or to use a less cumbersome phrase "way of thinking," if we remember that "way of thinking" means not only to grasp the significance of a situation but also to react in some way to it, and that the "way" may include emotion. Thus the Phaeacians have a "god-fearing way of thinking" (*Odyssey* vi, 121) and Achilles

Dipylon Vase (opposite), from Dipylon Cemetery, Athens, Eighth Century, B.C. The oldest surviving examples of Greek painting are found on vases such as this. The figures and geometric designs identify it as a piece from the Archaic period (eleventh century B.C. to early fifth century B.C.), during which time there developed an interest in the representation of the human figure and a search for the ideal form for the betrayal of gods and men. (Metropolitan Museum of Art, Rogers Fund, 1914)

Detail of *Dipylon Vase* (above): Funeral Scene. The artist's rendering of the figures in this scene as aggregates, or assemblages of parts, illustrates the Homeric perception of the body. The vase was painted in the black-figure style, that is, in black against the natural red of the clay. Internal details were incised with a sharp instrument. (Metropolitan Museum of Art, Rogers Fund, 1914)

has a "fierce way of thinking" (*Iliad* xxiii, 484). Agamemnon tried to appease the anger of Athena and did not realise that "the way of thinking of the immortal gods is not quickly turned" (*Odyssey* iii, 145f.). Secondly, just as *phatis* means "saying" in the sense of the words spoken, *noos* can mean the plan or thought which results from the appreciation.

Noos is rarely used to mean the agent or instrument of thought, and when it is so used its activity seems to be contrasted with some external activity. The clearest case is the contrast between speech and thought: "speak and do not hide it with your *noos*" (*Iliad* i, 363). As an extension of this, Penelope's public behaviour is contrasted with her private thoughts: "she makes promises to every man but her *noos* ponders other things" (*Odyssey* ii, 92, cf. viii, 78). But *noos* is also used of the poet's mind reviewing the events of which he sings but in which he did not take part (*Odyssey* i, 347) and of the man's mind visiting distant scenes while his body stays at home (*Iliad* xv, 80). Thus *noos* is a word which has a different origin from the other words that we have examined and already in Homer occasionally means an organ of private or mental as distinct from public or bodily behaviour.

Another peculiarity of psychological terminology in Homer may be called "open-field terminology." [According to one classical scholar] "a person in Homer is not a closed and compact entity but something like an open 'field' from which forces freely emanate and which is freely permeated by outside forces factual as well as spiritual." As developed by other scholars this would appear to mean that men in Homer are not responsible for their actions and that their behaviour is not predictable because they have not enduring propensities or characteristics. The second proposition is clearly impossible since the Homeric heroes are as distinct personalities as any in literature and Homer has ways of describing their enduring characteristics, e.g. Odysseus is a "man of many wiles." On the other hand when Homer is describing any kind of unusual condition, he habitually uses personification, or . . . "open-field" terminology: the poet can sing of events which he never saw because the Muse or Apollo taught him (*Odyssey* viii, 488); Agamemnon steals Achilles' girl because Zeus and Fate and

the Fury who walks in the dark cast wild Infatuation into his *phrenes* (*Iliad* xix, 86); Achilles starts up to kill Agamemnon but Athene catches hold of his hair (*Iliad* i, 188); Odysseus decides in his *thymos* to kill the Cyclops but another *thymos* holds him back (*Odyssey* ix, 299). In all these passages the terminology is "open-field," the character is acted on by a "person"; but he is also described in the same passages as responsible for his action: the poet sings "well and in good order." Agamemnon pays a ransom, Achilles is persuaded by Athene, and Odysseus waits groaning for the divine Dawn. The two methods of describing action are left side by side and Homer does not feel the need to reconcile them.

One final comment on Homeric psychology is necessary. As mentioned above, when a Homeric man died his *psyche* left him through his mouth or throat.

On leaving the body the *psyche* descends to Hades. And here man's last gasp becomes nothing more than the barest concession he can make to his innate fear of annihilation at death. For now that it has left the body, it retains its association with the man who has died only in so far as it is an "image" of him. In Hades it has no more power than it had in the living man, and is no more substantial than a shadow, a dream, or a puff of smoke. This is no place to discuss the nature of this *psyche*-belief, or such problems as its conflict with tendance of the dead, which seems to have been a permanent feature of Greek popular religion. But there are some points that are worth mentioning in view of the word's subsequent development.

(*a*) It alone, and not *thymos*, *phrenes*, or *noos*, is left behind when a man dies. Thus, although it is the weakest of strands stretching into the afterlife, it is still (as it were) the beginning of what can become a lifeline. And when religion and philosophy combine in finding an immortal soul in man, *psyche* alone has any qualification to describe it.

(*b*) The Homeric *psyche* in Hades was in theory such a nonentity that the very poet who presumably did much to reduce it to this state had himself to resuscitate it in order to bring it within the scope of his dramatic treatment: and here again (as in the case of the "omniscient" gods) doctrinal theory bowed to artistic requirements. This is important, for it means that the poems portray (in however restricted a fashion) various forms of personal survival, and do not really practice what they preach. And although the poet generally explains away the cases involved by utilising elements of popular belief and practice to justify them as exceptions, the picture of the dead Patroclus (e.g.) conversing intelligently with Achilles (and still identifiable, however remotely, as Patroclus), remains with us long after the explanation of how he was able to do so has been forgotten.

(*c*) On a purely linguistic level there are already signs of a confusion of *psyche* with *thymos* in the Homeric poems. And this is the beginning of an extremely important development whereby, with a carelessness that is typical of man's use of his mental terminology, *psyche* tended more and more to replace *thymos* in post-Homeric times, until it too became an important "mental-organ." The confusion in question (which was later to spread thus to all usages) is confined in Homer to death-phrases, and it can be detected by virtue of the anomalies it has produced. Thus: at death it is regularly the *psyche* that descends to Hades, and the *thymos* is simply lost; the *psyche* departs from an opening (the mouth or a wound), the *thymos* from the limbs; and the *psyche* is confined to human beings, the death of animals being described in terms of *thymos*. But in each case we find one exception to the rule,

brought about by a careless confusion of the two terms.[14]

In spite of the confusion in the use of certain words, Homer and his characters assume that there is an identity between a thing and its name. The characters in the *Iliad*, with the exception of Odysseus and Achilles in Book 9 (lines 307ff., especially 312–313), do not experience any discrepancy between the spoken word and the reality which the word represents. In other words, they all share very much the same image or world view.

. . . Everything in the world is regularly presented as all men (all men within the poem, that is) commonly perceive it. . . . Moral standards and the values of life are essentially agreed on by everyone in the Iliad. The unity of experience is . . . made manifest . . . by a common language. Men say the same things about the same things, and so the world to them, from its most concrete to its most metaphysical parts, is one. There is no need, as there is in Plato's day, for a man to "define his terms." [15]

Lack of space prevents the inclusion in these pages of *The Iliad* by Homer, Books 1, 3, 6, 9, 16, and 19–22.[16] At this point, however, these selections should be read. It is strongly recommended that a summary of the entire story of the war between the Achaians and the Trojans be read before students begin these selections in *The Iliad*.

[14] E. L. Harrison, "Notes on Homeric Psychology," *Phoenix*, Vol. XIV (1960), pp. 76–77. Reprinted by permission of *Phoenix* and E. L. Harrison. Footnotes have been omitted.

[15] Adam Parry, "The Language of Achilles," *Transactions of the American Philological Association*, Vol. LXXXVI (1956), pp. 3–4.

[16] One such account is provided in the Introduction to Richmond Lattimore's translation of *The Iliad of Homer* (University of Chicago Press, 1951; Phoenix paperback).

CHAPTER 4

THE TRANSITION FROM PRIMITIVE COMMUNITY TO POLITICAL SOCIETY IN THE ARCHAIC AGE:
Social Change and the Problem of Justice

[Hesiod] attempts to settle the complex relations existing among the gods and to place the activities of the divinities on a higher plane than they ever had in Homer, by associating them with the order of nature and by injecting certain new concepts, order and justice, into the heretofore rather roughhouse history of the gods. Hesiod's methodological device is the genealogy. He goes back to the primal gods and forces, and works down a time-scale, generation by generation, to the Olympian society known to us from Homer. In other words, for Hesiod, the key to understanding what to an intelligent Greek must have seemed a chaotic picture, a universe ruled by immortal and omnipotent gods who were yet something less than omnipotent and constantly frustrated and working at cross-purposes, was to go back to the very origins of all things, and by explaining the pedigree of the gods, systematize their relationships, and make intelligible their permanent meaning by embedding it in the order of nature. This is the first occasion known in European thought of a man who faced a theoretical problem, contrived a method for solving it, and put down his results in writing for the guidance of others.

Douglas J. Stewart, "Hesiod and the Birth of Reason," Antioch Review, *Vol. XXVI*

... Hesiod's [*Works and Days*] deals, in its first part, with the problem of evil, and no blacker, more despairing indictment of the injustice of the world has ever been written. Why, he asks, why is the world so full of evil? His first answer is mythical in its most traditional sense; he tells the story of Prometheus and Pandora: that is the answer, a typically mythical answer, the kind of answer Greeks continued to give to explain rites and beliefs all through their history. But now, he continues without pause, I will tell you another tale, and his second one, the alternative to the Pandora myth, is the account of the races of man. Clearly there is a new kind of thinking here, inchoate, poetic and not systematic, not followed through and not even properly linked with the rest of the poem, but nonetheless pointing to an entirely new line of intellectual endeavor and pointing away from myth and epic. "What is at the beginning?" [one classicist] said of Hesiod, "is the question of history precisely at the point where it turns into philosophy. . . . The question Hesiod poses is no longer about the historical past, but about the beginning of what exists, the question of philosophical origins. . . ." But "history" is wholly out of place here. Hesiod is foreshadowing the step from *mythos* to *logos*, and that step was not mediated by history.

It bypassed history altogether. It moved from the timelessness of myth to the time-lessness of metaphysics.

M. I. Finley, "Myth, Memory, and History," History and Theory, *Vol. IV*

The strength of snow and hail comes from the storm-cloud: *Causal relationships in nature*
    Thunder comes from out the lightning flame.
Great men destroy the city, and the people   *separation in responsibility — nature*
    Are the tyrant's slaves from ignorance.   *in relation to man's self-reliance*

Solon, Early Greek Elegists, *trans. C. M. Bowra*

logical construction — can't completely abandon patterns of previous ideas of order.

... The liberation of the individual from the bonds of clan and family is one of the major achievements of Greek rationalism, and one for which the credit must go to Athenian democracy. But long after the liberation was completed in law, religious minds were still haunted by the ghost of the old solidarity. . . .

E. R. Dodds, The Greeks and the Irrational

Accelerated social change in the middle of the eighth century B.C. marks the beginning of the Archaic Age (750–500 B.C.). Economic growth, as well as other factors, subsequently transformed the socio-political structure, world view, and self-image of the Greeks.

THE OPENING OF AN ERA OF EXPANSION
Tom B. Jones[1]

By 750 B.C. many of the Greek states along the east coast faced a serious crisis. The declining fertility of the soil and over-dependence on agriculture had resulted in overpopulation. A simple agrarian economy could not sustain the Greeks in Greece any longer. With so many people sunk in poverty and seething with dissatisfaction, something had to be done to re-

[1] Reprinted with permission from Tom B. Jones, *From the Tigris to the Tiber: An Introduction to Ancient History* (Homewood, Ill.: The Dorsey Press, 1969), pp. 90–97.

lieve pressures that might bring a political explosion. Overpopulation had to be dealt with and the Greek economy diversified. Colonization of lands outside of Greece, shipping off the surplus population, accomplished the first objective, while a gradual development of trade with the new colonies stimulated industry at home and created a diversified economy. . . .

Between 750–500 B.C., thousands of Greeks left their homes in Greece to settle in scores of colonies established in the north Aegean, around the Black Sea, in Sicily, southern Italy, southern France, northeastern Spain, and in Cyrene just west of Egypt in North Africa. Most colonies were formally organized, state-sponsored projects. The home government would select a site for the colony, choose a leader for the expedition, and arrange for the transport of the colonists. Once founded, however, the colony was usually politically independent; it ceased to have political ties with the metropolis, or parent state, unless some military or commercial treaty was later sought by both parties.

Even though political connections between metropolis and colony were rare, other bonds were not so easily severed. Kinship, common religious beliefs, and pure sentiment helped to maintain a feeling of cordiality between parent and offspring. Trade relationships developed because the colony, lacking economic self-sufficiency, tended to exchange its raw products and foodstuffs for special products and manufactures from the homeland. As trade grew and manufacturing for the colonial market was encouraged, the economy of the metropolis became diversified. A new growth of population was stimulated: states whose land was poor or limited in size could sustain only a small number of farmers, but they could easily accommodate many more traders and artisans whose activities made it possible to import food. Such states with converted economies flourished, and their villages grew into towns and cities.

As time passed, economic change altered phases of Greek life. The diversified economy led to the formation of a new socioeconomic class of traders and artisans which took its place between the big and small landholders. The growth of manufacturing brought an increase in slavery: since few of the Greeks at this time were skilled artisans, great numbers of slaves were purchased in Near Eastern markets and transported to Greece to serve as metal workers, potters, makers of textiles, and the like.

New social and economic patterns necessitated changes in governmental form. Of itself the growth of the city complicated problems of government. The new "middle" class, whose interests might clash with those of the landed aristocrats, would challenge the monopoly of the great landlords and demand a voice in government. Custom and religion were bound to be affected by the alterations in economics and society. All these changes as well as renewed contact with the outside world would influence and stimulate developments in literature, art, and thought. Accumulation of capital from the growing prosperity would encourage patronage of culture thus providing opportunity and support for creative activity.

Although colonization and its economic consequences brought Greece out of barbarism and back to civilization, the *form* that this new and complex Greek culture took was determined in large part by a renewal of contact with the Near East in the years following 750 B.C. Left to themselves, the Greeks might have developed a very different civilization, but as it was they borrowed heavily and adapted Near Eastern culture to their own needs. Economic development reached a point at which the Greeks had to make provision for a system of writing, certain business procedures, and an organized legal system. To satisfy these needs the Greeks adopted ready-made culture traits: they borrowed and adapted the Semitic alphabet, Near Eastern business methods, and the form of the Mesopotamian law codes along with the Babylonian system of weights and measures. These things were borrowed directly from the Phoenicians with whom the Greeks were now trading, but the trade with the Near East was not entirely a one-way affair since the Greeks had commenced to sail to the Syro-Palestinian coast and Egypt. Culture traits as well as foreign goods were brought home from the Near East; in art, literature, religion, science, mathematics, and other fields the Greeks received novel ideas and concepts from their more civilized neighbors.

The emergence of the Greeks from the

Dark Ages had very nearly coincided with the economic and cultural revival of the Near East. A rebirth of trade and industry had occurred in Syria and along the Phoenician coast in the 10th century. By 850, the Phoenicians were well embarked on a commercial career, conducting their growing trade with Cyprus, Asia Minor, and the western Mediterranean. It was not an accident that the so-called Asiatic or Eastern Greeks, who lived in western Asia Minor and the Aegean islands just offshore, were the first to become civilized and that the beginnings of Greek philosophy, certain types of sculpture and architecture, an "orientalizing" style of art, and a new poetry should appear in exactly those areas that were first in contact with Phoenicia. . . .

Certain island states, particularly Aegina and some of the towns of Euboea, along with the mainland towns of Corinth, Megara, and Sicyon, had been affected by developments on the other side of the Aegean and had followed the lead of the Asiatic Greeks. Aegina traded with Egypt, while Chalcis in Euboea began to trade with the north Aegean and also with the Etruscans in Italy; Corinth and Megara colonized and engaged in commerce with the west as well as with the north Aegean and the western end of the Black Sea beginning soon after 750 B.C. When the East Greek towns became subject to Persia, the rival trading powers across the Aegean simply took over their foreign trade and prospered even more.

Greek trade was often organized in triangular patterns. The Greeks wanted the spices, perfumes, foodstuffs, and other products of Egypt, but they had little of their own that was of interest to Egyptian buyers. On the other hand, Egypt was eager for silver and, to a lesser degree, gold. The Greeks solved this problem by taking their own manufactures to the north Aegean where they could be exchanged for silver and gold from the mines of that area. The precious metals were then shipped to Egypt to purchase the commodities wanted back home in Greece. The Corinthians followed a similar procedure in their trade with the western Mediterranean: Corinthian manufactures were traded through their colonies up the Adriatic for silver brought down from the mines of central Europe, and then the precious metal was exchanged for foodstuffs and raw products in Sicily and South Italy where silver was in great demand.

In order to facilitate this bullion trade in silver and gold, the Greeks borrowed from the Lydians the new invention of coined money. The precious metals, measured by weight, had long been used in the Near East as media of exchange, and in Greece a similar practice was beginning to replace the barter economy of the Dark Ages. Gold and silver ingots, nuggets, and gold dust were familiar forms, but coins did not appear until at least the end of the eighth century and possibly later. The coin, a piece of metal of definite shape and weight, bearing the symbol of the issuing authority as a guarantee of its weight and purity, was a great convenience in trade. Coins did not need to be weighed; they could be transported easily, quickly counted, and thus exchanged with facility. Most of the coins used in the international trade of the seventh and sixth centuries were large pieces of gold, silver, or electrum (an alloy of gold and silver). It is important to understand that they functioned not as money but as bullion. It was only later that coins were used as money for local transactions in the Greek states themselves; then, smaller denominations and

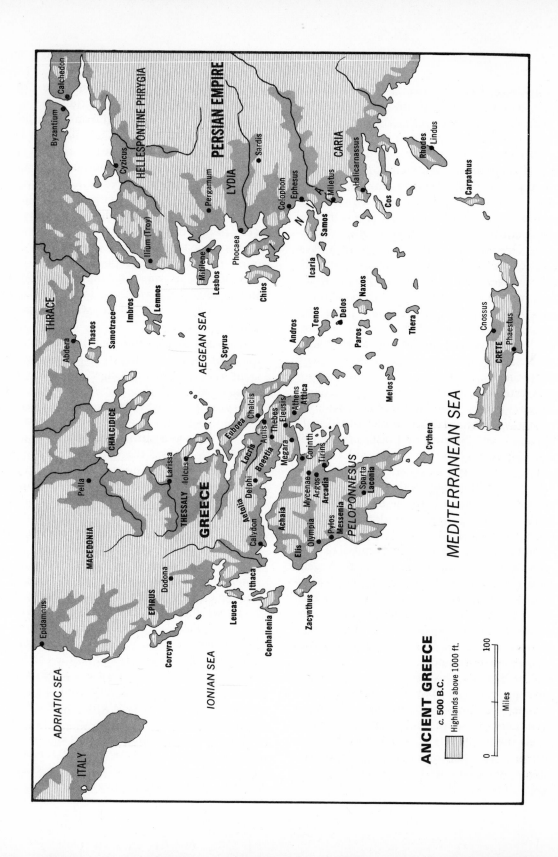

ADRIATIC SEA

ITALY

THRACE

Calchedon
Byzantium

HELLESPONTINE PHRYGIA

Cyzicus

PERSIAN EMPIRE

LYDIA

Sardis

Pergamum

CARIA

Rhodes
Lindus

Carpathus

Halicarnassus

Ilium (Troy)

Colophon
Ephesus
I
O
N
I
A
Miletus

Cos

Phocaea

Mitilene

Samos

Lesbos

Icaria

Chios

AEGEAN SEA

Abdera

Thasos

Samotrace

Imbros

Lemnos

Naxos

Paros

Tenos

Delos

Thera

Scyrus

Andros

Melos

Cnossus

Phaestus

CRETE

MEDITERRANEAN SEA

Epidamnus

EPIRUS

Dodona

Pella

MACEDONIA

Larissa

Iolcus

THESSALY

GREECE

Euboea

Chalcis

Aulis

Thebes

Athens

Eleusis

Attica

Cythera

Locris

Boeotia

Megara

Corinth

Delphi

Aetolia

Tiryns

Calydon

Mycenae

Argos

Arcadia

Sparta

Laconia

PELOPONNESUS

Achaia

Olympia

Elis

Pylos

Messenia

Leucas

Ithaca

Cephallenia

Zacynthus

Coreyra

IONIAN SEA

ANCIENT GREECE
c. 500 B.C.

Highlands above 1000 ft.

0   100

Miles

particularly bronze coins for small change made their appearance.

Turning now to political changes after 750 B.C., we have seen that the impending conflict between the big landholders and the impoverished small farmers in mainland Greece had been averted in many states by colonization, but the rise of a new socioeconomic class as a result of the growth of trade and industry created new political problems. When the great nobles ignored the demands of the middle class for reform and greater participation in government, revolutions sometimes occurred. Often, these uprisings against the aristocrats were led by men who were themselves of noble birth but who had chosen to join the opposing faction in order to gain power or wealth or even to satisfy patriotic impulses. Successful leaders of this type were known as *tyrants*.

Tyrannos, the Greek word for tyrant, appears to have been of Lydian origin; it originally meant "lord" or "leader" and did not have the modern connotation of "despot." The tyrants had first made their appearance among the Eastern Greeks. They were essentially dictators who seized power during periods of civil strife; some of them may have come to power in the crisis of the Cimmerian invasion of the early seventh century. Many became long-term heads of state who did not abolish the councils or assemblies but prolonged the existence of these bodies as part of the machinery of government. The tyrants promoted and gave direction to the economic development of the cities which they ruled. When the Lydian kingdom extended its sway over the East Greek towns in the late seventh and early sixth centuries, the tyrants fell, but tyranny was a culture trait diffused from Asia Minor to mainland Greece where it took a slightly different form.

In Greece, especially in the seventh and sixth centuries B.C., tyrants led the middle class, or the poor farmers, or both groups, against the entrenched aristocrats. Often, but not always, the tyrant was a political boss who did not change the constitution or hold state office but operated behind the scenes making sure that his candidates secured the magistracies and controlled the council. The great landholders were sometimes exiled and their lands confiscated. They were replaced in the government by representatives of the middle class with the frequent result that when the tyranny fell or the tyrant died the businessmen as a class would succeed to political supremacy. The mainland tyrants promoted trade and manufacturing; they also aided the poorer citizens with gifts of land or by setting up public works projects that not only beautified their cities but provided work for those who could not make a living by full-time farming. Many of the tyrants were patrons of culture; they subsidized the artists, literary men, and philosophers whom they invited to come to their towns. The Greek tyrant, like the 19th century (A.D.) Latin American *caudillo*, or dictator, was likely to appear when a state had reached a certain point in its political and economic development. His function was to bring about the overthrow of a political monopoly and to provide a measure of political stability, if not freedom, until the state in question gained sufficient economic and political maturity to get along without him.

The rise of the middle class to political power in Greece had been aided not only by the creation of new sources of wealth through business or by the immediate intervention of the tyrants, but also by a military development. During the Dark Ages the mainstay of the army had been the chariot warrior, with the spear-bearing foot soldier playing only a minor part. In this "Homeric" type of warfare the nobles with their horses and chariots did most of the fighting. We have already noted, however, the diminution of pasture land that brought a decrease in the numbers of cattle and horses. The shortage of horses and the consequent increase in their price made them almost too valuable to be risked in warfare. Then, in the seventh century, a new type of warfare came into Greece from Asia Minor; this was based on the phalanx, or packed mass of heavy-armed foot soldiers. Chariots tended to become obsolete because they were ineffective against the solid wall of the phalanx bristling with spears. The key to the phalanx was manpower. The nobles were too few to man it; consequently, the middle class whose members could afford the heavy armor and new weapons became indispensable to the state. Because of their growing numbers in the assembly and because of their value to the phalanx, the new class could not long be denied increased participation in the government. Sometimes the aristocrats were forced by military necessity to compromise and open the council and some of the offices to the businessmen; in such case, the intermediate step of tyranny could be avoided.

By the sixth century B.C., aristocracy as a form of government was the exception rather than the rule, just as monarchy had given way to aristocracy at the close of the Dark Ages. The prevailing governmental form was now *timocracy,* a government in which citizens participate in proportion to their wealth. Typically, in a timocracy the richest citizens would be able to hold any of the offices of state, be members of the council, and participate in the assembly; those of more moderate means would hold minor posts, be eligible for the council,

and vote in the assembly; the poorer citizens might be restricted to the assembly, and the poorest might well be excluded entirely from governmental participation. Timocracy had its origin in the development of sources of wealth other than land. Trade and industry had created new ways of acquiring wealth, and thus, according to Greek thinking, people of substance had a right to be represented in the government.

Hesiod, a poet-farmer who lived during the second half of the eighth century B.C. in central Greece in what was later to become the state of Boeotia,[2] provides us with perhaps the most detailed account of the early Archaic Age. Unlike Homer, who sang of the warrior aristocracy, Hesiod's concern was with the peasants' attitudes and way of life. He reflects in his poetry, too, the growing political unrest and the anxiety which was produced by the dissolution of the kinship-based society—an anxiety which seems to be experienced when any tribal society undergoes this kind of change.

In tribal societies kinship arrangements permeate the most diverse and basic involvements: they define a man's fundamental loyalties, determine when and against whom he is to wage war, establish the locales within which he will pursue his subsistence-getting activities, rigorously regulate whom he must or must not marry, from whom he gets justice, and from whom he learns ritual requirements and work skills.

With the decline of tribalism men leave a society in which their diverse activities are integrated within a single institutional framework, in which the bonds between men are multiple rather than segmentalized, and in which the basic paradigm of human relations is that of the family or of kinship ties. Leaving tribalism they come to live among those with whom they are, for the most part, un-

[2] See map on p. 76.

Black-figured Lekythos, c. 560 B.C. The more naturalistic treatment of the human form is a refinement of the Archaic portrayal of the body. Further, the concern with household activities (women folding cloth, top left; working wool on the loom, top right) indicates a less formal usage of art. (Metropolitan Museum of Art, Fletcher Fund, 1931)

related by real or fictive kinship ties, and thus in effect relinquish the support and protection of a group that is viewed much as if it were a large family.

To leave tribalism is to leave a world in which most decisions are closely regulated by a network of unexaminable rules. To leave tribalism is to enter a world of greater choices

—concerning marriage, trade, and personal and political alliances. It is to enter a world in which the very rules governing decisions are themselves regarded as things concerning which decisions may be made. Men increasingly view themselves as rule-makers, as "the measure of all things," rather than simply as rule-followers or rule-breakers. It is a move, therefore, toward an open and unstructured social situation which can be more exciting but, at the same time, more uncertain and anxiety inducing.

In this new world, one way that men for whom established tradition and its interpreters have lost authority may know the right and the real is by referring to the opinion of those around them. It becomes increasingly important for men to secure consensual validation of their impulses, beliefs, and, indeed, of their very worth, when the traditional verities wane and the ways of the world no longer seem ordained.

Under tribalism men might chafe and rebel against the traditional rules but these rules constitute, nevertheless, the visible pivot of their choices. With the breakdown of tribalism the choice is no longer the relatively simple one of conformity with or deviance from received rules, of rules that are taken as given; there is now a question of choices concerning the rules themselves. The rules become problematic. The diké, or "the way," of the group becomes unclear to the detribalized Greeks; they begin to ask themselves: What is diké? What is the right way? What is justice? What rules should we follow? What is the good? Are there any limits to the rules we can make? Is there a latent (or "natural") order underlying and limiting the diversity of the alternative rules by which one might be guided?

The growing concern with problems of ethics and morality—already evident in Hesiod and culminating in Socrates—marks the emergence of men who have to improvise new rules of the game even as they are playing it. . . .[3]

In both his *Theogony* and *Works and Days* Hesiod reveals his concern with right order and morality, especially as it is found in law. In the earlier of the poems, the *Theogony*, Hesiod orders the relationships between the gods by going back to their origins and then recording their history up to his own time.

THE STORY TOLD IN THE THEOGONY
Michael Grant[4]

First Chaos came into being, next wide-bosomed Gaea (Earth), Tartarus and Eros (Love). From Chaos came forth Erebus and black Night. Of Night were born Aether and Day (whom she brought forth after intercourse with Erebus), and Doom, Fate, Death, Sleep, Dreams; also, though she lay with none, the Hesperides and Blame and Woe and the Fates, and Nemesis to afflict mortal men, and Deceit, Friendship, Age and Strife, which also had gloomy offspring.

And Earth first bore starry Heaven (Uranus), equal to herself, to cover her on every side, and to be an ever-sure abiding place for the blessed gods. And Earth brought forth, without intercourse of love, the Hills, haunts of the Nymphs, and the fruitless Sea with his raging swell. And Earth lay with Heaven and bore their children the Titans: Oceanus (who had three thousand neat-ankled daughters, one of them the mother of Thetis), Hyperion, Iapetus, Themis, Memory (Mnemosyne), Phoebe (whose daughter by Coeus was Hecate, whom Zeus loved most of all),

[3] From *Enter Plato* by Alvin W. Gouldner, pp. 80–81. © 1965 by Basic Books, Inc., Publishers, New York, and reprinted by their permission.

[4] Reprinted by permission of The World Publishing Company from *Myths of the Greeks and Romans* by Michael Grant, pp. 87–90. Copyright © 1962 by Michael Grant.

also Tethys, and the one-eyed Cyclopes, and Cronus the wily—youngest and most terrible of her children.

Cronus hated his lusty sire Heaven (Uranus). And Heaven hated others whom Earth had borne him, the hundred-armed and fifty-headed Cottus and Briareus and Gyes; and Heaven would not let them come up into the light. But Cronus answered his mother's plea and, as his father Heaven lay upon Earth, he castrated his father with a jagged sickle. Cronus cast the severed members behind him, and from the bloody drops Earth conceived the Furies, Giants and Nymphs of the Ash-Trees. And as the members were swept away in the sea, the foam that spurted around them gave birth to Aphrodite.

To Cronus, Rhea bore Hestia, Demeter, Hera, Hades, Posidon. But Cronus devoured them all as soon as each had left its mother's womb, for he had learnt from Earth and Heaven that he was destined to be overcome by his own son. But when Rhea was about to bear Zeus to him, Earth and Heaven sent her to Lyctus in Crete; and there Zeus was born, and hidden in a mountain cave. To Cronus she gave instead of him a stone wrapped in swaddling clothes, and he swallowed it instead of his son. When Zeus grew to manhood, Cronus was conquered by him, and Cronus spewed up not only this stone, but the children he had devoured. Zeus also released the brothers of Cronus from beneath the earth; and they gave him the thunderbolt and lightning by which he rules.

To one of Cronus' brothers, Iapetus, a daughter of Ocean named Clymene bore Atlas who upholds the sky, and wily Prometheus. At Mecone the Field of Poppies, while gods and men were met together there, Prometheus sought to deceive Zeus. When Prometheus was cutting up a great ox to be divided among them, he separated the flesh and entrails from the bones. He enclosed the meat and entrails in the stomach, and the bones he concealed in a wrapping of fat. Then he gave Zeus his choice of the two portions, and Zeus, though in his wisdom he saw through the trick, chose the bones. Out of anger for what Prometheus had done, he deprived mankind of fire; but Prometheus stole it in a hollow fennel-stalk and gave it to men. So Prometheus was bound by Zeus to a rock, and each day an eagle flew over and ate his liver, which grew again during the night—until later Heracles, by the will of his father Zeus, released him from his bonds.

Zeus punished man in another way also, by creating an evil thing, woman, as the price of fire. Hephaestus made her out of clay; Athene adorned her, setting upon her head a golden crown which Hephaestus himself had devised; and Zeus brought her out to be shown to gods and men, and gave her to Prometheus' scatterbrained brother Epimetheus. "And wonder took hold of the deathless gods and mortal men when they saw that which was sheer guile, not to be withstood by men. For from her is the deadly race and tribe of women who live amongst mortal men to their great trouble."

But strife broke out between the young gods on one side—Zeus and his brothers and sisters, the children of Cronus dwelling on Mount Olympus—and on the other side the older gods, the Titans, children of Heaven and Earth, dwelling on Mount Othrys. With the help of the hundred-armed three, Cottus and Briareus and Gyes whom he had brought up from beneath the earth, Zeus assailed his Titan

The Temple of Poseidon (Neptune) at Paestum, Mid-fifth Century B.C. The Greek temple is believed to have served originally as a shelter for a statue devoted to a particular god or goddess. The unique structure was developed by borrowing from the Myceneans, Minoans, and particularly the Egyptians and Assyrians. The above temple was a place of worship for the devotees of the ruler of the sea. (J. Allan Cash from Rapho Guillumette)

enemies. "The thunderbolts flew thick and fast from his strong hand, with thunder and lightning, and flame unspeakable rose to the bright upper air; and his hundred-armed allies hurled three hundred rocks and felled the Titans to as far beneath the earth as heaven is above it." For so far is the distance from earth to Tartarus with its gates and walls of bronze, the murky home of Night, Sleep, Death, Hades, Persephone and their guardian hound, and of the eternal, primeval water of Styx. At the entrance to Tartarus stands Atlas upholding the sky, where Night and Day draw near and greet one another as they pass the brazen threshold.

After the Titans had been driven from heaven, Earth bore to Tartarus her youngest child Typhoeus. A hundred snakes' heads sprouted from his shoulders, and flames flashed from his eyes. At times his voices were understood by the gods, but sometimes they were like the roar of a lion or bull, or the baying of a hound; and sometimes there came from him a hissing or whistling that echoed from peak to peak. Typhoeus threatened the earth and the sea and Olympus itself, but Zeus struck at him with thunder and lightning until the whole universe seethed, and the earth was scorched and melted. His hundred heads perished in flames, and he was hurled down, a maimed wreck, to Tartarus.

Now that Zeus had overcome all his enemies, the gods chose him to be their

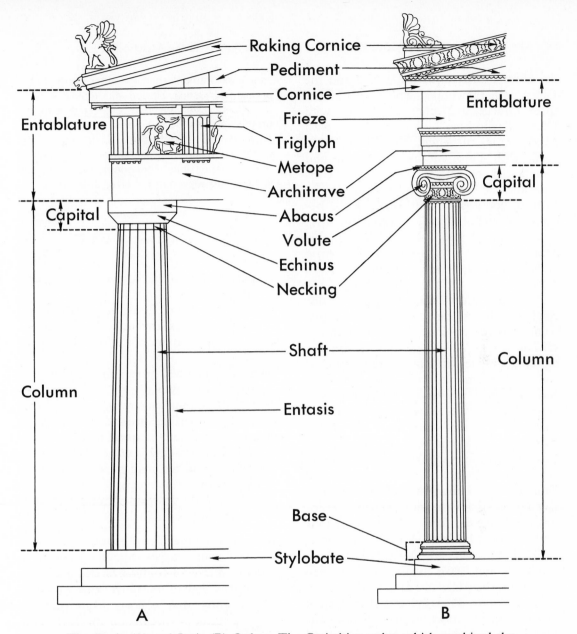

Raking Cornice
Pediment
Cornice
Frieze
Triglyph
Metope
Architrave
Abacus
Volute
Echinus
Necking
Shaft
Entasis
Base
Stylobate

Entablature

Capital

Column

Entablature

Capital

Column

A

B

The Doric (A) and Ionic (B) Orders. The Corinthian order, which combined the central features of the Doric and Ionic columns, emerged much later and received extensive use and elaboration in the Roman Empire. (Giraudon)

king, and he divided their powers and privileges among them. He made Wisdom (Metis) his first wife, but swallowed her before she could give birth to Athene so that none but he could be Athene's parent. Then he lay with Themis, who bore him the Hours, Order, Justice, Peace and the Fates; with Eurynome, who bore him the three Graces and other daughters; with Demeter who bore him Persephone; with Mnemosyne, of whom the Muses were born; with Leto, mother of Apollo and Artemis. Then lastly he made Hera his wife, and she bore him Hebe and Ares and Ilithyia, goddess of child-birth. Hebe became the wife of Heracles, son of Alcmene —"happy man! For he has finished his great work and lives among the undying gods, untroubled and unageing all his days."

But being angry with Zeus, Hera, conceiving without him, bore Hephaestus, "who is skilled in crafts more than all the sons of heaven."[5] And there were also immortal goddesses who lay with mortal men and bore them children who were like gods: Demeter whose son by Iasion, conceived in a thrice-ploughed fallow in the rich land of Crete, was Plutus who makes man rich; Harmonia wife of Cadmus and mother of Semele, who was to bear Dionysus to Zeus; Eos, who bore Memnon and Emathion to Tithonus, and Phaethon to Cephalus; Medea the daughter of heaven-nurtured Aeetes, from whom Jason took her; Thetis who bore Achilles to Peleus; Aphrodite (Cytherea) who loved the hero Anchises and gave birth to their son Aeneas on the peaks of Ida; and those who bore children to Odysseus—Circe gave birth to Agrius and Latinus, rulers of the Etruscans, and Calypso to Nausithous and Nausinous.

Having established a literary "right order" among the gods in the *Theogony*, Hesiod devoted his *Works and Days* to the right order that

should exist among men—in other words, to the problem of justice. Hesiod was moved to write this poem after he had quarreled with his brother, Perses. The dissension between them arose out of what Hesiod considered an inequitable division of property for which he held Perses responsible. The poem was addressed to Perses to show him the error of his ways.

WORKS AND DAYS
Hesiod[6]

Muses, who from Pieria give glory through
    singing,
come to me, tell of Zeus, your own father,
    sing his praises, through whose will
mortal men are named in speech or remain
    unspoken.
Men are renowned or remain unsung
    as great Zeus wills it.
For lightly he makes strong,
    and lightly brings strength to confusion,
lightly diminishes the great man,
    uplifts the obscure one,
lightly the crooked man he straightens,
    withers the proud man,
he, Zeus, of the towering thunders,
    whose house is highest.

Hear me, see me, Zeus: hearken:
    direct your decrees in righteousness.
To you, Perses, I would describe
    the true way of existence.

It was never true that there was only one
    kind
of strife. There have always
been two on earth. There is one
    you could like when you understand her.

---

[5] But Hephaestus has already appeared: here is an imperfect fusion of two stories.

[6] Reprinted from *Hesiod: The Works and Days* translated by Richmond Lattimore, lines 1–49 and 106–382 by permission of The University of Michigan Press. Copyright © 1959 by The University of Michigan Press.

The other is hateful. The two Strifes
  have separate natures.
There is one Strife who builds up evil war,
  and slaughter.
She is harsh; no man loves her, but under
  compulsion
and by will of the immortals men
  promote this rough Strife.
But the other one was born
  the elder daughter of black Night.
The son of Kronos, who sits on high and
  dwells in the bright air,
set her in the roots of the earth and among
  men;
  she is far kinder.
She pushes the shiftless man to work,
  for all his laziness.
A man looks at his neighbor, who is rich:
  then he too
wants work; for the rich man presses on
  with
  his plowing and planting
and the ordering of his state.
  So the neighbor envies the neighbor
who presses on toward wealth. Such Strife
  is a good friend to mortals.
Then potter is potter's enemy, and
  craftsman is craftman's
rival; tramp is jealous of tramp,
  and singer of singer.
      So you, Perses, put all this firmly
  away
  in your heart,
nor let that Strife who loves mischief
  keep you from working
as you listen at the meeting place
  to see what you can make of
the quarrels. The time comes short for
  litigations
  and lawsuits,
too short, unless there is a year's living
  laid away inside
for you, the stuff that the earth yields,
  the pride of Demeter.

When you have got a full burden of that,
  you can push your lawsuits,
scheming for other men's goods, yet you
  shall not be given another chance
to do so. No, come, let us finally settle
  our quarrel
with straight decisions, which are from
  Zeus,
  and are the fairest.
Now once before we divided our inheritance,
  but you seized
the greater part and made off with it,
  gratifying those barons
who eat bribes, who are willing
  to give out out such a decision.
Fools all! who never learned
  how much better than the whole the
  half is,
nor how much good there is
  in living on mallow and asphodel.
For the gods have hidden and keep hidden
  what could be men's livelihood.
It could have been that easily
  in one day you could work out
enough to keep you for a year,
  with no more working.
Soon you could have hung up your steer-
  ing oar
  in the smoke of the fireplace,
and the work the oxen and patient mules
  do
  would be abolished,
but Zeus in the anger of his heart hid it
  away
because the devious-minded Prometheus
  had cheated him;
and therefore Zeus thought up dismal sor-
  rows
  for mankind.
                    • • •
Or if you will, I will outline it for you
  in a different story,
well and knowledgeably—store it up

in your understanding—
the beginnings of things, which were the
same for gods
as for mortals.

In the beginning, the immortals
who have their homes on Olympos
created the golden generation of mortal
people.
These lived in Kronos' time, when he
was the king in heaven.
They lived as if they were gods,
their hearts free from all sorrow,
by themselves, and without hard work or
pain;
no miserable
old age came their way; their hands, their
feet,
did not alter.
They took their pleasure in festivals,
and lived without troubles.
When they died, it was as if they fell
asleep.
All goods
were theirs. The fruitful grainland
yielded its harvest to them
of its own accord; this was great and abundant,
while they at their pleasure
quietly looked after their works,
in the midst of good things
[prosperous in flocks, on friendly terms
with the blessed immortals].

Now that the earth has gathered over this
generation,
these are called pure and blessed spirits;
they live upon earth,
and are good, they watch over mortal men
and defend them from evil;
they keep watch over lawsuits and hard
dealings;
they mantle
themselves in dark mist
and wander all over the country;

they bestow wealth; for this right
as of kings was given them.
Next after these the dwellers upon
Olympos created
a second generation, of silver, far worse
than the other.
They were not like the golden ones either
in shape
or spirit.
A child was a child for a hundred years,
looked after and playing
by his gracious mother, kept at home,
a complete booby.
But when it came time for them to grow up
and gain full measure,
they lived for only a poor short time;
by their own foolishness
they had troubles, for they were not able
to keep away from
reckless crime against each other,
nor would they worship
the gods, nor do sacrifice on the sacred
altars
of the blessed ones,
which is the right thing among the customs of men,
and therefore
Zeus, son of Kronos, in anger engulfed
them,
for they paid no due
honors to the blessed gods who live on
Olympos.

But when the earth had gathered over this
generation
also—and they too are called blessed spirits
by men, though under
the ground, and secondary, but still
they have their due worship—
then Zeus the father created the third
generation
of mortals,
the age of bronze. They were not like
the generation of silver.

They came from ash spears. They were
   terrible
   and strong, and the ghastly
action of Ares was theirs, and violence.
   They ate no bread,
but maintained an indomitable and ada-
   mantine spirit.
None could come near them; their strength
   was big,
   and from their shoulders
the arms grew irresistible on their pon-
   derous bodies.
The weapons of these men were bronze,
   of bronze their houses,
and they worked as bronzesmiths. There
   was not yet
   any black iron.
Yet even these, destroyed beneath the
   hands
   of each other,
went down into the moldering domain of
   cold Hades;
nameless; for all they were formidable
   black death
seized them, and they had to forsake
   the shining sunlight.

Now when the earth had gathered over
   this generation
also, Zeus, son of Kronos, created yet another
fourth generation on the fertile earth,
   and these were better and nobler,
the wonderful generation of hero-men,
   who are also
called half-gods, the generation before our
   own
   on this vast earth.
But of these too, evil war and the terrible
   carnage
took some; some by seven-gated Thebes
   in the land of Kadmos
as they fought together over the flocks of
   Oidipous;

others
war had taken in ships over the great gulf
   of the sea,
where they also fought for the sake
   of lovely-haired Helen.
There, for these, the end of death was
   misted
   about them.
But on others Zeus, son of Kronos, settled
   a living
   and a country
of their own, apart from human kind,
   at the end of the world.
And there they have their dwelling place,
   and hearts free of sorrow
in the islands of the blessed
   by the deep-swirling stream of the
   ocean,
prospering heroes, on whom in every year
   three times over
the fruitful grainland bestows its sweet
   yield.
These live
far from the immortals, and Kronos
   is king among them.
For Zeus, father of gods and mortals,
   set him free from his bondage,
although the position and the glory still
   belong
   to the young gods.

After this, Zeus of the wide brows
   established yet one more
generation of men, the fifth, to be
   on the fertile earth.

And I wish that I were not any part
   of the fifth generation
of men, but had died before it came,
   or been born afterward.
For here now is the age of iron. Never by
   daytime
will there be an end to hard work and pain,
   nor in the night

to weariness, when the gods will send
   anxieties
   to trouble us.
Yet here also there shall be some good
   things
   mixed with the evils.
But Zeus will destroy this generation
   of mortals also,
in the time when children, as they are
   born,
   grow gray on the temples,
when the father no longer agrees with the
   children,
   nor children with their father,
when guest is no longer at one with host,
   nor companion to companion,
when your brother is no longer your friend,
   as he was in the old days.
Men will deprive their parents of all rights,
   as they grow old,
and people will mock them too,
   babbling bitter words against them,
harshly, and without shame in the sight of
   the gods;
   not even
to their aging parents will they give back
   what once was given.
Strong of hand, one man shall seek
   the city of another.
There will be no favor for the man
   who keeps his oath, for the righteous
and the good man, rather men shall give
   their praise
   to violence
and the doer of evil. Right will be in the
   arm.
   Shame will
not be. The vile man will crowd his better
   out,
   and attack him
with twisted accusations and swear an oath
   to his story.
The spirit of Envy, with grim face
   and screaming voice, who delights

in evil, will be the constant companion
   of wretched humanity,
and at last Nemesis and Aidos, Decency
   and Respect,
   shrouding
their bright forms in pale mantles, shall go
   from the wide-wayed
earth back on their way to Olympos,
   forsaking the whole race
of mortal men, and all that will be left by
   them
   to mankind
will be wretched pain. And there shall be
   no defense
   against evil.

Now I will tell you a fable for the barons;
   they understand it.
This is what the hawk said when he had
   caught
   a nightingale
with spangled neck in his claws and carried
   her
   high among the clouds.
She, spitted on the clawhooks, was wailing
   pitifully,
but the hawk, in his masterful manner,
   gave her an answer:
"What is the matter with you? Why
   scream?
   Your master has you.
You shall go wherever I take you,
   for all your singing.
If I like, I can let you go. If I like,
   I can eat you for dinner.
He is a fool who tries to match his strength
   with the stronger.
He will lose his battle, and with the shame
   will be hurt also."
So spoke the hawk, the bird who flies so
   fast
   on his long wings.

But as for you, Perses, listen to justice;
   do not try to practice

violence; violence is bad for a weak man;
   even a noble
cannot lightly carry the burden of her,
   but she weighs him down
when he loses his way in delusions; that
   other road
   is the better
which leads toward just dealings. For Justice
   wins over violence
as they come out in the end. The fool
   knows
   after he's suffered.
The spirit of Oath is one who runs
   beside crooked judgments.
There is an outcry when Justice is dragged
   perforce,
   when bribe-eating
men pull her about, and judge their cases
   with crooked decisions.
She follows perforce, weeping, to the city
   and gatherings of people.
She puts a dark mist upon her and brings
   a curse
   upon all those
who drive her out, who deal in her
   and twist her in dealing.
But when men issue straight decisions
   to their own people
and to strangers, and do not step at all
   off the road of rightness,
their city flourishes, and the people
   blossom inside it.
Peace, who brings boys to manhood, is in
   their land,
   nor does Zeus
of the wide brows ever ordain that hard
   war
   shall be with them.
Neither famine nor inward disaster comes
   the way
   of those people
who are straight and just; they do their
   work

as if work were a holiday;
the earth gives them great livelihood,
   on their mountains the oaks
bear acorns for them in their crowns,
   and bees in their middles.
Their wool-bearing sheep are weighted
   down
   with fleecy burdens.
Their women bear them children
   who resemble their parents.
They prosper in good things throughout.
   They need have no traffic
with ships, for their own grain-giving land
   yields them its harvest.
But when men like harsh violence
   and cruel acts, Zeus
of the wide brows, the son of Kronos,
   ordains their punishment.
Often a whole city is paid punishment
   for one bad man
who commits crimes and plans reckless
   action.
   On this man's people
the son of Kronos out of the sky
   inflicts great suffering,
famine and plague together, and the people die
   and diminish.
The women bear children no longer, the
   houses dwindle
by design of Olympian Zeus; or again at
   other times,
he destroys the wide camped army of a
   people,
   or wrecks
their city with its walls, or their ships
   on the open water.

You barons also, cannot even you
   understand for yourselves
how justice works? For the immortals
   are close to us, they mingle
with men, and are aware of those who
   by crooked decisions

break other men, and care nothing
　for what the gods think of it.
Upon the prospering earth there are
　thirty thousand immortal
spirits, who keep watch for Zeus and all
　that men do.
They have an eye on decrees given
　and on harsh dealings,
and invisible in their dark mist they hover
　on the whole earth.
Justice herself is a young maiden.
　She is Zeus's daughter,
and seemly, and respected by all the gods
　of Olympos.
When any man uses force on her by false
　impeachment
she goes and sits at the feet of Zeus Kron-
　ion,
　her father,
and cries out on the wicked purpose of
　men,
　so that their people
must pay for the profligacy of their rulers,
　who for their own greedy purposes
twist the courses of justice aslant
　by false proclamations.
Beware, you barons, of such spirits.
　Straighten your decisions
you eaters of bribes. Banish from your
　minds
　the twisting of justice.

The man who does evil to another does
　evil
　to himself,
and the evil counsel is most evil
　for him who counsels it.
The eye of Zeus sees everything. His mind
　understands all.
He is watching us right now, if he wishes
　to,
　nor does he fail
to see what kind of justice this community
　keeps

inside it.
Now, otherwise I would not myself
　be righteous among men
nor have my son be so; for it is a hard thing
　for a man
to be righteous, if the unrighteous man
　is to have the greater right.
But I believe that Zeus of the counsels
　will not let it end thus.

You, Perses, should store away in your
　mind all
　that I tell you,
and listen to justice, and put away
　all notions of violence.
Here is the law, as Zeus established it
　for human beings;
as for fish, and wild animals, and the flying
　birds,
they feed on each other, since there is no
　idea
　of justice among them;
but to men he gave justice, and she in the
　end
　is proved the best thing
they have. If a man sees what is right
　and is willing to argue it,
Zeus of the wide brows grants him pros-
　perity.
But when one, knowingly, tells lies and
　swears
　an oath on it,
when he is so wild as to do incurable dam-
　age
　against justice,
this man is left a diminished generation
　hereafter,
but the generation of the true-sworn man
　grows stronger.
I mean you well, Perses, you great idiot,
　and I will tell you.
Look, badness is easy to have, you can
　take it
　by handfuls

without effort. The road that way is
  smooth
and starts here beside you.
But between us and virtue the immortals
  have put
  what will make us
sweat. The road to virtue is long
  and goes steep up hill,
hard climbing at first, but the last of it,
  when you get to the summit
(if you get there) is easy going after the
  hard part.

That man is all-best who himself works
  out
  every problem
and solves it, seeing what will be best late
  and in the end.
That man, too, is admirable who follows
  one
  who speaks well.
He who cannot see the truth for himself,
  nor,
  hearing it from others,
store it away in his mind, that man
  is utterly useless.
As for you, remember what I keep telling
  you
  over and over:
work, O Perses, illustrious-born, work on,
  so that Famine
will avoid you, and august and garlanded
  Demeter
will be your friend, and fill your barn
  with substance of living;
Famine is the unworking man's most constant
  companion.
Gods and men alike resent that man who,
  without work
himself, lives the life of the stingless
  drones,
who without working eat away the substance

of the honeybees'
hard work; your desire, then, should be
  to put your works in order
so that your barns may be stocked with all
  livelihood in its season.
It is from work that men grow rich and
  own flocks
  and herds;
by work, too, they become much better
  friends
  of the immortals.
[and to men too, for they hate the people
  who do not labor].
Work is no disgrace; the disgrace is in not
  working;
and if you do work, the lazy man will soon
  begin
  to be envious
as you grow rich, for with riches go nobility
  and honor.
It is best to work, at whatever you have a
  talent
  for doing,
without turning your greedy thought toward what
  some other man
possesses, but take care of your own livelihood,
  as I advise you.
Shame, the wrong kind of shame, has the
  needy man
  in convoy,
shame, who does much damage to men.
  but prospers them also,
shame goes with poverty, but confidence
  goes with prosperity.

Goods are not to be grabbed; much better
  if God
  lets you have them.
If any man by force of hands wins him
  a great fortune,
or steals it by the cleverness of his tongue,
  as so often

happens among people when the intelligence
is blinded
by greed, a man's shameless spirit tramples
his sense of honor;
lightly the gods wipe out that man, and diminish
the household
of such a one, and his wealth stays with him
for only a short time.
It is the same when one does evil to guest or suppliant,
or goes up into the bed of his brother, to lie
in secret
love with his brother's wife, doing acts
that are against nature;
or who unfeelingly abuses fatherless children,
or speaks roughly with intemperate words
to his failing
father who stands upon the hateful doorstep
of old age;
with all these Zeus in person is angry,
and in the end
he makes them pay a bitter price
for their unrighteous dealings.
Keep your frivolous spirit clear of all such
actions.
As far as you have the power, do sacrifice
to the immortals,
innocently and cleanly; burn them the shining
thighbones;
at other times, propitiate them with libations
and burnings,
when you go to bed, and when the holy light
goes up the sky;
so They may have a complacent feeling
and thought

about you;
so you may buy someone else's land, not have someone
buy yours.

Invite your friend to dinner; have nothing to do
with your enemy.
Invite that man particularly who lives close
to you.
If anything, which ought not to happen, happens in your neighborhood,
neighbors come as they are to help; relatives
dress first.
A bad neighbor's as great a pain as a good one's
a blessing.
One lucky enough to draw a good neighbor
draws a great prize.
Not even an ox would be lost, if it were not
for the bad neighbor.
Take good measure from your neighbor,
then pay him back fairly
with the same measure, or better yet,
if you can manage it;
so, when you need him some other time,
you will find him steadfast.
No greedy profits; greedy profit is a kind
of madness.
Be a friend to your friend, and come to him
who comes to you.
Give to him who gives; do not give to him
who does not give.
We give to the generous man; none gives to him
who is stingy.
Give is a good girl, but Grab is a bad one;
what she gives is death.
For when a man gives willingly, though he gives
a great thing,
yet he has joy of his gift and satisfaction
in his heart,

while he who gives way to shameless greed
and takes
from another,
even though the thing he takes is small,
yet it stiffens his heart.
For even if you add only a little to a little,
yet if
you do it often enough, this little may yet
become big.
When one adds to what he has,
he fends off staring hunger.
What is stored away in a man's house
brings him no trouble.
Better for it to be at home, since what is
abroad
does damage.
It is fine to draw on what is on hand, and
painful
to have need
and not have anything there; I warn you
to be careful in this.
When the bottle has just been opened, and
when
it's giving out, drink deep;
be sparing when it's half-full; but it's useless
to spare the fag end.

Let the hire that has been promised to a
friend
be made good.
When you deal with your brother, be
pleasant,
but get a witness; for too much
trustfulness, and too much suspicion,
have proved men's undoing.
Do not let any sweet-talking woman be-
guile
your good sense
with the fascinations of her shape. It's
your barn
she's after.
Anyone who will trust a woman is trusting
flatterers.

One single-born son would be right to
support
his father's
house, for that is the way substance piles
up
in the household;
if you have more than one, you had better
live
to an old age;
yet Zeus can easily provide abundance
for a greater number,
and the more there are, the more work is
done,
and increase increases.
If the desire within your heart is for greater
abundance,
do as I tell you: keep on working with
work
and more work.

The arbitrariness of aristocratic rule against
which Hesiod inveighed was, as noted by Professor Jones, a source of social and political
unrest throughout the Archaic Age. The end
result was frequently revolution and the establishment of a tyranny. In the seventh century
B.C. Sparta, one of the strongest of the Greek
states, succeeded in avoiding this pattern of
development.

SPARTA IN THE ARCHAIC AGE
Tom B. Jones [7]

As the sixth century B.C. drew to a close,
mainland Greece was the home of several
states notable for political, military, or
economic strength. These were Athens,
Sparta, Corinth, Thebes, and Argos. All
were situated on the eastern side of
Greece, with Thebes and Athens in the

[7] Reprinted with permission from Tom B. Jones,
*From the Tigris to the Tiber: An Introduction to Ancient
History* (Homewood, Ill.: The Dorsey Press, 1969),
pp. 97–98 and 100–101.

central area and the other three in the southern peninsula, the Peloponnesus. Only a few score miles separated Thebes, farthest north, from Sparta, farthest south, yet in this tiny cockpit the main drama of Greek history was to be played out (550–350 B.C.). Very little is known of the internal history of Thebes, and certainly not enough about Corinth and Argos. Athens and Sparta we know better because they had the leading roles in the fifth century, a circumstance that led the ancient writers to deal copiously with them to the neglect of the history of the other states. Thebes was a land-locked city state in the midst of the fertile region of Boeotia. Corinth was a great commercial and industrial state possessed of considerable naval strength. Argos, important in Mycenaean times but declining at the end of the Dark Ages, was still a force to be reckoned with. Corinth typified the new era (750–500 B.C.), while Thebes and Argos seemed backward and atavistic by comparison. Sparta and Athens, each in their own way, were atypical; unlike Corinth, neither had followed the pattern of development already outlined for the Age of Colonization but both had arrived at greatness before the end of the sixth century.

Sparta differed from other Greek states in its size, resources, and historical development. The territory of Laconia controlled by Sparta was much larger than that of the ordinary Greek state, and it contained some of the most fertile land in Greece. It was in its political evolution, however, that Sparta could most justly claim to be unique.

The ruling element in Laconia was Dorian, as it was also in Corinth and Argos. The Dorian conquerors of Laconia had taken over the most fertile land and forced the natives to cultivate the soil as *helots*, or serfs. Before the end of the Dark Ages, the inhabitants of mountain and coastal areas had been made subject to Sparta; since their lands ringed the fertile Laconian plain, these people were known as *perioeci*, "dwellers around." The perioeci had local self-government, but their foreign relations were in Spartan hands, and they had to furnish contingents for the Spartan army in time of war.

Sparta itself was a *polis*, or city state, which controlled the surrounding area of Laconia. Spartan citizens who could perform military service participated in the assembly, or *apella* as it was called in Sparta. There was a council of the elders, composed of the senior representatives of 28 noble clans. What was truly remarkable was that the monarchy had not been abolished, but even more startling and unusual was the fact that Sparta had two royal families and two kings. We may guess that this dual monarchy had been the result of some ancient compromise.

In spite of its fertility, Laconia had known land hunger. Just before 700 B.C. colonists had been sent to Tarentum in southern Italy, and in the seventh century Laconia also participated in the colonization of Cyrene in North Africa. In a less conventional move to assuage the desire for land, Spartan aristocrats had invaded and conquered a fertile plain in Messenia, just across the mountains to the west of Laconia. About 630 B.C., however, the Messenians rose in revolt, drove out the Spartans, and invaded Laconia. In this extremity, the aristocrats were forced to seek the aid of the common people. Messenia was reconquered, but the nobles had to repay the commoners by acceding to an extensive reorganization of the Spartan economy and governmental system. These reforms, once credited to a semilegendary lawgiver named Lycurgus, we now know to have been gradually accomplished over a long period of years and still in progress in the mid-sixth century B.C. Sweeping changes made Sparta into a unique state dissimilar to any other in Greece. The completed arangements may be described as follows:

Private ownership of land was abolished. The state controlled the land and distributed farms of equal size to heads of families along with helots to work the land for the citizen tenants. Henceforth the adult male citizen had two responsibilities: to see that his farm maintained a certain rate of productivity, and to perform what amounted to nearly life-long, continuous military service. These citizen warriors had to be constantly alert to prevent a helot uprising or to fight off outside enemies who might wish to invade the rich country of Laconia and Messenia. The job of policing Laconia itself was not easy since the perioeci might become restive and the helots, always dangerous, outnumbered the Spartans about 12 to one. This was one reason why Spartan policy was generally isolationist; they had enough to worry about at home without getting involved in trouble abroad.

Sparta became completely militarized. Every man was a soldier, and his training, or indoctrination, began at the tender age of seven when he was taken from home and mother and put into barracks with other boys. Until a citizen was 30 years old he continued to live in the barracks where he underwent a regimen that developed his physique, made him skilled in the use of weapons, and trained him to execute military maneuvers with that precision that was essential for the effectiveness of the new phalanx formation. This made the Spartan army practically invincible since all other Greeks were, at best, summertime soldiers.

On the other hand, political, economic, and cultural evolution ended for Sparta. Time stood still. The reforms brought Sparta a strength and security that were temporarily beneficial, but the rest of the world moved on, and the Spartans were eventually left behind. Their state was overcome in the fourth century because they had not adapted themselves to the changing times.

The kings, the council of the elders, and the apella were left unchanged under the new system adopted after the Messenian war, but a new feature was added: this was the board of five *ephors* annually elected by the assembly. The ephors were supposed to guard the people's rights achieved by the reforms and to see that no alterations were made in the system now adopted. Possessing power superior to that of the kings, the ephors supervised the kings closely; they could even fine the kings or force them to abdicate. The ephors conducted the foreign relations of Sparta, and at home they had it in their power to oversee and regulate every phase of public and private life.

Once established, the Spartan system was unchanged for nearly 200 years. Only one important addition was made: this was the formation of the Peloponnesian League which began to be organized about 560 and was virtually completed by 500 B.C. The league consisted of a series of alliances contracted by Sparta on the one hand and individual Peloponnesian states on the other; each state was bound to Sparta by a separate treaty. The alliances were defensive in intent; the treaty makers were pledged to aid one another in case of enemy attack. This created a ring of buffer states around Laconia that would reinforce the protective shell provided by the perioeci. The Peloponnesian League made the Spartans the leaders of a powerful military machine which completely outclassed the land forces of any possible enemy or combination of enemies in Greece. When the Spartans broke the power of hostile Argos by a victory in 547 B.C., they became supreme in the Peloponnesus. It was fortunate for the rest of the Greeks that the policy of Sparta was isolationist and defensive and that the forces of the Peloponnesian League could be mobilized only for defense and not for aggression. If the Spartans had turned to imperialism in the sixth century, they might have subjected most of Greece to their rule.

Sparta was of great importance in the history of ancient Greece not only because it became a great landed military power but also because it was the first to be governed by a constitution. It was "the first state in Greece which we know consciously to have created a new social and political system with an authority greater than that of any member or class of members of the state."[8]

Athens, where the great drama of classical Greece was to be played out, also learned to deal with political unrest; but the manner in which it handled its social problems was substantially different from that of Sparta.

ATHENS IN THE EARLY ARCHAIC AGE
Tom B. Jones [9]

Attica, the territory in which Athens was situated, was neither as large nor as fertile as Laconia. It possessed some arable plains, good clay, fine marble, and forest reserves that lasted until the end of the fifth century. Two possessions of value

were not exploited by the Athenians before 500 B.C.: deposits of silver at Laurium and a fine harbor, the Piraeus. Attica is triangular in shape. Two sides are defined and defended by sea boundaries, but the landward side of the Attic peninsula posed some problems in antiquity. Adjoining Attica on the west was Boeotia, dominated by hostile Thebes; to the southwest was Megara, a tiny Dorian state that was not always an effective buffer between Athens and her other archenemy, Corinth.

According to recent opinion, Africa was fairly prosperous during the Dark Ages. At any rate, population pressures that promoted foreign colonization by Corinth and Megara in the eighth and early seventh centuries do not seem to have disturbed Attica until after 650 B.C. when it was too late for the Athenians to share in the colonization movement. This meant that Athens would have to solve its problems in a different way, and so, like Sparta, its history would not follow usual patterns.

The march of events at Athens is obscured from us until well into the second half of the seventh century B.C. By that time the monarchy had been abolished and the functions of the king divided among several annually elected magistrates chosen from the ranks of the landed aristocrats. These officials were called *archons*. One, known simply as *the* archon, headed the administration of Athens; another was the war-leader *(polemarch);* still another was a kind of high priest called the *archon basileus,* or king archon; by 620 B.C. six other archons, the *thesmothetai,* had been added to the list to serve as judges. A council manned by nobles was called the *Areopagus* because it met on the hill of that name just northwest of the Acropolis. All citizens able to perform military service were eligible to participate in the assembly *(ecclesia),* but a large number of

[8] W. G. Forrest, *The Emergence of Greek Democracy, 800–400 B.C.* (New York: McGraw-Hill Book Company, 1966), p. 143.
[9] Tom B. Jones, *From the Tigris to the Tiber: An Introduction to Ancient History* (Homewood, Ill.: The Dorsey Press, 1969), pp. 101–104.

people had already been excluded from this body by reason of their poverty.

Trouble had been brewing for some time. There had been an unsuccessful attempt to establish a tyranny perhaps even before 620, and about that date the aristocrats had been forced to consent to an elementary codification of the law, presumably because the administration of justice had been abused by the nobles. At last, a real crisis developed, and revolution was averted only at the cost of sweeping political and economic reforms. In 594 B.C., or possibly as late as 570, the constitution was suspended, and a single lawgiver, or *nomothete,* was given the authority to make changes that would save the state from chaos. Solon, a distinguished citizen trusted by both nobles and commons, was authorized to institute the necessary reforms. Emergency legislation enacted by Solon cancelled the mortgages that bound many small farmers to their own lands where they had been forced to labor for their creditors; other citizens who had been sold into slavery were redeemed and emancipated at public expense, and debt slavery in any form was henceforth prohibited in Attica.

These measures forestalled a revolution. They were remedies for an immediate situation, but Solon realized the necessity for more drastic changes in order to cure the basic ills of the country and prevent new crises from arising. Attica must be freed from her overdependence on agriculture; the economy must be diversified. To this end, Solon sought to encourage the development of trade and industry. He promoted the production and export of olive oil, a commodity of superior quality in Attica. This would be a cash crop that could be traded abroad for food and raw materials. To stimulate industry, Solon offered Athenian citizenship to foreign artisans who would settle in Attica and produce their wares for local consumption and export. Athenians were encouraged to apprentice their sons to these artisans in order that farm boys might learn a trade and find a place in the new economy.

Constitutional as well as economic reforms were made by Solon. He transformed the government from an aristocracy into a timocracy by arranging the citizens in census classes according to their wealth and fixing the degree of political participation for each class. The *thetes,* the poorest citizens, were admitted to the assembly even though they were unable to perform military service. People of moderate means were allowed to hold minor offices and perhaps be elected to the council as well as to participate in the assembly. The archonships, other offices, the council, and the assembly were of course all open to the wealthiest citizens. To forestall abuses of power by the masses who could now outvote the wealthier citizens in the assembly, Solon bestowed upon the Areopagus the privilege of reviewing legislation passed in the assembly; the Areopagus could invalidate measures which it deemed unconstitutional. Solon also promulgated a new law code less harsh and more comprehensive than the older one of the seventh century, and he created a court of appeal called the *heliaia.* Any citizen sentenced by a magistrate to the penalty of death, exile, or a heavy fine could appeal his case to the *heliaia.* The exact composition of this court is somewhat in doubt, but the evidence suggests that the *heliaia* was actually the *ecclesia* sitting as a court to hear such appeals.

Solon thus averted a revolution, liberalized the Athenian government, and reconstituted the Athenian economy. The export of olive oil stimulated the growth of a pottery industry. At first the potters made the containers in which the oil was exported, but later they also began to make and sell abroad extremely handsome painted vases used for tableware and other purposes. Other types of manufacturing developed as producers were able to exploit markets opened up by the oil trade. A middle class spawned by trade and industry soon appeared and, as elsewhere in Greece, entered the political arena.

While Solon's specific reforms were of great significance for both the political and social life of the Greeks, perhaps even more important was the new meaning he gave to the ideas of law and justice, both of which were dynamic elements in the historical development of the polis and Greek democracy. As already indicated, both before and during Solon's time Greece was beset

by social unrest and the striving for a better form of life. In these century-long disputes the idea of justice occupied a more and more prominent place. It is obvious that in the literature of the time the Homeric concept of right, *themis* (ordinance),[10] gives way gradually to Hesiod's favorite word, *diké*, which originally seems to have designated a share. In other words, the general trend was from an authoritative to a rational conception of right which stressed equality (*diké* was usually defined as "the equal") and mutual obligation.

At the same time the procedure of the administration was rationalized: the "custom" or *nomos* of the cities was codified by wise lawgivers appointed by the people, and thus *nomos* became the word for the written form in which the custom was laid down: it developed the new meaning "law." The social revolution which changed the feudal order of

the early Greek world during the seventh and sixth centuries was carried out under the slogans *diké* and *nomos,* or (to stress the equality of rights of the citizens *isonomia*.[11] This was the old word which the Greeks used instead of later *demokratia*. The ethical code of these centuries saw a new virtue added to the canon of civic virtues, *dikaiosyné*, which signified the moral quality of a man who is "just" and in this sense possesses "justice." The word was most often defined by the Greeks as obedience to the law. It is rather lawfulness than Plato's "justice" which is a condition within the human soul. This new virtue, which was characteristic of the time of the great Greek codifications and lawgivers, now became the highest standard of human perfection. Poets such as Phocylides and Theognis [in the mid-sixth century B.C.] described it as the virtue which comprises all the others. Even Aristotle retained it in this old sense in his *Ethics* as well as in the sense of fulfilling one's contractual obligations. We witness here the rise of new norms of human life and conduct which took the place of the vanishing old ones. Hesiod had complained when he pictured the "iron age" in which he was living that Aidos and Nemesis had left the earth and returned to Olympus. The concepts, which in the Homeric world had represented the traditional norms of human conduct and social responsibility, were now replaced by the spirit of the new commonwealth, the *polis*, as it was manifest in its written laws and in the obedience of the citizens to this supreme standard.

No other early Greek author illustrates this new legal ethos better than Solon, the great Athenian lawgiver, who (in his poems) reflects the principles of his legislative activity. In what seems to be one of the earliest documents of his thought, the political elegy *Our City*,[12] belonging to the period preceding his archonship (in 594 B.C.), he derives the present social unrest and the disrupting disturb-

[10] In Homer's time codified law did not exist and the later word for law, *nomos,* had not yet appeared. In the Homeric era it was believed that kings received their scepters and with them the *themistes* (ordinances which were actually customary usages) from Zeus, the source of earthly justice. [Ed.]

[11] Isonomia literally meant equality of dignity or status. [Ed.]

[12] See p. 99. [Ed.]

OUR CITY
Solon [13]

This city of ours will never be destroyed by the planning
   of Zeus, nor according to the wish of the immortal gods;
such is she who, great hearted, mightily fathered, protects us,
   Pallas Athene, who hands are stretched out over our heads.
But the citizens themselves in their wildness are bent on destruction
   of their great city, and money is the compulsive cause.
The leaders of the people are evil-minded. The next stage
   will be great suffering, recompense for their violent acts,
for they do not know enough to restrain their greed and apportion
   orderly shares for all as if at a decorous feast.

       . . .

   they are tempted into unrighteous acts and grow rich.

       . . .

   sparing the property neither of the public nor of the gods,
they do on stealing, by force or deception, each from the other,
   nor do the solemn commitments of Justice keep them in check;
but she knows well, though silent, what happens and what has been
      happening,
   and in her time she returns to extract a full revenge;
for it comes upon the entire city as a wound beyond healing,
   and quickly it happens that foul slavery is the result,
and slavery wakens internal strife, and sleeping warfare,
   and this again destroys many in the pride of their youth,
for from enemies' devising our much-odored city is afflicted
   before long by conspiracies so dear to wicked men.
Such evils are churning in the home country, but, of the impoverished,
   many have made their way abroad on to alien soil,
sold away, and shamefully going in chains of slavery . . .

       . . .

Thus the public Ruin invades the house of each citizen,
   and the courtyard doors no longer have strength to keep it away,
but it overleaps the lofty wall, and though a man runs in
   and tries to hide in chamber or closet, it ferrets him out.
So my spirit dictates to me: I must tell the Athenians
   how many evils a city suffers from Bad Government,
and how Good Government displays all neatness and order,
   and many times she must put shackles on the breakers of law.
She levels rough places, stops Glut and Greed, takes the force from
      Violence;
   she dries up the growing flowers of Despair as they grow;
she straightens out crooked judgments given, gentles the swollen
   ambitions, and puts an end to acts of divisional strife;
she stills the gall of wearisome Hate, and under her influence
   all life among mankind is harmonious and does well.
I gave the people as much privilege as they have a right to:
   I neither degraded them from rank nor gave them free hand;
and for those who already held the power and were envied for money,
   I worked it out that they also should have no cause for complaint.
I stood there holding my sturdy shield over both the parties;
I would not let either side win a victory that was wrong.

       . . .

Thus would the people be best off, with the leaders they follow:
   neither given excessive freedom nor put to restraint;
for Glut gives birth to Greed, when great prosperity suddenly
   befalls those people who do not have an orderly mind.

       . . .

   Acting where issues are great, it is hard to please all.

[13] Reprinted from *Greek Lyrics,* Richmond Lattimore, trans., pp. 20–22, by permission of the University of Chicago Press and Richmond Lattimore. Copyright 1949, 1955 and 1960 by Richmond Lattimore.

ances of the internal peace of the community from violation of justice committed by the political leaders who are guided by their own profit rather than by consideration of the common good. But Dike keeps a watchful eye on them, he asserts, even though she be silent, and eventually she will come to hold them responsible for their action. Dike appears as an all-powerful goddess here, as in Hesiod's poems; omniscient and all-seeing and independent of human justice when she comes to impose her retribution on the evildoer. It is impossible to escape her arm; it will reach even those who were able to outwit their human judges. All this recalls Hesiod's unshakable trust in divine justice; but Solon gives voice to his faith not as as a prophecy but as a common experience of human life. It is true he often expresses that experience, like Hesiod, in religious terms, and the firm belief in a just world order which is protected by divine power penetrates all his words and works. But he is far from the naive realism of Hesiod's religious faith. Hesiod lists as the god-sent punishments of his unjust city thunderstorms, floods, bad harvests, miscarriage, fire, war, loss of ships and cargo on the high sea, while their opposites are the blessings of heaven rewarding the just city. But Solon sees the vindicatory arm of Justice in all the kinds of *social* evil which befall the community: political unrest, party strife, riots, plots, bloodshed, and civil war; while her rewards for the just city are concord, peace, prosperity, good order, etc. In other words, his Justice works from within the political organism; it is a principle inherent in the social order itself. Like the physical life of the body, social life reacts with grave disturbances and diseases when its harmony is violated. There is in Solon's conception of justice the new awareness of a necessary connection of cause and effect between social phenomena. It corresponds to the causality which the Ionian philosophers of nature in Solon's time discovered in the cosmic phenomena. Justice is, in Solon's sense, the health of the community. We may doubt

whether this conception was in perfect harmony with the positive law of his age, which still followed the authority of tradition. For it was essentially a rational and philosophic conception of justice, and as such found its expression in Solon's whole work as a lawgiver: and the effect of this work was a revolution, though peaceful, of the existing forms of law in accordance with his ideal of the true social order. Solon's concept of justice was far from mere formal obedience to the law; he attempted to restore full harmony between the written law and that which appeared to his reason as the natural and logical order of things, and this he called *eunomia*.[14]

We have traced the development of the Greek concept of justice from Homer to Solon, and this brief survey has directed our attention to a feature which we shall find essential to Greek legal thought in all its phases: the relationship of justice and law to the nature of reality. We see it expressed first in religious terms which connect human justice with the divine government of the world and with the will of Zeus, the supreme wisdom. Gradually there rises a more rational concept of justice and its fundamental importance for human life; but the religious terminology is retained even by such legal thinkers as Solon, because he needs these categories in order to stress the close relationship between justice and the nature of reality. For his *diké* is only a more rationalized form of that early Greek idea of justice, which was in harmony with the divine order of the world itself. . . .[15]

Solon's reforms in 594 B.C. did not bring immediate political stability because the progressive disintegration of Athens' aristocratic-tribal society continued to produce social unrest. By 560 B.C. there were three factions . . .

[14] *Eunomia* refers to a human community which is ruled by moderation, unity, and order. [Ed.]
[15] Werner Jaeger, "Praise of Law: The Origin of Legal Philosophy and the Greeks," in *Interpretations of Modern Legal Philosophies,* Paul Sayre, ed. (New York: Oxford University Press, 1947), pp. 355–357.

locked in a struggle for political supremacy: the landed aristocrats who were trying to retain their ebbing power; a faction probably representing the new middle class; and a third group composed mainly of impoverished small farmers. The leader of this last faction was a noble named Peisistratus who established a tyranny in 546 B.C. after two previous and unsuccessful attempts. Peisistratus drove out the nobles and confiscated their lands, won the support of the business class, and directed the affairs of Athens until he died in 527. Cultivating close relations with states likely to increase Athenian commerce, and continuing the liberal citizenship policy of Solon so that more foreign traders and artisans settled in Athens, Peisistratus built up trade and industry until his state was more than a match for its main competitor, Corinth. Some of the landless were given land; others found employment on the public works program of Peisistratus which aimed at the adornment of the Acropolis, the religious center of Athens, and other parts of the town. Peisistratus was a notable patron of culture who brought artists, poets, and philosophers to Athens. He inaugurated dramatic contests in honor of the god Dionysus; these were the forerunners of the great Athenian tragedies and comedies of the next century. Peisistratus in addition enlarged and elaborated the Panathenaic festival which honored the goddess Athena, and this gave Athens a religious pageant rivalling the Isthmian, Nemean, and Delphic games in other parts of Greece and nearly competitive in fame with the Olympic festival which honored Zeus at Olympia in Elis.

Peisistratus gave Athens stable government and great prosperity, but the Athenians tired of tyranny and were not so docile when Hippias and Hipparchus, the sons of Peisistratus, tried to prolong the regime after their father died. Growing unpopularity at home, pressures exerted by the aristocrats in exile, and the hostility of Sparta finally brought about the overthrow of the tyranny. Hipparchus was killed in an uprising in 514 B.C., and at last Hippias was expelled with Spartan aid in 510.

The departure of Hippias left the Athenians free to fight among themselves once more. There was a conservative faction backed by Sparta that wanted to scrap the liberal reforms of Solon and rescind the policy of giving citizenship to foreigners; the absent Hippias had a sizable following still in Athens that plotted for his return; and there was a liberal party with democratic inclinations led by a young noble named Cleisthenes. After attacks and counterattacks and interference by the Spartans, the liberals were finally victorious. In 508 Cleisthenes was given powers resembling those of Solon with a mandate to revise the constitution. Perhaps following on the heels of a military reform, Cleisthenes divided the Athenian citizen body into 10 tribes—previously there had been only four. Each tribe then annually elected 50 councillors who took their places in a new council, or *boule*, called the Council of the 500; the councillors were chosen from persons enrolled in the middle and upper census classes. The old council, the Areopagus, was not abolished; it retained its power of legislative review, but henceforth its members were ex-archons. The army consisted of 10 tribal regiments, each of which elected annually its own general, or *strategos*. The 10 *strategoi* composed a military board which operated under the presidency of the war archon (*polemarch*).

The new Council of the 500 was larger and more representative than the Areopagus had been. It was supposed to supervise the activities of the magistrates and other officials; it deliberated on matters of policy previous to meetings of the assembly; and it also drafted legislative measures to be submitted to the assembly for enactment. The ancients believed that the Council of the 500 superseded a Council of the 400 introduced by Solon, but the matter is debatable.

Perhaps one of the most important changes effected by Cleisthenes was his introduction of *deme* membership as the test or badge of citizenship. A *deme* was a small geographic division or ward in Attica, and henceforth a citizen was registered as such in his own deme so that the presence of his name on the deme rolls constituted proof of citizenship. Formerly, citizenship had been based on membership in a clan or phratry (brotherhood, a sort of artificial clan), and apparently many foreigners who had been granted citizenship by Solon or Peisistratus had been prevented from acquiring full civic rights because religious or social obstacles had been set in their path by conservative Athenians who were not in sympathy with the liberal citizenship policies. Transferring the matter to the demes took it out of the realm of religion and traditional social organization and into that of the purely civic or political.

By the end of the sixth century, then, Athens had achieved a diversified economy and great prosperity. Solon's timocracy had been translated into a reality when Peisistratus broke the power of the nobles, while the reforms of Cleisthenes carried the Athenian constitution one more step toward the democracy which was to be created in the fifth century.[16]

The Archaic Age, which the reforms of Cleisthenes brought to a close, had been an era of far-reaching changes in every sphere of Greek life. While economic growth, the transformation of the kinship-based society, and the establishment of new genres of political life must be considered the most important of these, there were others which cannot be bypassed without comment. Values, as we have seen, had become confused, and the means by which they were enforced had been modified.

. . . In the Archaic Age the mills of God ground so slowly that their movement was practically imperceptible save to the eye of faith. In order to sustain the belief that they

moved at all, it was necessary to get rid of the natural time-limit set by death. If you looked beyond that limit, you could say one (or both) of two things: you could say that the successful sinner would be punished in his descendants, or you could say that he would pay his debt personally in another life.

The second of these solutions emerged, as a doctrine of general application, only late in the Archaic Age, and was possibly confined to fairly limited circles. . . . The other is the characteristic archaic doctrine: it is the teaching of Hesiod, of Solon and Theognis, of Aeschylus and Herodotus. That it involved the suffering of the morally innocent was not overlooked: Solon speaks of the hereditary victims of *nemesis* [retribution] as . . . "not responsible"; Theognis complains of the unfairness of a system by which "the criminal gets away with it, while someone else takes the punishment later"; Aeschylus, if I understand him rightly, would mitigate the unfairness by recognising that an inherited curse may be broken. That these men nevertheless accepted the idea of inherited guilt and deferred punishment is due to that belief in family solidarity which Archaic Greece shared with other early societies and with many primitive cultures today. Unfair it might be, but to them it appeared as a law of nature, which must be accepted: for the family was a moral unit, the son's life was a prolongation of his father's, and he inherited his father's moral debts exactly as he inherited his commercial ones. Sooner or later, the debt *exacted its own payment*: as the Pythia told Croesus, the causal nexus of crime and punishment was *moira* [Fate], something that even a god could not break; Croesus had to complete or fulfil . . . what was begun by the crime of an ancestor five generations back.

It was a misfortune for the Greeks that the idea of cosmic justice, which represented an advance on the old notion of purely arbitrary divine Powers, and provided a sanction for the new civic morality, should have been thus associated with a primitive conception of the

[16] Reprinted with permission from Tom B. Jones, *From the Tigris to the Tiber: An Introduction to Ancient History* (Homewood, Ill.: The Dorsey Press, 1969), pp. 104–106.

family. For it meant that the weight of religious feeling and religious law was thrown against the emergence of a true view of the individual as a person, with personal rights and personal responsibilities. Such a view did eventually emerge in Attic secular law . . . The liberation of the individual from the bonds of clan and family is one of the major achievements of Greek rationalism, and one for which the credit must go to Athenian democracy. But long after that liberation was complete in law, religious minds were still haunted by the ghost of the old solidarity. It appears from Plato that in the fourth century fingers were still pointed at the man shadowed by hereditary guilt, and he would still pay a *cathartes* to be given ritual relief from it. And Plato himself, though he accepted the revolution in secular law, admits inherited religious guilt in certain cases. A century later, Bion of Borysthenes still found it necessary to point out that in punishing the son for the father's offence God behaved like a physician who should dose the child to cure the father; and the devout Plutarch, who quotes this witticism, tries nevertheless to find a defence for the old doctrine in an appeal to the observed facts of heredity.

To return to the Archaic Age, it was also a misfortune that the functions assigned to the moralised Supernatural were predominantly, if not exclusively, penal. We hear much about inherited guilt, little about inherited innocence; much about the sufferings of the sinner in Hell or Purgatory, relatively little about the deferred rewards of virtue; the stress is always on sanctions. That no doubt reflects the juridical ideas of the time; criminal law preceded civil law, and the primary function of the state was coercive. Moreover, divine law, like early human law, takes no account of motive and makes no allowance for human weakness. . . . The proverbial saying popular in that age, that "all virtue is comprehended in justice," applies no less to gods than to men: there was little room for pity in either. That was not so in the *Iliad:* there Zeus pities the doomed Hector and the doomed Sarpedon; he pities Achilles mourning for his lost Patroclus, and even Achilles' horses mourning for their charioteer. . . . He says in *Iliad* 21: "I care about them, though they perish." But in becoming the embodiment of cosmic justice Zeus lost his humanity. Hence Olympianism in its moralised form tended to become a religion of fear, a tendency which is

Gorgonian Head (Head of Medusa), c. mid-sixth century B.C. This terracotta image of Medusa is one of the early pieces in the Greek tradition to depict emotion. The intensity of the bizarre visage and its mood reveals one aspect of the psychological tenor of the Archaic Age. (Metropolitan Museum of Art, Harris Brisbane Dick Fund, 1939)

reflected in the religious vocabulary. There is no word for "god-fearing" in the *Iliad*; but in the *Odyssey* to be *theoudes* [god-fearing] is already an important virtue, and the prose equivalent, *deisi-daimon* [god-fearing], was used as a term of praise right down to Aristotle's time. The love of god, on the other hand, is missing from the older Greek vocabulary: *philotheos* [god-loving] appears first in Aristotle. And in fact, of the major Olympians, perhaps only Athena inspired an emotion that could reasonably be described as love. "It would be eccentric," says the *Magna Moralia*, "for anyone to claim that he loved Zeus."

And that brings me to the last general trait which I want to stress—the universal fear of pollution (*miasma*),[17] and its correlate, the universal craving for ritual purification (*catharsis*). Here once again the difference between Homer and the Archaic Age is relative, not absolute; for it is a mistake to deny that a certain minimum of catharsis is practised in both epics. But from the simple Homeric purifications, performed by laymen, it is a long step to the professional *cathartai* of the Archaic Age with their elaborate and messy rituals. And it is a longer step still from Telemachus' casual acceptance of a self-confessed murderer as a shipmate to the assumptions which enabled the defendant in a late fifth-century murder trial to draw presumptive proof of his innocence from the fact that the ship on which he travelled had reached port in safety. We get a further measure of the gap if we compare Homer's version of the Oedipus saga with that familiar to us from Sophocles. In the latter, Oedipus becomes a polluted outcast, crushed under the burden of a guilt "which neither the earth nor the holy rain nor the sunlight can accept." But in the story Homer knew he continues to reign in Thebes after his guilt is

discovered, and is eventually killed in battle and buried with royal honours. . . .

There is no trace in Homer of the belief that pollution was either infectious or hereditary. In the archaic view it was both, and therein lay its terror: for how could any man be sure that he had not contracted the evil thing from a chance contact, or else inherited it from the forgotten offence of some remote ancestor? Such anxieties were the more distressing for their very vagueness—the impossibility of attaching them to a cause which could be recognised and dealt with. To see in these beliefs the *origin* of the archaic sense of guilt is probably an over-simplification; but they certainly expressed it, as a Christian's sense of guilt may express itself in the haunting fear of falling into moral sin. The distinction between the two situations is of course that sin is a condition of the will, a disease of man's inner consciousness, whereas pollution is the automatic consequence of an action, belongs to the world of external events, and operates with the same ruthless indifference to motive as a typhoid germ. . . .[18]

During the Archaic Age art, too, was influenced by the atmosphere of emotional insecurity and tension. Monsters and wild beasts became prominent themes for the first time. As one historian has observed: "Throughout Greek art from the middle of the eighth century down well into the seventh century death intrudes frequently, and man responds to the ultimate proof of his weakness not with dignified resignation but with fierce, macabre horror."[19] Yet it was during the same period that the Greeks created their first lyric poetry and laid the foundations for their achievements in philosophy and mathematics.

[17] Pollution is the supposed presence of some kind of substance which is believed to stand in the way of man's relations with the supernatural. [Ed.]

[18] From E. R. Dodds, *The Greeks and the Irrational* (Berkeley and Los Angeles: University of California Press, 1951), pp. 33–36. Reprinted by permission of University of California Press.

[19] Chester G. Starr, *The Origins of Greek Civilization, 1100–650 B.C.* (New York: Alfred A. Knopf, Inc., 1961), p. 283.

CHAPTER 5

THE SEPARATION OF MAN FROM NATURE:
The First Scientific Revolution

. . . Three scientific revolutions have been at the foundation of the metaphysics of the Western world. The first was the revolution of the Ionian nature-philosophers, which, in its search to identify the material properties of all natural substances, was led to seek in rational principles the explanation of the multiformities of change. This effort to establish reason in nature culminated not in a single system but in the construction of three great cosmologies: the system of Aristotle, emphasizing form and matter; the system of Democritus, establishing atomism; and the system of Plato, based on mathematical relations. . . .

Albert William Levi, Philosophy and the Modern World

[For the Ionian philosophers nature] . . . is subject to an immanent rule of law like mankind, and . . . it is this rule of law which regulates coming-to-be and passing-away throughout creation.

Werner Jaeger, Paideia, *Vol. I*

Only Being is; not-being cannot be. . . .

Parmenides

> I have gone gray at the temples,
> yes my head is white, there's nothing
> of the grace of youth that's left me,
> and my teeth are like an old man's.
> Life is lovely. But the lifetime
> that remains for me is little.
> For this cause I mourn. The terrors
> of the Dark Pit never leave me.
> For the house of Death is deep down
> underneath the downward journey
> to be feared, for once I go there
> I know well there's no returning.

Anacreon of Teos (a lyric poet of the late sixth century B.C.*), Greek Lyrics,*
trans. by Richmond Lattimore, 2d ed., pp. 46–47

Music is the arithmetic of the soul, which counts without its being aware of it.

Leibniz

The Archaic Age (750–500 B.C.), one of several troubled eras in the history of ancient Greece, witnessed a vast increase in the knowledge of both the physical world and the human personality. With this knowledge the stage was set for the supreme achievements of the fifth and fourth centuries. During the sixth century B.C. science was born in Ionia. Here for the first time nature was described in rational terms; natural phenomena were no longer conceived to be effected in any manner by supernatural forces. Despite the impressiveness of this intellectual feat, it must be remembered that the first scientists were not scientists in the modern sense.

> . . . They did not generalize cautiously from careful observation and experiment. On the contrary, they immediately proceeded by tenuous analogy to the most extensive generalization, thus exhibiting a characteristic of magical rather than scientific thinking.[1]

Nevertheless, their common-sense and non-mythical approach to nature is typical of the scientific spirit. Perhaps these first scientists are best understood if defined as natural philosophers and the precursors of both modern scientists and philosophers.[2]

These natural philosophers, it should be noted, are also referred to as the Pre-Socratic philosophers and include the Milesian or Ionian philosophers (Thales, Anaximander, and Anaximenes), Heraclitus, the Eleatics (Parmenides and Zeno), the Pythagoreans (who will be dealt with later in this chapter) and the pluralists (who will be discussed in Chapter 8).

NATURAL PHILOSOPHY
W. K. C. Guthrie[3]

"Pre-Socratic" is the term commonly used (and the one that will be used here) to cover those Greek thinkers from approximately 600 to 400 B.C. who attempted to find universal principles which would explain the whole of nature, from the origin and ultimate constituents of the universe to the place of man within it. Yet 400 was the last year of Socrates' life, and among the Sophists, who are also excluded, Protagoras and Gorgias were older than he and others were his contemporaries. "Pre-Socratic" therefore indicates not so much a chronological limit as an outlook and a range of interests. This outlook Protagoras and Socrates deliberately attacked, condemning natural philosophy as worthless compared with the search for a good life, the discussion of social and political questions, and individual morality. Socrates also dismissed its explanations as inadequate because expressed predominantly in terms of origins and internal mechanisms. In his view explanation should be functional, looking to the

---

[1] A. P. Cavendish, "Early Greek Philosophy," in *A Critical History of Western Philosophy,* D. J. O'Connor, ed. (New York: The Free Press, 1964), p. 3.

[2] When the term "philosophy" was first used (presumably by the Pythagoreans in the sixth century B.C.), it meant the rational explanation of anything or the general principles under which all facts could be explained. The sciences were not formally separated from the discipline of philosophy until the early nineteenth century.

[3] W. K. C. Guthrie, "Pre-Socratic Philosophy," *Encyclopedia of Philosophy,* Paul Edwards, ed. (New York: The Macmillan Company and The Free Press, 1967), Vol. VI, pp. 441–444.

end rather than the beginning. Thus, for the last sixty or so years of the fifth century, both points of view existed, and a lively controversy went on between them. It was not that the natural philosophers excluded human nature from their investigations but that they saw man and society in a larger framework, as a particular late stage in cosmic development, whereas the others deliberately turned their backs on the external world. The universal and speculative character of pre-Socratic thought was also combated by some of the fifth-century medical writers, and it was in the fields of physiology and hygiene that observational science reached its highest point in this period.

Nature of the Evidence

Before attempting to describe the pre-Socratic doctrines, it is necessary to emphasize the peculiar nature of our sources of knowledge. None of the pre-Socratics' works has survived independently. We have a few references in Plato, some more systematic discussion in Aristotle, and information from later compilers and commentators of which the greater part goes back to a history by Aristotle's pupil Theophrastus. Actual quotations occur and are in some cases extensive, as with the prose fragments of Heraclitus and the 450 surviving lines of Empedocles. Yet, from Aristotle onward, the men who passed on this information were not historians in the modern sense but wrote from a particular philosophical viewpoint . . . searching the past for anticipations of their own ideas and selecting and arranging their material accordingly. The task of reconstruction and interpretation is thus very different from and more precarious than that of interpreting a philosopher whose original writings are still available for study.

The Milesian School

Pre-Socratic philosophy differs from all other philosophy in that it had no predecessors. Philosophy has been a continuous debate, and even highly original thinkers can be seen developing from or reacting against the thought of a predecessor. Aristotle is unimaginable without Plato; Newton, without Descartes, Kepler, Galileo, and many others. But with the Greeks of the sixth century the debate begins. Before them no European had set out to satisfy his curiosity about the world in the faith that its apparent chaos concealed a permanent and intelligible order, and that this natural order could be accounted for by universal causes operating within nature itself and discoverable by human reason. They had predecessors of a sort, of course. It was not accidental that the first pre-Socratics were citizens of Miletus, a prosperous trading center of Ionian Greeks on the Asiatic coast, where Greek and Oriental cultures met and mingled. The Milesian heritage included the myths and religious beliefs of their own peoples and their Eastern neighbors and also the store of Egyptian and Babylonian knowledge—astronomical, mathematical, technological. The influence of this heritage was considerable. Yet the Milesians consciously rejected the mythical and religious tradition of their ancestors, in particular its belief in the agency of anthropomorphic gods, and their debt to the knowledge of the East was not a philosophic one. That knowledge was limited because its aim was practical. Astronomy served religion; mathematics settled questions of land measurement and taxation. For these purposes the careful recording of data and the making of certain limited generalizations sufficed, and the realm of ultimate causes was left to dogmatism. For the

Greeks knowledge became an end in itself, and in the uninhibited atmosphere of Miletus they gave free play to the typically Greek talent for generalization, abstraction, and the erection of bold and all-embracing explanatory hypotheses.

Consciously, the revolt of the Milesian philosophers against both the content and the method of mythology was complete. No longer were natural processes to be at the mercy of gods with human passions and unpredictable intentions. In their place was to come a reign of universal and discoverable law. Yet a whole conceptual framework is not so easily changed. Poetic and religious cosmogonies had preceded the schemes of the Milesians, and the basic assumptions of these can be detected beneath the hypotheses of their philosophic successors. Nevertheless, the achievement of abandoning divine agencies for physical causes working from within the world itself can hardly be overestimated.

It was common to the mythologies of Greece and neighboring civilizations (and, indeed, to others) that the world arose from a primitive state of unity and that the cosmogonic process was one of separation or division. This was the first act of the Hebrew Creator. In the Babylonian *Enuma Elish* the original state of the universe was an undefined mass of watery cloud. The Greek theogony of Hesiod speaks of Heaven and Earth, conceived as anthropomorphic figures, lying locked in an embrace until their son forced them apart as Marduk [in the *Enuma Elish*] formed heaven and earth by splitting apart the body of the monster Tiamat. Euripides relates an old tale according to which earth and heaven were once "one form" and after their separation brought to birth the whole variety of living things. In Egypt (like Babylonia, a river culture) everything arose out of the primeval waters.

Thales. It is not surprising, therefore, that the first men to seek a universal explanation of the world along rational lines assumed that it was in substance a unity from which its variety had been produced by some process of segregation. The key, they thought, lay in identifying the single substance which must satisfy the condition of being able to produce variety out of itself. Thales (active in 585 B.C.), who chose water or moisture, may still have had the myths at the back of his mind. For him the earth floated on water as it did for the Egyptians. Little else certain is known of him, and we can only guess at his reasons. Water can be seen as solid, liquid, and vaporous. Aristotle thought it more probable that Thales was influenced by the essential connection of moisture with life, as seen in such substances as semen, blood, and sap. With the removal of external personal agents, the world must initiate its own changes, and at this early stage of speculation the only possibility seemed to be that life of some kind is everywhere and that the universe is a growing, organic structure. This may be the explanation of the saying attributed to Thales: "Everything is full of gods."

Anaximander. With Anaximander, Thales' younger contemporary, there emerges the notion of the four primary opposites which later, when the concepts of substance and attribute had been distinguished, gave rise to the four elements adopted by Aristotle and destined for a long and influential history. Anaximander spoke of only the hot and the dry, which were inevitably in conflict with the cold and the wet. This led him to a momentous idea. The original substance of the universe could not be anything definitely qualified like water, for how could the cold and wet produce their opposites, the hot and dry? Water quenches fire; it cannot engender it. Prior to all perceptible body there must be an indefinite something with none of the incompatible qualities implied by perceptibility. Although still regarding all that exists as corporeal, Anaximander is the first to find ultimate reality in the nonperceptible.

This primary substance he called the apeiron, a word of many meanings all related to the absence of limits—everlasting, infinite, indefinite. Because it was imperishable, the origin of all things, and the author of their changes, he called it (says Aristotle) divine. From it all things have been "separated out," though in what sense they were previously "in" it while the apeiron itself remained a unity is a question which probably did not present itself to him. Somewhere in the apeiron, Theophrastus asserts, a "germ" or "seed" of hot and cold was separated off, and from the interaction of these two flowed the whole cosmic process. A sphere of flame enclosed a moist mass, more solid at the center where the earth formed, vaporous between. The sphere burst into rings around which the dark vapor closed, leaving holes through which we see what appear as sun, moon, and stars. Wet and dry continue to separate, forming land and sea, and finally life itself is produced by the same action of heat (sun) on the cold and moist portions of the earth. The first animals were born in water and crawled onto dry land. Human infants were originally born and nurtured within the bodies of fishlike creatures, for under primitive conditions unprotected babies could not have survived.

The earth, a flat cylinder, hangs freely in space because of its equal distance from all parts of the spherical universe. The sun is the same size as the earth. Eclipses are caused by the closing of the holes in the vapor tubes of the sun and moon. In this first of all attempts at a rational cosmogony and zoogony, the sudden freedom from mythical modes of thought is almost incredible.

Anaximenes. Further reflection led Anaximenes, the youngest member of the Milesian school, to a different conclusion about the primary substance: it was air. In its elusiveness and invisibility as atmospheric air, it could almost match the apeiron, and, whereas apeiron, once differentiated into a universe, could no longer be so called, air could become hotter and colder, rarer and denser, and still remain the same substance. Moreover, this theory allowed Anaximenes to break with the notion of separation, which was, at bottom, mythical, and account for the universe by the extension of a known natural process. This was condensation and rarefaction, the former of which he associated with cold and the latter with heat. Air as it rarefies becomes fire; condensed, it turns first to wind, then to cloud, water, earth, and stones. In other words, it is all a question of how much of it there is in a given space, and for the first time the idea enters science that qualitative differences are reducible to differences of quantity. This is Anaximenes' main achievement, although there is no evidence that he applied the principle with any mathematical exactness.

With air as his basic, self-changing substance, Anaximenes could find room for the ancient belief that life was identical with breath. Macrocosm and microcosm were animated by the same principle: "Just as our soul, which is air, integrates us, so breath and air surround the whole cosmos."

The few details that we have of his cosmology suggest that compared with Anaximander's, it was reactionary and timid. His contribution lies elsewhere. . . .

Heraclitus

Heraclitus [maintained that] . . . strife and opposition were the life of the world. Life was maintained by a tension of opposites fighting a continuous battle in which neither side could win final victory. Thus, movement and the flux of change were unceasing for individuals, but the structure of the cosmos remained constant. This law of individual flux within a permanent universal framework was guaranteed by the Logos, an intelligent governing principle materially embodied as fire, the most subtle element and identified with soul or life.

Philosophy had thus far meant the search for an essentially simpler reality underlying the bewildering confusion of appearances. The answers fell into two broad categories, matter and form: reality was a single material substance (the Milesians) or an integral principle of structure which could be expressed in terms of numbers (the Pythagoreans). Heraclitus, with a statement like "You cannot step twice into the same river," reaches the logical conclusion of the materialistic answer. The water will be different water the second time, and, if we call the river the same, it is because we see its reality in its form. The logical conclusion of form-philosophy is the opposite of flux—namely, a belief in an absolute, unchanging reality of which the world of change and movement is only a quasi-existing phantom, phenomenal, not real. (This conclusion was reached in the idealism of Plato. . . .)

Eleatic School: Unity of Reality

At this time the direction of philosophy was changed by the precocious and uncompromising logic of Parmenides of Elea, who was perhaps 25 years younger than Heraclitus. For the first time abstract, deductive reasoning is deliberately preferred to the evidence of the senses: "Ply not eye and ear and tongue, but judge by thought." He concluded that if there is any reality at all (in the language of his time, if "it is"), it must be (1) one only (for if more than one, its units could be separated only by "what is not"); (2) eternal and unchanging (for to speak of change or perishing is to say that reality at some time "is not" what it was, but to say of "what is" "it is not" is contradictory and impossible); (3) immovable (this follows from his statement that "all is full of what is"; since it cannot admit discontinuity or lack of homogeneity and since "what is not is not," the spatial requirements of locomotion cannot be provided). In this way he "proved" that, on the premise of his predecessors that reality is one, differentiation of the real can never occur. It remains one—a timeless, changeless, motionless, homogeneous mass, which he compared to a sphere. The multiple, changing world of appearances is an illusion of our senses. Only as a concession to human weakness, and in recognition of our practical need to come to terms with the show of a natural world, did he append a cosmology of the conventional type, beginning with two principles, heat-light and cold-darkness. Cosmogony from a single origin was no longer possible, yet he explicitly warns his hearers that reality is in truth a unity and that the cosmos is only a deceitful appearance to mortals.

It is disputed whether the One Reality of Parmenides is material. The question can hardly be answered, since we are still in a period before the distinction between material and nonmaterial could be drawn. The important thing is that it was nonsensible and could be reached only by thought. Parmenides was the first philosopher to distinguish explicitly between the sensible and the intelligible and to condemn the former as unreal. Plato himself, though fully aware of the distinction between material and spiritual, usually preferred to call them sensible and intelligible, and it is very doubtful whether the philosophy of Platonic idealism would ever have been possible without Parmenides.

Zeno and Melissus. Parmenides had two followers, who, with him, are known as the Eleatic school. Zeno of Elea (born c. 490) concentrated on a defense of the proposition that reality is one and immovable by the dialectical method of showing up absurdities in the contrary view. His famous paradoxes are aimed at demonstrating the impossibility of plurality and movement. Melissus of Samos (active in 440) modified Parmenides' ideas to the extent of sayng that reality is infinite. He explicitly denied the possibility of empty space (which Parmenides had only hinted at) and said that if there *were* many things, each would have to have the characteristics of the Parmenidean One. It is therefore probable that the atomists had him especially in mind when they boldly explained the world in terms of space plus tiny entities, each of which had many of the Eleatic qualities—indivisibility, homogeneity, unalterability.

The naïveté of Parmenides' logic and the purely linguistic nature of some of his difficulties seem obvious now, but at the time his questions appeared unanswerable. There were only two ways out: either to abandon monism and admit the ultimate plurality of the real or to admit the unreality of the natural world. The latter solution was Plato's, with his contrast between "what always is and never becomes" and "what is continually becoming (like the flux of Heraclitus) but never truly is." . . .

The Milesians, Heraclitus, and the Eleatics formulated rational, as opposed to mythical, explanations of the natural world in ontological terms.[4] Because they adopted this mode of explanation, they began the development of those concepts which have since been the central concern of Western philosophy:

being and becoming, sensible and intelligible, analytic and synthetic, appearance and reality, time and eternity, materialism and idealism, mechanism and teleology, and so forth. Once these stand out clearly, a philosopher may champion one or the other, but the pre-Socratics could not yet do this. One cannot speak realistically of a controversy among them between, say, materialists and idealists. The achievement of their intellectual effort and controversy was that by the end of this

---

[4] The word "ontology" derives "from the Greek terms *ontos* (being) and *logos* (theory, account). . . . When we inquire about the 'ontological status' of something, say, perception, we ask whether the data of perception are real or illusory, and, if real, what sort of reality they possess (e.g., whether they are mind-dependent or whether they exist independently of minds), and so on." Ontology is very close in meaning to metaphysics. "Metaphysics" refers to "the study of the ultimate nature of reality, or, as some philosophers would say, the study of 'being as such.' [It is] to be contrasted, therefore, with physics, which studies the 'being' of physical nature; with astronomy, which studies the 'being' of the solar system; with biology, which studies the 'being' of animate nature and so on. By 'being as such' these philosophers mean, not the special characteristics of special things (e.g., living things), but the most general and pervasive characteristics of all things." (W. T. Jones, *A History of Western Philosophy,* pp. 1017–1018)

period a clear notion of what was meant by matter and mind, sensible and intelligible, phenomenal and real, and the rest was at last emerging. . . . For the first of all philosophers, this was no mean achievement.[5]

They could also claim the distinction of having discovered one of the fundamental postulates of logic, the principle of noncontradiction (A cannot both be B and not be B).

In explicitly recognizing that noncontradiction is a fundamental property of existence, as well as of thought, Parmenides hit upon a most important principle. Once it is recognized that only consistent entities can exist, the truth of generalizations can be tested by examining their consistency. . . . Throughout nature—in philosophy, physics, everywhere—it became possible to show simply by examining their logical consequences that some generalizations cannot be true. Whenever precise deduction leads to a contradiction, we can be sure that the initial assumption is wrong. Being cannot tolerate anything internally contradictory. . . .[6]

What factors enabled these few Greeks to discard a mythical understanding of the universe and to explain the physical world in rational terms? This question cannot be answered with certainty, but reasons can be suggested. One of them almost certainly was the unique character of Greek religion.

. . . The supernatural powers had taken human shapes so concrete and well defined that a Greek could recognise any god by sight. . . . It was inevitable that, when the gods had become completely human persons, some sceptical mind should refuse to believe that a thunderstorm in Asia Minor was really due to the anger of a deity seated on the summit of Olympus. In the sixth century Xenophanes attacked anthropomorphic polytheism with devastating finality:

"If horses or oxen had hands and could draw or make statues, horses would represent the forms of the gods like horses, oxen like oxen."

Henceforth natural science annexed to its province all that went on "aloft" in the sky or "under the earth." Thunder and lightning, Anaximander said, were caused by the blast of the wind. Shut up in a thick cloud, the wind bursts forth, and then the tearing of the cloud makes the noise, and the rift gives the appearance of a flash in contrast with the blackness of the cloud. This is a typically scientific "explanation." There is no longer a supernatural background, peopled with fragmentary or complete personalities accessible to prayer and sacrifice or amenable to magical compulsion. Intelligence is cut off from action. Thought is left confronting Nature, an impersonal world of things, indifferent to man's desires and existing in and for themselves. The detachment of self from the object is now complete.[7]

The detachment of the self from the natural world was only a first step in the development of science. In order to explain the external world in rational terms a new vocabulary was also required. Luckily, Greek intellectuals had at their disposal a language which lent itself to the creation of the necessary abstract vocabulary. The Greek language must thus be considered another factor which made the first scientific revolution possible.

[5]Reprinted with permission of the publisher from W. K. C. Guthrie, "Pre-Socratic Philosophy," *Encyclopedia of Philosophy*, Paul Edwards, editor, Vol. VI, pp. 445–446. Copyright © USA 1967 by Crowell Collier and Macmillan, Inc. Copyright © in Great Britain and under International Copyright Union 1967 by Crowell Collier and Macmillan, Inc.

[6] Robert S. Brumbaugh, *The Philosophers of Greece* (New York: Thomas Y. Crowell Company, 1964), pp. 54–55.

[7] Francis MacDonald Cornford, *Before and After Socrates* (Cambridge: Cambridge University Press, 1932), pp. 16–17.

THE FORGING OF A LANGUAGE FOR SCIENCE
Bruno Snell [8]

The oldest philosophical and scientific term that we know of and which actually seems to have been the oldest known to the Greeks is the *ápeiron* of Anaximander, the "boundless" or "infinite." In Homer, Poseidon, using this word *(Iliad* 7. 446), says that men are scattered over "the boundless earth." And in the *Odyssey* (4. 510) Homer says that someone pushes forth on "the boundless sea." This means of course that one cannot see the end of the land or the sea, that, as far as the eye can reach, there is only land or sea. But then comes the first philosopher from whom we have his own words—that is, Anaximander—and he speaks of the *ápeiron,* the "boundless"; and this boundlessness is for him the beginning and principle of all being.

Something quite absurd occurs at this point: one word, which asserts nothing positive, but only affirms that something is *not* there, namely an end or boundary, loses its harmless obvious meaning. Indeed Anaximander openly and quite consciously cuts off the word from the sight and experience of men by transforming the adjective into a noun. Thus he creates something that doesn't exist in the empirical world. The most absurd thing, however, is that this artificially produced concept is by no means vague and indefinite, but lends itself well to exact and noncontradictory definition. One can even substitute it in calculation with the help

[8] Bruno Snell, "The Forging of a Language for Science in Ancient Greece," *The Classical Journal,* Vol. LVI (1960–1961), pp. 50–58. Reprinted by permission of *The Classical Journal.*

of a mathematical symbol: the figure 8 lying on its side.

Now exactly what has happened? Anaximander took language seriously in an entirely new way, and took the word at its face value. The word "endless" actually points beyond its simple, ordinary usage; strictly speaking, Homer dared not speak of "endless sea" or of "boundless earth." One can make clear to everyone that "endless" connotes more than the fact that the eye perceives no boundary. Homer himself knows that, even if one cannot see them, Crete and Egypt lie beyond the sea. Beyond that, whatever seems boundless to men is exceeded by what is endless in fact and in reality.

Anaximander, so we learn, made an abstract concept out of an extant word from the colloquial and literary language. The Greek language provided him, through the definite article, with a convenient tool for constructing such abstractions: *tò ápeiron,* "the endless"—in the same way that later philosophers continued to form such abstractions: *tò agathón,* "the good," etc. This is the beginning of that immeasurable development in which philosophers and scientists create new entities, the creations of their thought. The terminology which was developed for these new concepts is undoubtedly the crowning achievement of scientific language. . . .

Likewise in the field of meaning that concerns knowledge and recognition, the Greeks gradually drew whatever was usable and fruitful for scientific language out of common words existing in ordinary language, in the same artificial and yet very natural way.

The word "to know" in Greek, *eidénai,* really means "to have seen," and so originally denotes the result of a certain sense perception, the residue (so to speak) of what is "intellectual" in sight, and only later the pure intellectual condition of knowledge as independent of how this knowledge was acquired. To the Greeks . . . knowledge gained through sight was always a sort of model according to which they were inclined to interpret other knowledge. Even in Homer, *eidénai* meant "to understand something well," in the sense of "to be well versed in a matter" . . . , though often in his works and later the original meaning survives. Thus as early as Homer *eidénai* is a general concept of knowledge of so broad a compass that later philosophy and science could use it as a general term for "to know." The decisive step to free the word from its original sensuous connotation, however, had been made in times before Homer. . . .

From still another sphere comes the word *epistamai*, from which the Platonic concept of knowledge, *episté·me·*, is derived. In Homer *epístasthai* means "to know how to do something," and it implies primarily a knowledge that lies within practical ability. It refers to handicrafts and all arts, as well as to speaking and to situations that one has to manage. . . .

To imagine man as a being who works as a scientist, who thinks and investigates, is first possible when one begins to grasp the mind more abstractly. But what does "abstract" mean? It is platitudinous to say that abstraction is necessary for all scientific and philosophical thought and speech. We have already encountered this fact with Anaximander's "endless," as well as with . . . thinking. The whole theme of my lecture could be exhausted in this one sentence: the Greeks developed a scientific language by forming abstractions. . . .

It seems to me that there are three ways of forming abstractions in language. The first is that nouns can be formed out of verbs and adjectives, as we have seen with Anaximander's *ápeiron*. The second is that the designation of an organ can be used to denote its function, as one can say: "Someone has a good head," which means, "He has a good intellect or good thoughts." The third is that proper names, for instance of divine or demonic beings, can be used as abstractions. In Greek the abstract vocabulary has been formed in each of these three ways.

The special adaptability of the Greek language to abstract thinking is unquestionably one of the primary factors in any explanation of the first scientific revolution. In addition, we have already seen the special significance attached by some scholars to the fact that this language was based on a phonetic alphabet.[9] The following selection suggests the role played by writing in the social life of the polis, and the impact which the social order in turn had on the natural philosophers' depiction of the world-order.

THE INFLUENCE OF THE POLIS ON THE CHANGING CONCEPTION OF SPACE
J. P. Vernant[10]

. . . The Ionians saw the world-order in a spatial framework; they were able to represent the positions, sizes, distances and movements of the stars by geometrical constructions; they sometimes made mechanical models. In the second place, . . . [the astronomy] of the Greeks was presented at once as a *theoria,* a body of knowl-

[9]See p. 62.
[10] From *Scientific Change,* edited by A. C. Crombie, pp. 103–107. © 1963 by Heinemann Educational Books Ltd., Basic Books, Inc., Publishers, New York. Reprinted by permission of the publishers.

edge having as its aim the systematization of the universe, and with no end other than itself. . . .

The introduction of geometry to, and secularization of, astronomical thought, such were the two aspects which essentially characterized the Greek phenomenon. That these two aspects are interdependent is demonstrated, in a striking manner, by Anaximander's example. By placing the earth in the centre of the universe, by affirming that it thus remained motionless, not needing any support because, being at an equal distance from all points of the celestial circumference, it had no reason to move in one direction rather than in another, Anaximander made cosmology geometrical; he situated the physical world in a purely mathematical space, consisting of reversible and symmetrical relationships. But, at the same time, he separated himself from all the ancient cosmogonies which distinguished between cosmic "levels" devoted to different divine powers, which attributed religious virtues to the various directions of space, and which represented the earth as emerging from the primordial waters (as again did Thales) or as founded in the subterranean depths of Erebos (as did Hesiod). With Anaximander, this mythical imagery, now useless, disappears: to understand the position and the stability of the earth, it is sufficient to know that all the radii of a circle are equal.

How can this intellectual mutation be explained? . . . One will readily agree that the Greeks were geometers. . . . But why? It cannot be a mere question of ethnic characteristics: the other Indo-Europeans do not manifest analogous gifts; besides, the Ionian Greeks, who founded the first cosmology, were precisely the most hybrid: Herodotus attributed to Thales a "Phoenician" origin. The phenomenon is a cultural, not a racial, one. It arises out of a psycho-social analysis putting astronomy, and more generally Ionian physics of which it is a part, into its context of civilization, into the spiritual framework proper to the seventh-century Greek.

From this point of view, a primary factor is to be noted. In the system of the Greek *Polis,* writing, as an intellectual tool, assumed a social function and took on a psychological character quite different from that in the kingdoms of the Middle East. The Greek case was here a privileged one because it presented successively the two forms of writing; the Mycenean world used, indeed, a form of writing—the linear B—reserved for professionals, for a class of specialist scribes, whose role was to establish as accurate a computation as possible of the various aspects of social life, rigorously controlled and regulated by the palace: not only economic production and the exchange, but also the organization of the religious calendar, the celebration of prescribed dates with the requisite rites. With the downfall of Mycenean power, about the twelfth century, this writing disappeared at the same time as the class of scribes involved in the system of palace economy. When the Greeks re-introduced writing, between the ninth and eighth centuries, by borrowing it from the Phoenicians, it was not only a different type of writing, phonetic and no longer syllabic, but a radically different cultural fact: no longer the speciality of a class of scribes, but the instrument of a communal culture, the intellectual link between all those who constituted the human community of the city. The social and psychological significance of writing was thus, in some way, inverted: writing no longer had as its object the production of archives for the king, enclosed in the secrecy of the palace; it fulfilled henceforward the function of an agent of publicity; it revealed, exposed to all the citizens, knowledge formerly forbidden or reserved for certain religious "orders" *(gene)*. To use Greek expressions again, writing allowed the making communal, *es koinon*, of privileges which, until then, had rightfully belonged to certain individuals like the *basileus*. The need to draw up laws, manifested from the beginning of the *Polis*, was very significant in this respect. Drawn up, written on a *pinax* exposed to the view of everyone, the laws escaped from the private authority of the *basileis*, whose function was to "speak" the law, to become public property, truly communal, a general rule superior to each individual and applicable to all equally. Because of the publicity conferred by writing, *diké*, without ceasing to appear as an ideal value, was in a position to act on a properly human level, to be realized in a legal system, *nomos*, submitted to discussion and revision, modifiable by the decision of the assembly. When in their turn individuals decided to make public their learning by means of writing: either in the form of books like those that Pherecydes and Anaximander were the first to write; or in the form of *parapegma*, of monumental inscription on stone, analogous to those which the city erected in the names of its magistrates and its priests (certain citizens had astronomical abjurations or chronological tables inscribed); or in the form of a *pinax*, of a chart or annotated map of the world; their ambition was not to share with others a personal opinion, but, in giving their message *es to koinon*, to make it the common

property of the whole city, a standard, like the law, to be recognized by all. Divulged, their wisdom acquired objectivity; it became "truth." It was no longer a question of a religious secret, reserved for a few members of the elite, favoured by divine grace. It is certainly true that the truth of the sage, like the religious secret, was a revelation of the essential, the unveiling of a superior reality which was beyond by far the greater part of mankind: but by delivering it up to writing it was torn away from a closed circle of secrets and exposed in the full light of day to the eyes of the whole city; it showed a recognition that it was by right accessible to all men, an agreement to submit it, like political matters, to the judgement of all, with the hope that it would be definitively accepted and recognized by all. . . .

But perhaps one can go even further. To this secularization, to this rationalization of social life, seems aptly to correspond the advancement of a new conception of space. It will be observed that the expression *es koinon* applied to that which, being of common interest to the city, must be the object of a public debate, is duplicated by another which has the same meaning: *es meson*. The Greeks maintained that certain deliberations, or certain privileges of the king, or the power (the *arché*, the *kratos*, the *dunasteia*) could not belong to any particular person, but must be deposited "in the centre," "in the middle." The recourse to a spatial image to express the consciousness which the city has of itself, the sentiment of its existence as a political community, has no simple value of comparison. It reflects the birth of an entirely new social space. The urban constructions are no longer, in fact, grouped as formerly around a royal fortress, sur-

rounded by walls. The town is now centred on the *agora,* common land, seat of
the *Hestia Koiné*—a public place where
problems of general interest were debated.
It is the town itself which is surrounded
by walls, protecting and circumscribing in
its totality the human group which constitutes it. There, where the royal citadel
used to stand, a private and privileged
residence, it erected temples which were
opened for a public cult. On the ruins of
the palaces, on the Acropolis which it
henceforward consecrated to the gods, it
is still itself that the city projects on to the
plane of the sacred as it realizes itself, on
the profane level, in the space of the
Agora. This urban framework, which men
like Hippodamos of Miletus—town-plan-
ner and politician—still attempted to rationalize, defined in fact a mental space,
discovered a new spiritual horizon, which
we must define in a more precise manner.
In the centre of the city, the agora constitutes a public and common area: all
those who go there show themselves, inasmuch as they are citizens, to be equals:
homoioi, isoi. However different they may
be in the concrete terms of social life, they
find themselves, by their very presence in
that socialized and "political" space, in
relationships of symmetry, equality, and
reciprocity. It is what is implied, in particular, by the institution of the *Hestia
Koiné,* of the Common Hearth. Installed
in the *Prytaneion,* on the *agora,* the public
hearth is a symbol of the community: as
the centre, it is, in some measure, at an
equal distance from the domestic hearths
of the divers families, which it had to represent equally without identifying itself
with one rather than another. A central,
public, egalitarian, and symmetrical area,
but also a secularized one; made so by

confrontation and argument, and which
was in opposition to the religious space of
the acropolis as the realm of the *hosia,* of
the profane affairs of the human city, was
to that of the *hiera,* of the sacred interests
which concern the divine.

Thus was projected and expressed in
space the new conception of the social
order which characterized the city. Society
was no longer formed of a hierarchical
pyramid having the king at its summit,
an exceptional personage, intermediary
between the gods and men. All the citizens
were situated on the same level, and the
level was subject to a regular order, to a
law of symmetry and reciprocity, as is
fitting for equals.

Like the new conception of the social order,
the concept of *diké* also arose from the social
conditions of the Archaic Age, and it too was
used by the natural philosophers in their interpretation of the physical world.

. . . They understood the invariable succession of cause and effect, to the observation
of which they had devoted themselves, as a
kind of retribution or compensation imposed
on everything that exists by a supreme justice, inherent in nature itself. Anaximander
of Miletus wrote in the one much-discussed
fragment which is preserved of his book, *On
Nature,* that this justice is fulfilled by the
ceaseless process of coming to be and passing
away by which all individual things pay penalty and compensation to each other according to the ordinance of Time. He obviously
thinks of time as a judge who imposes his
verdict on the contesting parties before a law
court. That reminds us of Solon, who keeps
saying that *diké* comes "in time" sooner or
later and in one passage explicitly makes time
(*chronos*) the ultimate judge of all human actions. But Solon's *diké* is the order underlying

the *human* world, whereas Anaximander's *diké* is the *eternal* order that rules the whole universe. They both have in common their conception of *diké* as an objective principle inherent in the divine nature of things, either the social world of man or the universe as a whole. What they had in mind was not only the strict regularity of causation which we call the law of nature, although their achievement is often spoken of in these modern terms; but also they traced in the life of the universe a supreme *norm* to which they thought it subjected. The idea of justice (*diké*) was the only concept which offered itself to them for this purpose because it was the highest norm in the world of man and nothing could escape its ordinance. Anaximander's *diké* gives sense and order to the universe and redeems it from chaos.

A world thus "justified" could be called rightly by another term taken over from the sphere of social order, a *cosmos.* That word occurs for the first time in the language of the Ionian philosophers; by taking this step and extending the rule of *diké* to reality as a whole they clearly revealed the nature of Greek legal thought and showed that it was based on the relationship of justice to being. . . .[11]

Also associated with the social changes of the Archaic Age, and perhaps the most important factor in explaining the first scientific revolution, was the growing consciousness of self. The transformation of the family-based society into a social order comprised of individuals produced the kind of frustrations and tensions which tend to lead to a heightened awareness of self. This is nowhere better demonstrated than in the first Greek lyric poetry, which was composed in the sixth century B.C. The following two poems by Sappho, a poetess who lived on

the island of Lesbos and a contemporary of Solon, illustrate the nature of the new sense of self.

SAPPHO OF MYTILENE[12]

I

Throned in splendor, deathless, O Aphrodite,
child of Zeus, charm-fashioner, I entreat you
not with griefs and bitternesses to break my
    spirit, O goddess;

standing by me rather, if once before now
far away you heard, when I called upon you,
left your father's dwelling place and de-
    scended, yoking the golden

chariot to sparrows, who fairly drew you
down in speed aslant the black world, the
    bright air
trembling at the heart to the pulse of count-
    less fluttering wingbeats.

Swiftly then they came, and you, blessed lady,
smiling on me out of immortal beauty,
asked me what affliction was on me, why I
    called thus upon you,

what beyond all else I would have befall my
tortured heart: "Whom then would you have
    Persuasion
force to serve desire in your heart? Who is it,
    Sappho, that hurt you?

Though she now escape you, she soon will
    follow;
though she take not gifts from you, she will
    give them:
though she love not, yet she will surely love
    you even unwilling."

In such guise come even again and set me
free from doubt and sorrow; accomplish all
    those

[11] Werner Jaeger, "Praise of Law: The Origin of Legal Philosophy and the Greeks," in *Interpretations of Modern Legal Philosophers. Essays in Honor of Roscoe Pound,* Paul Sayre ed. (New York: Oxford University Press, 1947), pp. 357–358.

[12] Reprinted from *Greek Lyrics,* Richmond Lattimore, trans., pp. 38–39, by permission of The University of Chicago Press and Richmond Lattimore. Copyright 1949, 1955 and 1960 Richmond Lattimore.

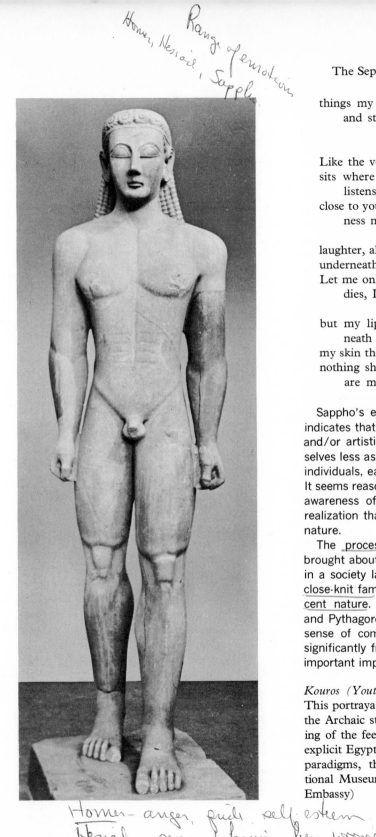

things my heart desires to be done; appear
and stand at my shoulder.

II

Like the very gods in my sight is he who
sits where he can look in your eyes, who
    listens
close to you, to hear the soft voice, its sweet-
    ness murmur in love and

laughter, all for him. But it breaks my spirit;
underneath my breast all the heart is shaken.
Let me only glance where you are, the voice
    dies, I can say nothing,

but my lips are stricken to silence, under-
    neath
my skin the tenuous flame suffuses;
nothing shows in front of my eyes, my ears
    are muted in thunder.

Sappho's exaltation of her personal feelings
indicates that the Greeks—at least the sensitive
and/or artistic Greeks—were thinking of themselves less as members of a group and more as
individuals, each with his own unique inner life.
It seems reasonable to assume that this growing
awareness of self in large part produced the
realization that man was in fact separate from
nature.

The process of individualization inevitably
brought about a reaction, for many felt isolated
in a society lacking the intimacy of the former
close-knit family and the friendship of a benefi-
cent nature. The mystery religions, Orphism,
and Pythagoreanism furnished for many a new
sense of community which, however, differed
significantly from that of earlier times and had
important implications for the future.

Kouros (Youth) from Sounian, c. 615–590 B.C.
This portrayal of the human form is sculpted in
the Archaic style. The static pose, the positioning of the feet, and the clenched fists reveal an
explicit Egyptian influence. Unlike the Egyptian
paradigms, the Kouros is free-standing. (National Museum, Athens, Courtesy Royal Greek
Embassy)

Homer - anger, pride, self-esteem, fear.
Hesiad - sense of having been wronged, sense of pride in work
Sappho - fears repressed feeling, great sadness (private emotion)
awareness of autonomy of self - leads religion community

. . . The rise of new religious groups, transcending the limits and ignoring the ties of kinship, is attended by consequences of great importance. On the social side, at least, the seed is sown of the doctrine that all men are brothers; the sense of solidarity, set free from its old limits, can spread to all living things. *Philia* ceases to mean kinship, and begins to mean love.[13]

These religious groups also reasserted the unity of all life, and from them, too, there emerged a new concept of the soul.

. . . In this period of social revolution and intellectual upheaval there is more than one group that seems to have contributed to the new conception of man's internal life and nature. The Orphic religion, the Pythagorean ideal of an ascetic life, and the religion of the so-called mysteries . . . are concerned with man's inner life, however material its symbolic representation. They all think of man as being much closer to the divine than was commonly assumed, even as being himself of divine origin. In these circles we find for the first time the belief in the soul of man as something different and separable from the body. Unfortunately we know very little of these sects or of the cult of the mysteries, which were kept secret by the members, and we must therefore try to form an idea of them from sources that are considerably later than the 6th century. The Orphic religion, the origin of which was attributed to the mythical person of Orpheus, the singer, was

[13] F. M. Cornford, "Mystery Religions and Pre-Socratic Philosophy," in *The Cambridge Ancient History,* Vol. IV: *The Persian Empire and the West* (Cambridge: Cambridge University Press, 1930), p. 534.

Kore (Maiden) of Auxerre, c. 630 B.C. Like the Kouros, this statue of a standing maiden has a static quality. Both the Kouros and the Kore were produced in large numbers in the seventh and sixth centuries B.C. For reasons unknown, the Kouros is always nude and the Kore is draped. (Hirmer)

a *Bios* or way of life to keep the soul pure and immaculate during its habitation in the body, in order to enable it to return to its divine home after death. Some speak of the body as the soul's prison or tomb. . . . Pindar, who encountered the Orphic religion in Sicily, in his second Olympian ode describes the religious faith of its followers and their expectation of a life after death: "Day and night the sun shines for the guiltless in the world beyond, they do not disquiet the earth with the strength of their hands, neither the water of the sea, but among the honored gods they enjoy a life without tears; while the wicked suffer pain the sight of which none can bear; but those who have kept their soul free from unjust deeds and have maintained an innocent state for the space of three lifetimes both here and beyond, they will walk the path of Zeus to Kronos' tower. There the ocean-breezes sweep across the Island of the Blessed. Flowers of gold flame from the radiant trees on the mainland, while the water nourishes others, and with garlands of these the blessed decorate themselves. . . ." Here we have the concept of soul in a quite un-Homeric sense, not as a shadow or idol in Hades, but living through three lives in both worlds, here and beyond, and this soul is the real subject of man's inner life. More descriptions of the soul's blessed life in the world beyond are to be found in the preserved fragments of a Pindaric *Threnos*, i.e., lament for somebody's death; but more important than these colorful pictures of eternal bliss is what is said there about the nature of the soul itself. "The body of all men is subject to all-powerful death, but there still remains alive an image of man's life, for this alone comes from the gods. It sleeps when the limbs are active, but to those that sleep, it presages in many a dream the decision of things delightful or doleful." . . . The ghostlike *psyche* in Homer is never referred to while man is alive, but only when he dies or is dead in the sense of Pindar's description. More recent scholarship, however, has shown that we have here two entirely different concep-

tions of the *psyche,* the Homeric and the Orphic. The former is not a soul at all in our sense but a ghostlike shadow, whereas the Orphic conception presupposes not only a soul in the later sense of the word but its continuing existence, both while still imprisoned in the body and after its release from it. But it is not identical with the conscious life of man; we might call it the dream soul, because it is only in his dreams that man has any indication of its existence within himself. It is this independent existence of the dream soul inside us and its intensified activity in the face of death that makes Pindar (or the people whose faith he describes) believe in its continued existence after death. . . .[14]

In addition to the belief in immortality the Orphics subscribed to a unique cosmogony and anthropology which were to be of great importance in the later development of Greek thought.

. . . At the head of the cosmogony was Chronos, the Time which never grows old; of him were born Aither, Chaos, and Erebus. Chronos formed an egg in the Aither and from this Phanes sprang forth, the creator and first king of the gods. His daughter Night assisted him and bore to him Uranus and Gaea. Then follows the common myth of Kronos and Zeus. Zeus was praised as the beginning, the middle, and the end of all; the contradiction thus implied to the creation by Phanes was solved by the statement that Zeus swallowed Phanes and all was created anew. By Demeter Zeus had the daughter Kore-Persephone who bore Dionysus, who was also named Zagreus. Zeus wanted to hand over his royal power to the child, but the wicked Titans lured it to them with toys, tore it to pieces, and devoured its limbs. Yet

[14] Reprinted by permission of the publishers from Werner Jaeger, "The Greek Ideas of Immortality," *Harvard Theological Review*, Vol. LII, pp. 139–141. Cambridge, Mass.: Harvard University Press. Copyright 1959 by the President and Fellows of Harvard College.

Athena saved its heart and brought it to Zeus, who ate it, and of him a new Dionysus, the son of Semele, was born. The Titans were struck by the lightning of Zeus and burned to ashes from which man was formed. . . .

The anthropogony is in fact the original contribution of Orphism to the development of religious thought. Plato speaks of the "Titanic nature" of man as a proverbial saying in the sense of his innate evil nature, which can only be understood as referring to the crime of the Titans as told by the Orphics. Because man had been formed of the ashes of the Titans who had devoured the Divine Child, he contains within himself something of the divine and something of the evil Titanic nature. Further, Plato says that the followers of Orpheus called the body a tomb, because the soul is punished for that for which it is punished and it seems to have this covering—the likeness of a prison—in order that it may be kept in custody. First it is to be noted that evidently the body is the evil and the soul the divine part of man. Abstinence from killing animals and eating their flesh was the best known feature of Orphic life, noted, e.g., by Euripides and Plato. The reason for this prohibition may be found in the uncleanness of the body or in the crime of the Titans or most probably in the belief in metempsychosis. This belief is not expressly ascribed to the Orphics, but it is to be remembered that Orphism is no isolated religious phenomenon but is in various ways related to the mystic movements and beliefs of the archaic age which it took up and systematized. Plato tells of sorcerers who produced books by Musaeus and Orpheus and through sacrifices according to these and pastimes called initiations promised deliverance and purification from guilt and from pains in the after-life: the righteous were to be rewarded by a symposium in the Nether World. The Orphics had appropriated the belief in punishments in the Underworld. Though it was not peculiar to them it had a special note: whosoever had not undergone the purifications in

this life was to lie in the mire in the Nether World; the initiated and righteous were to live in happiness. This belief appealed to the broad public and was important for Orphic practice. In the words quoted from Plato the soul is apparently punished by being imprisoned in the body. In the archaic age there was a tendency, opposed to general Greek ideas, to scorn this life and to attribute a higher value to the other life in which the soul is freed from the fetters of the body. . . .[15]

It seems more than likely that Pythagoras and his followers took over the beliefs in immortality and transmigration from Orphism. Their subsequent dissemination of these beliefs was of critical importance in the development of Greek philosophy. In addition, these beliefs stimulated that pioneering work in the field of mathematics which constituted another major phase of the first scientific revolution.

THE MATHEMATICAL DISCOVERIES OF PYTHAGORAS AND HIS FOLLOWERS
F. M. Cornford [16]

. . . In the island of Samos [in Ionia] towards the middle of the sixth century before Christ, Pythagoras was born. In early manhood he removed to southern Italy, and there founded a brotherhood, with some monastic features, which lasted for about two hundred years—through the lifetimes of Socrates, Plato, and Aristotle—and left a tradition which was still living in the earliest Christian centuries. Of his life we know little more; and that for a

[15] M. P. Nilsson, "Orphism," *The Oxford Classical Dictionary*, M. Cary, *et al.*, eds. (Oxford: Clarendon Press, 1949), pp. 627–628. Reprinted by permission of the Clarendon Press, Oxford.

[16] F. M. Cornford, *The Unwritten Philosophy* (Cambridge: Cambridge University Press, 1950), pp. 17–27. Reprinted by permission of Cambridge University Press.

significant reason. Already by his immediate followers he was recognised (like his contemporary, the Buddha) as one of those divine men of whom history knows least because their lives are at once transfigured into legend. He was, they said, the son of a God, Apollo, by a mortal woman; and Aristotle recorded some of the miracles ascribed to his more than human powers. His doctrines are commonly classed under two heads: the religious and the scientific or philosophical; but in fact they are only parts of a single vision of the universe.

The soul is of its own nature immortal, that is to say divine. When the body dies, the soul, according to its deeds, passes into other forms of life, of man or animal or plant. It is bound upon this wheel of reincarnation until it shall have become pure. It will then regain a place in the company of the immortal gods and heroes. The body is no better than a temporary prison-house or tomb of the living soul, thus grossly closed in the muddy vesture of decay. From this follows the unity of all life: there is a bond of kinship uniting man to the gods above him and the beasts below: for any soul may climb or descend to any rung upon the single ladder of existence. And the sin for which the fallen soul has been condemned to its round of mortal births was a breach of this unity, symbolised by the shedding of blood.

Reincarnation had been taught earlier by the votaries of Orpheus. . . . They too abstained from killing animals or eating flesh, holding the same belief that the unity of life should be inviolate. Upon secret sympathy between all creatures had rested the power of Orpheus, who, for them as for us, was a figure of the far legendary past. He was the enchanting son of the Muse Calliope; and his enchant-

ment was wrought by music, the sober Apolline music of the lyre:

> Such notes as, warbled to the string,
> Drew iron tears down Pluto's cheek
> And made Hell grant what love did seek.

Now the myth of Orpheus contains a thought that took shape in the mind of Pythagoras. How can music possess this magical influence? If the power of music is felt by all living things, and even . . . by trees, stones, and floods, there must be in the principle of life itself, in the soul of man and of universal nature, chords that can answer to the touch of harmonious sound. May it not be the most essential truth about the soul that it is, in some sort, an instrument of music?

Tradition, truly as I believe, reports that Pythagoras declared the soul to be, or to contain, a harmony—or rather a *harmonia*. For in Greek the word *harmonia* does not mean "harmony," if "harmony" conveys to us the concord of several sounds. The Greeks called that *symphonia*. *Harmonia* meant originally the orderly adjustment of parts in a complex fabric; then, in particular, the tuning of a musical instrument; and finally the musical scale, composed of several notes yielded by the tuned strings. What we call the "modes" would be to the Greek *harmoniai*.

Pythagoras turned to the study of the musical scales; and in this field he made a discovery which gave him a clue to the whole structure of the world. He found that the concordant intervals of the musical scale can be exactly expressed in terms of ratios between numbers. It was only later that Greek musicians guessed that these ratios hold between the numbers of vibrations corresponding to the several notes. Pythagoras simply measured the lengths on the string of a monochord, stopped by a movable bridge. It came to light that the ratio of the octave is 1:2; of the fourth, 4:3; of the fifth, 3:2. These (which are still known to musicians as the "perfect consonances") are the fixed intervals common to all the Greek scales, the variety of scales being obtained by varying the intervening or "movable" notes. Observe further that the numbers which occur in these ratios are 1, 2, 3, 4—the sum of which is 10, the perfect number. Pythagoras would never have made the experiment, if he had not already divined that the order and beauty evoked by the art of music from the weltering chaos of sound—a matter, plainly enough, of measure, proportion, rhythm—might be reducible to the pure abstractions of number. To discover that these fundamental proportions, on which every scale is built, could be expressed so simply in ratios between the first four numbers was enough to flood any mathematician's soul with joy. To Pythagoras it came as a revelation, lighting up the framework of the moral, no less than of the natural, world.

First, in the microcosm of the individual, not only are strength and beauty dependent on proportions and rhythms of form, of which the Greek sculptors might determine the canon, but health—the virtue of the body—was interpreted as a proportion or equipoise of contending elements, which any excess might derange or finally destroy. And virtue—the health of the soul—likewise lay in the golden mean, imposing measure on the turbulence of passion, a temperance which excludes both excess and deficiency. In virtue the soul achieves moral order and beauty; its *harmonia* is in tune.

> Dust as we are, the immortal spirit grows
> Like harmony in music, there is a dark

> Inscrutable workmanship that reconciles
> Discordant elements, makes them cling together
> In one society.

That the soul should be harmonised meant not only that its several parts should be in tune with one another, but, as one instrument in an orchestra must be in tune with all the rest, so the soul must reproduce the *harmonia* of the Cosmos. The phrase "in tune with the infinite" is one that no musician, least of all a Greek musician, would use. The very essence of order is a measure or limit imposed upon the infinite or unlimited; and looking out into the world of Nature, Pythagoras saw here the secret of beauty and of rational truth.

For in the field of the eye, no less than of the ear, there is harmony or discord in the relations of colour, and there is measure and proportion in form. Music has its being in time, not in space; but space is peopled with extended bodies having surfaces whose shapes and colours, confounded in the darkness, are, as it were, recreated daily by the dawn of light. From the measurement of these surfaces we can reach the theorems of geometry, simple, perfect, and unalterably true. Moreover, the truths of geometry can be yet more abstractly expressed in numbers. So numbers and their properties and relations underlie the whole fabric of the world in space and time; and Pythagoras, in the language of his day, declared that numbers—not formless matter—were the "nature of all things."

It was Pythagoras who first gave to the visible world the name of Cosmos, a word which equally signifies order and beauty. Of his cosmogony only a few traces survive. These indicate that the two great

Bronze Kouros from Piraeus, c. 530 B.C. The relaxed pose and more natural lines of this figure are an evolution from the earlier renderings of the male form. (See Kouros, p. 119) (Greek National Tourist Office)

Kore in Dorian Peplos ("The Peplos Kore"), c. 530 B.C. Produced one hundred years after the Auxerre Kore (see p. 120), this statue represents a less rigid female figure. The body is now distinguishable from the clothing and the hair is realistic. The calm mysterious smile is seen in many statues of this era. (Hirmer)

principles of Nature are Light and Darkness, concretely conceived as Fire and the dark, cold vapour of primaeval Night filling the abyss of space. Imagine a spark or seed of Fire planted in the womb of unlimited Darkness. By the self-propagating power of light spreading outwards from this centre, a spherical realm of order and form and colour is won from the dominion of Night. This is the universe, the Cosmos, extending from earth at the centre to the sphere of the fixed stars. Between centre and circumference, the seven known planets (including sun and moon) are set, each like a jewel in its ring, in material orbits which carry them round; and these are spaced according to the intervals of a musical scale, the celestial *harmonia*.

The Pythagoreans suppose, says Aristotle, that the motion of bodies so huge as these and moving with so great a speed must produce a sound. Arguing so, and from the observation that their speeds, as measured by their distances, are in the same ratios as the concords of the musical scale, they assert that the sound given forth by the revolution of the heavenly bodies is a *harmonia* or scale. They explain that we do not hear this music because the sound is constantly in our ears from the very moment of birth and so cannot be distinguished by contrast with silence.

Such, in its earliest form, is the harmony of the spheres. "The whole heaven," said the Pythagoreans, "is harmony and number"—number because the essence of harmony lies, not in the sound, but in the numerical proportions, and these (I think we may add) constitute the soul of Nature, which thus, like the human soul, is itself a harmony. So the moral world is interfused with the physical. The harmony of heaven is perfect; but its counterpart in human souls is marred with imperfection

and discord. This is what we call vice or evil. The attainment of that purity which is to release the soul at last from the wheel of incarnation, may now be construed as the reproduction, in the individual, of the cosmic harmony—the divine order of the world. Herein lies the secret of the power of music over the soul. . . .

Finally, the influence of the celestial harmony is absorbed and assimilated by the soul in contemplation (*theoria*). The soul in the presence of the Cosmos was compared to the spectator at a festival, who comes, not to compete for success or to traffic for gain, but to see and to enjoy. Contemplation is contrasted with practical activity. . . . But if contemplation is not for practical ends, it is not merely passive, but (as Aristotle taught) an activity. To the Pythagorean it meant, not only taking in the spectacle of order and beauty in the visible heaven, but the active operation of thought in all the mathematical sciences which reveal the truths of number and form. Contemplation is the search for wisdom, not only the fruition. Among those whom the Greeks honoured as wise men, Pythagoras was the first to refuse the title and to call himself, not wise, but a lover of wisdom (*philo-sophos*), not a sage but a philosopher.

Mathematics, and more especially geometry, was in many ways responsible for the direction which the development of Greek culture took. In addition, the Greek predilection for mathematics subsequently had an enormous impact on the intellectual life of Western man, for it was the Greeks who first equated mathematical—that is, a priori—knowledge with all knowledge. The following selection continues the discussion of the development of Greek mathematics and places it in the larger context of the nature of mathematics itself.

The Nature of Mathematics
Anatol Rapoport [17]

Mathematics exhibits one of the most curious aspects of the human mind. Most sciences are defined by their subject matter. Mathematics is defined by its method. Indeed, if by subject matter is meant a class of events, like "the living process" (the preoccupation of the biologist) or "the production and exchange of commodities" (the concern of the economist), then mathematics has no subject matter at all.

To be sure, old fashioned text books say that mathematics deals with numbers and magnitudes, but such a description misses the point. It is possible to deal with numbers without any idea of what mathematics is about. We now have machines that do the most complicated computations with unimaginable speed, but these machines are not mathematicians. On the other hand, it is commonplace for a great mathematician to have trouble in adding up a grocery check. Reckoning is not mathematics.

It has not always been this way, and the only means of understanding the new departures in mathematical thinking is to see clearly how we got where we are. There was a time when reckoning and measuring were all there was to mathematics. But there was also a time when the strongest and bravest were the best warriors. That time has passed. The whole concept of war has changed from a match of physical strength in battle to a vast coordination of production, transportation, diabolical

[17] From "Mathematics: The 'Empty' Science" by Anatol Rapoport in *Frontiers of Knowledge,* edited by Lynn White, Jr., pp. 232–242. Copyright © 1956 by Harper & Row, Publishers, Incorporated. Reprinted by permission of the publishers.

invention, and diplomacy, and so the old concept of the warrior has disappeared. In mathematics it was a similar story. The whole concept of mathematics has changed. The modern mathematician has no resemblance to his prototype who was clever at numbers and at surveying.

If numbers and magnitude are not the chief themes of mathematics, what are? As we said, mathematics has no subject matter. Bertrand Russell was not joking when he remarked that in mathematics we never know what we are talking about nor whether what we are saying is true. He meant it literally. How, then, if one takes Russell's epigram seriously, is one to avoid the notion that mathematics is an empty pursuit? If mathematics is as ambiguous as Russell's statement seems to imply, how is one to understand the eulogies which hail mathematics as the proudest achievement of the human mind and the assertions of some philosophers that God must be a mathematician?

The key to this paradox is found in the nature of abstraction and of symbols. Once one understands the nature of abstraction, one fathoms the soul of mathematics, and when one understands what mathematics is truly about, one cannot help exclaiming "What hath man wrought!"

Think of a small child's conception of a game of chess. The child sees the game as two people facing a checkered board, on which they shift the positions of the pieces. The child imagines that he too "plays chess" as he moves the pieces around on the board. After a while (probably not before the eighth year on the average) the child can be made to understand that he is not really playing chess unless he follows certain rules. But only considerably later the idea sinks in that the pieces and the board are not necessary.

The rules are the game. A chess game reported in the newspaper consists simply of letters and numbers indicating the moves, which need not have reference to any physical objects at all, but are only communicative symbols.

This progressive emancipation of concepts from *particular* situations depends on the maturation of a certain ability peculiar to human beings, the ability to abstract, that is, to perceive *relations* quite apart from the objects which are related. This ability appears also in the progressive mastery of language by the child. A young boy who has one brother, if asked "Have you a brother?" will say "Yes." But if asked "Has your brother a brother?" he may well say "No." He still does not think of *himself* as his brother's brother. He is he; the brother the brother. Only later he comes to understand that "brother" does not have to be any one in particular. "Brother" is not a name of a person; it is a name of a relation among persons. Abstraction, then, involves the ability to think and reason about relations apart from the things which are related. The maturation of mathematical ability follows a similar course.

First, there is counting, always with something to count. Two oranges and three oranges make five oranges. Two bicycles and three bicycles make five bicycles. It is an immense feat of abstraction to realize that two of *anything* and three of the same make five of the same. And since "anything" is nothing in particular, there is no point in mentioning it at all. Two and three make five. We still have words in our language inherited from a distant past when this leap into abstraction had not yet been made. We say a married *couple,* a *pair* of shoes, a *team* of

horses, *twin* sisters, *double*-u, and, if we want to be fancy, a *brace* of pheasants. All these words mean "two." The many words for "two" indicate that the words were in use before the common meaning of "two" in all the different contexts was recognized. There is no such multiplicity of names for "thirty-six," probably because we learned to count only after we could abstract number from the objects counted. There are still people in remote places whose only counting words are "one," "two," and "many."

The concept of number as something apart from and independent of the objects with which it is associated is then the first step in mathematics. Once we have torn the numbers away from the objects and from such intermediate aids as fingers or pebbles, we attain much greater freedom in manipulating numbers. You can't divide seven cows evenly among thirteen men as long as you think of whole cows. But once seven ceases to be a number of objects and becomes a "magnitude," you can slice it as finely as you wish. Fractions are born. If you think of how much money you have, you cannot imagine having less than nothing. But if you abstract from "money" to "assets and liabilities," you can represent your "worth" by a magnitude which is less than nothing (if liabilities exceed your assets). Negative numbers are born.

The abstraction from objects is now complete, but now the numbers themselves appear as particular things with particular names. Any statements made about particular numbers will pertain to those only and not necessarily to others. Now the way forward in any science is toward a situation where more and more *general* statements can be made, that is, statements pertaining to more and more things simultaneously. The mental mechanism which makes this possible is abstraction. After arithmetic abstracted numbers from their context, algebra performed the next step of abstraction by divorcing symbols for numbers from particular numbers, so that a symbol could stand for *any* number. Let us see how this is done.

When I write $3 + 5 = 5 + 3$, I am saying that whether I add 5 to 3 or 3 to 5, I get the same result. But when I say $a + b = b + a$, I am saying that if I add two numbers (*any* two numbers), I get the same sum whether I add the second to the first or vice versa. To take a somewhat more complicated example, if I say $(5 + 3)(5 - 3) = 5^2 - 3^2$, I am saying that the sum of 5 and 3 multiplied by their difference is the same as the difference of their squares. You can verify this and obtain 16 in both cases. But when I say $(a + b)(a - b) = a^2 - b^2$, I am saying that the sum of *any* two numbers multiplied by their difference is the same as the difference of their squares.

If now you ask, "How do you know?" you invite an answer about the very nature of mathematics. So let us pursue this question. How do I know that $(a + b)(a - b) = a^2 - b^2$? If I were worried about whether this was true, I could proceed to verify the statement by substituting "any" two numbers for *a* and *b*. We have seen that it is true for 5 and 3. Let us try 17 and 11. The product of the sum and difference is $28 \times 6 = 168$. The difference of the squares is $289 - 121 = 168$. It works. Let us try with two "ones." The product of the sum and difference is $2 \times 0 = 0$; the difference of the squares is $1 - 1 = 0$. It works again. If you are still in doubt, try two fractions, say ⅔ and ½. I assure you, you will get the same result.

Now does this settle the matter? If not, how many pairs of numbers shall we try before we can say with certainty that the formula $(a + b)(a - b) = a^2 - b^2$ is true in all cases? Let us see how we answer a similar question in other situations. How many times will you put your finger in the fire before you come to the conclusion that fire is hot? How many times must a chemist perform an experiment to be assured of the result? Your answers to such questions may be "once," "twice," or "many times." Experience may or may not justify your answers. But a mathematician gives an entirely different answer to such questions. Verification in special cases is never sufficient to establish the truth of a general mathematical statement, unless *all* cases have been verified.

Since we obviously cannot try all pairs of numbers to test our formula (there is an infinity of numbers), it follows that verification of the formula can never establish its truth for a mathematician. In this respect, the mathematician differs from all other scientists. The biologist, for example, having observed that in all observed instances rats give birth to rats and never to mice, and so on for other species, is able to assert his general proposition: Each organism reproduces after his own kind. When a chemist says that acids and bases react to produce water and salts; when the economist says that when a product which is in demand becomes rare, its price generally rises, they are stating generalizations from experience. True, if they are devoted to the spirit of science they will always have some reservations about any such general statements. They will be ready to modify them in the face of new evidence. However, in the face of repeated and consistent verification, a general statement in any science except mathematics will be at least provisionally accepted as "true." This method of establishing truth logicians call "induction," that is, arguing from many particular cases to the more general assertion. Because mathematics is not bound to the particular, this method is prohibited in mathematics. It violates the mathematician's rules of evidence. The only way a mathematical truth can be established (except where all cases can be verified, which is rarely) is by "deduction," that is, by arguing from the general to the particular.

To return to our example, the truth of the statement $(a + b) (a - b) = a^2 - b^2$ cannot be established from any number of verifications with particular numbers. It *can* be established from the more general rules of addition and multiplication. These state that to multiply $(a + b) (a - b)$, you sum all the paired products, affixing to each its proper sign (*plus* if both members of the pair are of like sign, *minus* otherwise), thus: $a^2 - ab + ba - b^2$. *Furthermore*, $ab = ba$, so that $ab - ba = 0$. This leaves $a^2 - b^2$. The crucial feature of this proof is that the particular numbers for which *a* and *b* may stand *never entered the argument*. The reasoning holds no matter what numbers *a* and *b* stand for. Therefore it becomes unnecessary to verify the formula in any particular case to establish its truth.

The preceding example was from algebra. Indeed, much of algebra deals with establishing the results of operating on any numbers in a prescribed way. However, the earliest recognition of the nature of deductive proof and its role in mathematics appeared not in algebra but in

geometry; so let us turn our attention to geometry.

The word "geometry" comes from the Greek words for "earth" and "measurement." It is said that geometry developed first as an art of determining land areas. We are told that it arose in ancient Egypt in response to the need of establishing field boundaries after they were erased by the annual overflows of the Nile. Now, just as reckoning was once simply a skill, involving only "know-how," not "know why," so was geometry. Many rules were known by which to compute lengths, areas, and volumes. The Egyptians knew that the area of a rectangular field equals the length times the width, that the circumference of the circle is about $3\frac{1}{7}$ times the diameter, that the volume of a pyramid is the area of the base times ⅓ the height, etc. We say this knowledge involved only "know-how," not "know why," because the rules were not proved but only tested. This is not to say that "know-how" is in any way "inferior" knowledge. To a people engaged in the pyramid-building business for fifteen centuries, knowledge of how to compute the volume of a pyramid must have been important, proof or no proof. However, as a *mathematical* achievement much more impressive is the early knowledge of the Babylonians who, more than a thousand years before Pythagoras and Euclid, were acquainted with general theorems such as that the angle inscribed in a semicircle is a right angle, or the theorem for which Pythagoras later became famous. This general intellectual interest of those early Mesopotamian mathematicians, as opposed to the practical problems of weighing, finding volumes, or computing areas, is shown by their search for methods of

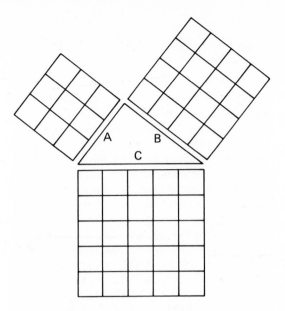

the axioms, one must accept the truth of the theorems. Then, using the propositions thus proved as "stepping stones" of reasoning, they proved still more complicated ones. Theirs was a process not unlike our building complicated machinery from manufactured parts. The parts are put together in subassemblies; these are united into assemblies, etc. Each step of the process starts where the last left off, making possible a division of labor and therefore an increase in complexity and efficiency. In the same way the introduction of the deductive method stimulated the rapid growth of mathematical knowledge. Such growth is not possible if knowledge depends on mere accumulation of facts and rules. The memory capacity of a single person is limited, and even if storage facilities (such as catalogues and libraries) are available, their usefulness diminishes as the bulk of accumulated information becomes unwieldy. If you want to get a feeling for the difference between logically connected and arbitrarily gathered information, try to memorize a hundred-word speech (the Declaration of Independence through "the pursuit of happiness" is 106 words) and then try to memorize one hundred randomly selected words and see the difference in the work involved.

Again it is time for an illustration. Let us prove the simplest of the propositions of geometry. If two straight lines intersect, the vertical angles are equal.

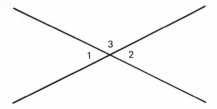

determining numbers satisfying the Pythagorean relation, $A^2 + B^2 = C^2$.

In Greece, the whole approach to geometry was different. The Greeks "built" their geometry. The "bricks" were the propositions (or theorems, as they were called) and the mortar was logic. Greek geometry was as different from the Egyptian as a temple is different from a pile of bricks. The foundation of their "temple" consisted of a few simple propositions, which they thought were "self-evident." Thus it seemed impossible to deny that the shortest line between two points is a straight line; that if the same quantity is subtracted from two equal quantities, the remainders are equal, etc. Starting with these "postulates" (statements about primitive geometric notions) and "axioms" ("self-evident" statements about relations among quantities), Greek mathematicians *proved* more complicated statements about geometric figures, that is, they showed by means of logical argument that if one accepted the truth of the postulates and

In the figure, one pair of vertical angles is labeled "1" and "2." Angles are measured by how much of a circle they span. Conventionally the circle is divided into 360 degrees, so that a "straight" angle, that is, one whose arms make a straight line and thus span half a circle, has 180 degrees. To prove the proposition, we need two axioms: (1) quantities equal to the same quantity are equal to each other; and (2) if the same quantity is subtracted from two equal quantities, the remainders are equal. We note that the sum of Angle 1 and Angle 3 is a straight angle, therefore we write: Angle 1 + Angle 3 = 180 degrees.

Similarly: Angle 2 + Angle 3 = 180 degrees.

Now we use axiom (1) and conclude that Angle 1 + Angle 3 = Angle 2 + Angle 3.

Now if we subtract Angle 3 from both of these quantities, we must conclude, because of axiom (2) that the remainders are equal, namely, Angle 1 = Angle 2 and our proof is complete. We are *forced* to say that the vertical angles are equal, not because we have measured them, but because their equality is a logical consequence of the axioms, which we have accepted. Note that the actual size of the angles does not enter the argument, any more than the values of a and b entered the proof of the formula $(a + b) (a - b) = a^2 - b^2$.

Simple as this simplest of geometric theorems is, it illustrates perfectly the nature of mathematics. Mathematical truths are arrived at by drawing necessary conclusions from propositions known or assumed or accepted as true. A mathematical proposition always says that *if* something is true, then something else must be true. The actual truth of the "if" part is not relevant. . . .

The realization that mathematical proof is not dependent on sensory experience constituted one of the great discoveries made by Greek mathematicians. An examination of the idea of incommensurability provides an insight into the significance of their discovery. After Pythagoras had demonstrated that the square of the hypotenuse of a right triangle is equal to the sum of the squares on the other sides,[18] he found that this theorem did not apply to an isosceles right triangle. The hypotenuse cannot be measured exactly, yet its length can be represented by the symbol for a square root ($\sqrt{\ }$) and by the concept of incommensurability (which simply means that the hypotenuse and sides cannot be measured by the same standards). Neither "square root" nor "incommensurability" exist outside the mind of man. This problem of "irrational" numbers, those numbers whose square root is a decimal fraction with an endless series of nonrepeating digits after the decimal point, was one of the factors which turned the Greek geometers away from numbers and measurement to the study of form (lines and areas), for here they encountered no obstacles which they could not overcome.

By the end of the sixth century B.C. two rational interpretations of natural phenomena had been formulated by the philosophers of Ionia and southern Italy. For many of them the reality of the physical world was materialistic (water, air, fire, and so on); the Pythagoreans, on the other hand, maintained that what we see, hear, and touch can be expressed in numbers and it is the latter which constitute the real. During the fifth century B.C. these philosophies provoked further speculation, but the scene of this intellectual activity was Athens rather than the Greek colonies.

[18]See above, p. 131.

CHAPTER 6

THE IMPACT OF ATHENIAN EXPANSION ON POLITICS, MORALS, AND THOUGHT:
The Sophists

When [Darius] was king of Persia, he summoned the Greeks who happened to be present at his court, and asked them what they would take to eat the dead bodies of their fathers. They replied that they would not do it for any money in the world. Later in the presence of the Greeks, and through an interpreter, so that they could understand what was said, he asked Indians, of the tribe called Callatiae, who do eat their parents' bodies, what they would take to burn them. They uttered a cry of horror and forbade him to mention such a dreadful thing.

Herodotus, The Histories

Man is the measure of all things.

Protagoras

[The Sophists assumed] that the political order had become removed from nature; and that its very separateness allowed men to perceive in what respects the political had become separate. By contrasting the conventions of political society with the principles of nature, [they were] implicitly allowing that the political order could be distinguished; that the political observer himself could gain a measure of detachment. . . .

In disengaging the political from the natural order, the Sophists were, in one sense, following the path of the earlier nature philosophers. The great contribution of the latter had been to approach the external world naturalistically; that is, as an order comprehensible to human reason and not as a mixture of natural and supernatural elements which defied rational explanation. This, in turn, was accompanied by still another claim: that the observer could, so to speak, "get outside" the object he was describing. But at this point certain differences, which were to assume great importance later, began to appear. The detachment of the nature philosopher consisted in his viewing nature as something to be understood, but not necessarily as something to be controlled. This form of detachment was not taken over by political philosophy. Instead, as the philosophy of Plato shows, the "nature" of politics was to be viewed as manipulable, as a bundle of forces from which order could be

133

fashioned. In this respect, political philosophy was to be armed with a bolder assumption than the scientific inquiry of that time.

Sheldon S. Wolin,
Politics and Vision: Continuity and Innovation in Western Political Thought

Ionian intellectual supremacy was terminated abruptly at the very end of the sixth century B.C. when Asia Minor came under the political and cultural control of a rapidly expanding Persian Empire. Persian leaders, especially Darius and Xerxes, were not content with the domination of Asia Minor, however, for the security of that area, they believed, depended on their control of the Aegean. The power they confronted there was Athens.

EARLY ATHENIAN EXPANSION AND THE PERSIAN WARS
James M. Powell [1]

The sixth century . . . witnessed the gradual expansion of Athenian hegemony over surrounding territories. Megara and Salamis, islands controlling the sea approaches to the city, fell into her hands. Moreover, Athens' ties with the Greek cities of Asia Minor grew closer because of her trade. These cities had been conquered by the Persians during the sixth century. Although Persian rule was far from harsh and even drew support from the aristocratic elements in the Greek cities of Asia Minor, there were also periodic attempts at revolt. Democratic Athens proved more receptive than conservative Sparta to requests for assistance and thus earned the enmity of the Persian kings. According to one story, the Persian

[1] Reprinted with permission of The Macmillan Company from *The Civilization of the West: A Brief Interpretation* by James M. Powell, pp. 47–49, 51. Copyright © J. M. Powell, 1967.

king Darius ordered his servants to repeat "Sire, remember the Athenians" lest he forget the manner in which they had aided his enemies.

In 493 B.C., a great Persian fleet crossed the Aegean and landed an army at the bay of Marathon across a narrow neck of land from Athens. Greece was unprepared. The Spartans promised aid, but held back because of religious scruples until it was too late. Only a small force from Plataea joined nine thousand Athenians on the plain of Marathon. Outnumbered almost two to one, the Greeks were nevertheless victorious. The Persians, unwilling to risk a siege of Athens, sailed away.

But victory at Marathon won only a respite for the Greeks, as they were well aware. Athens took the lead in arousing the other Greek cities to the danger of a renewed Persian attack. Under the inspired leadership of Themistocles, the Athenians began the construction of a great fleet. On the Persian side, Darius' son Xerxes began long preparations for a massive invasion of Greece. In 480 B.C., this great army crossed the Hellespont and descended on the peninsula while a fleet sailed along the coast. This time the Greeks were prepared. A small band of Spartans led a detachment northward to meet the Persian army while the Athenians completed their preparations for meeting the main force at sea. Leonidas, King of Sparta, and his handful of troops put up a gallant stand against the "Immortals," the best of the Persians. They chose for a battleground the narrow pass at Thermopylae, where the mountains press close to the sea. Greatly outnumbered, the Greeks were betrayed by one of their own, who led the Persians around to their rear by another route. Leonidas and three hundred Spartans fell in battle. Themopylae became a proud badge of courage in the ancient world. Yet, like many other battles in which the courage of brave men won the plaudits of those who remained, Thermopylae was futile. The Greeks would have accomplished more by a strategic withdrawal and continued harassment of the Persian army. As it was, Greece now lay open to the invaders.

The Spartans and their allies, fearful of the results of a Persian invasion of their homeland, fell back to defend the Peloponnesian peninsula leaving Athens and her allies to fend for themselves. Because the Athenians realized they could not defend their city they crossed to the island of Salamis and watched the burning of their city by the advancing Persians. Meanwhile, Themistocles made preparations to meet the Persian fleet. He divided the Greek fleet into two parts and, using half as a decoy, concealed the other half around the headland of the island of Salamis. As the Persian king watched from his throne, his fleet pursued the seemingly fearful Athenians through the narrow waters between Salamis and the mainland. Then, when the Persian fleet had entered the channel, the Greeks closed the opening. Aeschylus the playwright has described the destruction of the Persians: "The jutting shores and rocks were piled with dead, and every Persian ship that still survived rowed hard for refuge in disordered flight." Broken by the defeat, Xerxes hastened in retreat, spurred on by fear of further Greek attacks and news of uprisings among the Greeks of Asia Minor. But the danger to Greece was far from over, for Persian troops continued to hold the north of Greece and the mainland, including Athens. The Athenians managed to persuade the Spartans to assist them in ridding Greece of this danger. At Plataea (479 B.C.), the Greek allies administered a crushing defeat to the Persian army and forced the remaining Persians to withdraw from Greece.

Although the Greeks had succeeded in driving the foreigners from their soil, they realized that Persia still remained a great power that might decide to launch further attacks on Greek soil. Even after they had wrested control of the Hellespont from the Persians, they remained concerned about the possibilty of a renewed attack. This was especially true of the Athenians, who took the initiative in the formation of the Delian League in 478 B.C.

This league was chiefly a naval alliance of the Aegean powers, with Athens as the dominant partner. It drew its name from the fact that the treasury of the league was located on the sacred island of Delos. The purpose of the league was to enable the members to carry on joint naval operations against the Persians in the Aegean, but very quickly it took on the character of a commercial alliance. In the beginning, each member city was expected to contribute men and ships for the fleet, according to a prescribed rate. Smaller cities paid sums of money rather than men or ships and this soon became the usual manner of raising the levy. Thus the Athenians controlled the fleet of the entire league and reaped the advantage in her greatly strengthened naval power. As the danger from Persia subsided, Athens had to apply pressure to keep the alliance together and to maintain the fleet. Consequently, the character of the league gradually changed from a voluntary alliance against the Persians to a commercial league with Athens as the leader. This has led historians to speak of "The Athenian Empire," even though Athens was never able to exercise the kinds of controls generally associated with the term.

The empire was not without advantages to its members. The powerful Athenian navy, strengthened by contributions of the members, defended their trade from the attacks of the Persians as well as from the pirates who infested the waters of the Aegean Sea. Moreover, the alliance encouraged commercial exchanges within its framework. Of course, Athens became the metropolis, but all members shared in the prosperity. On the other hand, wealth came at the expense of freedom. The obligation to pay tribute and furnish rowers for the navy was probably not as onerous as Athens' interference in the internal government of the cities of the empire. In each city, the Athenians supported those elements most inclined to back their policy. Thus, they attempted to ensure that a "democratic" regime rather than an "oligarchic" or Spartan-sympathizing government ruled in these cities. There were also restrictions on the individual citizens of the "allies." In lawsuits where an Athenian was involved, the cases had to be tried in Athens. Obviously, the old equality of the Delian League had given way to a new equality of which the Athenians possessed a greater share than the citizens of their allies.

By the beginning of the fifth century B.C., Athens had made the transition from a kinship-based society to one in which the individual was the basic unit. This did not mean, however, that Athenian society was individualized to the degree that Western society is today. The polis—much larger than the family but certainly far smaller than the modern city or nation-state—had become the source of the intimacy, identity, and norms which had been furnished earlier by kinship groups.

The polis is the sum of all its citizens and of all the aspects of their lives. It gives each citizen much, but it can demand all in return. Relentless and powerful, it imposes its way of life on each individual, and marks him for its own. From it are derived all the norms which govern the life of its citizens. Conduct that injures it is bad, conduct that helps it is good. This is the paradoxical result of the passionate effort to obtain rights and equal status of each individual. All these efforts have forged the new chains of Law, to hold together the centrifugal energies of mankind, and to co-ordinate them far more successfully than in the old social order. Law is the objective expression of the state,[2] and now Law has become king, as the Greeks later said —an invisible ruler who does not only prevent the strong from transgressing and bring the wrongdoer to justice, but issues positive commands in all the spheres of life which had once been governed by individual will and preference. Even the most intimate acts of the private life and the moral conduct of its citizens are by law prescribed and limited and defined. Thus, through the struggle to obtain law, the development of the state brings into being new and more sharply differentiated principles of public and private life. . . .

The new factor in the development of the city-state, which at last made every man a political being, was the compulsion laid on each male citizen to take an active part in the public life of his community, and to rec-

---

[2] Once again it should be noted that the word "state" refers here to "polis," not to the state as it is understood today. [Ed.]

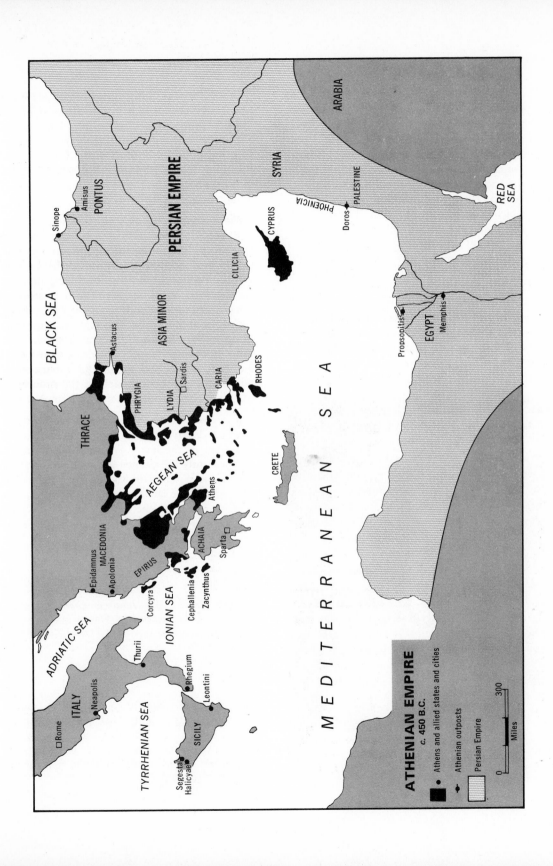

BLACK SEA

PERSIAN EMPIRE

ARABIA

SYRIA

Sinope
Amisus
PONTUS

PALESTINE
PHOENICIA
Doros

RED
SEA

CYPRUS

CILICIA

ASIA MINOR

Actacus

Sardis
PHRYGIA
LYDIA
CARIA

RHODES

Prosopitis
EGYPT
Memphis

THRACE

AEGEAN SEA

CRETE

M E D I T E R R A N E A N   S E A

Athens

Epidamnus
MACEDONIA
Apolonia
EPIRUS
Corcyra

ACHAIA
Sparta

ADRIATIC SEA

IONIAN SEA
Cephallenia
Zacynthus

Thurii

ITALY

Rome

Neapolis

Rhegium
Leontini

TYRRHENIAN SEA

SICILY

Segesta
Halicydae

ATHENIAN EMPIRE
c. 450 B.C.

Athens and allied states and cities

Athenian outposts

Persian Empire

300

Miles

0

ognize and accept his civic duties—which were quite different from his duties as a private person and a working man. Previously, it was only the nobleman who had possessed this "universal" political ability. For centuries power had been in the hands of the aristocrats, and they had a vastly superior system of political education and experience, which was still indispensable. The new city-state could not, without injury to itself, ignore the areté of the aristocracy; but it was bound to repress its selfish and unjust misuse. That was at least the ideal of the polis, as expressed by Pericles in Thucydides' [*History of the Peloponnesian War*]. Thus, . . . the culture of the city-state was based on the old aristocratic culture—on the ideal of areté which embraced the whole personality and all its

powers. The working-class morality of Hesiod was not abandoned; but the citizen of the polis aimed above all at the ideal which Phoenix had taught Achilles: to be a speaker of words and a doer of deeds. Certainly the leading men in each state were bound to move towards that ideal, and the ordinary citizen too came to sympathize with it.[3]

The ordinary citizens—the *demos*—of Athens had become an increasingly important force in political life after Cleisthenes' reforms in 507 B.C. Thereafter, though involved in the struggle with the Persians, the Athenian polis completed the transition to democracy. The final stage in this process was begun when, in 487 B.C., it was decided that the archons would be chosen by lot rather than by direct election. Subsequently, under the leadership of Ephialtes (? –461 B.C.) and Pericles (about 490–429 B.C.), both members of the democratic faction, the Areopagus was stripped of most of its powers. In 461 B.C.

a decree was pushed through the assembly which deprived the Areopagus of its "guardianship of the law," as Aristotle phrased it. Apparently the council lost its right to supervise the conduct of the magistrates and to safeguard the law against illegal decrees, that is, to prosecute the movers of such decrees. The new arrangement transferred supervision of the magistrates to the Council of Five Hundred and protection of the law to the *heliaea*, the popular courts.

This was the opening stroke of a legislative

[3] From *Paideia: The Ideals of Greek Culture* by Werner Jaeger, translated by Gilbert Highet. Copyright 1939 by Oxford University Press, Inc. Reprinted by permission.

Head of Pericles (Roman copy of a fifth-century B.C. Greek bust). This bust portrays Pericles (461–426 B.C.), the Athenian leader during the Golden Age of Greece. The use of civic funds for artistic projects was initiated during his term of office. (Ray Garner)

program by which Pericles extended the democracy and consolidated his popular support. In 457 B.C. the lower middle class gained access to the archonship when the property qualification for that office was lowered to Solon's third class, the *zeugitae.* The privileged area of archonship and, through it, the Areopagus, was now open to many more Athenians, for by the mid-fifth century the formal qualification for the third class, an income of 200 drachmas, had been greatly cheapened through inflation. It remained to make participation in government easier for the lower class. In the late 450's Pericles introduced the most significant of his measures, pay for the Athenian jurymen, who were drawn by lot from a panel of six thousand citizens to staff the law courts. Pay for service to the state was a new principle in Greece. When it was extended in the following years to officials, to members of the council, to soldiers and sailors, it attracted trenchant criticism from antidemocratic politicians. The pay was not large, only one-half drachma per day for jurors, and a drachma for councilors, but it did enable the poor Athenian citizen to serve his government without sacrificing his livelihood. Since Athenian citizenship had become more valuable, it had to be safeguarded. Consequently in 451 B.C. Pericles passed legislation limiting citizenship to those of Athenian birth on both sides of the family, not merely through the father, as previously. By these measures Pericles won solid support for his ambitious plans to extend Athenian power abroad.[4]

Pericles maintained a position of great prominence in Athenian political life from 461 B.C. until his death in 429. Though a strong leader and repeatedly elected a general, he was by no means a dictator.

[4] Reprinted with the permission of Charles Scribner's Sons from *The World of Ancient Times,* pp. 258–259, by Carl Roebuck. Copyright © 1966 Charles Scribner's Sons.

THE OPERATION OF ATHENIAN DEMOCRACY
A. R. Burn[5]

. . . Being annually elected general ensured that he was always near the centre of things, certainly; it also gave him, even in peace time, every encouragement to work long hours in an office on foreign affairs and imperial security. A surprising range of business might be said to affect state security, and scores of Decrees of the Council and People ended with a clause "Let the Generals see to it that" something be done (or prevented). Meanwhile the sovereign people went home to dinner with a feeling of duty done. But if Pericles' voice was heard about home affairs too, as about the regulations for a music festival or the choice of a sculptor, it was only because he was Pericles, a citizen of Athens, with one vote and some hard-earned influence.

The official centre of the state was not at the Generals' office; they were only important executives. Ambassadors or messengers with important news were conducted to the conical-roofed building called the Tholos (Round House) or Skias (Parasol—its official name), next to the Council Chamber, in the corner of the Agorá. There, unless the Council were in session, they would find the Epistates or Duty Officer of the day, with his quorum of sixteen other councillors of the tribe "presiding." In Pericles' time the Epistates was also chairman of the Council and Assembly. . . .

By one of the few rules which Demos al-

[5] From *The Pelican History of Greece* by A. R. Burn, pp. 238–243. Copyright © 1965 by A. R. Burn. Reprinted by permission of the publishers, Hodder and Stoughton Limited, outside the USA; and Funk & Wagnalls, New York, under the title *A Traveller's History of Greece,* inside the USA.

The Acropolis ("Upper City"), Athens. The buildings were dedicated to the virgin goddess Athena (patroness of Athens), other Olympians, and selected Greek heroes. (Greek National Tourist Office)

The Parthenon, the Acropolis, Athens, 447–432 B.C. This edifice is regarded as the ultimate architectural achievement utilizing the Doric order. In 480 B.C. the Persians had destroyed the temples and statues on the Acropolis. The rebuilding of the Parthenon under Pericles was completed prior to the Peloponnesian War (431–404 B.C.). (Greek National Tourist Office)

Model of the Acropolis (northwest view; scale 1:200) The Parthenon (center) dedicated to Athena, and the Erectheum (on its left) date from the fifth century B.C. This model shows the upper portion of the Acropolis cliffs. Farther down the slopes on the south side were numerous monuments such as the theater of Dionysus. (Royal Ontario Museum, Toronto)

Model of the Parthenon as it appeared c. 440 B.C. The Parthenon was designed by the architects Ictinus and Callicrates. No mortar was used; the stones were cut to fit together so that they formed a single smooth surface. There is a definite organization of verticals and horizontals and a relationship of length and breadth to height. (Metropolitan Museum of Art, Purchase, 1890, Levi Hale Willard Bequest)

Upper photo, the *Erechtheum* (viewed from the southeast), the Acropolis, Athens, 421–405 B.C. This temple was built in the Ionic order to house an ancient wooden statue of Athena. Note that the Ionic columns are more slender than the Doric columns of the Parthenon. The fundamental difference between the two can be seen in comparing the capitals of each. The Ionic has scroll-like volutes, an embellishment which heralds the more elaborate Corinthian order. (Giraudon)

Lower photo, the *Erechtheum*, south porch ("Porch of the Maidens"), the Acropolis, Athens, 421–405 B.C. An interesting variation on the conventional orders of columns appears on the south porch of the Erechtheum. Statues of maidens support the entablature. In order that the supporting figures would not appear over-burdened and that the classical sense of proportion be maintained, the frieze and the pediment were omitted. (Greek National Tourist Office)

Theater at Epidaurus (southeast Greece), c. 350 B.C. This Greek theater, one of the best preserved, has a seating capacity of 13,000. In such theaters, the Greeks attended plays written by the classical dramatists—Aeschylus (525–456 B.C.), Sophocles (496–404 B.C.), Euripides (480–406 B.C.), and Aristophanes (c. 444–380 B.C.). (Consulate General of Greece)

Procession of Maidens (detail of the Panathenaic procession relief), the Acropolis, Athens, c. 440 B.C. The scene depicted here is that of the Greater Panathenae, a procession held every four years to honor Athena. It served as a prelude to a festival which featured poetic and oratorical contests as well as competition in drama and athletics. (Hirmer)

ways faithfully kept, no business ever went before the Assembly without going before the Council first. This prevented the Assembly's time being wasted. The Council drew up the *programma* or order-paper, which might include detailed recommendations, though, once the debate was open, amendments might be moved. In an emergency, a mere statement of the situation or of the news received could suffice; the

Athena (relief from the Acropolis), Athens, c. 445 B.C. Athena is shown in this panel in a pensive yet dignified attitude. What might be a static, rigid form is given a certain mobility and softness by the positioning of the arms and head. (Royal Greek Embassy)

Girl with Pigeons (grave relief), Island of Paros, c. 455–450 B.C. This form (like those of the Procession of Maidens and Athena) manifests a crucial development in Greek relief sculpture: the rendering of depth. The figure of the girl has been freed from the stone surface as much as it might be without sculpting it in the full round. (Metropolitan Museum of Art, Fletcher Fund, 1927)

Generals would already have been alerted, and the democracy could move fast. . . .

When business was less exciting, there was no rush to take part; in fact, on these occasions the humorous device was adopted of sending the Scythian slave police, whom Athens employed so that no citizen might have to lay violent hands on another, to sweep up voters from the streets with ropes dipped in wet, red paint. There were in each year forty statutory or ordinary meetings for the transaction of routine business, often purely formal; e.g. at the first in each prytany votes of confidence in the magistrates were moved, and usually no doubt passed without discussion. If one were rejected, the magistrate was suspended and would probably be sent for trial by a jury for his alleged malpractices. At another any citizen might take the green bough of a suppliant and humbly petition to have "any cause, public or private" placed on the agenda; a right of initiative for the obscure. "Anyone who wished" could, moreover, take up the cause of a widow or orphan, or anyone else alleged to be suffering wrong.

It is clear that, except when business was particularly exciting, most citizens did not attend the assembly—especially the poor, and those who lived at Piraeus or in the country. Athens in 431 counted over 27,000 citizen-soldiers of the hoplite and cavalry classes; and the poor or "naval crowd" were presumably considerably more numerous. But for some classes of business, such as ostracism or other legislation on the status of an individual, it was laid down that at least 6,000 votes were necessary; which indicates that at a routine

Zeus (Poseidon?) from Cape Artemision, c. 460–450 B.C. This bronze statue depicts either Zeus hurling a thunderbolt or Poseidon about to throw his trident. Obviously, the Kouros form has been abandoned; in its place the sculptor has fashioned a powerful, lifelike figure. The precise anatomical detail and graceful mobility of this statue indicate that it is the creation of a master sculptor of the era. (Hirmer)

Discobulus (Discus Thrower), Roman copy after a Greek bronze original by Myron, c. 450 B.C. In the *Discus Thrower,* a genius for balance, harmony, and proportion is readily observed. In order to achieve these characteristics a unit of measure was employed to assure the orderly relation of the parts to the whole. This unit, the module, was not of a fixed size or dimension but varied according to the particular object involved (e.g., in architecture it could be the diameter of a column; in sculpture it could be the diameter of a limb).

The throwing of the discus was one of the competitive events in the Olympic games and was a central part of the festival held at the shrine of Zeus in Olympia. The games were inaugurated in 776 B.C. and drew participants from most of the Greek city-states.

meeting the attendance might be much smaller. In the fourth century those who attended meetings were paid for their time, but not yet in the fifth. In the circumstances, regular attenders were probably confined to a class of active politicians. There are indications that even councillors, who were paid, tended to be well-to-do or middle-class citizens rather than the poor; but since it was not permitted to sit on the council more than twice in a lifetime (and not in consecutive years), the demand for an average of at least 250 new councillors, and in practice more, per year, meant that some 12,000 or more different Athenians would have this experience within the forty years of a normal active life.

The "political world," as modern Greece calls its active politicians, naturally included all those who served as financial officials, who had to belong to the top property-class, or as generals, most of whom were of old-established landed families; and many of these were also frequent speakers. But to see that the gentry did not have things all their own way, there also grew up a class of speakers who did not hold office, and who claimed to speak for the masses; the Popular Leaders or *demagogues.* The first famous demagogue (though he had predecessors) came to the front at the end of Pericles' time: Kleon, a master-tanner. He gets a bad "press" from all our literary sources; Aristophanes[6] calls him a stinking exponent of a malodorous trade; Thucydides[7] (whose career he may have ruined, after

[6] Aristophanes (about 450–385 B.C.), an Athenian, was (as far as is known) the greatest writer of comedy in ancient Greece. [Ed.]

[7] Thucydides (about 460–400 B.C.) was the greatest of the Greek historians and will be treated at length in the next chapter. [Ed.]

Thucydides had failed in a military command) speaks of him as favouring war, because in it his evil deeds were less likely to be found out. He is also said to have introduced a new and vulgar style of oratory, stamping about on the platform, shouting and gesticulating. But Thucydides also shows him as not afraid to criticize his audience; he seems to have been a sincere if ferocious "jingo" patriot. Under such leadership a crowd of the poorer citizens could, if provoked, turn up to carry measures displeasing to Pericles, and still more to the conservatives. In imperial politics, it was the "naval crowd" and their leaders who were the quickest to demand strong measures against suspect allies; while the gentry, whose income came from their lands and not from the sea and who sympathized with their class-mates among the allies, stood for comparative gentleness and moderation.

Apart from well-known speakers, when the herald cried "Who wishes to speak?" the debate was open; but if the speaker was not very much to the point, the Assembly would soon show its impatience. References in Plato and Xenophon show that it expected sound knowledge of the subject of debate, which might be technical, e.g. architecture or ship-building. If the speaker were inadequate, and the meeting thought so, the chairman might order him down, and if necessary tell his

Scythian constables to remove him. It is a great mistake to think of the Assembly as a gullible body ready to listen to any smooth-tongued rhetorician; ready though they certainly were to savour and relish a play on words or a well-turned phrase.

Between meetings of the assembly, the Council had a heavy programme of routine work. It was responsible for inspecting new ships built for the navy, the horses of the cavalry—true cavalry, recruited among young men of the ancient "knightly class," having been introduced recently—

Dying Niobid, c. 450–440 B.C. A dramatic blending of action and emotion distinguishes this statue from Archaic Kore figures. The sculpture conveys pathos and arouses empathy in the viewer. This is the first instance in Greek sculpture of an undraped female body. The activity and movement of the Niobid is similar to that previously reserved for the male nude. (Hirmer)

and the candidates for the archonships and Council of the following year. . . . It supervised and advised the numerous boards of officials, all chosen by lot, except the military and some important financial officers. There were auditors, inspectors, and collectors of taxes, market-inspectors, police-chiefs, five in Athens and five in Piraeus; their duties included preventing householders from constructing verandas and trellises which obstructed the street, seeing that girl flute- and guitar-players, in demand for men's parties, did not receive more than a fixed maximum payment (twice that for a skilled workman—but to hire the most popular flute-girl was a status-symbol), and seeing that the scavengers dumped the garbage not less than a mile outside the walls. The Council also

had powers as a criminal court in matters arising out of its administrative duties. Later, these too were taken away, and it could only commit for trial by a jury. Altogether the Council was on duty on about 300 days in each year, that is on every day except the numerous festivals—one must remember that the Greeks had no Sunday.

Councillors, as has been said, were paid, with additional subsistence allowances when on night-and-day duty; and so were the other officials, who by the later fourth century numbered perhaps 350. Plato and other anti-democratic writers pour scorn on the practice of pay for public service—how much better that of other cities and of the Good Old Days, when gentlemen gave of their time freely! But looking at the matter dispassionately, it is clear that such pay . . . was essential if the democratic machinery was to function in a truly democratic way.

This applies particularly to the judicial branch: the 6,000 registered jurymen of any year, who were empanelled in juries of varying size according to the importance of the case—501 was common—on all working days, up to the number required. Commercial cases and appeals from the Empire, added to those arising in Athens, at this time kept the courts busy. Nevertheless, Aristophanes depicts jurymen getting up before dawn to queue and make sure of a place; by no means the whole 6,000 were employed every day. Moreover their day's pay was, in Pericles' time, a mere subsistence allowance, two obols, a third of a drachma. This would have made

Greek vase, attributed to "Eucharides Painter," red-figure style, 490 B.C. *Apollo and Artemis before an Altar*. (Metropolitan Museum of Art, Rogers Fund, 1907)

little appeal to the strong and active, and in fact, we gather from Aristophanes, it was chiefly old men who did this work. The allies objected to the whole principle of having to bring cases to Athens; but we have few complaints of Athenian commercial justice, and none at all of bribery; there was safety in numbers. Where the courts were open to criticism was in that they were prejudiced—in favour of Athens and in favour of democracy. When they handled cases from the empire, they were defending their own interests; and they too sympathized with their class-mates in the allied cities. There was no better way of keeping a check on aspirations to autonomy than by supporting the natural opponents of local leaders; and for local democrats there was no better way of resisting the rich than by representing them at Athens as disloyal.

The political conflicts of the fifth century B.C., the democratization of the polis, increasing literacy, commercial expansion and the establishment of an empire—in short, the growing complexity of Athenian society—created educational needs far different from what they had been in previous centuries. In early Greek society, as in all preliterate societies, instruction began in the home. When a boy learned all that could be provided by the family group, he was apprenticed to a more experienced and knowledgeable citizen (usually a member of the extended family) to learn a trade, or if he was an aristocrat, to learn the arts of war. By the middle of the sixth century B.C., however, even aristocratic education in Athens had lost its exclusively military character and a few elementary

schools had been founded to teach gymnastics (physical training) and music (including the study of lyric and epic poetry). By the time of the Persian Wars, reading and writing had been introduced into the curriculum. Although this represented an advanced level of education in the ancient Near East, it was available only to members of the privileged aristocracy, and the curriculum was still geared to their needs.

The first men who sought to replace this aristocratically oriented instruction with a more comprehensive system of education were the Sophists.

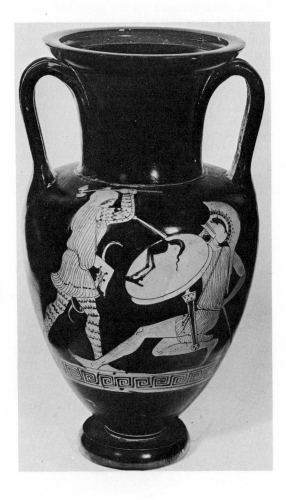

Greek vase, red-figure style, c. 460 B.C. *Combat of Amazon and Greek*. (Metropolitan Museum of Art Rogers Fund, 1941)

THE SOPHISTS
Eric Voegelin[8]

. . . The sophists were migratory teachers. In order to find an audience and an
income they had to dispense what their
public needed. Nature and form of their
teaching was inseparable from the needs
of the new democracy and in particular of
Athens. From our study of the tragedy we
are acquainted with the meaning of action
as well as with the necessity of translating
the decision reached by the political leader
into the will of the people through persua-
sive speech. The political supremacy of
the aristocratic clans was broken, and
while the aristocrats might transmit their

[8] Eric Voegelin, *Order and History*, Vol. II: *The
World of the Polis* (New Orleans: Louisiana State University Press, 1957), pp. 270–272. Reprinted by permission of the publisher.

traditional way of life to their sons through
education, such transmission had become
the private affair of a social class but did
not lead by itself to political success in a
polis of freemen. . . . The leading statesmen, generals, and magistrates might still
come from the old families but their political success depended on their ability to
gain the favor of the people against com-
petitors as well as to gain continued popular support for their policies in the face of
the intense criticism, gossiping, and intriguing of a compact, comparatively small
town. The mastery of typical situations
and arguments in public debate, a stock of
thorough knowledge with regard to the
public affairs of the polis in domestic and
imperial relations, a ready wit, a good
memory improved by training, a disciplined intellect ready to grasp the essentials of an issue, the trained ability of
marshalling arguments on the spur of the

Greek vase, red-figure style, c. 475–
450 B.C. *Odysseus Tied to the Mast of
a Galley.* This vase is painted in the
red-figure style, a reversal of black-
figure style (see p. 79). The red-
figure artist painted the background
of the vase black and left his figures
in the natural red color of the clay.
The internal details of his figures
convey the illusion of motion with
subtlety and naturalism. (Trustees of
the British Museum)

moment, a ready stock of anecdotes, para-digmata and sayings drawn from the poets for illustrating a point, general oratorical perfection, skill in debate leading to more or less graceful discomfiture of an oppo-nent, a good deal of psychological knowl-edge in handling people, good appearance and bearing, natural and trained charm in conversation—all these were required for success in the competitive game of the polis. Anybody would be welcome who could train the mind in arriving at sound decisions and in imposing them on others in this new form of politics through de-bate, speech, argument, and persuasion.

Obviously, neither Milesian cosmologi-cal speculation nor the study of Hera-clitean oracles could play an appreciable part in teaching that was calculated to satisfy such needs. A classified polyhis-tory[9] of a quite different type was re-quired. As far as the sources allow a judgment, the sophists in fact ordered the areas of knowledge that would be of serv-ice to a well-educated man in a cultivated, competitive society. They created some-thing like a curriculum of liberal education and their efforts in this respect have stood the test of time in so far as their ordering of subject matters in education was re-tained through the ages as the Quadrivium and the Trivium. The Quadrivium of arithmetic, geometry, music, and astron-omy met with certain misgivings at the time because the value of mathematical knowledge for a young gentleman who

[9] Polyhistory means a knowledge of all areas of learning. [Ed.]

Greek vase, *White Lekythos,* attributed to "Achilles Painter," red-figure style, said to be from Eretria, c. 450–440 B.C. (Metropolitan Museum of Art, Rogers Fund, 1908)

wanted to become a political leader seemed doubtful. . . . About the practical value of the Trivium of grammar, rhetoric, and dialectic there was never a doubt; the forms of language, speech, and thought had to be mastered under all circumstances.

Prodicus of Ceos[10] seems to have been the most notable philologist among the major sophists. According to tradition Socrates at some time was his pupil and we still can sense a distinct sympathy for him in the dialogues of Plato. He was concerned with semantic problems, with ascertaining the precise meanings of words and distinguishing shades of meanings of related terms. Moreover, it seems that his concern about meanings led to occupation with the objects denoted. That would go far to explain the Socratic and Platonic interest in him for, under one aspect, Platonic and Aristotelian philosophizing is the arduous process of developing the terms, which in retrospect have become "philosophical vocabulary," out of the meanings which the words had in everyday parlance. Plato's sympathy for Prodicus may well have been rooted in a craftsman's respect for the valuable work of a predecessor.

Beyond the fundamentals of the Quadrivium and Trivium the sophists developed the *techne politike*, the art of politics, as a special new discipline. It was the theory of an education from early childhood that would fit a man into the customs and cultural patterns of his community. And since the laws were the embodiment of the ultimate principles on which the order of the community rested, the process was crowned by imparting to the young

Greek vase, red-figure style, c. 465–460 B.C. *Pyxis with the Judgment of Paris*. A third vase-painting technique shown here and on p. 151 is the white-ground style which employs a wider range of colors. The vessels were coated by the artist with a white pigment upon which he sketched his figures; the outlines were then elaborately painted. This technique allowed the artist to achieve the effect similar to that of the modern artist working with pen and paper. (Metropolitan Museum of Art, Rogers Fund, 1907)

[10] A contemporary of Socrates. [Ed.]

man a thorough knowledge of the laws of his polis. At this point the decisive difference between the old aristocratic and the new democratic education perhaps becomes most clearly visible. The appeal to authority in education no longer goes to the conduct of honorable ancestors and heroes . . . ; it goes, rather, to the laws of the polis as the ultimately obligatory standards of conduct in command and obedience. The new education was bound by the horizon of the polis; its purpose was the formation of the responsible and successful citizen.

As indicated by this account, the most important subject taught by the Sophists was the art of communication, both written and spoken. Because this was their most important function as teachers, they were responsible for an intensified interest in oratory (that is, speaking itself) and rhetoric (the theory of speaking) and for the development of written prose. It is important to remember that

Greek society relied on oral expression. Although literacy was clearly extensive in fifth- and fourth-century Athens, even then reading and writing, whether on stone, bronze, clay, wood, wax, or papyrus, was difficult and unnatural. Both the mechanics of ancient civilization and its primary expression remained oral. The political system, for example, operated through the direct speech of the citizens among themselves and to their magistrates, and of the magistrates to their administrative assistants. Writing was used to record a vote, a law, a resolution, but rarely to achieve it in the first place. Political agitation was usually accomplished or defeated by word of mouth. The judicial system was similarly oral: verbal complaints were brought before magistrates, who held hearings; then the litigants pleaded their own cases in public before a jury of citizens. Documents were few. There were written business contracts, but they were negotiated and enforced by face-to-face argument rather than by prolonged correspondence. There were no newspapers, magazines, handbills, or circulars; information was spread orally. Entertainment was provided only to a limited extent by reading; informal conversation, the legitimate stage, or the sound of the human voice in some form constituted the commonest form of diversion. All literature was written to be heard, and even when reading to himself a Greek read aloud.

The oral nature of the society is evident in Greek literature, which flourished long before it was written down. The Homeric poems are undoubtedly the pinnacle of an oral tradition of epic verse that had sung of the deeds of the Trojan war and heroic Greece for generations, conforming extemporaneously to an exacting metrical form by the use of formulae and themes. Greek drama, both tragedy and comedy, grew out of the spontaneous oral traditions of festivals. The beginnings of philosophy are to be found in the traditional folk maxims and cosmologies which made the transition to writing in the poetry we attribute to Hesiod, and history reaches back to the beginnings of time through the tales told around a camp fire, the genealogies, real or fictitious, of famous families, and the advice imparted or the wonders reported by one traveler to another. No less does oratory go back to the beginnings of civilization. The Greeks have always loved to talk and even wrangle, and have felt the force of their own words. They still feel it. Their earliest oratory must have had many of the characteristics evident in oral poetry. The techniques were learned by listening and imitation, but the power was achieved by an inspiration which carried the speaker on without conscious observance of rules. As he spoke he used ancestors of the commonplaces of later oratory—the topics, the traditional examples, the maxims which he had heard and used before—in the same way that the oral poet used his devices of repetition, and he did so without notes and without verbatim memorization. . . .

The significance of oratory is as great in substance as in form. Wherever persuasion is the end, rhetoric is present. This is most marked in formal speeches in epic or drama or history, but it can be found in passages not formally oratorical both in lyric and in philosophy. The philosopher in weighing the evidence, drawing the conclusion, and presenting a literate exposition is fulfilling much the same functions as the orator in court, and so is the historian, who has similar problems of witnesses, psychological credibility, narration of incident, ascription of motive, weighing of evidence, and estimation of justice, expediency, or honor. The Greek philosopher and dramatist share the concern of the historian and orator with justice and responsibility.

The significance of rhetoric and oratory in Greek and Roman intellectual life is further evident in education and criticism. It is not too much to say that rhetoric played the central role in ancient education. . . .[11]

The techniques of speaking developed by the Sophists were strongly influenced by the law courts. After the judicial system was democratized in 462 B.C., litigants had to present their own cases to large juries of citizens chosen by lot. These juries had the power to determine both law and fact. There was no presiding judge and no public prosecutor. For the first time legal decisions were made on the basis of orally presented, logical proofs, though it should be remembered that emotion was by no

[11] George Kennedy, *The Art of Persuasion in Greece* (Princeton, N.J.: Princeton University Press, 1963), pp. 3–5 and 7. Reprinted by permission of Princeton University Press. Copyright © 1963 by Princeton University Press.

means absent from the courtroom. The power to persuade, therefore, was of critical importance.

One of the principal techniques of persuasion employed by the Sophists was to argue both sides of a question—that is, they made use of antithesis or, as it is also called, antilogy. The notion that there are two sides to every question was first enunciated by Protagoras. Within a short time it was generally held that informed decisions could only be made after both sides had been presented. The speaker arguing in this way was trained to switch easily from one line of reasoning to another, depending on how the case was going. Needless to say, such a technique put the emphasis on expediency and this could, and often did, lead to oratory without ethical content. In other words, for many the goal was winning an argument or a case for the sake of winning, not for the sake of proving that the argument or case was right.

The Sophists most frequently used two types of arguments, those from probability and from human nature. In the case of the former, for example, a man being tried for murder would argue in his defense that he was innocent because he was a small man, the victim was a big man, and it is improbable that small men attack big men. The court, in other words, was being asked to believe that what is often true is always true. Like the use of antithesis, arguing from probability could have serious ethical consequences, for probability need bear little relationship to fact. A man's size, for example, is only on very rare occasions completely responsible for his behavior. The other kind of argument—that from human nature—will be treated at some length later in this chapter.

The Sophists' disregard for the ethical consequences of the methods they were developing was in part a result of a growing uncertainty about traditional values. During the Archaic Age and well into the fifth century B.C. Athenian values had remained very similar to those of Homer's characters in the *Iliad*.

GREEK VALUES FROM THE HOMERIC AGE
TO THE FIFTH CENTURY B.C.
John Ferguson[12]

The predominant values of the age were aristocratic, and because aristocratic values tend to be conservative, they may properly be represented by the rather later figure of Pindar [about 515–435 B.C.]. His ideals in fact derive directly from the tradition of the Dorian aristocrats. The man who would achieve to the full that most untranslatable of Greek qualities, *arete* ("goodness"), must begin with the natural advantages of birth and wealth. Breed tells in the end, and wealth is among the greatest of external boons. But the mere possession of such external advantages is not of itself sufficient; success or failure still depends on what we do with the advantages which we possess. Inherited ability is a great thing, but it needs drawing out by education, training, discipline, work. The natural genius far outshines the technical expert, but natural genius will not of itself reach the highest point unless it is trained in the necessary techniques. Wealth and position should be used with courtesy and directed towards generosity and a liberal hospitality. Men must beware of that self-exaltation in face of heaven which the Greeks called *hubris* [pride]. These values reflect with greater poetical power and greater intellectual depth what may be found in the writings of an earlier aristocrat such as Theognis of Megara [in the mid-sixth century B.C.]. His lines show

12 John Ferguson, *Moral Values in the Ancient World* (London: Methuen & Company Ltd., 1959), pp. 19–23. Reprinted by permission of Associated Book Publishers Ltd.

moral contempt for those who lack both breed and riches, and he honours good-living and hospitality.

At this period *arete* means a capacity to do something. In its social context it naturally is linked with wealth, military (and athletic) prowess, and political authority. Homer can call Aegisthus *amumon* ("blameless") while at the same time condemning him for the murder of Agamemnon; this shows the connotation to be pragmatic, not moral. Mimnermus shrinks from old age because it makes a man *kakos* (conventionally "bad"), very nearly "impotent." Wealth and *arete* are so closely linked in Homer and Hesiod as to be at times indistinguishable. In Tyrtaeus and Callinus *aner agathos* (conventionally "a good man") is a successful warrior. Solon speaks of strength as the mark of *arete*. . . . Sometimes the prowess is intellectual. Even in the *Iliad* dominance in the political assembly is put alongside dominance on the battlefield. As the notion of morality itself becomes articulate it tends to be linked with the social solidarity of the dominant class. Thus in Homer it is characteristic of a good man to love and look after his wife. The moralization of the concept is increased as the aristocracy's power decays. Theognis, presented with the spectacle of impoverished aristocrats, cannot equate *arete* with wealth. Unhappily the emergence of moral concepts within this class at this period, though it did not stultify the ultimate development of moral philosophy, did have a profoundly adverse effect upon the whole future of Greek social thought, which remained consciously or unconsciously dominated by the ideas of a land-owning aristocracy. The working-man was *poneros* or *mochtheros*. Originally, perhaps, this meant little more than that he was socially impotent, lacking wealth, political privilege and any opportunity for outstanding military success. It remained as a moral stigma, and Greek thought never escaped from the delusion that there is something dishonourable attaching to manual labour, even when they exalted the virtue of toil itself. So too the merchants were stigmatized with the dislike that an ancient and established landed gentry always feel for the get-rich-quick methods of trade and commerce.

As the new democratic parties arose to challenge the *status quo* they introduced their own political catchwords of Liberty and Equality. It is important to notice that the second of these at least is an adaptation of an old aristocratic idea. *Homoios* ("equal") is in Homer a term of disapprobation, which is applied to war, death, old age and in general things which blot out the proper distinctions between man and man. The aristocrats however gradually took it up and applied it to themselves. At Sparta the ruling-class were known as the *Homoioi*. Herodotus speaks of the *isokratia* ("equality in power") of the Corinthian oligarchs. The picture is that of a ruling-class which allowed no individual member to domineer over the rest. The democrats took the same principles and applied them over a wider field. Greek democracy is in fact only an enlarged oligarchy, and the privileges which the democrats demanded for a wider citizenry they would not dream of extending to slaves or foreigners. . . .

The mere enunciation of these slogans is enough to make a modern student aware of a gap. The French Revolution bore on its banners LIBERTÉ, ÉGALITÉ and FRATERNITÉ. The impulses behind that revolution were in measure anti-Christian. But they were also post-Christian. Freedom and equality are assertions of rights, in the face of oppression. But brotherhood springs from a more philosophical reflection, and involves a moral judgement rather different from the other two. This the Greeks were not yet ready to make. They were to draw near to it under the influence of more mature philosophical speculation and a wider and more understanding experience of other peoples. But that lay in the future.

What did develop during this period [the sixth and fifth centuries B.C.] was a new sense of the importance of co-operative action, which may be drawn out of the writings of the lyric poets. It is interesting to trace the causes of this development. Primitive societies take social solidarity for granted. Such solidarity is the life of the people, and does not require any specific emphasis or expression. This is tribalism. An individual who dares to be unconventional is regarded in the strict sense as extra-ordinary, and cuts himself off from the life of the tribe. This excommunication is the worst possible fate in an age where everything depends on the life of the community. But when the order itself is challenged a different state of things emerges. One suspects that a potent factor in the change among the Greeks was the period of colonization. However conservative such colonies were in their original establishment, they acted on the framework of Greek ideology much as the fact of the "moving frontier" influenced the Americans. They encouraged individualism. Once individualism is there, not just in a solitary and isolated rebel, but as part of the accepted environment, it means that the old unthinking social solidarity has no longer any force. Co-operative enterprise has ceased to be automatic response. It has to become an act of will. This is precisely what we find.

Classical Greek knew literally thousands of words compounded with *sun* (anglicized as syn, as in synthesis) and indicating complete or co-operative action. In Homer there are not more than fifty, and in the verbal forms, almost if not quite without exception, the collectivity refers to the object not to the subject, and the word connotes action rather than emotion. Thus we find *sunhalein* to call together, *sunageirein,* to bring together, *sunelaunein,* to drive together, *sunorinein,* to move together. These are typical. But in the lyric period a new group of words comes into use. They refer to the inner life of mind and spirit, not the externalities of action, and the collectivity relates to the subject not the object. They relate in fact to what we should call "fellow-feeling." . . .

It will be noticed that though the actuality (and hence, once reflection sets in, the desirability) of such a communal sensitivity has now found expression, and though there is some transference of attention from external act to inward thought and feeling, language as yet reflects no moral judgement upon the nature of the communal experience itself. It is enough that we join together; the question has not yet been asked. "In what are we to join together?" . . .

This question was asked in the mid-fifth century B.C., after the Greeks had become increasingly familiar with foreign cultures. Relations with non-Greek peoples had revealed that there were many types of political systems and legal standards. It followed that Greek laws and political institutions—both of which embodied their values—did not have universal validity, and as a result the justification for their laws, political

system, and social conventions seemed to be no longer valid. One result of this situation was an intensification of the skepticism which had been created by the Eleatic philosophers' apparent demonstration that neither the senses nor reason could mediate the truth about the world.[13] This skepticism regarding both knowledge and values was clearly revealed in the protracted debate over the meaning of *nomos* (ancient rules, established customs, accepted moral standards, and positive law) and *physis* (the objective quality or essential property of a thing).

The *Physis-Nomos* Controversy
Glenn R. Morrow[14]

. . . The word *nomos* is as old as the epic poets, and seems originally to have been used to denote the ways of behavior characteristic of any group of living beings, whether men or wild beasts. Thus Hesiod uses it in *Works and Days:*

> The Son of Cronos has ordained this *nomos* for men. Fishes and beasts and winged fowl devour one another, for right (*dike*) is not in them; but to mankind he gave right, which proves far the best (ll. 276–280; Evelyn-White's translation).

In later days *nomos* was applied only to human ways of behavior; but it never lost its original meaning of custom, nor its association with justice. Whenever a later writer speaks of *nomoi,* he tends to imply not merely strict law, the law contained in published statutes, but also customary law. Likewise the *dike* which characterizes

[13] See pp. 110–111.
[14] Glenn R. Morrow, "Plato and the Law of Nature," in *Essays in Political Theory Presented to George H. Sabine,* Milton R. Konvitz and Arthur E. Murphy, eds. (Ithaca, N.Y.: Cornell University Press, 1948), pp. 20–25, 28–29. Reprinted by permission of the publisher.

nomos, as used by Hesiod, remains throughout all later history an inseparable part of the concept. Law is primarily an embodiment of justice, and conversely the just man is he who obeys the laws. But two other elements later came to be associated with the idea of *nomos:* the element of constraint, and the element of enactment. Customary law in its early stages is usually felt by a people as only vaguely compelling; conformity results without the machinery of courts and penalties. Similarly these customs are usually regarded as owing little to human contrivance; they are the gift of the gods, or a part of the unchanging order of things. For the Greeks this state of innocence was ended by the process of political unification and of colonization. When two or more communities found it expedient to join forces for mutual protection and benefit, their tribal and local customs had to be harmonized, and something like a common law, the law of the city, had to be set up, in some respects overriding the earlier and more familiar customs. Such a common law of the city was felt to have, and would need to have, more explicit power of constraining than the earlier customs; and furthermore it was seen to have arisen from something like explicit legislation or enactment, by the deliberate choice of "the best." . . . By the beginning of the fifth century the Greeks were well aware of this element of human judgment and positive enactment in the laws under which they lived. The course of political events in the fifth century only deepened this awareness. At Athens, for example, the successive changes in the constitution, the increasing resort to legislation, the growth of litigation, the widespread contacts with other peoples and other laws, and the heightened sense of individual interests

distinct from those of the community, all converged in their influence to give the Athenian citizen the conviction that his laws were to a great extent the result of legislation or enactment, and derived much of their authority from the sanctions explicitly attached to them.

Yet, so strong was the traditional association of law with justice, it appeared inconceivable that there should be justice apart from law. The relations of the two concepts had to a great extent been reversed. Whereas in the beginning law was regarded as finding its norm in justice, in the fifth century justice came to be defined in terms of law. Under these circumstances the only recourse open to one who felt the injustice of his city's law was to appeal to a higher law. Sometimes the appeal was made on religious grounds, as in the moving chorus of Sophocles' *Oedipus the King,* to

> the laws born of Olympus, that pace on high the heavenly ether,
> not begotten of mortal human nature (Il. 865–870).

Sometimes the appeal was made to *patrioi nomoi,* ancestral customs, as more authoritative than the innovations of later times. Again an appeal was often made to universal *nomima,* common to all mankind, or to the common laws of all Greeks. Finally, more vaguely, an appeal could be made to the "unwritten law," by which might be meant any one of the above-mentioned higher laws. These various protests testify to the uncertain moral foundations of positive law, but they provided no clearly defined alternative. The *patrioi nomoi,* and the universal *nomima,* were different in content, but not in formal character, from the *nomoi* from which appeal was made. To critical reflection they would reveal the same defects. The divine law was presumably free from the defects of human judgment, but the appeal to such a divine law could be (and was) effectively countered by the observation that belief in the gods is itself a convention supported by the sanctions of the city's laws. As Euripides' Hecuba declares:

> By law (*nomo*) we learn that there are gods, and mark out the bounds of justice and injustice (*Hecuba* 799f.).

In short, there seemed no escape from the "tyranny of *nomos*." The dilemma of the fifth-century thinker is nicely exemplified in the attitude of Socrates. Before the Athenian court he declares firmly that he must "obey God rather than men." Yet he was a loyal subject of the laws of Athens, and according to Xenophon he fully concurred in the current opinion that justice means conformity to the laws.

The notion of *physis* belongs to an entirely different context. The idea of *nomos* is the product of reflection on political and moral experience; the conception of *physis* was worked out by the early Greek scientists—those men of Miletus, Ephesus, Clazomenae, and Abdera, of Sicily and southern Italy, who attempted to explain, in terms of familiar elements and processes the phenomena of the heavens and all the other varied occurrences in the cosmos that surrounds human life. The speculations of these early thinkers were universally designated, from the fifth century onward and perhaps even earlier, as inquiries into *physis*. . . . These inquiries were introduced into Athens in the fifth century by Anaxagoras, and the shock they gave to the older beliefs of the Athenians is one of the major events of that century. The meaning of the term *physis*, universally used to designate the object of these

inquiries, varied somewhat with the thinker and with the context in which the term was used. Sometimes it referred to the primary stuff, or kinds of stuff, of which the ordered cosmos is constituted; sometimes it denoted that ordered cosmos itself . . . ; sometimes the form or constitution of any person or thing within that cosmos; and sometimes the originating power or agency through which this order came about, whether in the cosmos as a whole, or in its separate parts. . . . But these varied meanings had a common core. Underlying all these investigations into *physis* was the assumption that there are certain enduring primary characters or elemental forces which, if understood, would explain the origin and behavior of the cosmos and all its parts.

The contrast between *nomos* and *physis* is therefore unmistakable. *Nomos* varies from place to place and from time to time, whereas *physis* has the character of necessity . . . and is therefore invariable. *Nomos* is transitory, while *physis* is "ageless and deathless." *Nomos* is the product of human contriving; but the forces at work in nature, and the order they bring about, are independent of human agency. Furthermore *physis* is primary, not merely in the order of being, but also in time; for *nomos,* together with all other human institutions, is a late occurrence in cosmic history. A fragment of Archelaus, a pupil of Anaxagoras, tells us that living beings arose "where the warm and the cold were first mingled together in the earth; men were then separated off from the other animals, and set up kings and laws and the arts and cities and all the rest." For all these reasons *physis* came inevitably to be identified with the real and the true, whereas *nomos* is merely convention, what is accepted or acknowledged, whether rightly or wrongly. . . . Thus *nomos* comes to stand for the whole complex of human opinions, beliefs, and traditions; and the contrast between *nomos* and *physis* is generalized into a distinction between popular belief and what we would call scientific understanding. The former is relative, transitory and unstable, whereas the latter is sure and abiding, since it rests upon the real nature of things. . . .

It was only natural that this generalized distinction between *nomos* and *physis* should have been used as a tool for the analysis of human institutions themselves. But here the partisans of *physis* seem to have confronted an unpleasant dilemma. Strictly interpreted, the distinction between the just and the unjust should have been denied any standing in the order of nature, just as the distinction between the hot and the cold was regarded as merely a matter of convention. Archelaus followed this course, so it seems, and declared roundly that "the just and the shameful exist not by nature but by law." A similar doctrine is implied by Thrasymachus, as he is represented in the first book of Plato's *Republic*. From this point of view all possible moral and political rules would be merely institutions, in the literal sense of the word, existing *thesei* [by arbitrary establishment], not *physei* [by nature]. But to drop the inquiry here was to leave unsatisfied one important purpose widely cherished by the partisans of nature. A large part of the appeal of this concept lay in the prospect it afforded of finding a standard of judgment more reliable than inherited opinions and traditions. If nature is the criterion of truth, can we not also find in nature a standard of justice? The traditional opinion was that law is somehow the embodiment of a justice beyond the law. What then could be more logical than to attempt to do, by means of the concept of *physis*, what had been impossible with *nomos*, i.e., to distinguish between real justice, a justice that exists by nature, and the more or less imperfect embodiments of justice found in the law? . . .

Two different solutions to this problem were worked out in the fourth century, leading to two distinct conceptions of "natural justice," based respectively upon what later came to be called the Law of Nature and the Social Contract. The former conception of natural justice was arrived at by a transformation of the concept of *physis*, so as to permit the incorporation of the peculiarly human conception of law, as an intelligent ordering of events for the achievement of an end, into the very structure of the cosmos. This is the conception of natural justice that is familiar to us from the Stoics, and for which, as I think it can be shown, Plato provided the indispensable philosophical foundation. The other conception of natural justice is quite different. It takes over without essential modification the impersonal and indifferent cosmos of the fifth-century physiologers, and founds justice upon an agreement made by human beings to abstain from injuring one another. This is the doctrine we find in Epicurus. "Natural justice," he says, "is a contract of mutual expediency, to prevent one man from harming or being harmed by another." With the origins of this doctrine we are not here concerned, but it is fairly certain that it had its advocates in the fourth century before Epicurus espoused it. The important thing for us to note is its divergence from the doctrine of Natural Law. It bases justice on a contract between human beings, a contract springing presumably from man's natural impulse to protect his vital interests; the other finds justice in the cosmos, and its authority is independent of any agreement between human beings. These two views were universally regarded in antiquity as antithetical; the partisans of the one were sharply opposed to those who espoused the other. As in later days the Stoics were arrayed against the Epicureans on this issue, so in the fourth century we find Plato and Aristotle on the one side, and the "sophists" on the other. . . .

Developments in Greek medicine played a vital role in the *nomos-physis* debate and in the formation of the concept of human nature which many Sophists employed. Rationalism began to penetrate Greek medicine in the sixth century B.C. at the same time that the natural philosophers were working out rational interpretations of natural phenomena. Perhaps the most fruitful aspect of Greek medicine was its reliance on observation and, to a lesser extent, on experiment. The use of the inductive method led physicians to conclude that the human physical organism was not subject to the laws external to it—to the laws that governed the cosmos—but to rules dictated by its own nature. Though each patient was treated on the basis of his specific physical constitution, temperament, and so on, Greek physicians did discover that there were regularities which characterized the biological functioning of man. These together constituted the *physis* of man.

Man is subject to certain rules prescribed by *his own* nature, which must be known if he is to live correctly in health and recover properly from illness. This was the first recognition of the fact that the physis of man is a physical organism, with a particular structure to be understood in a particular way. From that medical conception of physis, the Greeks soon reached a wider application of the word, which was the basis of the educational theories of the sophists: it now came to mean the whole man, made up of body and soul together, and in particular man's spiritual nature. . . . The idea of human nature, now formulated for the first time, should not be regarded as a simple or natural idea: it was a great and fundamental discovery of the Greek mind.[15]

For many of the second-generation Sophists this concept of human nature became the justification for almost any kind of conduct. It was argued by Antiphon, for instance, that a man ought to do whatever he conceived to be natural.

. . . The majority of just acts according to law are prescribed contrary to nature. For there is legislation about the eyes, what they must see and what not; and about the ears, what they must hear and what not; and about the tongue, what it must speak and what not; and about the hands, what they must do and what not; and about the feet, where they must go and where not. Now the law's prohibitions are in no way more agreeable to nature and more akin than the law's injunctions. But life belongs to nature, and death too, and life for them is derived from advantages, and death from disadvantages. And the advantages laid down by the laws are chains upon nature, but those laid down by nature are free. So that the things which hurt, according to true reasoning, do not benefit nature more than those which delight; and things which grieve are not more advantageous than those which please; for things truly advantageous must not really harm, but must benefit. . . .[16]

The ethical relativism which issued from this kind of reasoning was but one feature of a moral crisis that was to become pronounced during

[15] Werner Jaeger, *Paideia: The Ideals of Greek Culture*, trans. Gilbert Highet, Vol. I: *Archaic Greece: The Mind of Athens*, 2nd ed. (New York: Oxford University Press, 1939), pp. 306–307. Reprinted by permission of Oxford University Press.
[16] Antiphon, "Truth," in *Ancilla to the Pre-Socratic Philosophers*, trans. Kathleen Freeman (Oxford: Basil Blackwell, 1948), p. 147.

Observation + recording observations
Discerning an order in diseases

the Peloponnesian Wars (431–404 B.C.). In general, the situation which existed in Athens in the closing decades of the fifth century B.C. was what sociologists describe as anomic. The origin of this word is Greek, and it meant "broken customs or laws." Today it is used to refer to a state of normlessness.

. . . . In the state of anomie . . . "the most reprehensible acts are . . . frequently rendered pure by success." "The limits are unknown between the possible and the impossible, what is just and what is unjust, legitimate claims and hopes and those which are immoderate. Consequently there is no restraint upon aspirations." What is anarchy in government is anomie in society.

. . . In its largest meaning, anomie refers to a state of deregulation in which social norms—mutually agreed upon goals and means—do not control men's actions. The individual participants may be clear in their own minds what the appropriate means and goals are, but if they are interacting with others who accept different norms, the social situation which they jointly share is normless. . . . Anomie in [another] sense exists when there is little agreement on appropriate means to approved goals, or when many persons are caught in circumstances where appropriate means are inaccessible, or institutional crises—business cycles or group conflict—block the road to expected satisfactions by approved means. What one is supposed to do, under these conditions, is unclear, for the pursuit of culturally approved goals may be possible

only by illegitimate means, or the refusal to employ illegitimate means may entail repudiation of goals.

It is the normless condition, however, and not individual responses to it, which constitutes anomie. It cannot be defined independently of a group. Anomie represents a loss of pattern in the *mutual* expectations for social action. The various ways in which individuals react to loss of pattern require different terms, although they do not always . . . get them.[17]

The Sophists' responsibility for the cultural malaise experienced by Athenian society must not be exaggerated. As we have seen, they made substantial and lasting contributions to education and to the development of intellectual tools with which man could understand and organize his experience. On the other hand, there is no doubt that they compounded the moral confusion of the late fifth century B.C. by enunciating, and in some cases actively espousing, a doctrine of ethical relativism. This negative aspect of their work might have been partially avoided if the Sophists had addressed themselves to the problem which was in pressing need of clarification, that of value itself. As it was, this task, complicated by the Peloponnesian War, was left to Socrates.

[17] J. Milton Yinger, "On Anomie," *Journal for the Scientific Study of Religion,* Vol. III (1964), p. 158, including a quotation from Emile Durkheim, *Suicide* (New York: The Free Press, 1951), p. 253.

CHAPTER 7

THE IMPACT OF ATHENIAN EXPANSION ON POLITICS, MORALS, AND THOUGHT:

The Uses of Analysis in the History of Thucydides

. . . The absolute prerequisite of historical consciousness is an unrelenting exploration of the self as it does exist and may be imagined to exist. . . . The conceptualization of another culture or of another period in history . . . is the result of interaction of the sense of self with the artifacts of another time and place.

Stanley Diamond, "Introduction:
The Uses of the Primitive," in Primitive Views of the World

. . . [The] capacity for generalization, [the] insistence on the typical, remained characteristic of the Greek mind, because, being secular, it was compelled to draw its leading ideas almost entirely from observation. One must remember that the Greeks had no organized priesthood and no accepted theology, and that through the formative centuries of their development they further lacked any such sense of scientific law as in modern times supplies the basis of thought. The poets rather . . . were the teachers of Greece. . . . When after the middle of the fifth century the sophists to some degree took over the poets' earlier function in society, they could not and did not abandon the latter's essential attitude of mind. The Greeks still relied not on scientific or religious truths but on truths drawn from human observation, and, however novel the precise views of the sophists may have been, the character of those views was inevitably generic, inevitably more concerned with the laws than the occurrence, the type than the individual.

John H. Finley, Jr., Thucydides

The plain fact is that the classical Greeks knew little about their history before 650 B.C. (or even 550 B.C.), and that what they thought they knew was a jumble of fact and fiction, some miscellaneous facts and much fiction about the essentials and about most of the details. One need only consider Thucydides' introduction [to the *History of the Peloponnesian War*]. . . . In [this] first part he had nothing to go on other than Homer and other "old poets," tradition, contemporary evidence, and a very powerful and disciplined mind. The result is a sweeping theory, namely, that Hellenic power and greatness emerged only in consequence of the systematic development of navigation and commerce, which were followed by an accumulation of resources, stable community organization, imperialism (to use an anachronistic word), and finally the greatest of all Greek power struggles, the Peloponnesian War. This theory may be right, in whole or in part. . . . What is crucial is that it is a theory derived from prolonged meditation about the world in which Thucydides lived, not from a study of history. True, there is something here which is history in a conceptual sense: Thucydides has made the bold suggestion that there was a continuity and a development in Greece from the most ancient (mythical) times to his own. I do not underestimate this new conception, but its actual working out by Thucydides in his opening pages is not history in any meaningful sense of that word. Instead he has given us what amounts to a general sociological theory, a theory about power and progress, applied retrospectively to the past. . . .

M. I. Finley, "*Myth, Memory, and History*," History and Theory, Vol. IV

One of the most important intellectuals of the late fifth century B.C. to be influenced by the Sophists' rhetorical techniques, ethical relativism, and the work of the physicians was Thucydides (460–400 B.C.), the first rationalist historian and the first writer in the Western tradition to employ an explicit analytical technique. Thucydides also left the most detailed and accurate account of the Peloponnesian War, a conflict which initiated the demise of Athenian culture. One of the sources of this struggle arose from the attempt by Pericles to extend Athenian influence over central Greece. The result was endemic warfare from 459 to 445 B.C.[1] Once both sides realized that a victory could not be achieved, they signed a thirty-year truce.

FROM THE FIRST TO THE SECOND PELOPONNESIAN WAR
Carl Roebuck[2]

. . . Greece was formally divided into two power zones, when Sparta recognized the Athenian maritime empire and pledged not to interfere with its members, and

[1] The first clash, which occurred between 459 and 454 B.C., is usually referred to as the First Peloponnesian War.

[2] Reprinted with the permission of Charles Scribner's Sons from *The World of Ancient Times*, pages 261–264, by Carl Roebuck. Copyright © 1966 Charles Scribner's Sons.

Athens agreed not to interfere with the Peloponnesian League and the allies of Sparta. Provision was made for the settlement of disputes by arbitration, but no clear procedure was laid down for the process. While Pericles had failed in his grandiose schemes to put Athens in control of Central Greece and the whole of the eastern Mediterranean, he had established an Athenian Empire which was recognized by Persia and Sparta. The peace was an uneasy stalemate, but it provided the opportunity for reorganization of the Empire and the further development of Athens itself.

After the peace with Sparta, Pericles extended the influence and power of Athens by diplomacy and the founding of Athenian colonies. Control of Thrace was secured by new settlements at Brea in 444 B.C. and at Amphipolis in 437 B.C. When the latter venture was successful that time, Athens gained access to the timber, grain and metals of the northern Aegean and could supervise shipping along the coast from the Hellespont. Also in 437 B.C. a detachment of the Athenian fleet paraded along the shore of the Black Sea in a goodwill tour. Alliances were made with the larger Greek city-states there, and a small Athenian colony was placed at Amisus on the south coast. Since Persian interest in the Black Sea was evidently slight at this time, the result of these ventures was that Athens had control of the grain shipped from Thrace and the Black Sea.

In South Italy and Sicily, where Athenian trade had been growing since the early sixth century, the power of Syracuse prevented any real extension of Athenian political influence, but Pericles established a new and interesting settlement at Thurii in South Italy. In 443 B.C. a colonizing expedition was sent out as a Panhellenic venture under Athenian auspices. Prominent Greek intellectuals, among them Herodotus, the historian, and Hippodamus, the architect and town planner, were invited to participate in a model foundation. The colonists, however, rejected Athenian leadership in a few years, and Athens' interest in the west had to remain commercial for the time being. The Empire itself was disturbed in 441 B.C. by the revolt of Samos, which was joined by Byzantium on the Bosporus. The reduction of Samos required a major effort by Athens, but in 439 B.C. the island was forced to surrender and became a subject ally. Only Lesbos and Chios then remained as free partners of Athens. Pericles also took steps to tighten the organization of the Empire and link it more closely to Athens.

After 445 B.C. the Empire included about three hundred members, fanning out in a great semicircle from Athens along the coastline of the Aegean, from Macedonia to the southern coast of Asia Minor. Athenian sea power held the small scattered subject states easily and without excessive administrative expense. We know a considerable amount about the Empire from a series of documents called the tribute lists. From 454 to 415 B.C. the

Athenians recorded the annual quota of money paid to Athena's treasury by each state on marble slabs, which were set up on the Athenian Acropolis. Many have survived, and their study throws a useful light on the administrative history of the Empire. In 443 B.C. a reorganization was made which grouped the members into five districts: Ionia, the Islands of the Aegean, Thrace, the Hellespont and Caria. Within each district large cities were assessed individually, but the smaller grouped into a single tribute unit. In 438 B.C. Caria and Ionia were merged into a single district, with some inland cities given up to Persian control. Athens exercised care to make adjustments in the assessments, according to changing circumstance. The money was collected by the member-states themselves and paid over to Athens, except when the exaction of arrears made Athenian intervention necessary. An annual sum of 350 to 400 talents was collected, which left a useful excess above the costs of administration for the use of Athens.

Not only the states of the Empire but all of Greece received very tangible benefits, when the Aegean area was knitted together under the protection of Athenian sea power. The Aegean was kept clear of Persian ships and pirates. The city of Athens became an important metropolitan market, to which traders and craftsmen flocked to make a good living. Athens had agreed to the freedom of the seas for all Greeks in the peace with Sparta in 445 B.C., but, despite this, the Athenians drew the Empire together into a close economic unit. Commercial treaties were made with their subject states, which guaranteed protection of commerce on favorable terms and turned their trade to Athens. In 425 B.C., in the course of the Peloponnesian

War, the Athenians issued a decree to standardize the weights and measures of the Empire to Athenian standards and closed local mints. This, of course, was partly a war measure and, when Athens' position deteriorated in the course of the fighting, did not prove effective. Yet Athenian silver coinage did become the medium for general Greek exchange and for trade into the Persian Empire. Despite the very real benefits of economic integration, both the subject states of the Empire and the free trading states of Greece realized the threat latent in Athenian naval power and resented Athenian leadership. They knew that Athens could close the sea lanes and control the flow of grain, timber, and metals into the Aegean. So long as Athens observed the peace, however, the chief difficulties were with the members of the Empire, who desired complete autonomy.

The degree of Athenian interference in the local affairs of the subject states varied, but, when Athens felt her own security was involved, her control was very far-reaching. For example, in Erythrae and Miletus in Ionia, Athenian garrisons were stationed and a governor appointed, whose task it was to install a system of government patterned on that of Athens. Important law suits, where cases involved tribute, treason and murder, had to be referred to Athenian courts. After a revolt Athens imposed severe penalties, as she did in Euboea in 445. The opponents of Athens were exiled and their lands confiscated to be made available for Athenian *cleruch* colonists. Athenians were invited to enroll for such a colony and to the members of the group so formed lots of land, *kleroi*, were assigned. The *cleruch* thus became a member of a privileged Athenian community in the territory of a

subject state, retaining Athenian citizenship and helping to protect Athenian interests.

These harsh methods by which Athens assured its control of the Empire bulked large among the complaints of the subject states and seem to have outweighed the material benefits which they enjoyed, although in each state a pro-Athenian faction formed. The supporters of Athens were the middle- and lower-class citizens, who favored a democratic system of government and were alive to the benefits of increased trade. Opposed to them and to Athenian control were the conservative upper-class landowners. Athenian aggressiveness was producing a revolution in Greece, but it could not break out into fighting until the Peloponnesian War gave the anti-Athenian groups some expectation of aid from Sparta. . . .

The specific incidents which led to the second outbreak of hostilities between Athens and Sparta are recorded in Thucydides' *History of the Peloponnesian War.* Though Thucydides' account of the causes and course of this conflict cannot be considered either unbiased or thoroughly factual, it does represent a striking redefinition of the meaning of history and the methods employed by the historian. Thucydides was not, it should be noted, the first Greek historian; he was preceded by Herodotus (about 484–425 B.C.), another member of the very productive Ionian intellectual community. Herodotus traveled widely in the civilized world of his time and studied the folklore and customs of the foreign peoples whom he met. In his *History of the Persian Wars* he used this material to contrast Greek culture with the cultures of the Near Eastern peoples who had been at war with Greece just prior to his birth. In many ways Herodotus' writings reflected the aristocratic culture which in the mid-fifth century B.C.

was being superseded. His *History*, for example, includes many tales of the exploits of great men intended as moral lessons for the reader. In addition, the gods still play a role in the actions of the most important leaders in the wars. For him history was far more a colorful drama than a process. In short, though Herodotus is considered the "Father of History," his work, because it remains heavily dependent on myth, lacks the kind of rationalism which has since come to characterize historical studies.

Thucydides, by laying aside the supernatural, produced the first purely rationalistic history. As he himself wrote in the first chapter of his *History of the Peloponnesian War*:

> And it may well be that my history will seem less easy to read because of the absence in it of a romantic element. It will be enough for me, however, if these words of mine are judged useful by those who want to understand clearly the events which happened in the past and which (human nature being what it is) will, at some time or other and in much the same ways, be repeated in the future. My work is not a piece of writing designed to meet the taste of an immediate public, but was done to last for ever.[3]

Thucydides was born about 460 B.C. of a prominent Athenian family which belonged to the oligarchic, antidemocratic tradition, and in this political milieu he was reared. Later, however,

> his orderly and impartial mind was impressed by the genius of Perikles, and so he became a Periklean, though not a democrat; nor could he admit that by so doing he was, in essence, approving of democracy. Later, the oligarchic tradition of his family, that had never been abandoned, reasserted itself, as he saw Periklean ideals forgotten, Periklean warnings ignored. He witnessed, with a brutally piercing eye, what seemed to him the evils of democracy run to seed, its moral fibre

weakening. He ended his life as he had begun it, a confirmed oligarch who had never renounced the creed of his fathers.[4]

After war broke out with Sparta in 431 B.C., Thucydides fought in the Athenian army for seven years. During an ensuing one-year generalship his troops failed to hold a certain city, and as a result he was sentenced to twenty years banishment. At the end of that time he returned to Athens where only a few years later he died.

During his exile, he traveled and gathered materials for the history of the wars then in progress. A description of the wars, their causes, and their impact on Greek society will best be left to Thucydides himself. The kind of history which he wrote, however, requires a few comments. While he was a careful observer and paid due attention to the accuracy of his facts, his *History* is not impartial: both interpretation and value judgments inform it. His opinion of Athens and Sparta illustrate this point. According to Thucydides

> . . . Sparta is a land power, agricultural, oligarchic, traditional in habit and outlook, loath to jeopardize her control of helots at home or her long-held priority abroad; Athens is a sea power, mercantile, democratic, recently risen through the energy that is the fruit of freedom to a position that endangers Sparta's ancient hegemony. The two antagonists enter the war at the head of leagues, and the example that Thucydides sees for posterity is of a world that has partly merged national states into bigger spheres, yet has missed the final step toward unity—a world, moreover, that was divided between settled and rising states, between traditional and novel forms of government, and, not least important, between simpler and more complex economies. The war is not at bottom an encounter between two states but a struggle for direction and unity within a civilization.

---

[3] Thucydides, *The Peloponnesian War* (Baltimore, Md.: Penguin Books, 1954), pp. 24–25.

[4] Malcolm F. McGregor, "The Politics of the Historian Thucydides," *Phoenix*, Vol. X (1956), p. 102.

As the History advances, Athens' true antagonist proves to be not Sparta but herself. To Thucydides, Athens' naval power not only expresses a far richer and more complex economy, but also, being fitly joined with a democratic constitution, elicits an energy and openness that amount to a new stage of civilization. Sparta's long dominance had been achieved by heavily armed infantry, the so-called hoplites, who, since most Greek cities depended on local grain, could force the choice of battle or starvation. But Athens by her long walls and command of the sea had outflown this dilemma. The contrast then becomes one between a sea-culture and a land-culture: the former unregimented, versatile, skeptical, inventive; the other disciplined, traditional, and relatively immobile. The crux lies within the sea-mind itself—whether, with all its vigor, it will remain sufficiently restrained in policy and constant in leadership—and it is this question that sets the second antithesis, between Pericles and his successors. . . . Thucydides seems to have been a young man, perhaps in his middle twenties, at the outbreak of the war in 431, and being connected with one of the chief conservative families, he was apparently drawn to Pericles by a kind of intellectual conversion. Greek opinion, he says, expected Sparta to win easily because she always had, but the young future historian evidently accepted Pericles' belief that Athens had put herself beyond Sparta's attack and would win if for the present she simply sought equality with Sparta, not further conquest. Of the three speeches of Pericles that he reports, the famous Funeral Oration takes added luster as our sole full statement of democratic theory from the great period. . . . "We love beauty with simplicity and pursue wisdom without softness," said Pericles, and the words convey an ideal of taste unhedged by privilege and of intelligence unclouded by suspicion. Athenians, he goes on, reach policies by open debate and believe bravery to consist not in ignorance but in facing dangers consciously undertaken. Imperfect as any actual democracy, the Athenian included, may be, this is democracy's first and perhaps its clearest statement, unrivaled in grasp of that individual self-respect, mental and moral, which democracy fosters and which makes it work.

Yet not even the intellectual Pericles foresaw the plague that would attend the crowding of the city in the face of the first Spartan invasion. He himself died of it, and there may be no sharper contrast in literature than that between the lucent reason of Pericles' speeches and the city's helplessness before the epidemic. . . . His successors, says Thucydides, being more on a level with one another, courted the demos for their personal gain; hence they led Athens to adventures which, when successful, aggrandized the leaders but when unsuccessful imperiled the city. The rest of the History recounts the mounting series of these adventures. . . .[5]

CHRONOLOGY OF THE PELOPONNESIAN WAR
433–432 B.C.

Corcyra, a colony of Corinth, offered to become an ally of Athens. Subsequently Athens made a defensive alliance with Corcyra and then defended it against Corinth, a member of the Spartan-dominated Peloponnesian League. A year later Corinth and Athens once again came into conflict. Under the prodding of the members of the League Sparta declared war on Athens.

431–421 B.C.

Athens, attacked by Sparta and her Peloponnesian allies, did not attempt to defend Attica. Instead, the Athenians brought the farmers from outlying regions within the city walls and depended almost exclusively on

[5] Reprinted from *Four Stages of Greek Thought* by John H. Finley, Jr., pp. 73–75, with the permission of the publishers, Stanford University Press. © 1966 by the Board of Trustees of the Leland Stanford Junior University.

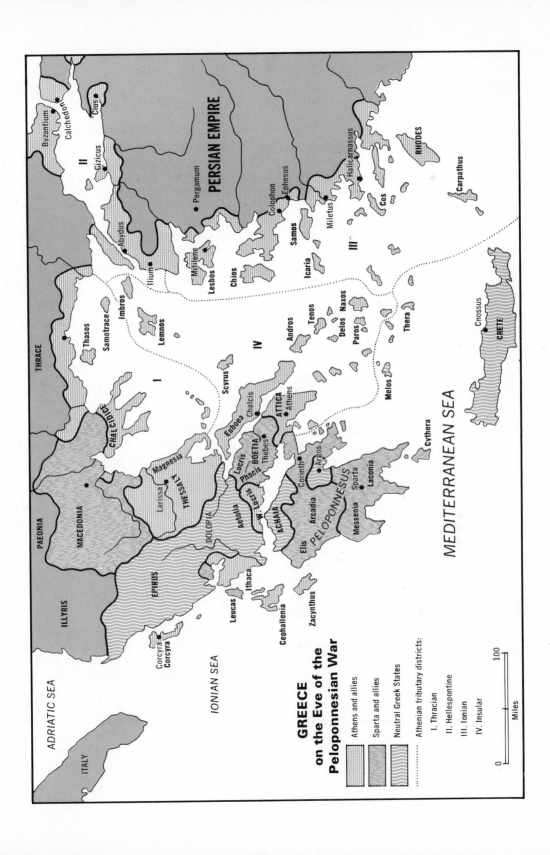

GREECE
on the Eve of the
Peloponnesian War

Athens and allies

Sparta and allies

Neutral Greek States

Athenian tributary districts:

I. Thracian
II. Hellespontine
III. Ionian
IV. Insular

0   100

Miles

ADRIATIC SEA

ITALY

IONIAN SEA

Corcyra
Corcyra

ILLYRIS

EPIRUS

PAEONIA

MACEDONIA

Larissa

THESSALY

DOLOPIA

Aetolia

W. Locris

ACHAIA

Elis

Arcadia

Messenia

PELOPONNESUS

Laconia

Sparta

Cythera

Corinth

Argos

Ithaca

Cephallenia

Zacynthus

Leucas

THRACE

Thasos

Samotrace

Imbros

Lemnos

Scyrus

Magnesia

Locris

Phocis

BOETIA

Thebes

CHALCIDICE

Euboea

Chalcis

ATTICA

Athens

MEDITERRANEAN SEA

I

IV

Andros

Tenos

Delos

Naxos

Paros

Thera

Melos

CRETE

Cnossus

Carpathus

RHODES

Cos

Halicarnassus

Miletus

Samos

Icaria

Colophon

Ephesus

Pergamum

PERSIAN EMPIRE

III

II

Byzantium

Calchedon

Cius

Cizicus

Abydus

Ilium

Mitilene

Lesbos

Chios

the navy for defense. The Spartans and their allies could do little to defeat this strategy.

430–429 B.C.: Athens was struck by a plague which took about one-third of the population. Pericles was perhaps its most tragic victim. His position of leadership was taken over by Cleon, a demagogue who represented the interests of those who were profiting from the war and therefore wanted it prolonged.

428 B.C.: Mytilene, the largest city on the island of Lesbos, attempted to withdraw from its alliance with Athens.

427 B.C.: In Corcyra the oligarchs who favored the cause of Sparta rose in revolt.

421–415 B.C.

By 421 B.C. the war had reached a stalemate and the Peace of Nicias, a treaty which resolved none of the differences between Athens and Sparta, was negotiated.

416 B.C.: Until 416 B.C. the southwest Aegean island of Melos, which was of no strategic importance, had succeeded in ignoring Athenian attempts to incorporate it in the Empire. In that year Athens decided it could no longer tolerate Melian neutrality. Melos was ordered to join the Empire voluntarily or be forced to join. Melos refused and suffered the consequences.

415–404 B.C.

415 B.C.: Sparta renewed the war.

411 B.C.: Dissatisfied with the war, an oligarchical group of conservative members of the upper class and of farmers seized control in Athens. Subsequently they turned the government over to a committee of Four Hundred which began secret peace negotiations with Sparta. Within a short time it was overthrown by the democratic majority which wanted to continue the war. A government similar to the former democracy was then installed.

404 B.C.: Athens was starved into surrender after Sparta had improved its fleet and gained control of the seas. Under the terms of the peace treaty Athens agreed to give up her

navy, destroy the fortifications surrounding the city, and become an ally of Sparta.

THE PELOPONNESIAN WAR
Thucydides

(The first page references are those in the Penguin edition; the Modern Library edition references are in parentheses.)

Book One:

1. Chapter 1, pp. 13–25 (3–15): Introduction, Methods, and Aims.
2. Chapter 6, pp. 48–62 (37–50): The Debate at Sparta and the Declaration of War.
3. Chapter 9, pp. 77–81 (65–70): The Second Congress at Sparta.
4. Chapter 11, pp. 91–96 (78–83): The Spartan Ultimatum and Pericles' Reply.

Book Two:

5. Chapter 4, pp. 115–123 (102–109): Pericles' Funeral Oration.
6. Chapter 5, pp. 123–129 (109–115): The Plague and Its Effects.
7. Chapter 6, pp. 129–135 (115–121): Justification for the Policy of Pericles.

Book Three:

8. Chapter 3, pp. 180–191 (163–173); Mytilene Debate.
9. Chapter 5, pp. 203–212 (184–192): Revolution in Corcyra.

Book Five:

10. Chapter 7, pp. 358–366 (330–337): Melian Debate.

N.B. There are two particular subjects in these selections which are of special importance: Thucydides' methodology (Book One, Chapter 1; Book Two, Chapter 5; and Book Three, Chapter 5) and the information he provides concerning the problem of values (Book Two, Chapter 4; Book Two, Chapter 5; Book Three, Chapter 3; Book Three, Chapter 5; and Book Five, Chapter 7).

CHAPTER   8

THE HUMAN PSYCHE DEFINED:
Socrates' Search for Ethical Certainty Through Self-Knowledge

. . . And then Socrates came forward, to be the Solon of the moral world. For it was from the moral world that state and society were being undermined, and through it they must be saved. . . . Solon had discovered the natural laws of the social and political community. Socrates now explored the moral cosmos in the human soul.

. . . [Through Socrates] the word *psyche*, soul, acquired the particular character which made it truly representative of all values implicit in the intellectual and moral personality of western man.

Werner Jaeger, Paideia, *Vol. II*

Socrates' discovery was that the true self is not the body but the soul. And by the soul he meant the seat of that faculty of insight which can know good from evil and infallibly choose the good. Self-knowledge implies the recognition of this true self. Self-examination is a discipline constantly needed to distinguish its judgment from the promptings of other elements in our nature, closely attached to the body and its distracting interests. Self-rule is the rule of the true self over those other elements—an absolute autocracy of the soul. For this inner judge of good and evil is also a ruler. The true self is a faculty, not only of intuitive insight, but of will—a will that can override all other desires for pleasure and seeming happiness. The soul which sees what is really good infallibly desires the good it has discerned.

F. M. Cornford, Before and After Socrates

. . . It is only in our immediate intercourse with human beings that we have insight into the character of man. We must actually confront man, we must meet him squarely face to face, in order to understand him. Hence it is not a new objective content but a new activity and function of thought which is the distinctive feature of the philosophy of Socrates. Philosophy, which had hitherto been conceived as an intellectual monologue, is transformed into a dialogue. Only by way of dialogical or dialectic thought can we approach the knowledge of human nature. . . . Truth is by nature the offspring of dialectic thought. It cannot be gained, therefore, except through a constant cooperation of the subjects in mutual interrogation and reply. It is not therefore like an empirical object; it must be understood as the outgrowth of a social act. Here we have the new, indirect answer to the question "What is man?"

Man is declared to be that creature who is constantly in search of himself—a creature who in every moment of his existence must examine and scrutinize the conditions of his existence. In this scrutiny, in this critical attitude toward human life, consists the real value of human life. . . . We may epitomize the thought of Socrates by saying that man is defined by him as that being who, when asked a rational question, can give a rational answer. Both his knowledge and his morality are comprehended in this circle. It is by this fundamental faculty, by this faculty of giving a response to himself and to others, that man becomes a "responsible" being, a moral subject.

Ernst Cassirer, An Essay on Man

Thucydides' account of the Peloponnesian War makes it readily apparent that both values and the traditional means of enforcing them had broken down by the end of the fifth century B.C. While Thucydides was not a first-hand observer at the time this occurred, there was a man present in Athens who diagnosed the causes of the cultural malaise and offered a solution. That man was Socrates.

Born sometime around 470 B.C. of a seem-ingly well-to-do Athenian family, Socrates, until the age of forty, was a prominent member of Athenian intellectual circles. During the years prior to the outbreak of the Peloponnesian War he studied with those natural philosophers who were known as the pluralists. This philosophical school attempted to resolve the problems that had been left by Parmenides.[1]

[1] See pp. 137.

Socrates (469–399 B.C.). (Anderson)

THE PLURALISTS
W. K. C. Guthrie[2]

The first of the pluralistic systems was that of Empedocles (c. 490–430), a Sicilian poet-philosopher steeped in the Western tradition, with its combination of rationalism and mystical religion so different from the purely scientific outlook of the Ionians. His proposal was the first clear enunciation of the four-element theory. Fire, air, water, and earth are the ultimate roots of all things, themselves ungenerated and indestructible. Everything in nature comes into being and perishes by the mixture and separation of these substances. The first premise is no longer "It is" but "They are." Thus, trees and animals, clouds and rocks, are not mere illusion. However, since they are only temporary combinations of the four "realities" in varying proportions, we can admit that they themselves are not "real." Nor need the forbidden concepts of "becoming" and "perishing" be invoked; mixture and separation will account for all. Locomotion is, of course, necessary, and, although he accepts the Eleatic denial of empty space, Empedocles seems to have thought that this could occur by some reciprocal and simultaneous exchange of place, the whole remaining full.

The four elements are not self-moving (another concept which Parmenides had rendered difficult), and the blend of mys-

[2]Reprinted with permission of the publisher from W. K. C. Guthrie, "Pre-Socratic Philosophy," *Encyclopedia of Philosophy*, Paul Edwards, editor. Vol. VI, pp. 444–445. Copyright © U.S.A. 1967 by Crowell Collier and Macmillan, Inc. Copyright © in Great Britain and under International Copyright Union 1967 by Crowell Collier and Macmillan, Inc.

tic and rationalist in Empedocles appears especially in his motive causes. These were two, Love and Strife, the former bringing disparate elements together and the latter drawing them apart. They are in endless opposition and prevail in turn, bringing about a double evolutionary cycle. Under Love all four elements are indistinguishably fused in a sphere; under Strife the same sphere contains them in separate layers. During the contest, when neither Love nor Strife is in complete control and when the elements are partly joined and partly separated, a world like our own is formed. Nothing existent is as yet incorporeal, though Love and Strife are of finer and more tenuous substance than the elements. Their names are no metaphors, nor is their action purely mechanical. Under Love the elements are dear to and desired by one another; Strife makes them grim and hostile. Nothing is purely inanimate, and everything has its share of consciousness. Besides his poem on nature, Empedocles also wrote a religious one, in which the moral character of Love and Strife is emphasized—Love is good, Strife evil. In the present world Strife is gaining, and men have fallen from a previous blessed state by giving themselves to Strife and sin, above all the sin of killing and eating animals. All life is akin, as it was to the Pythagoreans, and our souls are fallen spirits which must undergo a series of incarnations before they can win back their former state by abjuring Strife and cultivating Love. What the substance of the spirits was is not clearly stated, but most probably in their pure state they were portions of Love which are now contaminated with Strife.

Anaxagoras of Clazomenae (c. 500–428) brings us back to Ionia both geographically and in spirit. His motive is rational curiosity entirely uncomplicated by religious preoccupations. Even Parmenides, a Westerner like Empedocles, had written in verse and represented his deductive arguments as a revelation from a goddess. In his return to prose, as in his purely scientific aims, Anaxagoras is the heir of the Milesians. At Athens, where he lived until exiled for atheism, he was a member of the brilliant and freethinking circle of Pericles. His prosecution seems to have had a political flavor, but the charge is nevertheless significant: he declared the sun to be not a living divinity but a lump of incandescent rock larger than the Peloponnese.

To save the phenomena without admitting the coming into being or destruction of what exists, he adopted an extreme form of pluralism plus a first cause of motion, which he called Mind. It is described as knowing all things and having the greatest power, and, in order to control the material world, it is entirely outside the mixture of which the material world is formed. It is not easy to be sure whether Anaxagoras is at last trying to express the notion of incorporeal being without an adequate vocabulary or whether he still thinks of Mind as an extremely subtle and tenuous form of matter. At any rate, its separateness from the constituents of the cosmos is emphasized at every turn. In spite of the references to its knowledge and power, its action seems to be confined to the earliest stages of cosmogony. except in the case of living creatures. They are an exception to the rule that Mind is in nothing else, and them it still controls.

In the beginning "all things were together," a stationary mass in which nothing could be distinguished. Mind is the agent which has produced from this an ordered cosmos. It did so by starting a rotatory movement or vortex, which by its own increasing speed brought about the gradual separation of different forms of matter. Anaxagoras' highly subtle and ingenious theory of matter seems to have been especially prompted by the need to explain nourishment and organic growth: how can flesh and hair come out of the not-flesh and not-hair of the food we eat? After Parmenides the coming into being of new substances is disallowed. Anaxagoras answered that there is a portion of everything in everything—that is, every distinguishable substance, in however small a quantity, contains minute particles of every other but is characterized by that which predominates. He boldly asserted the existence of the infinitesimal (which Zeno had denied) in the words: "Of the small there is no smallest."

Perhaps around 430 Leucippus promulgated the much simpler theory of atomism, which was further developed by his famous pupil Democritus of Abdera (born c. 460). Like the other theories, this one arose in direct response to the Eleatic challenge. Its most striking innovation for its time was the assertion of the existence of genuine empty space. Thus far, everyone had believed that "what is" must be some form of body, and, when Parmenides brought into consciousness the implicit consequence that space, not being "what is," must be "what is not" (that is, nonexistent), his conclusion seemed logically inescapable. Hence, even the atomists had to use the paradoxical expression that it is no more correct to say of "what is" than of "what is not" that it *is*. At this particular point in the philosophic debate, this was the only way of expressing the conviction that, though not any kind of stuff, space must be assumed if the plain facts are to be explained. Democritus, said Aristotle, is to be commended for refusing to be dazzled by the abstract logic of Parmenides and for relying on the kind of argument more proper to a natural scientist. Reality consists of innumerable microscopic and indivisible (*a-tomos* = uncuttable) bodies in motion in infinite space. They are solid and homogeneous but infinitely variable in size and shape. At different places in the infinite, they have collided and become entangled. Projections hook together, convex fits into concave, and so on. Their continued motion sets up a vortex in which the larger and heavier fall into the center and the smaller and lighter are extruded to the circumference; in this way a cosmos is formed. There are many worlds, and not all are similar to our own. The first atomists appear to have provided no separate cause of motion, perhaps because they deemed it sufficient to free the atoms by setting them loose in infinite space. After all, the chief Eleatic arguments against motion had been the continuity of being and the nonexistence of a void.

Only atoms and the void exist. Sensible qualities other than size and shape are subjective, caused by interaction between the atoms of external objects and those in our own bodies. This was worked out in considerable detail. For instance, hard objects have their atoms more closely packed than do soft. Sweet flavors are caused by smooth atoms, bitter and astringent by sharp or hooked. Colors vary according to the positions of surface atoms, which cause them to reflect in different ways the light that falls upon them. Objects are continually throwing off films of atoms, and sight is the reception of these films by the eye. The soul, or life principle, is composed of smooth, round atoms that are even more mobile than the rest and impart to the body the power of motion and cognition, for "soul and mind are the same"—that is, composed of the same kind of atoms. Soul is dispersed throughout the body, alternating with body atoms, but the mind appears to have been a collection of these finest particles that is located probably in the breast. Although the direct objects of sight and hearing, taste and smell, are unreal, they lead the mind to the truth about reality, and Democritus quoted with approval a saying of Anaxagoras: "Phenomena are a glimpse of the unseen."

Ancient atomism (including its revival by Epicurus a century or more after Democritus) has acquired a partly adventitious reputation through its resemblances to nineteenth-century physical theories, but its hard, solid, unbreakable particles have little in common with the ultimate entities of modern science. Its most striking features are the distinction between primary and secondary qualities (upheld by Descartes, Galileo, and Locke), the explanation of directly observable objects by hypothetical constituents below the level of perception, and the outspoken championship of discrete quanta as opposed to a continuum. Its inadequacy in allowing no mode of action other than direct contact, collision, and interlocking was evident in some physical problems—for example, in its attempted explanation of magnetism and, most of all, in the effort to include within its purview the phenomena of life and thought. The atomic structure of matter has indeed been a fruitful hypothesis, but the intention of its authors is best understood in the context of their time and as an attempt to escape the Eleatic dilemma, rather than as an anticipation of postmedieval science.

As indicated by Plato in one of his dialogues, Socrates was not content with the philosophical answers at which the pluralists had arrived. The following selection from Plato's *Phaedo* provides what is generally considered to be an autobiographical account of this early stage in Socrates' intellectual life—that is, sometime prior to the outbreak of the Peloponnesian War in 431 B.C.

SOCRATES' REACTION AGAINST THE PLURALISTS
Plato[3]

". . . When I was young, Cebes, I had a remarkable enthusiasm for the kind of wisdom known as natural science; it seemed to me magnificent to know the causes of everything, why a thing comes into being, why it perishes, why it exists. Often I used to shift backwards and forwards trying to answer questions like this, to start with: Is it when the conjunction of the hot and the cold results in putrefaction that living creatures develop? Is it blood that we think with, or air or fire? Or is thought due to something else, namely the brain's providing our senses of hearing, sight and smell, which give rise to memory and judgement, and ultimately, when memory and judgement have acquired stability, to knowledge?

"Next I tried to investigate how things perish, and what went on in the heavens and on the earth, until in the end I decided that I had simply no gift whatever for this sort of investigation. To show how right I was about that, I may tell you that, whereas there were some things which up till then I had, as I thought myself and other people thought too, definitely un-

derstood, I was now smitten with such complete blindness as the result of my investigations that I unlearnt even what I previously thought I knew, including more particularly the cause of a human being's growth. I had supposed that to be obvious to anybody: he grew because he ate and drank; on taking food flesh was added to flesh, bone to bone, and similarly the appropriate matter was added to each part of a man, until in the end his small bulk had become a large one, and so the little child had become a big man. That was what I used to believe: reasonably enough, wouldn't you say?"

"I would," said Cebes.

"Now see what you think about this. I used to find it perfectly satisfactory when a tall man standing beside a short one appeared to be taller just by a head; similarly with two horses. And to take an even plainer case, I thought that ten was more than eight because of the addition of two, and that an object two yards long was greater than one only one yard long because the one extended by half its own length beyond the other."

"And what do you think about it all now?"

"I assure you I am very far from supposing that I know the cause of any of these things; why, I am dubious even about saying that, when we add one to one, either the one to which the addition is made becomes two, or that the one and the other together become two by reason of the addition of this to that. What puzzles me is that when the units were apart from each other each was one, and there was as yet no two, whereas as soon as they had approached each other there was the cause of the coming into being of two, namely the union in which they were put next to each other. Nor again can I any

[3] *Plato's Phaedo*, trans. R. Hackforth (Cambridge: Cambridge University Press, 1955), pp. 122–127 [96A–99D]. Reprinted by permission of the publisher.

longer persuade myself that if we divide one it is the division this time that causes two to come into being; for then the cause of two would be the opposite of that just suggested: a moment ago it was because the units were brought into close proximity each to each, and now it is because they are kept away and separated each from each. And for that matter I no longer feel sure that by adhering to the old method I can understand how a unit comes into being or perishes or exists; that method has lost all atraction for me, and in its place I am gaily substituting a new sort of hotch-potch of my own.

"One day, however, I heard someone reading an extract from what he said was a book by Anaxagoras, to the effect that it is Mind that arranges all things in order and causes all things; now there was a cause that delighted me, for I felt that in a way it was good that Mind should be the cause of everything; and I decided that if this were true Mind must do all its ordering and arranging in the fashion that is best for each individual thing. Hence if one wanted to discover the cause for anything coming into being or perishing or existing, the question to ask was how it was best for that thing to exist or to act or be acted upon. On this principle then the only thing that a man had to think about, whether in regard to himself or anything else, was what is best, what is the highest good; though of course he would also have to know what is bad, since knowledge of good involves knowledge of bad. With these reflexions I was delighted to think I had found in Anaxagoras an instructor about the cause of things after my own heart; I expected him to tell me in the first place whether the earth is flat or round, and then go on to explain the cause why it must be the one or the other,

using the term 'better,' and showing how it was better for it to be as it is; and then if he said the earth is in the centre of the universe, he would proceed to explain how it was better for it to be there. If he could make all these things plain to me, I was ready to abandon the quest of any other sort of cause. Indeed I was ready to go further, applying the same principle of inquiry to sun, moon and stars, their relative velocities and turnings and so forth: I would ask which is the better way for these bodies to act or be acted upon. For I never supposed that when Anaxagoras had said that they are ordered by Mind he would bring in some other cause for them, and not be content with showing that it is best for them to be as they are; I imagined that in assigning the cause of particular things and of things in general he would proceed to explain what was the individual best and the general good; and I wouldn't have sold my hopes for a fortune. I made all haste to get hold of the books, and read them as soon as ever I could, in order to discover without delay what was best and what was worst.

"And then, my friend, from my marvelous height of hope I came hurtling down; for as I went on with my reading I found the man making no use of Mind, not crediting it with any causality for setting things in order, but finding causes in things like air and aether and water and a host of other absurdities. It seemed to me that his position was like that of a man who said that all the actions of Socrates are due to his mind, and then attempted to give the causes of my several actions by saying that the reason why I am now sitting here is that my body is composed of bones and sinews, and the bones are hard and separated by joints, while the sinews, which can be tightened or relaxed, envelop the bones along with the flesh and skin which hold them together; so that when the bones move about in their sockets, the sinews, by lessening or increasing the tension, make it possible for me at this moment to bend my limbs, and that is the cause of my sitting here in this bent position. Analogous causes might also be given of my conversing with you, sounds, air-currents, streams of hearing and so on and so forth, to the neglect of the true causes, to wit that, inasmuch as the Athenians have thought it better to condemn me, I too in my turn think it better to sit here, and more right and proper to stay where I am and submit to such punishment as they enjoin. For, by Jingo, I fancy these same sinews and bones would long since have been somewhere in Megara or Boeotia, impelled by their notion of what was best, if I had not thought it right and proper to submit to the penalty appointed by the State rather than take to my heels and run away.

"No: to call things like that causes is quite absurd; it would be true to say that if I did not possess things like that—bones and sinews and so on—I shouldn't be able to do what I had resolved upon; but to say that I do what I do because of them—and that too when I am acting with my mind—and not because of my choice of what is best, would be to use extremely careless language. Fancy not being able to distinguish between the cause of a thing and that without which the cause would not be a cause! It is evidently this latter that most people, groping in the dark, call by the name of cause, a name which doesn't belong to it. Hence we find one man making the earth be kept in position by the heavens, encompassing it with a rotatory movement; and another treating it as a flat lid supported on a base of air; but the

power thanks to which heaven and earth are now in the position that was the best possible position for them to be set in, *that* they never look for, and have no notion of its amazing strength; instead they expect to discover one day a stronger and more immortal Atlas, better able to hold things together; for they don't believe in any good, binding force which literally binds things together and holds them fast.

"Well, I for my part should be most happy to be instructed by anybody about a cause of this sort; but I was baulked of it: I failed to discover it for myself, and I couldn't learn of it from others: and so I have had recourse to a second-best method to help my quest of a cause; would you like me to give a formal account of it, Cebes?

"Yes, indeed: I should like that immensely."

This "second-best method" which Socrates developed and subsequently taught to a circle of prominent and dedicated young Athenians was in part the product of the linguistic confusion which had arisen as the Greeks had acquired an increasing facility to think in abstract terms. While the natural philosophers had had little difficulty in creating a vocabulary of abstract terms for the description of the constituents and phenomena of nature, the same had not been true of terms with a value content, especially the language of ethics. Thucydides' commentary on the changing meaning of words in his depiction of the Corcyran revolution vividly illustrates this.[4] As we have seen, too, *nomos* had accumulated the multiple meanings of custom, positive law, convention, and, finally, the abstract meaning of law. Socrates clearly perceived this state of confusion and proposed

---

[4] See Book Three, Chapter 5, Thucydides, *The Peloponnesian War*.

that the definition of ethical terms be clarified. Defining ethical concepts, he believed, would have the advantage of countering the ethical relativism espoused by many of the Sophists—whose ideas and methods both Socrates and Plato deplored—for definition would fix a meaning and, as a result, everyone would understand the same thing when any given word were used. This, then, would be a first step toward the resolution of the moral crisis, for only when men *knew* the true (clearly defined) values which should guide their conduct could these values be realized in their behavior. In other words, it was his conviction

that knowledge was the key to virtue and happiness, and that it was to be obtained by means of a search for definitions. . . .

Socrates gave no formal rules for making definitions; rather, he tested suggested definitions in a number of ways. He would not accept a list—of just actions, for example, as a definition of justice. He supposed that because all members of the list were called "just," there must be something they had in common, apart from the name, and it was this that was to be defined. Further, he would not accept as a definition a phrase that itself contained, either explicitly or tacitly, the word to be defined. This is illustrated by his criticism of Theaetetus' definition of knowledge as geometry, the craft of shoemaking, and carpentry. According to Socrates, such a definition is unacceptable both because it is a mere list and because the craft of shoemaking may be defined as "knowing how to make shoes." Other suggestions fail on the grounds of vagueness or ambiguity or because they can easily be shown to be too narrow or too broad.

If a suggestion did not fail on any of these grounds, it was then tested by reasoning. Socrates took the definition as one of the premises of an argument, and the remaining premises were agreed on, some explicitly and many tacitly, between himself and his interlocutor. Deductions were then made from this set of premises, and the result might be un-

satisfactory either because a contradiction was reached or because a conclusion could be drawn which was in conflict with the obvious facts. In either case, it followed that there was something wrong with the premises. As the rest of these had been agreed upon, it had to be the definition itself that was faulty; it therefore had to be rejected.[5]

In a very real sense, therefore, Socrates was the first man in Western civilization to enjoin those with whom he conversed to define their terms, and in so doing he had discovered the concept.[6]

. . . We are all familiar with the word "courage," but how many of us are ready to say just what it includes and does not include? Until we can do so we have no clear *concept* of courage. We may determine and exhibit concepts in Socratic fashion by defining the terms already in popular or at least current usage. By this procedure we seek a definition that will include all the uses to which a given term is put. This we do by eliminating any definition suggested that will not fit instances of usage which can be cited. . . . Socrates believes that if we practice such analysis so that we learn to know just what we mean when we say—for instance, "Aristogeiton was a brave man"—in other words, if we have a clear concept of our topic, we will avoid that most frequent type of human error which arises when we fall unconsciously into using a word in more than one sense. . . .[7]

This process of definition is the "second-best method"—the Socratic or dialectic method—

[5] Reprinted with permission of The Macmillan Company from "Socrates and Plato," by Pamela M. Huby, in *A Critical History of Western Philosophy*, ed. by D. J. O'Connor, p. 15. Copyright © 1964 by The Free Press of Glencoe, a Division of The Macmillan Company.

[6] Review pp. 15–16.

[7] Newton P. Stallknecht and Robert S. Brumbaugh, *The Spirit of Western Philosophy* (New York: Longmans, Green and Company, 1950), pp. 24–25.

which Socrates referred to at the end of the autobiographical account in the *Phaedo*. Since the method consists of a verbal exchange between two individuals—a dialogue—it can be considered a product of the oral tradition which dominated Greek culture until the end of the fifth century B.C.[8] The following selection from Plato's dialogue, the *Meno*, furnishes an illustration of the method and also reveals the nature of Socrates' concern with ethics.

What is virtue? Socrates view + Meno's view.

MENO
Plato[9]

MENO. Can you tell me Socrates—is virtue something that can be taught? Or does it come by practice? Or is it neither teaching nor practice that gives it to a man but natural aptitude or something else?

SOCRATES. Well Meno, in the old days the Thessalians had a great reputation among the Greeks for their wealth and their horsemanship. Now it seems they are philosophers as well—especially the men of Larissa, where your friend Aristippus comes from. It is Gorgias who has done it. He went to that city and captured the hearts of the foremost of the Aleuadae for his wisdom (among them your own admirer Aristippus), not to speak of other leading Thessalians. In particular he got you into the habit of answering any questions you might be asked, with the confidence and dignity appropriate to those who know the answers, just as he himself invites questions of every kind from anyone in the Greek world who wishes to

ask, and never fails to answer them. But here at Athens, my dear Meno, it is just the reverse. There is a dearth of wisdom, and it looks as if it had migrated from our part of the country to yours. At any rate if you put your question to any of our people, they will all alike laugh and say: "You must think I am singularly fortunate, to know whether virtue can be taught or how it is acquired. The fact is that far from knowing whether it can be taught, I have no idea what virtues itself is."

That is my own case. I share the poverty of my fellow-countrymen in this respect, and confess to my shame that I have no knowledge about virtue at all. And how can I know a property of something when I don't even know what it is? Do you suppose that somebody entirely ignorant who Meno is could say whether he is handsome and rich and well-born or the reverse? Is that possible, do you think?

MENO. No. But is this true about yourself, Socrates, that you don't even know what virtue is? Is this the report that we are to take home about you?

SOCRATES. Not only that; you may say also that, to the best of my belief, I have never yet met anyone who did know.

MENO. What! Didn't you meet Gorgias when he was here?

SOCRATES. Yes.

MENO. And you still didn't think he knew?

SOCRATES. I'm a forgetful sort of person, and I can't say just now what I thought at the time. Probably he did know, and I expect you know what he used to say about it. So remind me what it was, or tell me yourself if you will. No doubt you agree with him.

MENO. Yes I do.

SOCRATES. Then let's leave him out of it, since after all he isn't here. What do you

---

[8] It should be noted that Socrates left no written works.

[9] Plato, *Protagoras and Meno*, trans. W. K. C. Guthrie (Baltimore, Md.: Penguin Books, 1956), pp. 115–128 [70A–80D]. Reprinted by permission of Penguin Books Ltd.

yourself say virtue is? I do ask you in all earnestness not to refuse me, but to speak out. I shall be only too happy to be proved wrong if you and Gorgias turn out to know this, although I said I had never met anyone who did.

MENO. But there is no difficulty about it. First of all, if it is manly virtue you are after, it is easy to see that the virtue of a man consists in managing the city's affairs capably, and so that he will help his friends and injure his foes while taking care to come to no harm himself. Or if you want a woman's virtue, that is easily described. She must be a good housewife, careful with her stores and obedient to her husband. Then there is another virtue for a child, male or female, and another for an old man, free or slave as you like; and a great many more kinds of virtue, so that no one need be at a loss to say what it is. For every act and every time of life, with reference to each separate function, there is a virtue for each one of us, and similarly, I should say, a vice.

SOCRATES. I seem to be in luck. I wanted one virtue and I find that you have a whole swarm of virtues to offer. But seriously, to carry on this metaphor of the swarm, suppose I asked you what a bee is, what is its essential nature, and you replied that bees were of many different kinds, what would you say if I went on to ask: "And is it in being bees that they are many and various and different from one another? Or would you agree that it is not in this respect that they differ, but in something else, some other quality like size or beauty?"

MENO. I should say that in so far as they are bees, they don't differ from one another at all.

SOCRATES. Suppose I then continued: "Well, this is just what I want you to tell me. What is that character in respect of which they don't differ at all, but are all the same?" I presume you would have something to say?

MENO. I should.

SOCRATES. Then do the same with the virtues. Even if they are many and various, yet at least they all have some common character which makes them virtues. That is what ought to be kept in view by anyone who answers the question: "What is virtue?" Do you follow me?

MENO. I think I do, but I don't yet really grasp the question as I should wish.

SOCRATES. Well, does this apply in your mind only to virtue, that there is a different one for a man and a woman and the rest? Is it the same with health and size and strength, or has health the same character everywhere, if it is health, whether it be in a man or any other creature?

MENO. I agree that health is the same in a man or in a woman.

SOCRATES. And what about size and strength? If a woman is strong, will it be the same thing, the same strength, that makes her strong? My meaning is that in its character as strength, it is no different, whether it be in a man or in a woman. Or do you think it is?

MENO. No.

SOCRATES. And will virtue differ, in its character as virtue, whether it be in a child or an old man, a woman or a man?

MENO. I somehow feel that this is not on the same level as the other cases.

SOCRATES. Well then, didn't you say that a man's virtue lay in directing the city well, and a woman's in directing her household well?

MENO. Yes.

SOCRATES. And is it possible to direct anything well—city or household or anything else—if not temperately and justly?

MENO. Certainly not.

SOCRATES. And that means with temperance and justice?

MENO. Of course.

SOCRATES. Then both man and woman need the same qualities, justice and temperance, if they are going to be good.

MENO. It looks like it.

SOCRATES. And what about your child and old man? Could they be good if they were incontinent and unjust?

MENO. Of course not.

SOCRATES. They must be temperate and just?

MENO. Yes.

SOCRATES. So everyone is good in the same way, since they become good by possessing the same qualities.

MENO. So it seems.

SOCRATES. And if they did not share the same virtue, they would not be good in the same way.

MENO. No.

SOCRATES. Seeing then that they all have the same virtue, try to remember and tell me what Gorgias, and you who share his opinion, say it is.

MENO. It must be simply the capacity to govern men, if you are looking for one quality to cover all the instances.

SOCRATES. Indeed I am. But does this virtue apply to a child or a slave? Should a slave be capable of governing his master, and if he does, is he still a slave?

MENO. I hardly think so.

SOCRATES. It certainly doesn't sound likely. And here is another point. You speak of "capacity to govern." Shall we not add "justly but not otherwise"?

MENO. I think we should, for justice is virtue.

SOCRATES. Virtue, do you say, or *a* virtue?

MENO. What do you mean?

SOCRATES. Something quite general. Take roundness, for instance. I should say that it is a shape, not simply that it is shape, my reason being that there are other shapes as well.

MENO. I see your point, and I agree that there are other virtues besides justice.

SOCRATES. Tell me what they are. Just as I could name other shapes if you told me to, in the same way mention some other virtues.

MENO. In my opinion then courage is a virtue and temperance and wisdom and dignity and many other things.

SOCRATES. This puts us back where we were. In a different way we have discovered a number of virtues when we were looking for one only. This single virtue, which permeates each of them, we cannot find.

MENO. No, I cannot yet grasp it as you want, a single virtue covering them all, as I do in other instances.

SOCRATES. I'm not surprised, but I shall do my best to get us a bit further if I can. You understand, I expect, that the question applies to everything. If someone took the example I mentioned just now, and asked you: "What is shape?" and you replied that roundness is shape, and he then asked you as I did, "Do you mean it is shape or *a* shape?" you would reply of course that it is *a* shape.

MENO. Certainly.

SOCRATES. Your reason being that there are other shapes as well.

MENO. Yes.

SOCRATES. And if he went on to ask you what they were, you would tell him.

MENO. Yes.

SOCRATES. And the same with colour—if he asked you what it is, and on your replying "White," took you up with: "Is white colour or *a* colour?" you would say that it is *a* colour, because there are other colours as well.

MENO. I should.

SOCRATES. And if he asked you to, you would mention other colours which are just as much colours as white is.

MENO. Yes.

SOCRATES. Suppose then he pursued the question as I did, and objected: "We always arrive at a plurality, but that is not the kind of answer I want. Seeing that you call these many particulars by one and the same name, and say that every one of them is a shape, even though they are the contrary of each other, tell me what this is which embraces round as well as straight, and what you mean by shape when you say that straightness is a shape as much as roundness. You do say that?"

MENO. Yes.

SOCRATES. "And in saying it, do you mean that roundness is no more round than straight, and straightness no more straight than round?"

MENO. Of course not.

SOCRATES. "Yet you do say that roundness is no more a shape than straightness, and the other way about."

MENO. Quite true.

SOCRATES. "Then what is this thing which is called 'shape'? Try to tell me." If when asked this question either about shape or colour you said: "But I don't understand what you want, or what you mean," your questioner would perhaps be surprised and say: "Don't you see that I am looking for what is the same in all of them?" Would you even so be unable to reply, if the question was: "What is it that is common to roundness and straightness and the other things which you call shapes?" Do your best to answer, as practice for the question about virtue.

MENO. No, you do it, Socrates.

SOCRATES. Do you want me to give in to you?

MENO. Yes.

SOCRATES. And will you in your turn give me an answer about virtue?

MENO. I will.

SOCRATES. In that case I must do my best. It's in a good cause.

MENO. Certainly.

SOCRATES. Well now, let's try to tell you what shape is. See if you accept this definition. Let us define it as the only thing which always accompanies colour. Does that satisfy you, or do you want it in some other way? I should be content if your definition of virtue were on similar lines.

MENO. But that's a naïve sort of definition, Socrates.

SOCRATES. How?

MENO. Shape, if I understand what you say, is what always accompanies colour. Well and good—but if somebody says that he doesn't know what colour is, but is no better off with it than he is with shape, what sort of answer have you given him, do you think?

SOCRATES. A true one; and if my questioner were one of the clever, disputatious and quarrelsome kind, I should say to him: "You have heard my answer. If it is wrong, it is for you to take up the argument and refute it." However, when friendly people, like you and me, want to converse with each other, one's reply must be milder and more conducive to discussion. By that I mean that it must not only be true, but must employ terms with which the questioner admits he is familiar. So I will try to answer you like that. Tell me, therefore, whether you recognize the term "end"; I mean limit or boundary—all these words I use in the same sense. Prodicus might perhaps quarrel with us, but I assume you speak of something being bounded or coming to an end. That is all I mean, nothing subtle.

MENO. I admit the notion, and believe I understand your meaning.

SOCRATES. And again, you recognize "surface" and "solid," as they are used in geometry?

MENO. Yes.

SOCRATES. Then with these you should by this time understand my definition of shape. To cover all its instances, I say that shape is that in which a solid terminates, or more briefly, it is the limit of a solid.

MENO. And how do you define colour?

SOCRATES. What a shameless fellow you are, Meno. You keep bothering an old man to answer, but refuse to exercise your memory and tell me what was Gorgias's definition of virtue.

MENO. I will, Socrates, as soon as you tell me this.

SOCRATES. Anyone talking to you could tell blindfold that you are a handsome man and still have your admirers.

MENO. Why so?

SOCRATES. Because you are for ever laying down the law as spoilt boys do, who act the tyrant as long as their youth lasts. No doubt you have discovered that I can never resist good looks. Well, I will give in and let you have your answer.

MENO. Do by all means.

SOCRATES. Would you like an answer *à la* Gorgias, such as you would most readily follow?

MENO. Of course I should.

SOCRATES. You and he believe in Empedocles's theory of effluences, do you not?

MENO. Whole-heartedly.

SOCRATES. And passages to which and through which the effluences make their way?

MENO. Yes.

SOCRATES. Some of the effluences fit into some of the passages, whereas others are too coarse or too fine.

MENO. That is right.

SOCRATES. Now you recognize the term "sight"?

MENO. Yes.

SOCRATES. From these notions, then, "grasp what I would tell," as Pindar says. Colour is an effluence from shapes commensurate with sight and perceptible by it.

MENO. That seems to me an excellent answer.

SOCRATES. No doubt it is the sort you are used to. And you probably see that it provides a way to define sound and smell and many similar things.

MENO. So it does.

SOCRATES. Yes, it's a high-sounding answer, so you like it better than the one on shape.

MENO. I do.

SOCRATES. Nevertheless, son of Alexidemus, I am convinced that the other is better; and I believe you would agree with me if you had not, as you told me yesterday, to leave before the mysteries, but could stay and be initiated.[10]

MENO. I would stay, Socrates, if you gave me more answers like this.

SOCRATES. You may be sure I shan't be lacking in keenness to do so, both for your sake and mine; but I'm afraid I may not be able to do it often. However, now it is your turn to do as you promised, and try to tell me the general nature of virtue. Stop making many out of one, as the humorists say

[10] Evidently the Athenians are about to celebrate the famous rites of the Eleusinian Mysteries, but Meno has to return to Thessaly before they fall due. Plato frequently plays upon the analogy between religious initiation, which bestowed a revelation of divine secrets, and the insight which comes from initiation into the truths of philosophy.

when somebody breaks a plate. Just leave virtue whole and sound and tell me what it is, as in the examples I have given you.

MENO. It seems to me then, Socrates, that virtue is, in the words of the poet, "to rejoice in the fine and have power," and I define it as desiring fine things and being able to acquire them.

SOCRATES. When you speak of a man desiring fine things, do you mean it is good things he desires?

MENO. Certainly.

SOCRATES. Then do you think some men desire evil and others good? Doesn't everyone, in your opinion, desire good things?

MENO. No.

SOCRATES. And would you say that the others suppose evils to be good, or do they still desire them although they recognize them as evil?

MENO. Both, I should say.

SOCRATES. What? Do you really think that anyone who recognizes evils for what they are, nevertheless desires them?

MENO. Yes.

SOCRATES. Desires in what way? To possess them?

MENO. Of course.

SOCRATES. In the belief that evil things bring advantage to their possessor, or harm?

MENO. Some in the first belief, but some also in the second.

SOCRATES. And do you believe that those who suppose evil things bring advantage understand that they are evil?

MENO. No, that I can't really believe.

SOCRATES. Isn't it clear then that this class, who don't recognize evils for what they are, don't desire evil but what they think is good, though in fact it is evil; those who through ignorance mistake bad things for good obviously desire the good.

MENO. For them I suppose that is true.

SOCRATES. Now as for those whom you speak of as desiring evils in the belief that they do harm to their possessor, these presumably know that they will be injured by them?

MENO. They must.

SOCRATES. And don't they believe that whoever is injured is, in so far as he is injured, unhappy?

MENO. That too they must believe.

SOCRATES. And unfortunate?

MENO. Yes.

SOCRATES. Well, does anybody want to be unhappy and unfortunate?

MENO. I suppose not.

SOCRATES. Then if not, nobody desires what is evil; for what else is unhappiness but desiring evil things and getting them?

MENO. It looks as if you are right, Socrates, and nobody desires what is evil.

SOCRATES. Now you have just said that virtue consists in a wish for good things plus the power to acquire them. In this definition the wish is common to everyone, and in that respect no one is better than his neighbour.

MENO. So it appears.

SOCRATES. So if one man is better than another, it must evidently be in respect of the power, and virtue, according to your account, is the power of acquiring good things.

MENO. Yes, my opinion is exactly as you now express it.

SOCRATES. Let us see whether you have hit the truth this time. You may well be right. The power of acquiring good things, you say, is virtue?

MENO. Yes.

SOCRATES. And by good do you mean such things as health and wealth?

MENO. I include the gaining both of gold and silver and of high and honourable office in the State.

SOCRATES. Are these the only classes of goods that you recognize?

MENO. Yes, I mean everything of that sort.

SOCRATES. Right. In the definition of Meno, hereditary guest-friend of the Great King, the acquisition of gold and silver is virtue. Do you add "just and righteous" to the word "acquisition," or doesn't it make any difference to you? Do you call it virtue all the same even if they are unjustly acquired?

MENO. Certainly not.

SOCRATES. Vice then?

MENO. Most certainly.

SOCRATES. So it seems that justice or temperance or piety, or some other part of virtue, must attach to the acquisition. Otherwise, although it is a means to good things, it will not be virtue.

MENO. No, how could you have virtue without these?

SOCRATES. In fact lack of gold and silver, if it results from failure to acquire it—either for oneself or another—in circumstances which would have made its acquisition unjust, is itself virtue.

MENO. It would seem so.

SOCRATES. Then to have such goods is no more virtue than to lack them. Rather we may say that whatever is accompanied by justice is virtue, whatever is without qualities of that sort is vice.

MENO. I agree that your conclusion seems inescapable.

SOCRATES. But a few minutes ago we called each of these—justice, temperance, and the rest—a part of virtue?

MENO. Yes, we did.

SOCRATES. So it seems you are making a fool of me.

MENO. How so, Socrates?

SOCRATES. I have just asked you not to break virtue up into fragments, and given you models of the type of answer I wanted, but taking no notice of this you tell me that virtue consists in the acquisition of good things with justice; and justice, you agree, is a part of virtue.

MENO. True.

SOCRATES. So it follows from your own statements that to act with a part of virtue is virtue, if you call justice and all the rest parts of virtue. The point I want to make is that whereas I asked you to give me an account of virtue as a whole, far from telling me what it is itself you say that every action is virtue which exhibits a part of virtue, as if you had already told me what the whole is, so that I should recognize it even if you chop it up into bits. It seems to me that we must put the same old question to you, my dear Meno—the question: "What is virtue?"—if every act becomes virtue when combined with a part of virtue. That is, after all, what it means to say that every act performed with justice is virtue. Don't you agree that the same question needs to be put? Does anyone know what a part of virtue is, without knowing the whole?

MENO. I suppose not.

SOCRATES. No, and if you remember, when I replied to you about shape just now, I believe we rejected the type of answer that employs terms which are still in question and not yet agreed upon.

MENO. We did, and rightly.

SOCRATES. Then please do the same. While the nature of virtue as a whole is still under question, don't suppose that you can explain it to anyone in terms of its parts, or by any similar type of explanation. Understand rather that the same question remains to be answered; you say this and that about virtue, but what *is* it? Does this seem nonsense to you?

MENO. No, to me it seems right enough.

SOCRATES. Then go back to the beginning and answer my question. What do you and your friend say that virtue is?

MENO. Socrates, even before I met you they told me that in plain truth you are a perplexed man yourself and reduce others to perplexity. At this moment I feel you are exercising magic and witchcraft upon me and positively laying me under your spell until I am just a mass of helplessness. If I may be flippant, I think that not only in outward appearance but in other respects as well you are exactly like the flat sting-ray that one meets in the sea. Whenever anyone comes into contact with it, it numbs him, and that is the sort of thing that you seem to be doing to me now. My mind and my lips are literally numb, and I have nothing to reply to you. Yet I have spoken about virtue hundreds of times, held forth often on the subject in front of large audiences, and very well too, or so I thought. Now I can't even say what it is. In my opinion you are well advised not to leave Athens and live abroad. If you behaved like this as a foreigner in another country, you would most likely be arrested as a wizard.

SOCRATES. You're a real rascal, Meno. You nearly took me in.

MENO. Just what do you mean?

SOCRATES. I see why you used a simile about me.

MENO. Why, do you think?

SOCRATES. To be compared to something in return. All good-looking people, I know perfectly well, enjoy a game of comparisons. They get the best of it, for naturally handsome folk provoke handsome similes. But I'm not going to oblige you. As for myself, if the sting-ray paralyses others only through being paralysed itself, then the comparison is just, but not otherwise. It isn't that, knowing the answers myself,

I perplex other people. The truth is rather that I infect them also with the perplexity I feel myself. So with virtue now. I don't know what it is. You may have known before you came into contact with me, but now you look as if you don't. Nevertheless I am ready to carry out, together with you, a joint investigation and inquiry into what it is.

Socrates spent the greater part of the later years of his life questioning and clarifying ethical concepts in quite the same manner as he did in the dialogue with Meno. This activity had two results. As far as philosophy is concerned his work constituted the discovery that values can be categorized as either intrinsic or instrumental.

SOCRATES' MISSION
Robert S. Brumbaugh [11]

[Socrates insisted] that his fellow citizens usually made the classification in exactly the wrong way. The things that have intrinsic value are the qualities of being that make a person excellent and happy. Things that may be used as means to this end but may also be misused have instrumental value—they are prized because of some further use they can be given. Property, physical beauty, and strength fall in the instrumental category. Neither wealth nor physical fitness can in itself make its possessor either a good person or a happy one. Wisdom, justice, and courage, on the other hand, have intrinsic value. Someone who knows what these virtues are will

[11] From *The Philosophers of Greece* by Robert S. Brumbaugh, pp. 129–131. Copyright © 1964 by Robert S. Brumbaugh. Reprinted by permission of the publishers, Thomas Y. Crowell Company, New York.

prize them for themselves, not as means to some other goal.

The ordinary Athenian, Socrates saw, set up his scale of values in exactly the opposite way. He commended justice because it was a means to a good reputation, which in turn was a means to political and financial success. Or else he told his sons they should be just because they would be punished—by human law courts, or by the gods—if they were not. The ends for which virtue was commended as a means were exactly those that were really external to happiness and true character: money, beauty, strength, prestige, and so on. Socrates found that the reason for this fundamental error in evaluation was ignorance: ignorance of the true nature of the soul, and ignorance of the true dignity that realization of an ideal brought to its possessor. And so Socrates was convinced that "virtue is knowledge" and that "the virtues are one." Anyone who knows the good—in Socrates' sense of knowledge, which involves really evaluating a thing itself, not just memorizing a slogan about it—will always choose it. And, in every situation, human excellence results from "knowledge," that is, from intelligent evaluation.

Since virtue is a condition of the inner self and this alone is intrinsically good, the popular notion that a person can be harmed by being deprived of property or of physical comfort is mistaken. The only real harm that can befall is for something to occur that will make one a worse person; and this can only be the result of a mistaken choice that leads one to give up dignity and act wickedly. Consequently, Socrates argued, faced with the choice, it is better to be treated unjustly than to act unjustly oneself.

Socrates believed that the only hope

for Athens lay in correcting the ignorance of the Athenian statesmen and their followers. The history of Athens during his life showed the need for such a correction. Athenian expansion had collided with Sparta and her allies, and for many years the long, drawn-out Peloponnesian War continued, ending finally in 404 B.C. with the defeat of Athens. An interim dictatorship of thirty oligarchs established itself, led by the Sophist Critias. They drove out the leaders of the democratic faction and, for a time, subjected Athens to an unprincipled reign of terror. In 403, however, the democratic group invaded the city and drove out the Thirty. The democratic leader Anytus had a law passed that no one could be prosecuted for actions before this democratic restoration, and the democracy tried to sustain its precarious position and regain some of the lost power and trade.

Socrates' first encounter with a government that wanted him to stop talking occurred when the Thirty were in power. Presumably some of his comparisons of their behavior with that of bad craftsmen angered Critias and his colleagues. At any rate, Critias took Socrates aside and told him to "give your cobblers and donkeys a rest . . ."—that is, stop talking! (My own guess would be that Socrates compared the Thirty to shepherds who spent all their time barbecuing the sheep they were guarding.) This warning was not heeded, and presently, in an attempt to implicate him, they ordered Socrates to help arrest a wealthy man, Leon of Salamis—an arbitrary arrest prior to the assassination of Leon and the confiscation of his property. Socrates quietly went home; and only the return of the democracy saved him from assassination by the oligarchic dictators.

But, in spite of the moderation Anytus

showed in his law of general pardon for earlier offenses, he too found Socrates a public danger and brought charges against him intended to frighten him into leaving Athens or to stop criticizing the democracy. Anytus had some justification for his feeling that the democratic government in Athens was in a precarious position and that Socrates' criticism was not the sort of uncritical patriotism that Anytus wanted. But obviously Socrates, convinced that intelligence was the only hope for human improvement, could not agree to give up his mission for the sake of the government's ideas of temporary expediency.

Anytus made the same mistake about Socrates that many other Greeks did: he assumed that Socrates did not really believe what he said. The city was full of people who *talked* idealistically, but who *acted* to increase their own property and comfort. But Socrates did, in fact, believe that it was better to suffer injustice than to commit it. He believed that his questions were essential and beneficial to society, and that he would be wrong to run away or keep silent.

Thus the second result of Socrates' labors: In 399 B.C. he was charged with corruption of the youth and the introduction of strange gods meant to replace those of the traditional pantheon. In the course of his defense, which is recorded in Plato's *Apology,* Socrates indicated what he considered to be the sanction for the values which he had been giving linguistic clarification. By so doing, he revealed a new understanding of the human psyche.

> . . . Athenians, I hold you in the highest regard and affection, but I will be persuaded by the god rather than you. As long as I have breath and strength I will not give up philosophy and exhorting you and declaring the truth to every one of you whom I meet. . . .

> This, you must recognize, the god has commanded me to do. And I think that no greater good has ever befallen you in the state than my service to the god. For I spend my whole life in going about and persuading you all to give your first and greatest care to the improvement of your souls, and not till you have done that to think of your bodies or your wealth. . . .

> Perhaps it may seem strange to you that, though I go about giving this advice privately and meddling in others' affairs, yet I do not venture to come forward in the assembly and advise the state. You have often heard me speak of my reason for this, and in many places: it is that I have a certain divine guide. . . . I have had it from childhood. It is a kind of voice which, whenever I hear it, always turns me back from something which I was going to do, but never urges me to act. It is this which forbids me to take part in politics. . . .[12]

The jury did not understand the meaning of these remarks, nor did they sympathize with the other arguments used in Socrates' behalf. As a result, he was found guilty and condemned to death. After the verdict he addressed his supporters at the trial:

> With you who have acquitted me I should like to discuss this thing that has happened, while the authorities are busy, and before I go to the place where I have to die. So, remain with me until I go: there is no reason why we should not talk with each other while it is possible. I wish to explain to you, as my friends, the meaning of what has happened to me. An amazing thing has happened to me, judges—for I am right in calling you judges. The prophetic guide has been constantly with me all through my life till now, opposing me

[12] From Plato: *Euthyphro, Apology, Crito,* translated by F. J. Church, pp. 35–36. Copyright © 1948, 1956 by The Liberal Arts Press, Inc. Reprinted by permission of The Liberal Arts Press Division of The Bobbs-Merrill Company, Inc.

even in trivial matters if I were not going to act rightly. And now you yourselves see what has happened to me—a thing which might be thought, and which is sometimes actually reckoned, the supreme evil. But the divine guide did not oppose me when I was leaving my house in the morning, nor when I was coming up here to the court, nor at any point in my speech when I was going to say anything; though at other times it has often stopped me in the very act of speaking. But now, in this matter, it has never once opposed me, either in my words or my actions. I will tell you what I believe to be the reason. This thing that has come upon me must be a good; and those of us who think that death is an evil must needs be mistaken. I have a clear proof that that is so; for my accustomed guide would certainly have opposed me if I had not been going to meet with something good.

And if we reflect in another way, we shall see that we may well hope that death is a good. For the state of death is one of two things: either the dead man wholly ceases to be and loses all consciousness or, as we are told, it is a change and a migration of the soul to another place. And if death is the absence of all consciousness, and like the sleep of one whose slumbers are unbroken by any dreams, it will be a wonderful gain. For if a man had to select that night in which he slept so soundly that he did not even dream, and had to compare with it all the other nights and days of his life, and then had to say how many days and nights in his life he had spent better and more pleasantly than this night, I think that a private person, nay, even the Great King of Persia himself, would find them easy to count, compared with the others. If that is the nature of death, I for one count it a gain. For then it appears that all time is nothing more than a single night. But if death is a journey to another place, and what we are told is true—that all who have died are there—what good could be greater than this, my judges? Would a journey not be worth taking, at the end of which,

in the other world, we should be delivered from the pretended judges here and should find the true judges who are said to sit in judgment below, such as Minos and Rhadamanthus and Aeacus and Triptolemus, and the other demigods who were just in their own lives? Or what would you not give to converse with Orpheus and Musaeus and Hesiod and Homer? I am willing to die many times if this be true. And for my own part I should find it wonderful to meet there Palamedes, and Ajax the son of Telamon, and the other men of old who have died through an unjust judgment, and to compare my experiences with theirs. That I think would be no small pleasure. And, above all, I could spend my time in examining those who are there, as I examine men here, and in finding out which of them is wise, and which of them thinks himself wise when he is not wise. What would we not give, my judges, to be able to examine the leader of the great expedition against Troy, or Odysseus, or Sisyphus, or countless other men and women whom we could name? It would be an inexpressible happiness to converse with them and to live with them and to examine them. Assuredly there they do not put men to death for doing that. For besides the other ways in which they are happier than we are, they are immortal, at least if what we are told is true.

And you too, judges, must face death hopefully, and believe this one truth, that no evil can happen to a good man, either in life or after death. His affairs are not neglected by the gods; and what has happened to me today has not happened by chance. I am persuaded that it was better for me to die now, and to be released from trouble; and that was the reason why the guide never turned me back. And so I am not at all angry with my accusers or with those who have condemned me to die. Yet it was not with this in mind that they accused me and condemned me, but meaning to do me an injury. So far I may blame them.

Yet I have one request to make of them.

When my sons grow up, punish them, my friends, and harass them in the same way that I have harassed you, if they seem to you to care for riches or for any other thing more than excellence; and if they think that they are something when they are really nothing, reproach them, as I have reproached you, for not caring for what they should, and for thinking that they are something when really they are nothing. And if you will do this, I myself and my sons will have received justice from you.

But now the time has come, and we must go away—I to die, and you to live. Which is better is known to the god alone.[13]

[13] From Plato: *Euthyphro, Apology, Crito,* translated by F. J. Church, pp. 47–49. Copyright © 1948, 1956 by The Liberal Arts Press, Inc. Reprinted by permission of the Liberal Arts Press Division of The Bobbs-Merrill Company, Inc.

CHAPTER 9

THE HUMAN SOUL AS THE SOURCE OF KNOWLEDGE:
Plato's Epistemology

The aim of the historian is to understand Plato in the context of his own time and problems. Those who approach him with problems of their own—philosophical, scientific or political—are each true to something in Plato, but as they pursue their diverse aims his own may be neglected or obscured. His primary purpose was not logical, scientific or political. It was rather the provision of a metaphysical basis for the moral life, adequate to counteract both the actual decline of morals in his day and the prevailingly sceptical and relativist attitude to knowledge which gave it, as he thought, a spurious intellectual respectability. . . .

W. K. C. Guthrie, Twentieth Century Approaches to Plato

Platonism . . . is not a dogma once promulgated but a living attitude. It manifests an eager concern with the world about us, but reads this world as an imperfect and changing expression of an eternal order, and bids us do in our time what lies in our power to reshape it. Never content to believe that material and automatic forces, that custom and statistics, have the last word, it appeals to reason and the will as final arbiters. Recognizing the gap between the lowest and the highest levels of human ability, it is cautious, even pessimistic, about the possibility of reshaping society; but it is hopeful of individuals building the "state within us," of a Socrates living, or dying, for the consistency of his faith in the Good, and not dying in vain.

This Platonism is not a quaint and timid academic survival, but a bold infiltration of philosophy itself into all our contemporary activities and disciplines, a criticism of their trends and standards and objectives. It does not offer itself as an all-sufficient substitute for any or all of them; it does not seek to displace modern philosophy, or modern literature, or the various natural and social sciences, or the religions that claim man's allegiance. It has no solution of our complex problems of war and peace. But it does bid men examine the very foundations and assumptions of their various speculations and activities in the light of the Good, at the same time that it invites their criticism of itself. Such a seasoned and open-minded Platonism we need today.

William Chase Greene,
"Platonism and Its Critics," Harvard Studies in Classical Philology

In the history of philosophical thought one may discern three basic types of approach to the analysis of the nature and validity of the idea of God, namely, the Aristotelian, the Platonic and the Democritean. . . . Philosophers who followed in the

192

Platonic tradition tended on the whole to adopt a psychological and epistemological approach and attempted to demonstrate that the idea of God was innate in some form since the idea of a most perfect being could not possibly be derived from sense experience. . . . All forms of the "Ontological Proof" for the existence of God may be traced to this Platonic presupposition that the concept of a most perfect being necessarily requires some transcendental cause other than man as the ground of its origin in the human mind. . . . The ethnological implication of this Platonic, ontological argument is that all peoples have the idea of a supreme being whatever the name by which it is called. . . .

David Bidney, "The Ethnology of Religion and the Problem of Human Evolution," American Anthropologist, *Vol. LVI*

Socrates' work was carried on after his death by his most devoted student, Plato. Plato was born in Athens in 428 B.C. of a prominent aristocratic family. Before the age of twenty he came under the influence of Socrates and remained his most devoted and outstanding student until Socrates' death in 399 B.C. In fact, Plato devoted his entire life to the continuation of the work begun by Socrates.

For a decade or so after Socrates' death Plato seems to have remained in Athens. During that time it is likely that he served briefly in the army during one of the many wars in which Athens was involved in the first half of the fourth century B.C. In 389 B.C. he made his first trip to Sicily. This visit was one of the major factors in giving his philosophy its unique direction, for there he met the members of the Pythagorean school.

Upon his return to Athens Plato established the Academy, generally considered the first formal school in Europe. The foundation of the Academy was, in many ways, the product of the frustration of political ambitions which he suffered early in his life. Late in his life Plato recounted his youthful impressions of the conduct of politics at the time he was considering a political career.

When I was young, I had the same experience that comes to so many: I thought that, as soon as I should be my own master, I should enter public life. This intention was favoured by certain circumstances in the political situation at Athens. The existing constitution was generally condemned, and a revolution took place.[1] . . . Some of the leaders were relatives and friends of mine, and they at once invited me to co-operate, as if this were the natural course for me to take. No wonder that, young as I was, I imagined they would bring the state under their management from an iniquitous to a right way of life. Accordingly I watched closely to see what they would do. It was not long before I saw these men make the former constitution seem like a paradise. In particular they tried to send Socrates, my friend, then advanced in years—a man whom I should not hesitate to call the most righteous man then living—with other persons, to arrest one of the citizens by violence for execution. Their purpose, no doubt, was to implicate Socrates, with or without his will, in their proceedings. He refused, preferring to face any danger rather than be a party to their infamous deeds. Seeing all this and other things as bad, I was disgusted and drew back from the evils of the time.

Not long afterwards the Thirty fell and the whole constitution was changed. Once more I was attracted, though less eagerly, towards taking an active part in politics. In these unquiet times much was still going on

[1] See pp. 170, 188–189.

that might move one to disgust, and it was no wonder that, during the revolutionary changes, some took savage vengeance upon their enemies; but on the whole the returning exiles showed great moderation. Unfortunately, however, some of the men in power brought my friend Socrates to trial on an abominable charge, the very last that could be made against Socrates—the charge of impiety. He was condemned and put to death—he who had refused to share the infamy of arresting one of the accusers' own friends when they themselves were in exile and misfortune.

When I considered these things and the men who were directing public affairs, and made a closer study, as I grew older, of law and custom, the harder it seemed to me to govern a state rightly. Without friends and trustworthy associates it was impossible to act; and these could not readily be found among my acquaintance, now that Athens was no longer ruled by the manners and institutions of our forefathers; and to make new associates was by no means easy. At the same time the whole fabric of law and custom was going from bad to worse at an alarming rate. The result was that I, who had at first been full of eagerness for a public career, when I saw all this happening and everything going to pieces, fell at last into bewilderment. . . .[2]

The political deterioration to which Plato refers had begun, as we have seen, during the Peloponnesian War. After Athens was defeated by Sparta, the Athenian empire was broken up. Until 371 B.C. Spartan control of Greece was maintained, but at the cost of intermittent wars and reliance upon foreign powers (such as Persia) to settle disputes between the Greek city-states. Thebes, after crushing Sparta, in that year became the dominant power among the poleis. When Theban hegemony was terminated by war in 362 B.C., chaos ensued, and order was restored only when Philip II of Macedon conquered Greece in 338 B.C.

[2] From *The Republic of Plato* translated by F. M. Cornford, "Seventh Epistle," pp. xvii–xviii. Oxford University Press, 1941. Reprinted by permission.

Within Athens itself political developments followed the same general pattern of disintegration. Participation in civic affairs declined and, as a result, both the military establishment and the administration of the polis were gradually professionalized. The individual's commitment to, and identity with, the polis community quite logically diminished. There appeared for the first time in the later fourth century B.C. a distinction between public and private life and consequently a separation of the ethical from the political. Because of the devastation caused by the many wars, small farmers had to sell their property, thus giving rise to larger and larger landholdings. This in turn led to extremes of wealth and poverty, a development which also took place in urban areas, and ultimately class warfare broke out.

Matters had by no means reached this low point when Plato returned from his first trip to Sicily to establish the Academy in 387 B.C. The circumstances which had made him abandon a political career did not diminish his concern with the political, nor did he ever cease regarding the political art as superior to all others. This was but a logical consequence of his belief that ethics and politics did not constitute two different spheres of conduct. Since his initial intellectual concern was ethics, politics necessarily had to figure in his solutions to the ethical problem. The Academy was one such solution. In it he established a curriculum of study designed to produce statesmen and rulers. The course of studies included mathematics, astronomy, harmonics, and philosophy. The curriculum, thus, was purely scientific. It was not designed to provide the student with useful knowledge, but with the opportunity to pursue knowledge of those eternal truths which, he believed, the statesman must possess if he were to govern a community wisely.

Plato's own personal intellectual efforts were devoted to the problems which Socrates had left unresolved. As was indicated in the previous chapter, Socrates had attempted to fix ethical concepts by applying inductive definitions. In other words, in the discussion of any given term the participants would move from inadequate to more adequate definitions or from particular examples to universal definitions by testing the truth or falsity of statements.

Because his tools of reasoning were limited and his interests confined to ethics, Socrates' efforts to clarify ethical concepts most frequently ended in negative definitions. He could, for example, determine what virtue was not, but not what it was. Plato continued the search for ethical absolutes and finally succeeded in creating a philosophical weapon which could combat the skepticism and moral relativism of the Sophists.

PLATO'S THEORY OF THE FORMS
W. T. Jones[3]

Plato saw that in order to answer the Sophists satisfactorily he had to find solutions to the various apparently insoluble dilemmas, growing out of earlier theories, that had convinced the Sophists of the hopeless inadequacy of human reason. It was impossible simply to treat the Sophists like naughty children, to spank them and put them to bed. Many of them were sincere and honest men, and their arguments were not easy to dispose of. One could say that the complete scepticism of a Gorgias was self-defeating and absurd, but until one could resolve the dilemmas which had led Gorgias to this conclusion and could justify the claims of reason as an instrument of knowledge, one could hardly hope to halt the descent into scepticism and subjectivism which Plato viewed with so much alarm.

We must therefore turn to Plato's effort to vindicate the power of reason, by showing that there are public facts, espe-

cially in morals and politics, and that man can learn what they are. Once he had proved this Plato could go on to examine and record the nature of these facts, that is, work out in detail his own moral and political theories. Into this further inquiry we must eventually follow Plato, but for the present let us concentrate on his theory of knowledge.

Plato realized that the problems which had baffled the Sophists—the problem of the one and the many, the problem of appearance and reality, the problem of change—grew inevitably out of the questions asked by earlier philosophers. All of these tricky problems were implied in Thales's apparently innocent question, "What is the one out of which everything comes?" When we say everything is really one, and that this is water, or air, or whatever, it is obvious that things look different from what they are—what is *really* water *appears* to be ships, sealing wax, cabbages, and kings. Thus we get the "problem of appearance": How can reality appear to be different from what it is? And to say that everything is really one also involves us in the problem of the one and the many, for we are saying that what is one (water) is a plurality (ships, cabbages, kings), which sounds like a contradiction. Suppose we attempt to get around this by saying that the one changes into the many and that reality undergoes some sort of alteration or transformation in the course of which it becomes appearance. But this is not at all helpful since change is itself a puzzle and apparent contradiction. To say that something changes is to say that while it remains itself it becomes something different. This, surely, is nonsense, yet it seems that we must assert both when we say that something changes. A thing that changes must become something different; otherwise, of course, it does not change.

[3] From *A History of Western Philosophy* by W. T. Jones, pp. 101–105, 109–114. Copyright 1952 by Harcourt, Brace & World, Inc. and reprinted with their permission.

But it must remain itself, for it is *it* that changes. That is, what we have is not mere difference—not a rabbit where before there was an empty hat—but a continuing something which alters. It this is difficult to follow, consider what you mean when you say you are the same person now (only, of course, also different!) that you were at birth. Since we are obviously different as adults from what we were as newborn infants, and since we nevertheless feel that we are somehow the same, we say that we have changed. But though we are certainly different, how are we the same? How could we be the same if we are different?

The reader may be disposed at this point to fling down his book and inquire what all this talk is about, since "of course change occurs and everybody knows that it does." But to take this line is to miss the point. We need, perhaps, to remind ourselves that we do not solve problems by ignoring them. Of course change occurs; nobody, unless he were as exclusively a logician as Parmenides, would deny it. Change is one of the most pervasive and obvious facts about life. Because it is so pervasive, we usually take it for granted, but when we are set to think about it we find it anything but easy to understand. It is precisely the fact that change does occur, even though it is a puzzle, that created the dilemma for these early Greek philosophers. It will not do, therefore, to reply to them by loftily reaffirming that things obviously change. It is just because change does occur that they were puzzled. Nobody is puzzled by the contradiction "round square," but we would be puzzled if, despite the contradiction, we were constantly running into round squares. Since this is the kind of puzzlement that these early Greek philosophers experienced

about change, we can perhaps sympathize a bit with the Sophists in their scepticism.

We can now also better understand, perhaps, why Heraclitus and Parmenides developed their peculiar theories. Each was concentrating on just one side of what we have called the dilemma of change. We have said that things obviously change, and that this seems to mean they must remain the same and yet be different. It would seem that both Heraclitus and Parmenides saw that this is a contradiction. Hence each tried to get away with an explanation of the universe in terms of one of the conflicting concepts. Thus Heraclitus, since he saw that difference is required, rejected identity (which seemed to him incompatible with difference) and tried to explain everything in terms of flux. But this is of course unsatisfactory. Parmenides, on the other hand, realizing that whatever changes must be identical throughout its change, took identity as the basic concept and was therefore forced to deny change, since the two concepts seemed to him, too, incompatible. . . .

Plato realized that these problems about change, the one and the many, and appearance and reality, had to be solved before he could satisfactorily answer the Sophists, since as long as change was incapable of rational explanation it did indeed look as if reason was, as the Sophists maintained, a hopelessly fallible instrument.

The main lines of Plato's solution are quite simple; it is their development that is difficult and complex. What Plato said, in effect, was this: Both Heraclitus and Parmenides were correct, for they were talking about different types of objects. The Sophists had supposed them both, as indeed they had probably supposed themselves, to be talking about the same type of objects, viz., the objects of sense perception in the physical world, and it is of course a contradiction to assert of the same object the completely different predicates that Heraclitus and Parmenides were attributing to "reality." But what if reality is not single, as the Milesians had supposed? What if it is dual, as the Pythagoreans had maintained? We could then say that one of these realities was in a constant flux, as Heraclitus had asserted, and that the other was eternally one, as Parmenides had claimed. This would resolve the dilemma, for there is no problem about asserting contradictory predicates (e.g., "round" and "square") of different objects. But *are* there two worlds, and, if so, what are they? There is no doubt, surely, about the world of sense perception —it obviously exists and, what is more, it seems to have Heraclitean characteristics. It is a flux, but a flux that conforms to the "measures." Acorns never remain the same, they are always changing, growing, decaying, but they grow into oak trees, not lions; and they decay into humus, not brass buttons. If we can never step into the same river twice, the ever flowing river in the main keeps its banks and flows in the same direction to the sea.

So much, then, for Heraclitus. But what of Parmenides? Of what world are we to assert Parmenidean properties? According to Plato, reality is not exhausted by the world of sense perception. This world of sense perception is the world of physical objects in space and time; but besides this world, different from it but standing in intimate relation to it, is another world— nonphysical, nonspatial, nontemporal. This world Plato called the world of *ideai* or of *eide*. The latter is the Greek term from which our word "idol" (an image or a picture) is derived; the former is, of course, the Greek word from which our word "idea" is derived. On this account people sometimes speak of Plato's "world of ideas" and call his account of this world his "theory of ideas." Though a natural usage, this is misleading, for we commonly talk in English of an idea as something that exists only as a thought in somebody's mind. Take away the mind and you take away the idea. Thus we contrast the idea of a hamburger with a real, independently existing hamburger, and attribute much less reality to the former than to the latter. But, according to Plato, his *eide* or *ideai* were not only real, but much more real than anything else. Thus, while our word "idea" is like Plato's term in that it stands for something not a physical object, the difference between the two is greater than the similarity. We shall do better, therefore, to avoid it. Instead, we shall use the English word "form" to translate *idea* or *eidos,* and hence we shall talk of Plato's "theory of forms," not of his "theory of ideas." The use of "form" in this connection has ample precedent, and while it may be said to suggest nothing very positive, it at least does not suggest something very false.

So far, then, all we have said is that Plato believed that there is a world of forms, over and beyond the sensible world, and that these forms are nonphysical, nonspatial, and nontemporal, yet very real. This, it must be allowed, is certainly not to say very much, and we must try to do better. A nonspatial and nontemporal "something" is not an object at all in the ordinary sense. It cannot, for instance, be seen (for anything visible is spread out in space), nor touched (space again), nor heard (for anything audible endures through some time, however short a duration), and so on. If, then, the forms cannot be known in sense perception, how can they be known? Plato's reply is that they are known in thought; they are, in fact, *the* objects of thought. When we are thinking, what we are thinking *about* are forms. Hence, if we wish to get hold of a form, let us take an example of thought at its best. Thought at its best is, Plato made no doubt, mathematical thinking, and the most obvious examples of forms are mathematical ones.

What, for instance, is a geometrician thinking about when he is working out a theorem—say, the theorem that the interior angles of a Euclidean triangle equal two right angles? It seems clear (Plato held) that the geometrician is not *inventing* something. He is *discovering* something. If, for instance, he were to say that the interior angles of a triangle equal three right angles he would be mistaken. About triangles, if not about taste, there *is* [no] disputing. In this field, at least, every man is *not* the measure of all things for himself. It follows, Plato argued, that there is a public object, *triangle*, with public properties which are independent of the geometrician.

The next question is, What is this public object whose properties it is the function of mathematical thinking to reveal? Surely, Plato maintained, the object of mathematical thought is not the physical triangle drawn in chalk or ink which the geometrician is looking at. To begin with, the mathematical triangle is a plane figure enclosed by three straight lines. But blackboards and pieces of paper are not perfect planes; the drawn lines of chalk or ink have some breadth, fine though they may be, while the mathematical line enclosing the mathematical triangle has only one dimension, length. It is obvious, therefore, that the physical object drawn in ink or

chalk is really not a triangle. Nevertheless, it is somehow "like" a triangle (which justifies us, when we speak loosely, in calling it one), and it stands in some sort of relation to the real triangle, for looking at it helps us think mathematically about the real triangle. (What this relation is, we shall have to investigate later.) It is clear, also, to pursue this matter a bit further, that the object of the mathematician's thought is not a *particular*. The properties he is asserting hold, he believes, universally, not just here and now, but everywhere and at all times. Now this universal object, nonphysical, nonspatial, nontemporal, the object of thought, not of sense, is what Plato called a form (*idea, eidos*). Plato believed that whenever we are *thinking* (in distinction from daydreaming, imagining, or perceiving) what we are thinking about is a form, in the sense described.

The scientist (the botanist or zoologist or chemist) may use some physical object—a primrose, a horse, a test tube of hydrogen—to help him think, as the mathematician uses the drawn triangle in thinking about the mathematical triangle. But what the scientist is thinking *about* always is a universal, nonphysical, nontemporal object, or form. If I look at a horse and see only this particular horse, old Dobbin, with a brown coat, a cast in his right eye, and a wicked dislike of motor cars, I am only perceiving, and what I am perceiving is a world of Heraclitean flux. Old Dobbin never for a moment remains the same; he is getting older, blinder, and wickeder all the time. But if I look at old Dobbin as a trained zoologist might what I see is more than old Dobbin. What I see is not just an old friend or enemy, or a mode of conveyance. What I, as zoologist, see is *horse,* that is, a set of universal properties which are probably only very poorly exemplified in Dobbin (just as the properties of triangle may be poorly exemplified in some hastily scrawled figure on a blackboard), the properties, that is, which distinguish horses from all other animals. And the totality of these properties, the possession of which makes Dobbin a horse, is what Plato would call the form "horse." These properties are what the trained zoologist explores and discovers. And we may say in general that unless there were forms, there could be no science, for a science is nothing but a method for getting at these universal and pervasive properties of things which make them what they are.

This world of universal and pervasive properties has all the characteristics of the Parmenidean one. Each form is eternal and unchanging. While Dobbin is, as we have seen, Heraclitean, "horse" is Parmenidean. Even if disease were to kill off Dobbin and all other flesh-and-blood horses, the properties that constitute horseness would still be what they are, just as the property of having interior angles equal to 180° would still belong to plane figures enclosed by three straight lines, even if there were no triangle drawn in chalk, stamped out of bronze, or incised in marble. In this physical world, then, everything is changing and nothing is ever exactly what it is; it is always becoming something different. In the world of forms, however, everything . . . is always what it is and not another thing. It is, Plato would argue, just the fact of its being Parmenidean—of its being eternally and unchangeably itself—that makes it possible for us to fix a form in knowledge. . . .

. . . [On the other hand,] the physical world is a shadow of the form world (and a lower form is a shadow of a higher form), just as the shadow cast by old Dobbin is a shadow of old Dobbin. Let us explore a little the relation between old Dobbin and his shadow, bearing in mind that our purpose is to discover corresponding facts about the relation between higher and lower forms and between the physical world as a whole and the world of forms as a whole.

The first thing to observe is that any shadow of old Dobbin tells us *something* about old Dobbin, that some shadows tell us more than others, but that no shadow tells us much about Dobbin. Thus though Dobbin's shadow in the morning or late afternoon hopelessly exaggerates the length of Dobbin's legs, it is reliable enough to enable us (merely from the shadow, without seeing Dobbin himself) to recognize this as the shadow of a horse (not of a table, which also has four legs), and perhaps also to distinguish it from the shadow of a cow or a lion. So, too, though the cow's legs will be elongated in the shadow, we will be able to say whether the real Dobbin is taller than the real Bess, for the distortion is relative to the real length and not completely arbitrary. Of course, not all shadows of Dobbin are equally reliable. Dobbin's shadow at noon and those of the table and of Bess may be almost indistinguishable "blobs." Again, although an isolated shadow of Dobbin tells us something, but not much, about Dobbin, a *collection* of Dobbin's shadows tells us more, if we are patient enough to study them. Suppose we collect the succession of shadows made by Dobbin as the sun advances from dawn to the meridian and sinks to the western horizon in the evening. These shadows constitute two series: first we have a very long shadow which becomes successively smaller until we reach the blob at noon, when the sun is overhead; then we get a second and expanding series, which is the mirror image of the other. Thus we have already introduced a kind of order in the succession of passing shadows—an order which is itself permanent, though the shadows are constantly changing, and which makes it possible for us, once we know it, to make predictions about the shapes and other characteristics of subsequent shadows. In other words, we have a crude science, entirely at the level of shadows. And we have this much of a science, it is important to observe, only because there is a real Dobbin who is casting the shadows. Dobbin is, as it were, the central point, or focus, about which the shadows are arranged.

Well, there are, of course, other things we could do in our shadow science. We could collect shadows of Dobbin standing, lying, galloping, and compare them. But it is unnecessary for us to pursue this metaphor further. It will be more profitable to apply what we have learned about the relation between Dobbin and his shadows to the problem of the relation between form and physical objects. The relation between some one of the forms, say the form "horse," and all *its* physical objects, is the same as the relation between one of these physical objects, say Dobbin, and all of *his* shadows. Thus we can say that any physical horse will be a more or less adequate shadow of the form "horse," that some physical horses tell us more about "horse" than others, but that no one by itself tells us really very much about "horse." Dobbin, a rather decrepit, ill-used beast, will probably tell us no more about "horse" than Dobbin's shadow-blob at noon tells us about him. Man o' War, or Traveller, on the other hand, being more respectable shadows of "horse," tell us considerably more about the real nature of "horse."

But rather than limiting ourselves to some one particular horse, whether Dobbin or Man o' War, we shall do better, certainly, to study a number of horses. And if we do so, even without ever passing beyond a purely empirical level, we shall be able to observe sequences and regularities and, on the basis of these observations, make predictions useful for ordinary living. This is the kind of science the veterinarian or the racing fan has. I may have observed that, in general, a certain shadow is followed by another shadow (e.g., that a certain chest formation, say, is an indication of speed, so I put my money on the horse with this chest formation). Similarly, in the treatment of disease the veterinarian, having observed the relation between certain bodily symptoms and drugs, proceeds to diagnose and to treat the disease accordingly. He knows that the animal "responds" (that certain events are followed in general by others), but *why* that should be the case he does not and cannot know until he passes beyond the physical to the form, any more than the student of Dobbin's shadows could know why the shadows follow each other in this orderly sequence, without passing beyond the shadows to look at Dobbin himself. And, finally, just as Dobbin is the central point around which the shadows are ordered, so the form "horse" is the focus on which the various particular horses are ordered. Just as Dobbin is the source of these shadows and their order, so the form is the source of these horses and their order.

So far we have been discussing a world made up of shadows of Dobbin, with Dobbin in the background, unknown and unseen by the student of his shadows. Suppose, now, after a long and careful study of, and generalization from, Dobbin's shadows, the student suddenly sees Dobbin himself. What a difference! And if one had given the name "Dobbin" to this collection of shadows (for want of knowing anything else), would one not now exclaim, seeing for the first time the flesh-and-blood animal, "So that's what Dobbin really is!" Dobbin, the flesh-and-blood animal, when finally known, illumines the shadows we have heretofore called by his name and makes them more intelligible. In the same way, Plato would have us think, the form "horse" when finally known illumines and makes intelligible all the individual flesh-and-blood horses, which indeed we call "horses" (as we called the shadows "Dobbin") only because we do not know the form which is *really* horse and of which they, the flesh-and-blood animals, are only the inadequate and partial shadows.

We can say, then, that anything which, when known, illumines something else and makes it intelligible, is, so far, "higher." That which is illumined is, so far, "lower." Since in Plato's view it is the general which illumines the particular, he customarily speaks of the forms as "higher" and the physical objects as "lower."[4] The way in

which successively higher (in this sense) and more general bodies of knowledge illumine lower and less general ones may be readily seen if one thinks of the different ways in which different people with different backgrounds of general knowledge know the same object—say, the motor of my car. What I see when I look under the hood of my car is hardly more than shadow—a jumble of wires and gadgets in which I may perhaps be able to distinguish something called a carburetor or a spark plug. As to what these things do or why they do it I have only the vaguest idea, and as to *knowledge* of the engine, clearly I have none. Plato would not allow that I even have so much as "opinion." Let us, therefore, call my state of mind about the engine "recognition." Like the man looking at and recognizing Dobbin's shadow, I recognize this gadget as a carburetor, but that is as far as I can go. Most of us, outside of the one or two limited fields in which we happen to be especially trained and proficient, never get beyond this level of recognition. To reach the level of opinion, we need to do more than recognize. A good motor mechanic not only recognizes the various gadgets, he knows how to fix them. A certain squeak, rattle, or thump *means* something to him. What it means is a function of previous experiences of similar rattles, thumps, or squeaks. He knows, for instance, that if he tightens this nut or screw he can stop that squeak (which is more than I know), and so on. When a man knows what will stop the rattle, or squeak, but does not know *why* it will do so, let us say that he has "opinion." Such a man may be an extremely good mechanic in the sense that he has learned by trial and error that doing thus-and-so will cure such-and-such symptoms. But for an instance

[4] The terms "higher" and "lower" are dangerous since they suggest a moral scale. It does not follow, because *x* makes *y* more intelligible, that it makes *y* better. Unfortunately Plato constantly made this illegitimate inference. He also assumed that illumination always operates from general to particular. But actually there is no fixed order, or direction, of illumination. Sometimes particulars are illuminated by generals, sometimes generals by particulars. (Thus an abstract, dictionary definition of horse may be made real and significant by our becoming acquainted with some particular horse, with the pleasures of riding him, the need of caring for him, and so on.) What illumines what in any given context depends on what we already know and what we want to know. But considerations like these take us far beyond Plato's own formulation of the view.

of real knowledge we must go a step further, to someone who not only has an empirical acquaintance with motor cars but who knows the theory of heat engines; who has, say, studied thermodynamics, and who therefore can see the gasoline engine as an example of certain general and mathematically statable laws which express the nature of heat energy.

Each successively "higher" knowledge is thus higher just because it illumines, or makes sense of, the experience which we call "seeing the engine." Each higher level is more general and more abstract, all the way from the almost bare particularity of my experience (of course if it were *wholly* bare I shouldn't even be able to recognize it as an experience of an engine) to the very great generality and abstraction of a theory of heat.

So far we have been discussing the realm of forms as a whole in its relation to the physical world. It is perhaps time now to try to examine the relationship between . . . the lower and higher forms. . . . We can make a beginning by noting that when we have reached a knowledge of thermodynamics and a theory of heat, we are still not at an end of the knowledge which, if we but had it, would throw light on and illumine our experience of the motor-car engine. For thermodynamics is but a small part of physics, and in order really to understand the phenomenon of heat we have to see it in its relation to the rest of physics, just as, in order to understand the engine we have to see *it* in relation to thermodynamics. But, since nobody can cover all this ground, every special science puts up more or less arbitrary boundaries, at which there are signs reading in effect, "No need to go further (we hope!)." Consider, for instance, the case of the geometrician. Geometry, at

least Euclidean geometry, which is the only kind Plato knew, begins with certain definitions, axioms, and postulates: "A straight line is the shortest distance between two points," "Parallel lines will never meet," and so on. Plato calls these *principles;* his point is that, while the Euclidean geometer assumes them and, having assumed them, goes on to see what he can do with them, there is a kind of study which would begin from them and work backwards, trying to *prove* the basic assumptions of the Euclidean geometer. How much sense there is to Plato's position here can be seen from the fact that when, centuries later, mathematicians made a determined effort to prove one of these principles—the so-called postulate of parallels—whole new geometries undreamed of before were discovered, and the basis was laid for a completely new understanding of the nature of mathematics. Here was new light and illumination indeed!

Every science, then, starts from certain assumptions. It must not forget that its starting point is only a set of assumptions and that study of them might radically alter the science's notion of itself. Another way of saying this is to say that all thinking —all knowing—is *conditioned*. We have, for instance, to decide whether to vote for the Democratic or the Republican candidate at the next election, but our attempt to decide operates within the assumption that we should do our duty as citizens and vote. It is fair to say, then, that our thought about how to cast our vote is conditioned on our acceptance of representative government. Of course, if we are going to vote in the coming election we cannot wait until we have explored and verified the bases of representative government! But though practical considerations often interfere with a rigorous pursuit of the conditions of our thinking, we would do well never to state a conclusion, even to ourselves ("I have decided to vote for so-and-so") except as a hypothetical proposition: "So-and-so is the better candidate, if . . ." To list some of the hidden assumptions on which this conclusion rests would give us a proper sense of our finitude, which is precisely what Plato wanted us to realize.

It is not just my knowledge of politics which is finite and conditioned; the geometer's knowledge of geometry, as we have seen, is similarly conditioned; so are the physicist's, the chemist's, and the biologist's. All the sciences, for instance, attempt to discover natural causes in the physical world. This means that each starts from the assumption, which no one of them attempts for a moment to prove, that every event does have a cause.

. . . [I]n this scheme, knowledge forms a kind of pyramid. The nearer we are to the base . . ., the more conditioned our knowledge is. The higher we rise, the more we free ourselves from conditions, until finally —this seems to be Plato's view—we reach a single point from which everything else depends and which itself is unconditioned. If we could know it, it would illumine and throw into proper scale and perspective all the rest of our knowledge. Being completely knowable in itself it could not be made more meaningful by knowing something else. This summit to the pyramid of knowledge Plato called the "Form of the Good." This is not an easy notion to understand. Indeed, . . . Plato held it to be inexplicable to anyone who has not actually studied dialectic and traversed the long path from [the lower forms to the higher forms].

This is probably correct. Any experience--not necessarily a great one like that of the Form of the Good—is something unique. A description, no matter how detailed, of being under fire or being torpedoed, is utterly different from, and inadequate to, the actual experience itself. There are only two ways of knowing what being torpedoed or being under fire is really like. One, of course, is being torpedoed or being under fire. The other is through the imaginative recreativity of an artist.

If the artist is good enough, he may give us an even better grasp of the experience than we would get by living through it. Being under fire or being torpedoed is too dangerous, too confusing, too transitory for us to grasp the meaning of what is happening; we are too busy looking out for our necks to attend very closely to the flavor of the experience. But the artist, if he is great enough, preserves it for us in its purity and, at the same time, gives it a kind of distance, or objectivity, so that we can look at it without being a part of it. Art, then, we may say, is (among other things) a substitute for firsthand experience.

This may help to explain the role of myth in Plato's writings.[5] Plato thought that none of the really important things— the real essence of goodness, nobility of spirit, humanity—could be condensed into neat copybook maxims. They elude us as the real flavor of Paris eludes the composer of Baedeker guidebooks. The best way, Plato thought, to learn the meaning of such concepts was to live close to someone who already knows them (just as the best way to know Paris is to go there, walk the streets and sit in the sidewalk cafés, stroll along the banks of the Seine and in the Luxembourg gardens). If one lives with such a great-souled man for a long time, one may pick up what he knows—not

[5] See pp. 20–24. [Ed.]

through formal lectures, not even so much through example as through a kind of intellectual and moral osmosis. This would be direct experience. To those who are not fortunate enough to participate in such an experience directly, Plato can offer only a *myth*, which is, as it were, an imitation of the experience; not a description of it, but an artistic re-creation of it. Hence, whenever in our reading of the dialogues we come to a myth, we can be sure we have reached a point of great importance for Plato. A good rule to follow is to take the myth seriously but not literally. It is not a fairy tale designed to amuse; it is designed to say in the language of poetry and art what is too subtle and elusive to be said in any other way.

What then, in lieu of a direct experience through a study of dialectic, can myth tell us about the Form of the Good? There are three "points" Socrates tries to bring out in his comparison of the Form of the Good with the sun. One is that, just as the sun makes physical things on the earth visible, the Form of the Good illumines and makes meaningful lower levels of knowledge and opinion. We have already, perhaps, said enough on this point. Second, Socrates says that the sun sustains and nourishes plants and other living things. In an analogous way, we must suppose, the Form of the Good is not just a cold, lifeless, and indifferent searchlight illumining our knowledge, but is somehow also an active and creative power.

Thirdly, there is an "affinity" between our eyes and the sun. Plato probably had in mind here a contemporary physiological theory according to which the eye contains fire (because it shines and is bright) just as the sun does. If we want to bring Plato's analogy up to date we might state the affinity between eye and sun by saying that the eye is so constructed that it per-

ceives at least a part of the range of light emitted by the sun. If this were not the case we could not see. Thus it is an affinity between the sun and our eyes that makes visible things visible. In the same way there is an affinity between the Form of the Good and our minds, such that the Form of the Good satisfies the kinds of questions minds such as ours ask. The realm of forms might conceivably be indifferent to us, static and aloof. It might be that there is an objective, public reality but that this reality stands in no particular relation to us. If this were the case, though we could know, our knowledge would do us no good. This was the kind of world Atomism revealed and it is the kind of world modern science discloses: a world of energy which, by some curious coincidence, behaves in ways our mathematical minds can understand but which is utterly indifferent to the questions our moral natures ask—a world in which human hopes and fears and expectations get no answer.

This conception of reality Plato denied. Man is not merely, he thought, a thinking machine. He is not a neutral knower, indifferent to everything except knowing what reality is, but a moral, esthetic, social, and religious creature as well. For his final satisfaction, therefore, the world in which he lives cannot be merely a neutral reality. It must be one which has affinities with him and which somehow satisfies the demands which his complex nature makes. This is why Plato called the highest reality the Form of the Good; it is something which, when known, satisfies our ultimate questionings. In other words, what Plato is affirming here is the old Greek notion of Cosmos. The world and man form a real organic unity. The reality out there waiting to be known is somehow consonant with the moral knower. The world of forms, then, satisfies not merely our demands for knowledge but also, Plato maintained, our demands for justice, for beauty, and for religious and moral meaning. Since what truly satisfies is truly good, it is quite correct to describe the highest of all forms as the Form of the Good.

The best known exposition of the theory of the forms is "The Allegory of the Cave" in Plato's *Republic*.

THE ALLEGORY OF THE CAVE
Plato[6]

Next, said I, here is a parable to illustrate the degrees in which our nature may be enlightened or unenlightened. Imagine the condition of men living in a sort of cavernous chamber underground, with an entrance open to the light and a long passage all down the cave.[7] Here they have been from childhood, chained by the leg and also by the neck, so that they cannot move and can see only what is in front of them, because the chains will not let them turn their heads. At some distance higher up is the light of a fire burning behind them; and between the prisoners and the fire is a track[8] with a parapet built along it, like the screen at a puppet-show, which hides the performers while they show their puppets over the top.

I see, said he.

Now behind this parapet imagine persons carrying along various artificial objects, including figures of men and animals in wood or stone or other materials, which project above the parapet. Naturally, some of these persons will be talking, others silent.[9]

It is a strange picture, he said, and a strange sort of prisoners.

Like ourselves, I replied; for in the first place prisoners so confined would have seen nothing of themselves or of one another, except the shadows thrown by the fire-light on the wall of the Cave facing them, would they?

Not if all their lives they had been prevented from moving their heads.

And they would have seen as little of the objects carried past.

Of course.

Now, if they could talk to one another, would they not suppose that their words referred only to those passing shadows which they saw?[10]

Necessarily.

And suppose their prison had an echo from the wall facing them? When one of the people crossing behind them spoke, they could only suppose that the sound came from the shadow passing before their eyes.

No doubt.

[7] The *length* of the "way in" (*eisodos*) to the chamber where the prisoners sit is an essential feature, explaining why no daylight reaches them.

[8] The track crosses the passage into the cave at right angles, and is *above* the parapet built along it.

[9] A modern Plato would compare his Cave to an underground cinema, where the audience watch the play of shadows thrown by the film passing before a light at their backs. The film itself is only an image of "real" things and events in the world outside the cinema. For the film Plato has to substitute the clumsier apparatus of a procession of artificial objects carried on their heads by persons who are merely part of the machinery, providing for the movement of the objects and the sounds whose echo the prisoners hear. The parapet prevents these persons' shadows from being cast on the wall of the Cave.

[10] . . . The prisoners, having seen nothing but shadows, cannot think their words refer to the objects carried past behind their backs. For them shadows (images) are the only realities.

In every way, then, such prisoners would recognize as reality nothing but the shadows of those artificial objects.

Inevitably.

Now consider what would happen if their release from the chains and the healing of their unwisdom should come about in this way. Suppose one of them set free and forced suddenly to stand up, turn his head, and walk with eyes lifted to the light; all these movements would be painful, and he would be too dazzled to make out the objects whose shadows he had been used to see. What do you think he would say, if someone told him that what he had formerly seen was meaningless illusion, but now, being somewhat nearer to reality and turned towards more real objects, he was getting a truer view? Suppose further that he were shown the various objects being carried by and were made to say, in reply to questions, what each of them was. Would he not be perplexed and believe the objects now shown him to be not so real as what he formerly saw? [11]

Yes, not nearly so real.

And if he were forced to look at the fire-light itself, would not his eyes ache, so that he would try to escape and turn back to the things which he could see distinctly, convinced that they really were clearer than these other objects now being shown to him?

Yes.

And suppose someone were to drag him away forcibly up the steep and rugged ascent and not let him go until he had hauled him out into the sunlight, would he not suffer pain and vexation at such treatment, and, when he had come out into the light, find his eyes so full of its radiance that he could not see a single one of the things that he was now told were real?

Certainly he would not see them all at once.

He would need, then, to grow accustomed before he could see things in that upper world.[12] At first it would be easiest to make out shadows, and then the images of men and things reflected in water, and later on the things themselves. After that, it would be easier to watch the heavenly bodies and the sky itself by night, looking at the light of the moon and stars rather than the Sun and the Sun's light in the day-time.

Yes, surely.

Last of all, he would be able to look at the Sun and contemplate its nature, not as it appears when reflected in water or any alien medium, but as it is in itself in its own domain.

No doubt.

And now he would begin to draw the conclusion that it is the Sun that produces the seasons and the course of the year and controls everything in the visible world, and moreover is in a way the cause of all that he and his companions used to see.

Clearly he would come at last to that conclusion.

Then if he called to mind his fellow prisoners and what passed for wisdom in his former dwelling-place, he would surely think himself happy in the change and be sorry for them. They may have had a practice of honouring and commending one another, with prizes for the man who had the keenest eye for the passing shadows and the best memory for the order in which they followed or accompanied one another, so that he could make a good guess as to

---

[11] The first effect of Socratic questioning is perplexity.

[12] Here is the moral—the need of habituation by mathematical study before discussing moral ideas and ascending through them to the Form of the Good.

which was going to come next.[13] Would our released prisoner be likely to covet those prizes or to envy the men exalted to honour and power in the Cave? Would he not feel like Homer's Achilles, that he would far sooner "be on earth as a hired servant in the house of a landless man"[14] or endure anything rather than go back to his old beliefs and live in the old way?

Yes, he would prefer any fate to such a life.

Now imagine what would happen if he went down again to take his former seat in the Cave. Coming suddenly out of the sunlight, his eyes would be filled with darkness. He might be required once more to deliver his opinion on those shadows, in competition with the prisoners who had never been released, while his eyesight was still dim and unsteady; and it might take some time to become used to the darkness. They would laugh at him and say that he had gone up only to come back with his sight ruined; it was worth no one's while even to attempt the ascent. If they could lay hands on the man who was trying to set them free and lead them up, they would kill him.[15]

Yes, they would.

Every feature in this parable, my dear Glaucon, is meant to fit our earlier analysis. The prison dwelling corresponds to the region revealed to us through the sense of sight, and the fire-light within it to the power of the Sun. The ascent to see the things in the upper world you may take as standing for the upward journey of the soul into the region of the intelligible; then you will be in possession of what I surmise, since that is what you wish to be told. Heaven knows whether it is true; but this, at any rate, is how it appears to me. In the world of knowledge, the last thing to be perceived and only with great difficulty is the essential Form of Goodness. Once it is perceived, the conclusion must follow that, for all things, this is the cause of whatever is right and good; in the visible world it gives birth to light and to the lord of light, while it is itself sovereign in the intelligible world and the parent of intelligence and truth. Without having had a vision of this Form no one can act with wisdom, either in his own life or in matters of state.

So far as I can understand, I share your belief.

Then you may also agree that it is no wonder if those who have reached this height are reluctant to manage the affairs of men. Their souls long to spend all their time in that upper world—naturally enough, if here once more our parable holds true. Nor, again, is it at all strange that one who comes from the contemplation of divine things to the miseries of human life should appear awkward and ridiculous when, with eyes still dazed and not yet accustomed to the darkness, he is compelled, in a law-court or elsewhere, to dispute about the shadows of justice or the images that cast those shadows, and to wrangle over the notions of what is right in the minds of men who have never beheld Justice itself.

It is not at all strange.

No; a sensible man will remember that the eyes may be confused in two ways— by a change from light to darkness or from darkness to light; and he will recognize

---

[13] The empirical politician, with no philosophic insight, but only a "knack of remembering what usually happens." He has *eikasia* = conjecture as to what is likely (*eikos*).

[14] This verse, being spoken by the ghost of Achilles, suggests that the Cave is comparable with Hades.

[15] An allusion to the fate of Socrates.

that the same thing happens to the soul. When he sees it troubled and unable to discern anything clearly, instead of laughing thoughtlessly, he will ask whether, coming from a brighter existence, its unaccustomed vision is obscured by the darkness, in which case he will think its condition enviable and its life a happy one; or whether, emerging from the depths of ignorance, it is dazzled by excess of light. If so, he will rather feel sorry for it; or, if he were inclined to laugh, that would be less ridiculous than to laugh at the soul which has come down from the light.

That is a fair statement.

If this is true, then, we must conclude that education is not what it is said to be by some, who profess to put knowledge into a soul which does not possess it, as if they could put sight into blind eyes. On the contrary, our own account signifies that the soul of every man does possess the power of learning the truth and the organ to see it with; and that, just as one might have to turn the whole body round in order that the eye should see light instead of darkness, so the entire soul must be turned away from this changing world, until its eye can bear to contemplate reality and that supreme splendour which we have called the Good. Hence there may well be an art whose aim would be to effect this very thing, the conversion of the soul, in the readiest way; not to put the power of sight into the soul's eye, which already has it, but to ensure that, instead of looking in the wrong direction, it is turned the way it ought to be.

Yes, it may well be so.

It looks, then, as though wisdom were different from those ordinary virtues, as they are called, which are not far removed from bodily qualities, in that they can be produced by habituation and exercise in a soul which has not possessed them from

the first. Wisdom, it seems, is certainly the virtue of some diviner faculty, which never loses its power, though its use for good or harm depends on the direction towards which it is turned. You must have noticed in dishonest men with a reputation for sagacity the shrewd glance of a narrow intelligence piercing the objects to which it is directed. There is nothing wrong with their power of vision, but it has been forced into the service of evil, so that the keener its sight, the more harm it works.

Quite true.

And yet if the growth of a nature like this had been pruned from earliest childhood, cleared of those clinging overgrowths which come of gluttony and all luxurious pleasure and, like leaden weights charged with affinity to this mortal world, hang upon the soul, bending its vision downwards; if, freed from these, the soul were turned round towards true reality, then this same power in these very men would see the truth as keenly as the objects it is turned to now.

Yes, very likely.

Is it not also likely, or indeed certain after what has been said, that a state can never be properly governed either by the uneducated who know nothing of truth or by men who are allowed to spend all their days in the pursuit of culture? The ignorant have no single mark before their eyes at which they must aim in all the conduct of their own lives and of affairs of state; and the others will not engage in action if they can help it, dreaming that, while still alive, they have been translated to the Islands of the Blest.

Quite true.

It is for us, then, as founders of a commonwealth, to bring compulsion to bear on the noblest natures. They must be made to climb the ascent to the vision of Goodness, which we called the highest object of knowledge; and, when they have looked upon it long enough, they must not be allowed, as they now are, to remain on the heights, refusing to come down again to the prisoners or to take any part in their labours and rewards, however much or little these may be worth.

Shall we not be doing them an injustice, if we force on them a worse life than they might have?

You have forgotten again, my friend, that the law is not concerned to make any one class specially happy, but to ensure the welfare of the commonwealth as a whole. By persuasion or constraint it will unite the citizens in harmony, making them share whatever benefits each class can contribute to the common good; and its purpose in forming men of that spirit was not that each should be left to go his own way, but that they should be instrumental in binding the community into one.

True, I had forgotten.

You will see, then, Glaucon, that there will be no real injustice in compelling our philosophers to watch over and care for the other citizens. We can fairly tell them that their compeers in other states may quite reasonably refuse to collaborate: there they have sprung up, like a self-sown plant, in despite of their country's institutions; no one has fostered their growth, and they cannot be expected to show gratitude for a care they have never received. "But," we shall say, "it is not so with you. We have brought you into existence for your country's sake as well as for your own, to be like leaders and king-bees in a hive; you have been better and more thoroughly educated than those others and hence you are more capable of playing your part both as men of thought and as men of action. You must go down, then, each in his turn, to live with the rest and let your eyes grow accustomed to the dark-

ness. You will then see a thousand times better than those who live there always; you will recognize every image for what it is and know what it represents, because you have seen justice, beauty, and goodness in their reality; and so you and we shall find life in our commonwealth no mere dream, as it is in most existing states, where men live fighting one another about shadows and quarrelling for power, as if that were a great prize; whereas in truth government can be at its best and free from dissension only where the destined rulers are least desirous of holding office."

Quite true.

Then will our pupils refuse to listen and to take their turns at sharing in the work of the community, though they may live together for most of their time in a purer air?

No; it is a fair demand, and they are fair-minded men. No doubt, unlike any ruler of the present day, they will think of holding power as an unavoidable necessity.

Yes, my friend; for the truth is that you can have a well-governed society only if you can discover for your future rulers a better way of life than being in office; then only will power be in the hands of men who are rich, not in gold, but in the wealth that brings happiness, a good and wise life. All goes wrong when, starved for lack of anything good in their own lives, men turn to public affairs hoping to snatch from thence the happiness they hunger for. They set about fighting for power, and this internecine conflict ruins them and their country. The life of true philosophy is the only one that looks down upon offices of state; and access to power must be confined to men who are not in love with it; otherwise rivals will start fighting. So whom else can you compel to undertake the guardianship of the commonwealth, if not those who, besides understanding best the principles of government, enjoy a nobler life than the politician's and look for rewards of a different kind?

There is indeed no other choice.

Since Plato insisted that the Forms had an independent existence, he was confronted with the necessity of explaining how the human mind attains knowledge of them. The solution to this problem was suggested to him by the Pythagorean doctrine of the immortality of the soul. Pythagoras

. . . taught that the soul was immortal and suffered many reincarnations. This Plato accepted in all seriousness and adapted to be an integral part of his theory of knowledge. Soul is alien to body and in its pure being akin to the gods; but early Greek mythology had its own story of the Fall, and the punishment for original sin was the cycle of incarnations. The body is for the soul as a prison, or a tomb which holds it away from its true life. Socrates had taught Plato to think of the soul as essentially the mind, whose faculties (he now believed) are dulled, and its power of cognition impaired, by the body with its material needs and gross appetites. In its original state as a divine essence it had a clear and direct vision of the eternal Forms. Between incarnations it may see them again, with more or less clarity of apprehension depending on its attitude to the body in this life. If it has indulged the body by giving way to the lower appetites, something of the body's pollution will still cling to it and impair its faculties after death.

. . . The soul became acquainted with the Forms before it entered bodily life. To see things which are all imperfect—whether moral actions, triangles, or instances of physical beauty—could not of itself implant in our minds the knowledge of perfection nor a standard by which to judge them; but given that the vision preceded, they can assist us

to recover it. The experience of birth and bodily life has made the soul forgetful, and what the imperfect copies can do is to remind it of what it once knew.

The acquisition of knowledge in this life is thus explained by the fact that it is the recollection of knowledge once possessed.[16]

The recovery of knowledge is begun when the individual is moved by a force which Plato referred to as Eros.

. . . Eros in Plato is the motive force behind all human thought and action, the drive of longing after a good unattained which impels the soul on without rest till it is satisfied. There is nothing in the nature of Desire in itself to specify the good at which it aims. Its force can be used by any of the three parts of the soul[17] which gains power in the man. It can be squandered on the base ends of the lower lusts, or directed by the higher "spirited" part to such ends as the acquiring of honour. And it can drive the philosopher on from the desire of mortal beauty till at last he reaches the "great sea of beauty," the absolute and unchanging beauty of the World of Forms. Then it will be serving reason and attaining its true end.[18] Plato thus provides

[16] Reprinted with permission of The Macmillan Company from "Socrates and Plato" by Pamela Huby in *A Critical History of Western Philosophy,* ed. by D. J. O'Connor, p. 26. Copyright © 1964 by The Free Press of Glencoe, a Division of The Macmillan Company.

[17] Plato's psychological theory will be discussed at greater length in the next chapter. [Ed.]

[18] One classical scholar has diagramed these gradations of Eros in the following manner. "The left-hand column states the type of eros, while the object of that specific type is found in the right-hand column."

(i)	sensual eros	a beautiful body
(ii)	humanitarian eros	all beautiful bodies
(iii)	spiritual eros	*psyche* or spiritus
(iv)	social eros	institutions and laws
(v)	epistemic eros	intellectual studies
(vi)	formal philosophic eros	The Forms

Jerry Stannard, "Socratic Eros and Platonic Dialectic," *Phronesis*, 4 (1959), p. 124. [Ed.]

his tripartite soul with a single rightful ruler, the reason, and a single driving force, Eros or Desire; and he would have said that man was not truly one or truly man unless reason ruled in him, illumined by the eternal truths of the Forms, and his desire was directed to its proper end, the attainment of that transcendent world. . . .[19]

After the desire for knowledge has been aroused, recollection is set in motion by a heightened awareness of similarities and differences in any given set of particulars, and this recognition constitutes the first step in the process of definition and classification. The second step involves the application of the dialectic, Socrates' "second-best method," which Plato had greatly refined. Plato's dialectic included the methods of Collection and Division. In a Collection

the dialectician apprehends the similarities between things and sees that they partake in a common Form. The job of the dialectician, then, is . . . first "to collect the things that are everywhere scattered about under one Form . . ." and then "to be able to divide them up again according to their Forms, according to their natural articulations" (*Phaedrus*, 265 de). Elsewhere in the late dialogues a similar account of dialectic is given. In the *Sophist* the aim of dialectic is said to be to show "what kinds agree with what others, and what kinds do not admit one another" and then the dialectician is described as the man who can discern "clearly *one* Form everywhere extended throughout many, where each one lies apart, and *many* Forms, different from one another, embraced from without by one Form; and again *one* Form connected in a unity through many wholes, and *many* Forms, entirely marked off apart" (253 bcd). Finally, in the *Politicus* the method is again

described in similar terms: it is necessary "first to perceive the *community* existing between the many, and then not to desist before seeing in it all the differences that there are among the Forms; and then having seen the manifold *dissimilarities* in the groups of many, not to be put out of countenance or stop until, bringing all the common features within a single *likeness*, one encloses them in the essence of a Form" (285 ab).

The idea that the central task of dialectic is to distinguish the essential similarities and again the essential differences between things is a point to which Plato returns again and again.[20]

An example of division is to be found in one of Plato's late dialogues, the *Sophist*. Note that in each step of the following excerpt a genus is repeatedly divided into two species—that is, a class is divided into two smaller classes which comprise it, until the essence or definition is found.

THE METHOD OF DIVISION ELABORATED IN THE *Sophist* Plato[21]

STRANGER.[22] Meanwhile you and I will begin together and enquire into the nature of the Sophist. . . . I should like you to make out what he is and bring him to light in a discussion; for at present we are only agreed about the name, but of the thing to which we both apply the name possibly you have one notion and I another; whereas we ought always to come to an understanding about the thing itself in terms of

[19] A. H. Armstrong, *An Introduction to Ancient Philosophy*, 3rd ed. (London: Methuen and Co. Ltd., 1957), pp. 42–43. Reprinted by permission of Associated Book Publishers Ltd.

[20] G. E. R. Lloyd, *Polarity and Analogy: Two Types of Argumentation in Early Greek Thought* (Cambridge: Cambridge University Press, 1966), pp. 432–433.

[21] Plato, *Sophist*, in *The Dialogues of Plato*, trans. B. Jowett, Vol. II (New York: Random House, Inc., 1892), pp. 223–226 [218D–220A and 221B].

[22] The Stranger presents Plato's views. [Ed.]

a definition, and not merely about the name minus the definition. Now the tribe of Sophists which we are investigating is not easily caught or defined; and the world has long ago agreed, that if great subjects are to be adequately treated, they must be studied in the lesser and easier instances of them before we proceed to the greatest of all. And as I know that the tribe of Sophists is troublesome and hard to be caught, I should recommend that we practise beforehand the method which is to be applied to him on some simple and smaller thing, unless you can suggest a better way.

THEAETETUS. Indeed I cannot.

STR. Then suppose that we work out some lesser example which will be a pattern of the greater?

THEAET. Good.

STR. What is there which is well known and not great, and is yet as susceptible of definition as any larger thing? Shall I say an angler? He is familiar to all of us, and not a very interesting or important person.

THEAET. He is not.

STR. Yet I suspect that he will furnish us with the sort of definition and line of enquiry which we want.

THEAET. Very good.

STR. Let us begin by asking whether he is a man having art or not having art, but some other power.

THEAET. He is clearly a man of art.

STR. And of arts there are two kinds?

THEAET. What are they?

STR. There is agriculture, and the tending of mortal creatures, and the art of constructing or moulding vessels, and there is the art of imitation—all these may be appropriately called by a single name.

THEAET. What do you mean? And what is the name?

STR. He who brings into existence something that did not exist before is said to be a producer, and that which is brought into existence is said to be produced.

THEAET. True.

STR. And all the arts which were just now mentioned are characterized by this power of producing?

THEAET. They are.

STR. Then let us sum them up under the name of productive or creative art.

THEAET. Very good.

STR. Next follows the whole class of learning and cognition; then comes trade, fighting, hunting. And since none of these produces anything, but is only engaged in conquering by word or deed, or in preventing others from conquering, things which exist and have been already produced—in each and all of these branches there appears to be an art which may be called acquisitive.

THEAET. Yes, that is the proper name.

STR. Seeing, then, that all arts are either acquisitive or creative, in which class shall we place the art of the angler?

THEAET. Clearly in the acquisitive class.

STR. And the acquisitive may be subdivided into two parts: there is exchange, which is voluntary and is effected by gifts, hire, purchase; and the other part of acquisitive, which takes by force of word or deed, may be termed conquest?

THEAET. That is implied in what has been said.

STR. And may not conquest be again subdivided?

THEAET. How?

STR. Open force may be called fighting, and secret force may have the general name of hunting?

THEAET. Yes.

STR. And there is no reason why the art of hunting should not be further divided.

THEAET. How would you make the division?

STR. Into the hunting of living and of lifeless prey.

THEAET. Yes, if both kinds exist.

STR. Of course they exist; but the hunting after lifeless things having no special name, except some sorts of diving, and other small matters, may be omitted; the hunting after living things may be called animal hunting.

THEAET. Yes.

STR. And animal hunting may be truly said to have two divisions, land-animal hunting, which has many kinds and names, and water-animal hunting, or the hunting after animals who swim?

THEAET. True. . . .

I suspect that we have now discovered the object of our search.

STR. Then now you and I have come to an understanding not only about the name of the angler's art, but about the definition of the thing itself. One half of all art was acquisitive—half of the acquisitive art was conquest or taking by force, half of this was hunting, and half of hunting was hunting animals, half of this was hunting water animals—of this again, the under half was fishing, half of fishing was striking; a part of striking was fishing with a barb, and one half of this again, being the kind which strikes with a hook and draws the fish from below upwards, is the art which we have been seeking, and which from the nature of the operation is denoted angling or drawing up.

The development of Collection and Division constituted a major step in the evolution of Greek thought. For the first time . . .

a systematic way of reaching a definition had been discovered, and as such it was a great advance on Socrates' method of trial and error. Socrates depended on suggestions made out of the blue, but now Plato could give formal rules for definition, even if they still needed common sense and judgment in their application. That is, collection must cover the right things to get the correct *summum genus* (highest genus), and the division must be carried out along natural lines of cleavage, for which no rules can be given. But the *form* is laid down. . . .

Why did Plato think this type of definition particularly satisfactory? He had now developed the theory of the forms beyond its original scope; he believed that the forms were related among themselves in a number of ways, one of which is like a pyramid. One higher form embraces a number of subordinate ones as "animal" embraces "man," "dog," "horse," and so on. A definition then serves to map out the world of forms and shows exactly the place in it of the form being defined. . . .[23]

Aristotle later developed this method into the syllogism, a deduction of one proposition from another which shows the connection (or dependence) of the particular upon the general; and it was the syllogism which provided the necessary technique for a science of deductive proof (formal logic). Before turning to a more comprehensive examination of Aristotle's work, consideration must first be given to several other outstanding contributions made by his teacher, Plato.

[23] Reprinted with permission of The Macmillan Company from "Socrates and Plato" by Pamela M. Huby in *A Critical History of Western Philosophy,* ed. by D. J. O'Connor, p. 30. Copyright © 1964 by The Free Press of Glencoe, a Division of The Macmillan Company.

CHAPTER 10

THE GOAL OF HUMAN KNOWLEDGE:
Plato's Politics, Ethics, and Cosmology

At last I perceived that the constitution of all existing states is bad and their institutions all but past remedy without a combination of radical measures and fortunate circumstances; and I was driven to affirm, in praise of true philosophy, that only from the standpoint of such philosophy was it possible to take a correct view of public and private right, and that accordingly the human race would never see the end of trouble until true lovers of wisdom should come to hold political power, or the holders of political power should, by some divine appointment, become true lovers of wisdom.

Plato, Epistle VII

. . . You mean this commonwealth we have been founding [is only] in the realm of discourse; for I think it nowhere exists on earth.

No, I replied; but perhaps there is a pattern set up in heaven for one who desires to see it and seeing it, to found one in himself. But whether it exists anywhere or ever will exist is no matter, for this is the only commonwealth in whose politics he can ever take part.

Plato, Republic

. . . O my friends, how can there be the least shadow of wisdom where there is no harmony? There is none; but the noblest and greatest of harmonies may be truly said to be the greatest wisdom; and of this he is a partaker who lives according to reason; whereas he who is devoid of reason is the destroyer of his house and . . . is utterly ignorant of political wisdom.

Plato, Laws

. . . The god invented and gave us vision in order that we might observe the circuits of intelligence in the heaven and profit by them for the revolutions of our own thought, which are akin to them, though ours be troubled and they are unperturbed; and that by learning to know them and acquiring the power to compute them rightly according to nature, we might reproduce the perfectly unerring revolutions of the god and reduce to settled order the wandering motions in ourselves.

Plato, Timaeus

214

... The human mind cannot reach the dimension to which the soul of man belongs by way of ordinary logic. Even though Plato makes repeated attempts to rationalize faith, it is "in the form of myth" that he gives humanity the lasting symbol of his experience of ultimate reality. He became the creator of the new myth after the primitive myth of a bygone age had had its last great revival in Greek tragedy. The point around which Plato's new myth crystallized is the soul. At the very moment when the Greek mind seemed to arrive at the stage of its final [demythologization], a super-myth arose and ushered in a new age of the world. It was in this atmosphere that the religion of Christianity was able to establish itself and so find the new justification for the great paradox of its own supermundane faith. . . . It was possible [only] in a world that spoke the spiritual language of Plato.

Werner Jaeger, "The Greek Ideas of Immortality," Harvard Theological Review *Vol. 52*

Plato's *Republic* is cast in the form of a dialogue narrated by Socrates the day after it took place not far from Athens in the home of Cephalus. The participants, in addition to Socrates, were Glaucon and Adeimantus (both sons of Ariston and elder brothers of Plato); Polemarchus, Lysias, and Euthydemus (all sons of Cephalus); Thrasymachus, a prominent teacher of rhetoric; and other young followers of Socrates. In this imaginary discussion Plato deals with three questions: What is justice? Can justice be achieved through the socio-political community (the polis)? What changes have to be made in order to achieve justice? The discussion of the first question, with which the dialogue begins, is broken off when Socrates declares that he is unable to define justice in the abstract. He then suggests a new approach: Why not examine what justice is in the polis, since justice is the same both for the polis and for individuals?

. . . Justice . . . , or in Greek *dikaiosyne,* is in ordinary speech primarily a matter of relations between man and man. Hence the reasonableness of seeking it first in a community. To determine what are the right and just relations between men living in the same community will put one in a better position to determine what is meant by *a just man:* for by that phrase one means above all a man of such a character that he will naturally tend to keep the right relations between himself and his neighbor. That is what is meant by justice in the individual.[1]

To ascertain what justice is in the polis the participants in the dialogue turn to a consideration of the origins of the polis (that is, of the socio-political community in general). Socrates maintains that men live together in societies because of their need for mutual support. In a communal form of life men can perform tasks which they do best. This in turn gives rise to specialization and the division of labor, both of which make the economic order more productive. As a result of greater efficiency, the polis flourishes, a class of intellectuals and artists arises, the population increases, and the polis is ultimately compelled to annex adjoining lands. This creates the need for warriors, and from this class the rulers of the ideal commonwealth—the Guardians—will eventually be drawn.

[1] W. K. C. Guthrie, *The Greek Philosophers From Thales to Aristotle* (London: Methuen & Co. Ltd., 1950), p. 110. Reprinted by permission of Associated Book Publishers International.

THE IDEAL COMMONWEALTH
AND ITS LEADERS
F. M. Cornford [2]

. . . In Plato's century the citizen militia was found to be no match for professional soldiers; so the Guardians are, in the first instance, to be specialists, fitted by a certain combination of qualities to be at once fierce to the country's enemies and gentle to the citizens in their charge.

The fierceness is characteristic of the "spirited element" in the soul. This term covers a group of impulses manifested in anger and pugnacity, in generous indignation allied to a sense of honour, and in competitive ambition. Its virtue is courage. Spirit needs to be tamed and controlled by the rational or philosophic element, which will later be seen to predominate in the nature of the higher section of Guardians, the philosophic Rulers, whom the lower section, the warriors, will obey. But for the present the Guardians form a single group, whose elementary education and manner of life will presently be described. The philosophic Rulers will be selected from among them at a later stage and subjected to a more advanced training.

At this point the lowest order—farmers, artisans, and traders—drops almost entirely out of sight. No radical change in their mode of life is proposed. They are already performing their function of satisfying the economic needs of the whole state, and any improvements will be consequent upon the reform of their rulers. No explicit provision is made for their

[2] From *The Republic of Plato* translated by F. M. Cornford, the translator's running commentary pp. 63–64, 66–67, 88–89, 92–93, 102–103, 111–112. Oxford University Press, 1941. Reprinted by permission.

education; but unless they share in the early education provided for the Guardians, there could hardly be opportunities for promoting their most promising children to a higher order. . . .

The education of Athenian boys, for which the family, not the state, was responsible, was carried on at private day-schools. It mainly consisted of reading and writing ("Grammatic"); learning and reciting epic and dramatic poetry, lyre-playing and singing lyric poetry, the rudiments of arithmetic and geometry ("Music"); and athletic exercises ("Gymnastic"). "Music" included all the arts over which the Muses presided: music, art, letters, culture, philosophy. Since the word has now a much restricted meaning, the translation substitutes a paraphrase. This education might cease at about the age of 15 or be prolonged to 18, when the youth had two years' military training. Plato adopts the system, only removing features which will not help to produce the type of character his Guardians are to have. These simplifying reforms are part of the process of ridding the luxurious state of unhealthy elements in contemporary civilization. . . .

The ultimate end of all education is insight into the harmonious order (*cosmos*) of the whole world. This earliest stage ends here in the perception of those "images" of moral or spiritual excellences which, when combined with bodily beauty in a living person, are the proper object of love (*eros*). They are apparitions, in the sensible world, of the Forms ("Ideas"), their archetypes in the world of unseen reality, beyond the threshold which the future philosopher will cross at the next stage of his advance. . . .

The physical training suitable for a

citizen soldier is briefly contrasted with that of the professional athlete. Simplicity in life produces bodily health, just as it produced temperance in the soul. This analogy leads to the thought that an educated man should be able to manage his own life physically and morally, seldom having recourse to a doctor or a court of law. . . . Finally, it appears that physical training, no less than education in literature and the arts, really has to do with the soul. The two together should produce a harmonious development of the spirited and the philosophic elements in human character.

. . . The education above described will be given to all the Guardians up to the age of twenty. Plato next indicates the tests (recalling ordeals to which candidates for initiation are subjected) whereby a few will be selected to undergo the higher training . . . and to become Rulers whom the lower order of Guardians, now called Auxiliaries, will obey.[3]

There will thus be three orders in the state: Rulers (legislative and deliberative), Auxiliaries (executive), and Craftsmen (productive). This institution is based, not on birth or wealth, but on natural capacities and attainments; children born in any class are to be moved up or down on their merits. It is to be recommended for popular acceptance by an allegorical myth, the materials for which are drawn partly from the current belief that certain peoples were literally "autochthonous," born from the soil, partly from Hesiod's account of the Golden, Silver, and Bronze races which had succeeded one another before the present age of Iron. The ancients sup-posed all myths to be the work of poets, inspired by the Muses or consciously invented. As we have seen, myths are to convey important truths in a form that will appeal to the imagination of young or untrained minds.

The Guardians are to live with Spartan simplicity under a kind of military monasticism. The absence of private property (for the Guardians only) will remove the chief temptations to sacrifice the welfare of the whole commonwealth to personal interests. . . . They will not use their power . . . to get the best of everything for themselves. They will be happy in the exercise of their natural gifts; and in any case our aim is not the exclusive happiness of any one class of citizens. . . .

The community of goods is prescribed for the Guardians only; the industrial order, concerned with economic needs, will have private property. But the Guardians must exclude from the state both riches and poverty. Great wealth will not strengthen the state against its enemies, but weaken it by setting up an internal class-war of rich against poor. Unity is all-important, and must further be maintained by not allowing the state to grow too large, and by preserving the principle of promotion by merit; there must be no purely hereditary governing class.

The one essential is to maintain unchanged a system of education which will forestall the growth of lawlessness. To rightly educated rulers may be safely left all the usual subjects of legislation. Religious institutions will be regulated by the recognized national authority, the Oracle at Delphi, which was normally consulted before the foundation of a new city.

Once the participants in the dialogue have

[3] The training of the Rulers is discussed on pp. 224–226 [Ed.]

outlined the constitution of the ideal polis, they return to the subject of justice in the commonwealth.

The original aim in constructing an ideal state was to find in it justice exemplified on a larger scale than in the individual. Assuming that four cardinal qualities make up the whole of virtue, Plato now asks wherein consist the wisdom, courage, temperance, and justice of the state, or, in other words, of the individuals composing the state in their public capacity as citizens.

Wisdom in the conduct of state affairs will be the practical prudence or good counsel of the deliberative body. Only the philosophic Rulers will possess the necessary insight into what is good for the community as a whole. They will have "right belief" grounded on immediate knowledge of the meaning of goodness in all its forms. The Auxiliaries will have only a right belief accepted on the authority of the Rulers. Their functions will be executive, not deliberative.

The Courage of the state will obviously be manifested in the fighting force. Socrates had defined courage as knowledge of what really is, or is not, to be feared, and he had regarded it as an inseparable part of all virtue, which consists in knowing what things are really good or evil. If the only real evil is moral evil, then poverty, suffering, and all the so-called evils that others can inflict on us, including death itself, are not to be feared, since, if they are met in the right spirit, they cannot make us worse men. . . . This knowledge only the philosophic Rulers will possess to the full. The courage of Auxiliaries will consist in the power of holding fast to the conviction implanted by their education.

Temperance is not, as we might expect, the peculiar virtue of the lowest order in the state. As self-mastery, it means the subordination of the lower elements to the higher; but government must be with the willing consent of the governed, and temperance will include the unanimous agreement of all classes as to who should rule and who obey. It is consequently like a harmony pervading and uniting all parts of the whole, a principle of solidarity. . . .

Justice is the complementary principle of differentiation, keeping the parts distinct. It has been before us all through the construction of the state since it first appeared on the economic level as the division of labour based on natural aptitudes. "Doing one's own work" now has the larger sense of a concentration on one's peculiar duty or function in the community. This conception of "doing and possessing what properly belongs to one" is wide enough to cover the justice of the law-courts, assuring to each man his due rights. Injustice will mean invasion and encroachment upon the rights and duties of others.[4]

Having established the nature of justice in the polis, Plato goes on to discuss

> . . . the individual man, the original object of the inquiry. In him too three parts may be observed. Unlike the beasts, he has *nous*, the power to think and deliberate. Secondly he may exhibit courage, and it is from the same spiritual source that he feels righteous anger when he sees what appears to him a wrong. The Greeks called it *thymos*, and it may be described generally as the spirited part of

[4] From *The Republic of Plato* translated by F. M. Cornford, the translator's running commentary pp. 119–120. Oxford University Press, 1941. Reprinted by permission.

Soul

Mind – nous
spirit – thymos,
desires   eros

human character. Thirdly he has a natural
desire for material welfare and physical satisfactions. In any conflict between the reason
and the desires, the function of the *thymos*
is to side with the reason, and it is then
equivalent to strength of will. We may say
therefore that in the healthy soul, organized
for the best possible performance of the function of living, the reason must be in command, guiding and directing the policy of the
whole. The *thymos* will give a man courage to
follow out in action what reason tells him is
the best course. Likewise the physical desires
have their function to perform in the nourishment of the body and the perpetuation of
the race, but must be kept subject to the
direction of the intellect.

That is the answer to our question: "What
is justice?" in its application to the individual.
It is a state of inner harmony, of the balance
and organization of the different elements of
character. Such a balanced and organized
character cannot fail to show itself outwardly
in the performance of the kind of action which
is ordinarily considered just. On this view,
justice is a healthy condition of the spirit,
and injustice a kind of disease. With the mind
running on a line of thought like this, which
is totally different from the one pursued by
the Sophists, their questions fade into sheer
irrelevance. If justice is this healthy organization of the soul, admitting even of such a
precise description as Plato has given, the
question whether justice or injustice brings
more benefit to the man who pursues them
can scarcely any longer be raised.[5]

Somewhat later in the dialogue Socrates and
Glaucon begin to discuss whether or not the
ideal commonwealth that has previously been
described has any real chance of being established.

[5] W. K. C. Guthrie, *The Greek Philosophers: From
Thales to Aristotle* (London: Methuen & Co. Ltd.,
1950), pp. 112–113. Reprinted by permission of Associated Book Publishers International.

The Possibility of Creating the Ideal Commonwealth
Plato[6]

But really, Socrates, Glaucon continued,
if you are allowed to go on like this, I am
afraid you will forget all about the question you thrust aside some time ago:
whether a society so constituted can ever
come into existence, and if so, how. No
doubt, if it did exist, all manner of good
things would come about. I can even add
some that you have passed over. Men who
acknowledged one another as fathers, sons,
or brothers and always used those names
among themselves would never desert one
another; so they would fight with un-
equalled bravery. And if their womenfolk
went out with them to war, either in the
ranks or drawn up in the rear to intimidate
the enemy and act as a reserve in case of
need, I am sure all this would make them
invincible. At home, too, I can see many
advantages you have not mentioned. But,
since I admit that our commonwealth
would have all these merits and any number more, if once it came into existence,
you need not describe it in further detail.
All we have now to do is to convince ourselves that it can be brought into being
and how.

This is a very sudden onslaught, said I;
you have no mercy on my shilly-shallying.
Perhaps you do not realize that, after I
have barely escaped the first two waves,
the third, which you are now bringing
down upon me, is the most formidable of
all. When you have seen what it is like

[6] From *The Republic of Plato* translated by F. M.
Cornford, pp. 176–179, 205–211. Oxford University
Press, 1941. Reprinted by permission. Footnotes have
been omitted.

and heard my reply, you will be ready to excuse the very natural fears which made me shrink from putting forward such a paradox for discussion.

The more you talk like that, he said, the less we shall be willing to let you off from telling us how this constitution can come into existence; so you had better waste no more time.

Well, said I, let me begin by reminding you that what brought us to this point was our inquiry into the nature of justice and injustice.

True; but what of that?

Merely this: suppose we do find out what justice is, are we going to demand that a man who is just shall have a character which exactly corresponds in every respect to the ideal of justice? Or shall we be satisfied if he comes as near to the ideal as possible and has in him a larger measure of that quality than the rest of the world?

That will satisfy me.

If so, when we set out to discover the essential nature of justice and injustice and what a perfectly just and a perfectly unjust man would be like, supposing them to exist, our purpose was to use them as ideal patterns: we were to observe the degree of happiness or unhappiness that each exhibited, and to draw the necessary inference that our own destiny would be like that of the one we most resembled. We did not set out to show that these ideals could exist in fact.

That is true.

Then suppose a painter had drawn an ideally beautiful figure complete to the last touch, would you think any the worse of him, if he could not show that a person as beautiful as that could exist?

No, I should not.

Well, we have been constructing in dis-

course the pattern of an ideal state. Is our theory any the worse, if we cannot prove it possible that a state so organized should be actually founded?

Surely not.

That, then, is the truth of the matter. But if, for your satisfaction, I am to do my best to show under what conditions our ideal would have the best chance of being realized, I must ask you once more to admit that the same principle applies here. Can theory ever be fully realized in practice? Is it not in the nature of things that action should come less close to truth than thought? People may not think so; but do you agree or not?

I do.

Then you must not insist upon my showing that this construction we have traced in thought could be reproduced in fact down to the last detail. You must admit that we shall have found a way to meet your demand for realization, if we can discover how a state might be constituted in the closest accordance with our decription. Will not that content you? It would be enough for me.

And for me too.

Then our next attempt, it seems, must be to point out what defect in the working of existing states prevents them from being so organized, and what is the least change that would effect a transformation into this type of government—a single change if possible, or perhaps two; at any rate let us make the changes as few and insignificant as may be.

By all means.

Well, there is one change which, as I believe we can show, would bring about this revolution—not a small change, certainly, nor an easy one, but possible.

What is it?

I have now to confront what we called the third and greatest wave. But I must state my paradox, even though the wave should break in laughter over my head and drown me in ignominy. Now mark what I am going to say.

Go on.

Unless either philosophers become kings in their countries or those who are now called kings and rulers come to be sufficiently inspired with a genuine desire for wisdom; unless, that is to say, political power and philosophy meet together, while the many natures who now go their several ways in the one or the other direction are forcibly debarred from doing so, there can be no rest from troubles, my dear Glaucon, for states, nor yet, as I believe, for all mankind; nor can this commonwealth which we have imagined ever till then see the light of day and grow to its full stature. This it was that I have so long hung back from saying; I knew what a paradox it would be, because it is hard to see that there is no other way of happiness either for the state or for the individual.

Socrates, exclaimed Glaucon, after delivering yourself of such a pronouncement as that, you must expect a whole multitude of by no means contemptible assailants to fling off their coats, snatch up the handiest weapon, and make a rush at you, breathing fire and slaughter. If you cannot find arguments to beat them off and make your escape, you will learn what it means to be the target of scorn and derision.

Well, it was you who got me into this trouble.

Yes, and a good thing too. However, I will not leave you in the lurch. You shall have my friendly encouragement for what it is worth; and perhaps you may find me more complaisant than some would be in answering your questions. With such backing you must try to convince the unbelievers.

I will, now that I have such a powerful ally. . . .

Well then, I went on, enough has been said about the prejudice against philosophy, why it exists and how unfair it is, unless you have anything to add.

No, nothing on that head. But is there any existing form of society that you would call congenial to philosophy?

Not one. That is precisely my complaint: no existing constitution is worthy of the philosophic nature; that is why it is perverted and loses its character. As a foreign seed sown in a different soil yields to the new influence and degenerates into the local variety, so this nature cannot now keep its proper virtue, but falls away and takes on an alien character. If it can ever find the ideal form of society, as perfect as itself, then we shall see that it is in reality something divine, while all other natures and ways of life are merely human. No doubt you will ask me next what this ideal society is.

You are mistaken, he replied; I was going to ask whether you meant the commonwealth we have been founding.

Yes, in all points but one: our state must always contain some authority which will hold to the same idea of its constitution that you had before you in framing its laws. We did, in fact, speak of that point before, but not clearly enough; you frightened me with your objections, which have shown that the explanation is a long and difficult matter; and the hardest part is still to come.

What is that?

The question how a state can take in hand the pursuit of philosophy without disaster; for all great attempts are hazardous, and the proverb is only too true, that what is worth while is never easy.

All the same, this point must be cleared up to complete your account.

If I fail, it will not be for want of goodwill; "yourself shall see me do my uttermost." In proof of which I shall at once be rash enough to remark that the state should deal with this pursuit, not as it does now, but in just the opposite way. As things are, those who take it up at all are only just out of their childhood. In the interval before they set up house and begin to earn their living, they are introduced to the hardest part—by which I mean abstract discussions—and then, when they have done with that, their philosophic education is supposed to be complete. Later, they think they have done much if they accept an invitation to listen to such a discussion, which is, in their eyes, to be taken as a pastime; and as age draws on, in all but a very few the light is quenched more effectually than the sun of Heraclitus,[7] inasmuch as it is never rekindled.

And what would be the right plan?

Just the opposite. Boys and youths should be given a liberal education suitable to their age; and, while growing up to manhood, they should take care to make their bodies into good instruments for the service of philosophy. As the years go on in which the mind begins to reach maturity, intellectual training should be intensified. Finally, when strength fails and they are past civil and military duties, let them range at will, free from all serious business but philosophy; for theirs is to be a life of happiness, crowned after death with a fitting destiny in the other world.

You really do seem to be doing your

uttermost, Socrates. But I fancy most of your hearers will be even more in earnest on the other side. They are not at all likely to agree; least of all Thrasymachus.

Don't try to make a quarrel between Thrasymachus and me, when we have just become friends—not that we were enemies before. You and I will spare no effort until we convince him and the rest of the company, or at least take them some way with us, against the day when they may find themselves once more engaged in discussions like ours in some future incarnation.

Rather a distant prospect!

No more than a moment in the whole course of time. However, it is no wonder that most people have no faith in our proposals, for they have never seen our words come true in fact. They have heard plenty of eloquence, not like our own unstudied discourse, but full of balanced phrases and artfully matched antitheses;[8] but a man with a character so finely balanced as to be a match for the ideal of virtue in word and deed, ruling in a society as perfect as himself—that they have never yet seen in a single instance.

They have not.

Nor yet have they cared to listen seriously to frank discussion of the nobler sort that is entirely bent on knowing the truth for its own sake and leaves severely alone those tricks of special pleading in the law-court or the lecture-room which aim only at influencing opinion or winning a case.

Quite true.

These, then, were the obstacles I fore-

---

[7] Heraclitus said "there is a new sun every day," since all things change and nothing remains the same.

[8] Refers to the political speeches and tracts of Isocrates, whose school for future statesmen was a rival of Plato's Academy, and who taught his pupils a very elegant style. Plato contrives to parody one of its artificial devices with a play upon words that defies translation.

saw when, in spite of my fears, truth compelled me to declare that there will never be a perfect state or constitution, nor yet a perfect man, until some happy circumstance compels these few philosophers who have escaped corruption but are now called useless, to take charge, whether they like it or not, of a state which will submit to their authority; or else until kings and rulers or their sons are divinely inspired with a genuine passion for true philosophy. If either alternative or both were impossible, we might justly be laughed at as idle dreamers; but, as I maintain, there is no ground for saying so. Accordingly, if ever in the infinity of time, past or future, or even to-day in some foreign region far beyond our horizon, men of the highest gifts for philosophy are constrained to take charge of a commonwealth, we are ready to maintain that, then and there, the constitution we have described has been realized, or will be realized when once the philosophic muse becomes mistress of a state. For that might happen. Our plan is difficult—we have admitted as much—but not impossible.

I agree to that.

But the public, you are going to say, think otherwise?

Perhaps.

My dear Adeimantus, you must not condemn the public so sweepingly; they will change their opinion, if you avoid controversy and try gently to remove their prejudice against the love of learning. Repeat our description of the philosopher's nature and of his pursuits, and they will see that you do not mean the sort of person they imagine. It is only ill-temper and malice in oneself that call out those qualities in others who are not that way inclined; and I will anticipate you by declaring that, in my belief, the public with

a few exceptions is not of such an unyielding temper.

Yes, I agree with you there.

Will you also agree that, if it is ill-disposed towards philosophy, the blame must fall on that noisy crew of interlopers who are always bandying abuse and spiteful personalities—the last thing of which a philosopher can be guilty? For surely, Adeimantus, a man whose thoughts are fixed on true reality has no leisure to look downwards on the affairs of men, to take part in their quarrels, and to catch the infection of their jealousies and hates. He contemplates a world of unchanging and harmonious order, where reason governs and nothing can do or suffer wrong; and, like one who imitates an admired companion, he cannot fail to fashion himself in its likeness. So the philosopher, in constant companionship with the divine order of the world, will reproduce that order in his soul and, so far as man may, become godlike; though here, as everywhere, there will be scope for detraction.

Quite true.

Suppose, then, he should find himself compelled to mould other characters besides his own and to shape the pattern of public and private life into conformity with his vision of the ideal, he will not lack the skill to produce such counterparts of temperance, justice, and all the virtues as can exist in the ordinary man. And the public, when they see that we have described him truly, will be reconciled to the philosopher and no longer disbelieve our assertion that happiness can only come to a state when its lineaments are traced by an artist working after the divine pattern.

Yes, they will be reconciled when once they understand. But how will this artist set to work?

He will take society and human character as his canvas, and begin by scraping it clean. That is no easy matter; but, as you know, unlike other reformers, he will not consent to take in hand either an individual or a state or to draft laws, until he is given a clean surface to work on or has cleansed it himself.

Quite rightly.

Next, he will sketch in the outline of the constitution. Then, as the work goes on, he will frequently refer to his model, the ideals of justice, goodness, temperance, and the rest, and compare with them the copy of those qualities which he is trying to create in human society. Combining the various elements of social life as a painter mixes his colours, he will reproduce the complexion of true humanity, guided by that divine pattern whose likeness Homer saw in the men he called godlike. He will rub out and paint in again this or that feature, until he has produced, so far as may be, a type of human character that heaven can approve.

No picture could be more beautiful than that.

Are we now making any impression on those assailants who, you said, would fall upon us so furiously when we spoke in praise of the philosopher and proposed to give him control of the state? Will they be calmer now that we have told them we mean an artist who will use his skill in this way to design a constitution?

They ought to be, if they have any sense.

Yes, for what ground is left for dispute? It would be absurd to deny that a philosopher is a lover of truth and reality; or that his nature, as we have described it, is allied to perfection; or again, that given the right training, no other will be so completely good and enlightened. They will hardly give the preference to those impostors whom we have ruled out.

Surely not.

So they will no longer be angry with us for saying that, until philosophers hold power, neither states nor individuals will have rest from trouble, and the commonwealth we have imagined will never be realized.

Less angry perhaps.

I suggest that, if we go farther and assume them to be completely pacified and convinced, then, perhaps, they might agree with us for very shame.

Certainly they might.

Granted, then, that they are convinced so far, no one will dispute our other point, that kings and hereditary rulers might have sons with a philosophic nature, and these might conceivably escape corruption. It would be hard to save them, we admit; but can anyone say that, in the whole course of time, not a single one could be saved?

Surely not.

Well, one would be enough to effect all this reform that now seems so incredible, if he had subjects disposed to obey; for it is surely not impossible that they should consent to carry out our laws and customs when laid down by a ruler. It would be no miracle if others should think as we do; and we have, I believe, sufficiently shown that our plan, if practicable, is the best. So, to conclude: our institutions would be the best, if they could be realized, and to realize them, though hard, is not impossible.

Yes, that is the conclusion.

If, as Plato assumes, the philosopher-king can be found, what program of studies would lead him to that knowledge of the Good which he must possess if he is to rule? The most important subjects of study were to be geometry, solid geometry, arithmetic, astronomy, and music. These subjects have the . . .

power of turning the soul's eye from the material world to objects of pure thought. They are the only disciplines recognized by Plato as sciences in the proper sense, yielding *a priori* certain knowledge of immutable and eternal objects and truths. For him there could be no "natural science," no exact knowledge of perishable and ever-changing sensible things. The modern technique of seeking laws of phenomena in the sensible world by observation and experiment was unknown to the ancients. Knowledge, Plato thought, was to be found, not by starting from "facts" observed by the senses, framing tentative generalizations, and then returning to the facts for confirmation, but by turning away and escaping as fast as possible from all sensible appearances. Mathematical knowledge might be even better achieved by a disembodied soul which had no sensible experience. Information about the facts or events of human or natural history was not knowledge in the strict sense.

. . . After a ten-years' training in mathematics the philosophers are to be exercised from the age of 30 to 35 in Dialectic. The brief description given [earlier] is now expanded in terms of the imagery of the Cave. Mathematics will drag the prisoner out of the darkness to the point where he can look at the shadows and reflections of real things, but not yet at the things themselves or the Sun. The defect of these studies is that the various branches are not seen "synoptically" as one connected whole, but pursued separately, each starting from the assumption of its own unquestioned premises. Thus each mathematical science is a separate chain of deductive reasoning, self-consistent but not linked at the upper end to any absolutely self-evident and unconditional principle. The object of Dialectic, as applied in this field, is to secure this final confirmation and the synoptic view of all mathematical knowledge in connexion with the whole of reality. It may be conjectured that Plato contemplated a possible deduction of all pure mathematics starting from the concept of Unity, one aspect of the Good. . . .

Dialectic is also applicable to the moral Forms, which are more obviously partial aspects of the Good. Astronomy and Harmonics have just been represented as useful in so far as they conduce to a knowledge of beauty and goodness. They lead the mind to contemplate the beautiful and harmonious order manifested in the visible heavens and in the harmonies of sound. Since the purpose is the assimilation of the philosopher's soul to this order, harmony has both a physical and a moral significance and provides a transition to moral philosophy. In this field the Forms will be studied by the method of question and answer which Plato inherited from Socrates, the respondent putting forward his "hypothetical" attempts at definition, the questioner demanding an "account" of his meaning and subjecting his suggestions to examination and refutation and so leading him on to amend them. Such a procedure, covering the whole field of moral conceptions, would ideally lead up to a perfect vision of the nature of Goodness itself. Plato refuses to give a detailed account of this method for the same reasons that made him refuse to give a definition of Goodness. . . .

The whole course of education has now been traced. It remains to fix the age for entering on each successive stage.

(1) Up to 17 or 18, the early training in literature and music and in elementary mathematics will be carried on with as little compulsion as possible. (2) From 17 or 18 to 20, an intensive course of physical and military training will leave no leisure for study. (3) From 20 to 30, a select few will go through the advanced course in mathematics . . . ,

with a view to grasping the connexions between the several branches of mathematics and their relation to reality. (4) After a further selection, the years from 30 to 35 will be given wholly to Dialectic, and especially to the ultimate principles of morality. Plato once more insists on the danger of a too early questioning of these principles. (5) From 35 to 50, practical experience of life will be gained by public service in subordinate posts. (6) At 50 the best will reach the vision of the Good and thereafter divide their time between study and governing the state as the supreme council.

The question, asked [earlier] how, if ever, the ideal state might come into being, is now answered. It can exist, if the philosophic statesman can be produced and educated and given a free hand to remould society.[9]

Later in his life Plato abandoned the hope that the philosopher-king could either be found or created. In the *Laws*, one of his last dialogues, Plato hinted at one of the reasons for his abandonment of this ideal.

. . . If anyone gives too great power to anything, too large a sail to a vessel, too much food to the body, too much authority to the mind, and does not observe the mean, everything is overthrown, and, in the wantonness of excess runs in the one case to disorders, and in the other to injustice, which is called the child of excess. I mean to say, my dear friends, that there is no soul of man, young and irresponsible, who will be able to sustain the temptation of arbitrary power—no one who will not, under such circumstances, become filled with folly, that worst of diseases, and be hated by his nearest and dearest friends: when this happens his kingdom is undermined, and all his power vanishes from

him. And great legislators who know the mean should take heed of this danger.[10]

While there can be little doubt that Plato's experiences with Dionysius II in Sicily were in part responsible for this view, it has been suggested that his high regard for the rationality of man had greatly diminished. In the *Laws*, for example, Plato explicitly admitted the existence of an evil man as opposed to one who merely behaved badly out of ignorance.

. . . As to the actions of those who do evil, but whose evil is curable, in the first place, let us remember that the unjust man is not unjust of his own free will. For no man of his own free will would choose to possess the greatest of evils, and least of all in the most honourable part of himself. And the soul, as we said, is of a truth deemed by all men the most honourable. In the soul, then, which is the most honourable part of him, no one, if he could help, would admit, or allow to continue the greatest of evils. The unrighteous and vicious are always to be pitied in any case; and one can afford to forgive as well as pity him who is curable, and refrain and calm one's anger, not getting into a passion, like a woman, and nursing ill-feeling. But upon him who is incapable of reformation and wholly evil, the vials of our wrath should be poured out; wherefore I say that good men ought, when occasion demands, to be both gentle and passionate.[11]

The political implications of these observations were twofold. On the one hand, Plato concluded that "men are as unfit to rule themselves as a flock of sheep, that God, not man, is the measure of things, that man is the gods' property, and that if he wishes to be happy, he should be . . . 'abject,' before God. . . ."[12] On the

[9] From *The Republic of Plato* translated by F. M. Cornford, the translator's running commentary pp. 236, 250–251, 256. Oxford University Press, 1941. Reprinted by permission.

[10] Plato, *Laws*, in *The Dialogues of Plato*, trans. B. Jowett, Vol. II (New York: Random House, Inc., 1892), p. 466 [691D].

[11] Plato, *Laws*, in *The Dialogues of Plato*, Vol. II, p. 499 [731C].

[12] E. R. Dodds, "Plato and the Irrational," *Journal of Hellenic Studies*, Vol. LXV (1945), p. 19.

other hand, having rejected the idea of the philosopher-king, he had to find something else or someone else to govern the political community. That he found in law.

> . . . We must not entrust the government . . . to any one because he is rich, or because he possesses any other advantage, such as strength, or stature, or again birth: but he who is most obedient to the laws of the state, he shall win the palm; and to him who is victorious in the first degree shall be given the highest office and chief ministry of the gods; and the second to him who bears the second palm; and on a similar principle shall all the other offices be assigned to those who come next in order. And when I call the rulers servants or ministers of the law, I give them this name not for the sake of novelty, but because I certainly believe that upon such service or ministry depends the well- or ill-being of the state. For that state in which the law is subject and has no authority, I perceive to be on the highway to ruin; but I see that the state in which the law is above the rulers, and the rulers are the inferiors of the law has salvation, and every blessing which the Gods can confer.[13]

According to Plato, lawmakers should have certain aims and criteria in mind when legislating. Laws should

> make those who use them happy; and . . . confer every sort of good. Now goods are of two kinds: there are human and there are divine goods, and the human hang upon the divine; and the state which attains the greater, at the same time acquires the less, or, not having the greater, has neither. Of the lesser goods the first is health, the second beauty, the third strength, including swiftness in running and bodily agility generally, and the fourth is wealth. . . . Wisdom is the chief and leader of the divine class of goods, and next follows temperance; and from the union of

these two with courage springs justice, and fourth in the scale of virtue is courage. All these naturally take precedence of the other goods, and this is the order in which the legislator must place them, and after them he will enjoin the rest of his ordinances on the citizens with a view to these, the human looking to the divine and the divine looking to their leader, mind.[14]

Though Plato had come to recognize the element of irrationality that existed in man and had, for that reason, replaced the philosopher-king with the law, he did not for a moment waver in his belief that man did have the ability to use his reason to discern those divine laws which would produce right conduct and therefore happiness. Reason alone, however, was not enough. Other psychological capacities also had to play a role in the interpretation of experience.

> . . . While reason can lead us to a knowledge *about* man, or poetry, or the universe, reason cannot fill in the sketch, cannot tell what a thing is in itself. If we ask why not, Plato will answer that the word *truth* has a deeper meaning for him than we usually give it. For us, perhaps unfortunately, a "truth" is something which appears at the end of a syllogism rightly cast, an equation truly balanced and resolved, or an experiment properly controlled. Plato would, and did, call such things merely "facts," and for him a fact is not the same thing as a truth. Plato's world is, in modern terms, "value-centered"—particular facts are not perhaps false, but they do not in themselves constitute "truth," which lies rather in relevancies and relationships which have value. Thus truth and falsehood are in some sense agents: they both *produce* something in the world: the one, goodness and beauty, whether of geometical proofs, artistic reproductions or just governments; the other, evil, whether of tyrannical regimes or debauched lives. Truth belongs to a trinity of

[13] Plato, *Laws*, in *The Dialogues of Plato*, Vol. II, p. 487 [715C–D].

[14] Plato, *Laws*, in *The Dialogues of Plato*, Vol. II, p. 413 [631B–D].

values, which are at once a unity: the good, the true, and the beautiful. Perhaps, then, we can entertain in these terms a justification of Plato's everlasting gravitation toward myth: reason can lead us to the recognition of the *existence* of what is true, but it cannot really say anything about the *essence* of what is true. Despite Plato's own repeated statements that knowledge is virtue, his own actions show that he fully understood the incapacity of knowledge cast in negative and intellectualist terms (such as the proof that the soul is immortal) to lead anyone to embrace the good or act upon his knowledge.

Aristotle put it in his prosy way: the reasoning intellect knows neither motive nor fear—it cannot be inspired to action nor feel revulsion; it is the appetite which moves towards a real or apparent good or away from an evil. Without being so clinical, Plato says the same thing: no one, not even a philosopher, can be moved to contemplate the truth and to adjust his life to it simply because the reasoning faculty is operative; truth can only move men when appealing to them in the form of one of the other hypostatically united parts of Plato's trinity—as the good, or as the beautiful, or as both at once.

The myth, then, is an enactment of the *motivating* aspects of truth. . . .[15]

In the *Timaeus,* the dialogue in which Plato disclosed his cosmology and cosmogony, man's contradictory nature is expressed in mythical form.

. . . Man needs protection not really against a part of nature which threatens his life, but against the irrational part of himself which wars against his divine part, for man's soul is divine. We might call Plato's theory of purpose "opportunistic," for it contains a worldview that does not place man on the apex of creation, but nearer the bottom; yet it is cal-

culated to entice and assist him to reach the peak. Immortality and perfection are available to all.

Plato, then, views man as almost a potential god, and the universe, for all its artistic perfection, as primarily a gymnasium and academy for the human intellect. But all this is expressed in myth, and myth is the creation of poets under the influence of inspiration. Myth is, moreover, an invitation to act and think in a certain way. What is the invitation of the *Timaeus*? Its intent is plainly to lead man from what he thinks he knows to what he has forgotten (for he has seen truth face to face before birth). . . . His bodily existence is merely the compromise made with necessary causes so that divine causes may lead him to become what he is meant to be. Man, as he is today or tomorrow, in this place and time, is no more than a mythical statement of what he can become.[16]

The *Timaeus* is not only instructive regarding Plato's use of myth. It also demonstrates his reconciliation of the sensible and nonsensible worlds of Becoming and Being. The participants in the dialogue are Socrates and Timaeus, and the subject with which they begin is that of Becoming and Being.

TIMAEUS
Plato[17]

[TIMAEUS]. We must, then, in my judgment, first make this distinction: what is that which is always real and has no becoming, and what is that which is always becoming and is never real? That which is

[15] Douglas J. Stewart, "Man and Myth in Plato's Universe," *Bucknell Review*, Vol. XIII (1965), pp. 73–74. Reprinted by permission of Douglas J. Stewart.

[16] Stewart, "Man and Myth in Plato's Universe," pp. 89–90. Reprinted by permission of Douglas J. Stewart.

[17] From *Plato's Cosmology*, translated by Francis MacDonald Cornford. Reprinted by permission of the Liberal Arts Press Division of the Bobbs-Merrill Company, Inc. and Routledge & Kegan Paul Ltd.

apprehensible by thought with a rational account is the thing that is always unchangeably real; whereas that which is the object of belief together with unreasoning sensation is the thing that becomes and passes away, but never has real being. Again, all that becomes must needs become by the agency of some cause; for without a cause nothing can come to be. Now whenever the maker of anything looks to that which is always unchanging, and uses a model of that description in fashioning the form and quality of his work, all that he thus accomplishes must be good. If he looks to something that has come to be and uses a generated model, it will not be good.

So concerning the whole Heaven or World—let us call it by whatsoever name may be most acceptable to it—we must ask the question which, it is agreed, must be asked at the outset of inquiry concerning anything: Has it always been, without any source of becoming; or has it come to be, starting from some beginning? It has come to be; for it can be seen and touched and it has body, and all such things are sensible; and, as we saw, sensible things, that are to be apprehended by belief together with sensation, are things that become and can be generated. But again, that which becomes, we say, must necessarily become by the agency of some cause. The maker and father of this universe it is a hard task to find, and having found him it would be impossible to declare him to all mankind. Be that as it may, we must go back to this question about the world: After which of the two models did its builder frame it—after that which is always in the same unchanging state, or after that which has come to be? Now if this world is good and its maker is good, clearly he looked to the eternal; on the

contrary supposition (which cannot be spoken without blasphemy), to that which has come to be. Everyone, then, must see that he looked to the eternal; for the world is the best of things that have become, and he is the best of causes. Having come to be, then, in this way, the world has been fashioned on the model of that which is comprehensible by rational discourse and understanding and is always in the same state.

Again, these things being so, our world must necessarily be a likeness of something. Now in every matter it is of great moment to start at the right point in accordance with the nature of the subject. Concerning a likeness, then, and its model we must make this distinction: an account is of the same order as the things which it sets forth—an account of that which is abiding and stable and discoverable by the aid of reason will itself be abiding and unchangeable (so far as it is possible and it lies in the nature of an account to be incontrovertible and irrefutable, there must be no falling short of that); while an account of what is made in the image of that other, but is only a likeness, will itself be but likely, standing to accounts of the former kind in a proportion: as reality is to becoming, so is truth to belief. If then, Socrates, in many respects concerning many things—the gods and the generation of the universe—we prove unable to render an account at all points entirely consistent with itself and exact, you must not be surprised. If we can furnish accounts no less likely than any other, we must be content, remembering that I who speak and you my judges are only human, and consequently it is fitting that we should, in these matters, accept the likely story and look for nothing further.

SOCRATES. Excellent, Timaeus; we must

certainly accept it as you say. Your prelude we have found exceedingly acceptable; so now go on to develop your main theme.

THE MOTIVE OF CREATION

TIM. Let us, then, state for what reason becoming and this universe were framed by him[18] who framed them. He was good; and in the good no jealousy in any matter can ever arise. So, being without jealousy, he desired that all things should come as near as possible to being like himself. That this is the supremely valid principle of becoming and of the order of the world, we shall most surely be right to accept from men of understanding. Desiring, then, that all things should be good and, so far as might be, nothing imperfect, the god took over all that is visible—not at rest, but in discordant and unordered motion— and brought it from disorder into order, since he judged that order was in every way the better.

Now it was not, nor can it ever be, permitted that the work of the supremely good should be anything but that which is best. Taking thought, therefore, he found that, among things that are by nature visible, no work that is without intelligence will ever be better than one that has intelligence, when each is taken as a whole, and moreover that intelligence cannot be present in anything apart from soul. In virtue of this reasoning, when he framed the universe, he fashioned reason within soul and soul within body, to the end that the work he accomplished might be by nature as excellent and perfect as possible. This, then, is how we must say, according to the likely account, that this world came to be, by the god's providence, in very truth a living creature with soul and reason.

[18] The Demiurge or creator. [Ed.]

THE CREATOR'S MODEL

This being premised, we have now to state what follows next: What was the living creature in whose likeness he framed the world? We must not suppose that it was any creature that ranks only as a species; for no copy of that which is incomplete can ever be good. Let us rather say that the world is like, above all things, to that Living Creature of which all other living creatures, severally and in their families, are parts. For that embraces and contains within itself all the intelligible living creatures, just as this world contains ourselves and all other creatures that have been formed as things visible. For the god, wishing to make this world most nearly like that intelligible thing which is best and in every way complete, fashioned it as a single visible living creature, containing within itself all living things whose nature is of the same order. . . .

THE FOUR KINDS OF LIVING CREATURE. THE HEAVENLY GODS

Now so far, up to the birth of Time, the world had been made in other respects in the likeness of its pattern; but it was still unlike in that it did not yet contain all living creatures brought into being within it. So he set about accomplishing this remainder of his work, making the copy after the nature of the model. He thought that this world must possess all the different forms that intelligence discerns contained in the Living Creature that truly is. And there are four: one, the heavenly race of gods; second, winged things whose path is in the air; third, all that dwells in the water; and fourth, all that goes on foot on the dry land.

The form of the divine kind he made for the most part of fire, that it might be most bright and fair to see; and after the likeness of the universe he gave them well-rounded shape, and set them in the intelligence of the supreme to keep company with it, distributing them all round the heaven, to be in very truth an adornment (*cosmos*) for it, embroidered over the whole. And he assigned to each two motions: one uniform in the same place, as each always thinks the same thoughts about the same things; the other a forward motion, as each is subjected to the revolution of the Same and uniform. But in respect of the other five motions he made each motionless and still, in order that each might be as perfect as possible.

For this reason came into being all the unwandering stars, living beings divine and everlasting, which abide forever revolving uniformly upon themselves; while those stars that having turnings and in that sense "wander" came to be in the manner already described. . . .

THE TRADITIONAL GODS

As concerning the other divinities, to know and to declare their generation is too high a task for us; we must trust those who have declared it in former times: being, as they said, descendants of gods, they must, no doubt, have had certain knowledge of their own ancestors. We cannot, then, mistrust the children of gods, though they speak without probable or necessary proofs; when they profess to report their family history, we must follow established usage and accept what they say. Let us, then, take on their word this account of the generation of these gods. As children of Earth and Heaven were born Oceanus and Tethys; and of these Phorkys and Cronos and Rhea and all their company; and of Cronos and Rhea, Zeus and Hera and all their brothers and

sisters whose names we know; and of these yet other offspring.

THE ADDRESS TO THE GODS

Be that as it may, when all the gods had come to birth—both all that revolve before our eyes and all that reveal themselves in so far as they will—the author of this universe addressed them in these words:

"Gods, of gods whereof I am the maker and of works the father, those which are my own handiwork are indissoluble, save with my consent. Now, although whatsoever bond has been fastened may be unloosed, yet only an evil will could consent to dissolve what has been well fitted together and is in a good state; therefore, although you, having come into being, are not immortal nor indissoluble altogether, nevertheless you shall not be dissolved nor taste of death, finding my will a bond yet stronger and more sovereign than those wherewith you were bound together when you came to be.

"Now, therefore, take heed to this that I declare to you. There are yet left mortal creatures of three kinds that have not been brought into being. If these be not born, the Heaven will be imperfect; for it will not contain all the kinds of living being, as it must if it is to be perfect and complete. But if I myself gave them birth and life, they would be equal to gods. In order, then, that mortal things may exist and this All may be truly all, turn according to your own nature to the making of living creatures, imitating my power in generating you. In so far as it is fitting that something in them should share the name of the immortals, being called divine and ruling over those among them who at any time are willing to follow after righteousness and after you—that part, having sown it as seed and made a beginning, I will hand over to you. For the rest, do you, weaving mortal to immortal, make living beings; bring them to birth, feed them, and cause them to grow; and when they fail, receive them back again."

THE COMPOSITION OF HUMAN SOULS. THE LAWS OF DESTINY

Having said this, he turned once more to the same mixing bowl wherein he had mixed and blended the soul of the universe, and poured into it what was left of the former ingredients, blending them this time in somewhat the same way, only no longer so pure as before, but second or third in degree of purity. And when he had compounded the whole, he divided it into souls equal in number with the stars, and distributed them, each soul to its several stars. There mounting them as it were in chariots, he showed them the nature of the universe and declared to them the laws of Destiny. There would be appointed a first incarnation one and the same for all, that none might suffer disadvantage at his hands; and they were to be sown into the instruments of time, each one into that which was meet for it, and to be born as the most god-fearing of living creatures; and human nature being twofold, the better sort was that which should thereafter be called "man."

Whensoever, therefore, they should of necessity have been implanted in bodies, and of their bodies some part should always be coming in and some part passing out, there must needs be innate in them, first, sensation, the same for all, arising from violent impressions; second, desire blended with pleasure and pain, and besides these fear and anger and all the feelings that accompany these and all that are of a contrary nature; and if they should master these passions, they would live in righteousness; if they were mastered by them, in unrighteousness.

And he who should live well for his due span of time should journey back to the habitation of his consort star and there live a happy and congenial life; but failing of this, he should shift at his second birth into a woman; and if in this condition he still did not cease from wickedness, then according to the character of his depravation, he should constantly be changed into some beast of a nature resembling the formation of that character, and should have no rest from the travail of these changes, until letting the revolution of the Same and uniform within himself draw into its train all that turmoil or fire and water and air and earth that had later grown about it, he should control its irrational turbulance by discourse of reason and return once more to the form of his first and best condition.

HUMAN SOULS SOWN IN EARTH AND THE PLANETS

When he had delivered to them all these ordinances, to the end that he might be guiltless of the future wickedness of any one of them, he sowed them, some in the Earth, some in the Moon, some in all the other instruments of time. After this sowing he left it to the newly made gods to mold mortal bodies, to fashion all that part of a human soul that there was still need to add and all that these things entail, and to govern and guide the mortal creature to the best of their powers, save in so far as it should be a cause of evil to itself.

THE CONDITION OF THE SOUL WHEN NEWLY INCARNATED

When he had made all these dispositions, he continued to abide by the wont of his own nature; and meanwhile his sons took heed to their father's ordinance and set about obeying it. Having received the immortal principle of a mortal creature, imitating their own maker, they borrowed from the world portions of fire and earth, water and air, on condition that these loans should be repaid, and cemented together what they took, not with the indissoluble bonds whereby they were themselves held together, but welding them with a multitude of rivets too small to be seen and so making each body a unity of all the portions. And they confined the circuits of the immortal soul within the flowing and ebbing tide of the body.

STRUCTURE OF THE HUMAN BODY: HEAD AND LIMBS

Copying the round shape of the universe, they confined the two divine revolutions in a spherical body—the head, as we now call it—which is the divinest part of us and lord over all the rest. To this the gods gave the whole body, when they had assembled it, for its service, perceiving that it possessed all the motions that were to be. Accordingly, that the head might not roll upon the ground with its heights and hollows of all sorts, and have no means to surmount the one or to climb out of the other, they gave it the body as a vehicle for ease of travel; that is why the body is elongated and grew four limbs that can be stretched out or bent, the god contriving thus for its traveling. Clinging and supporting itself with these limbs, it is able to make its way through every region, carrying at the top of us the habitation of the most divine and sacred part. Thus and for these reasons legs and arms grow upon us all. And the gods, holding that the front is more honorable and fit to lead than the back, gave us movement for the most part in that direction. So man must needs have

the front of the body distinguished and unlike the back; so first they set the face on the globe of the head on that side and fixed in it organs for all the forethought of the soul, and appointed this, our natural front, to be the part having leadership.

THE EYES AND THE MECHANISM OF VISION

First of the organs they fabricated the eyes to bring us light. . . .

ACCESSORY CAUSES CONTRASTED WITH THE PURPOSE OF SIGHT AND HEARING

. . . Sight . . . in my judgment is the cause of the highest benefits to us in that no work of our present discourse about the universe could ever have been spoken, had we never seen stars, Sun, and sky.[19] But as it is, the sight of day and night, of months and the revolving years, of equinox and solstice, has caused the invention of number and bestowed on us the notion of time and the study of the nature of the world; whence we have derived all philosophy, than which no greater boon has ever come or shall come to mortal man as a gift from heaven. This, then, I call the greatest benefit of eyesight; why harp upon all those things of less importance, for which one who loves not wisdom, if he were deprived of the sight of them, might "lament with idle moan"? For our part, rather let us speak of eyesight as the cause of this benefit, for these ends: the god invented and gave us vision in order that we might observe the circuits of intelligence in the heaven and profit by them for the revolutions of our own thought, which are akin to them, though ours be troubled and they are un-

[19] Compare with the remarks made by Bruno Snell in Chapter 5, pp. 113–114. [Ed.]

perturbed; and that, by learning to know them and acquiring the power to compute them rightly according to nature, we might reproduce the perfectly unerring revolutions of the god and reduce to settled order the wandering motions in ourselves.

Of sound and hearing once more the same account may be given: they are a gift from heaven for the same intent and purpose. For not only was speech appointed to this same intent, to which it contributes in the largest measure, but also all that part of Music that is serviceable with respect to the hearing of sound is given for the sake of harmony; and harmony, whose motions are akin to the revolutions of the soul within us, has been given by the Muses to him whose commerce with them is guided by intelligence, not for the sake of irrational pleasure (which is now thought to be its utility), but as an ally against the inward discord that has come into the revolution of the soul, to bring it into order and consonance with itself. Rhythm also was a succor bestowed upon us by the same hands to the same intent, because in the most part of us our condition is lacking in measure and poor in grace.

There is one final aspect of the *Timaeus* which deserves attention. In it Plato reveals what he considers to be the ultimate constituents of matter. Like many thinkers in the fifth century B.C., he thought that everything in the visible world was made up of the four elements —earth, water, air, and fire. He did not believe, however, that these were the *ultimate* constituents of matter. In the words of a twentieth-century classical scholar, Plato was convinced that each of the four elements

consists of minimum particles in the shape of one of the regular solids, which for this reason were later known as the Platonic figures: fire is composed of tetrahedra or three-sided pyra-

mids, air of octahedra, water of icosahedra, and earth of cubes. Now the surfaces of the first three are equilateral triangles and that of the cube can be divided into two right-angled isosceles triangles. These latter, and the right-angled scalene which is half an equilateral triangle, Plato takes as the simplest forms of plane figure. The chemical transformation of one element into another is possible because the particles of three of the elements are composed of identical surfaces, so that, if they should be broken up, the surfaces can re-combine in different ways to form any other of the regular solids so constructed. When the heat of fire dries up a puddle of water, the small, sharp, mobile fire-pyramids have pierced the icosahedra of water and split them into their component triangles, and in Plato's own words, "When water is divided into parts by fire, it can give rise to one particle of fire and two of air by combination." In this case the twenty faces of each water-particle are regrouped as two octahedra and one pyramid.

. . . The particles of each element have the same shape, but they exist in different sizes, related to each other in strict mathematical proportion, because composed of a different number of identical triangles. This accounts for the different sub-forms of each main element, for the element "water" in fact stands for all liquids, and "air" for all gases or vapours. Thus water, oil, wine, acid have the same atomic shape but different atomic size.

These geometrical shapes are imposed by the controlling Reason on what Plato calls the Receptacle of becoming, a mysterious conception, as he admits himself. It is "of a nature invisible and characterless, all-receiving, partaking in some puzzling way of the intelligible and very hard to apprehend." Now he calls it space, and again he compares it to a plastic material or matrix. It is not empty space, for it is full of random and disorderly motion, a field of undisciplined energy. This it is which is reduced to order by the imposition upon it of geometrical figures which cause it to appear now fiery, now watery, now airy and now earthy.[20]

While many scientists long decried this view of nature as a bane to scientific advance, it has now been demonstrated that, in fact, Plato's belief that nature can ultimately be reduced to geometrical forms (or mathematical formulae) was one of the most powerful stimuli of the second scientific revolution (which occurred in the seventeenth century). If Plato's view of the nature and arrangement of the constituents of the visible world received only overdue praise from scientists and historians, it did at least have the immediate effect of resolving the problem of the relationship between *nomos* and *physis*. He accomplished this by bringing the two concepts together. Once united they constituted an embryonic form of natural law—a concept which has played a dynamic role in the Western cultural tradition from classical antiquity until today.

PLATO'S RESOLUTION OF THE
Nomos-Physis CONTROVERSY
W. K. C. Guthrie[21]

. . . Far from there being any contrast between nature and the world of law and order, nature and law [according to Plato] are the same thing. Reason and order are not merely human characteristics, for the nature of the universe is such that it can only have been the product of a reason existing antecedently to make it. But if

[20] W. K. C. Guthrie, *Twentieth Century Approaches to Plato,* University of Cincinnati Classical Lectures in Memory of Louise Taft Semple, Vol. I, 1967, pp. 11-12. Reprinted by permission of Princeton University Press.
[21] W. K. C. Guthrie, *In the Beginning: Some Greek Views on the Origins of Life and the Early State of Man* (London: Methuen & Co. Ltd., 1957), pp. 107–109. Reprinted by permission of American Book Publishers International.

the origin of the Universe can be revealed as the unfolding of an ordered plan, then to make any distinction between life according to nature and life according to law, and try to exalt either at the expense of the other, is to talk nonsense. Law, order and art are the products of intelligence and intelligence is the first and highest manifestation of nature. Such a metaphysic, if it can be proved, will have an obvious bearing on the significance of human life.

We can now see better what Plato is aiming at in the cosmogony of the *Timaeus*. He was summoning all the resources of contemporary science to prove that the major events of the cosmos could only be explained on the assumption that behind them lay a conscious and designing Mind, in other words that they were a divine creation. If in this he was in conflict with the Ionians, he had on his side the mathematical and astronomical studies of the Pythagoreans, whose whole outlook was more sympathetic to his own. Both he and they went further. Not only was the Universe created by a god, it was itself a living creature, and the sun, moon and stars the highest forms of life within it. The divinity of the heavenly bodies was of course a traditional article of Greek belief, and it had been a truly shocking thing when the Ionian scientist Anaxagoras announced that the sun was only an incandescent lump of rock.

There is a contrast here between the Greek way of thinking and our own. We tend to associate life and reason with freedom of action. Instead of following a regular and to all appearances predestined track, the living creature will exhibit a multiplicity of movements and activities. When we see something everlastingly revolving in a circle, we do not jump to the conclusion that it is a living and divine being. For Plato on the other hand there was a perfect analogy between rational thought and circular motion. If like him we wanted to argue that the planets, as well as the fixed stars, were alive and divine, we might think it evidence in favour of our view that they do not appear to travel monotonously in circles, but can be seen to deviate, go back on their tracks, and even stand still. Yet to Plato this was the scandal that had to be removed. In order to show that their movements were inspired by reason, he had to explain away their irregularities and demonstrate that, contrary to appearances, they were really moving all the time in perfect circles.

In this world-view of Plato's, the blindly mechanistic force of "necessity," which governed the Ionian cosmogonies, is not abolished altogether. It persists, but is almost entirely subordinated by the mind of the divine creator. Almost, but not quite. Plato is not a monist, nor is his god omnipotent. He has to work on a pre-existing material with certain given characteristics, and although in general he impresses it with the stamp of his own reason and goodness, there remains an irreducible minimum of resistance which accounts for the disorder and evil in the world. As for man, his possession of reason relates him to God and gives him infinite possibilities, but being associated with a material body he is subject also to the "necessity" of physical forces and finds it difficult to realize his potentialities completely.

The Greeks drew the analogy between microcosm and macrocosm, man and the Universe, with a seriousness and a literalness which we have outgrown. Plato fol-lowed the Pythagoreans in holding that the pre-eminent characteristic of the world was its ordered beauty (that is the meaning of the Greek word *cosmos*), and that the soul of man, being rational, was capable of becoming a *cosmos* in miniature. The order and regularity in the world were evidence of its divine origin, an origin in which human beings shared. Hence the true end of man, as Plato puts it elsewhere, was to "assimilate himself to God."

To sum up, his aim in the *Timaeus* was to make use of the regularities of the heavenly bodies, and their effects in the cosmos as a whole, in order to demonstrate that the whole Universe works in accordance with a rational and moral law. By showing forth the same rational and moral law in terms of human life, men will not be acting contrary to nature as the Sophists thought; they will be fulfilling their own being as parts of nature, and in this true self-fulfilment is to be found the greatest happiness both for individuals and communities.

Plato, then, leaves us with a number of questions: Are all men capable of acquiring knowledge of the rational law which governs the universe? Will such knowledge lead to right conduct and happiness for the individual and to the rule of justice within the body politic? And, finally, what are the specific rules of conduct embodied in this law? Because the Platonic heritage as a whole has been of supreme importance in shaping the intellectual techniques with which Western man organizes his experience, Western intellectuals from Plato's time until today have had to grapple with the many problems which he left unresolved. The first to undertake this task was his greatest student, Aristotle.

CHAPTER 11

THE SEARCH FOR KNOWLEDGE IN THE SENSORY WORLD:

The Philosophy of Aristotle

It is impossible for the same thing at the same time both to belong and not to belong to the same thing and in the same respect.

Aristotle's Law of Noncontradiction

. . . My argument is that the breakdown of religion and law stimulated the growth of the methodological or procedural aspect of logic which ultimately came to fruition in the Aristotelian syllogism as a decision-making technique for ordinary language, and that this formalization of logic was foreshadowed by the cruder decision-making procedures of rhetoric and informal logic as they were used by Cleon and Diodotus in the Mytilene Debate, when, in the midst of mass death and despair, the force of moral precept and legal precedent was no longer binding on men.

John M. Schram, "Prodicus' 'Fifth-Drachma Show Lecture' and 'The Mytilene Debate' of Thucydides: An Account of the Intellectual and Social Antecedents of Formal Logic," Antioch Review, *Vol. XXV*

. . . It does not seem to be merely a matter of ethnocentric prejudice to say that in two areas at least the Greeks developed intellectual techniques that were historically unique, and that possessed intrinsic empirical advantages which led to their widespread adoption by most subsequent literate cultures: the first area is epistemological, where the Greeks developed a new kind of logical method; and the second area is that of taxonomy, where the Greeks established our accepted categories in the fields of knowledge—theology, physics, biology, and so forth.

In the former, Plato is essentially an heir of the long Greek enterprise of trying to sort out truth, *episteme,* from current opinion, *doxa.* This epistemological awareness seems to coincide with the widespread adoption of writing, probably because the written word suggests an ideal of definable truths which have an inherent autonomy and permanence quite different from the phenomena of the temporal flux and of contradictory verbal usages. In oral cultures, words . . . may hardly be conceived of as separate entities, divorced from the rest of the sentence and its social context. But once given the physical reality of writing, they take on a life of their own; and much Greek thought was concerned with attempting to explain their meanings satisfactorily and to relate these meanings to some ultimate principle of rational order in the universe, to the *logos.*

It was, of course, Plato and Aristotle who conceived that there might be a special intellectual procedure for this process; who imagined the possibility of a system of rules for thinking itself, rules which were quite distinct from the particular problem being thought about and which offered a more reliable access to truth than current opinion. . . . [For Plato this method involved] analysis of a problem into its constituent elements, and . . . subsequent rational synthesis. . . .

The same process of dissection into abstract categories, when applied not to a particular argument but to the ordering of all elements of experience into separate areas of intellectual activity, leads to the Greek division of knowledge into autonomous cognitive disciplines which has since become universal in Western culture and which is of cardinal importance in differentiating literate and non-literate cultures. Plato made one important step in this direction, for he developed both the word and the notion of theology to designate a separate field of knowledge. . . .

Plato, however, was too much the disciple of Socrates to take the compartmentalization of knowledge very far. This was left to his pupil, Aristotle, and to his school; by the time of the death of Aristotle in 322 B.C. most of the categories in the field of philosophy, natural science, language and literature had been delineated, and the systematic collection and classification of data in all of them had begun.

Jack Goody and Ian Watt, "The Consequences of Literacy." Reprinted by permission of the editors from Comparative Studies in Society and History, *Vol. V*

In a sense, with Aristotle, the achievement of the thinkers of the Hellenic Age had been completed. Once human reason sees clearly the ideal of system, which can order the many generalizations and conceptions that man derives from sensation and memory, there can be an attempt to find a master plan for discovering or creating a systematic order. In the beginning of the history of Greek thought, philosophers had brilliant insights. They began to recognize different aspects of being—matter, form, flux, substance—abruptly realized in vivid and original expressions of new thought. Their insights are not accompanied by very clear analysis, and they did not make the distinctions which by now have become so firmly embedded in our language and common sense.

As later thinkers continued their exploration and consolidated earlier gains, four ways of ordering concepts systematically came into the foreground. And the history of philosophy from ancient Greece to the present day seems to confirm the notion that the four most effective and persistently attempted ways of ordering our many concepts are just these four. (1) Analysis into elements, (2) synthesis into formal hierarchies that converge at some highest law or form, (3) intuitive recognition of creativity and process in their continuity, and (4) classification as type-specimens without regard for size of these or their relation to a single hierarchical scheme. These four ways are destined to endure as man applies reason to understanding the total range of being throughout later Western philosophy.

Robert S. Brumbaugh, The Philosophers of Greece

. . . [Aristotle's physics] was a serious physics, a consistent and highly elaborated ideation of natural phenomena. It started from experience apprehended by common

sense, and moved through definition, classification, and deduction to logical demonstration. Its instrument was the syllogism rather than the experiment or the equation.
Its goal was to achieve a rational explanation of the world by showing how the myriad
subordinate means are adapted to the larger end of order. Its operations were suited
to these interests. Direct and minute observation, classification of forms by species,
analysis of how the part serves the whole—these are useful acts up to a point in natural
history, as the description of life and its environment was called until the nineteenth
century. Not till then was biology ready to transcend the Aristotelian sense of purpose
in nature and follow physics into objectivity. Aristotelian physics, too, had immense
humane advantages denied to that which has supervened since Galileo. It easily fell
in with a sense of Providence in nature. As the physical system sheltering the world
view of Islam, Judaism, and Christianity, it became the scientific orthodoxy of all
three religions which shaped the West in its emergence from the dark centuries after
Rome. For Aristotelian physics made sense of the world and strengthened the hands
of men of God and all those striving to redeem civilization, culture, and truth from
barbarism.

There was only one trouble. It was wrong. For however congenial Aristotelian physics was to the self-knowledge of the minds that elaborated it, nature is not like that,
not an enlargement of common sense arrangements, not an extension of consciousness
and human purposes. . . .

Charles Coulston Gillispie, The Edge of Objectivity

During the fourth century B.C. the polis-
community gave way to an empire. In the first
half of the century, as we have seen, the political
and military obligations of the citizens were
taken over by professionals. Conflicts between
the city-states did not end, and Persian interference and threat of invasion was a factor with
which the Greeks had constantly to reckon. In
spite of internecine warfare, attempts were
made to unite poleis in regional federations.

Economic decline continued throughout most
of the century, largely as a result of former
colonies establishing their own industries and
producing their own wine and olive oil. While
mainland Greece experienced a contraction of
its export markets, the population which had to
be supported increased. The economic reces-
sion was made worse by the fact that the Greeks
more and more looked upon work as a dis-
honorable form of activity.

The middle of the fourth century B.C. witnessed the rise of two new powers in the Mediterranean. In the west, Carthage was beginning
to emerge as an economic and military power,
while to the north the Macedonians were being
united by Philip II. The Macedonians were a
Greek-speaking people, but they had not shared
the historical experience of the Greeks living in
the city-states. Their society had remained on
the more primitive agrarian-tribal level. The
Macedonian Greeks were considered "barbarians" (that is, non-Greeks) by their southern
cousins. Once Philip had united his people, he
invaded and conquered the city-states (338
B.C.). The poleis were allowed to maintain a high
degree of autonomy under the hegemony of
Macedonia.

When Philip was assassinated in 336 B.C., he
was succeeded by his son, Alexander, a young
man of eighteen who was deeply devoted to
Greek culture. A war against Persia, originally
planned by Philip as a means of uniting the

Greeks firmly under Macedonian leadership, launched Alexander on a series of military campaigns that were to result in the conquest and Hellenization of the Near East and earn him the title of Alexander the Great. During the course of his thirteen-year career he subdued a territory that extended from Greece and Egypt to Turkestan and northern India. To this vast area Alexander, his army, and retinue of officials brought Greek culture. In addition, he and his successors founded a large number of new cities, Alexandria in Egypt being the most important of them. Alexander made himself an oriental despot as King of Persia, thus introducing into the Western tradition a new kind of kingship—one which was divinely sanctioned. With Alexander's transformation of the eastern Mediterranean world there began that period which historians designate as the Hellenistic Age.[1]

Aristotle, who was born in Stagira (Ionia) in 384 B.C., was a witness to this momentous transformation. Yet his work does not seem to reflect the changes that were taking place. This is surprising at first glance for a number of reasons. Aristotle's interest in the materially real world has always made him appear far more down-to-earth than the Greek philosophers of the late fifth and early fourth centuries B.C.

[1] While most historians agree that this particular historical period began during Alexander's reign (336–323 B.C.), there is no consensus regarding its termination. Some argue that it ended in the second century B.C. while others maintain that it lasted until the second century A.D.

"Hellenistic" should not be confused with "Hellenic." This latter term refers to Greece during the fifth and early fourth centuries B.C. The former designates the period which began during the reign of Alexander.

The Alexander Mosaic, first century B.C. This floor mosaic from Pompeii is almost certainly a copy of a Greek painting of the late fourth century B.C. The Battle of Issus, in which Alexander defeated Darius of Persia, is depicted in a range of four colors: red, brown, black, and white. By using tiny bits of colored stone, the mosaicist was able to achieve natural perspective effects. (Alinari)

Furthermore, his father, once court physician of the rulers of Macedonia, had been close to those who were transforming the socio-political environment. In addition, Aristotle himself served as Alexander's tutor for six years. It also seems that he was expected to follow in his father's footsteps and become a physician.

In spite of this background, Aristotle's thought was a product of the classical Greek polis that had in fact lost those very characteristics which had made it a unique way of life. The decisive reason for his being something of an anachronism was almost certainly his relationship with Plato. At the age of seventeen (367 B.C.) he went to Athens to study at the Academy. He remained there until Plato's death in 347 B.C. It was this twenty years under the direct influence of Plato that determined the direction his thought was to take.

After Plato's death the Academy was led by Speusippos, a man who was interested primarily in mathematics and Pythagoreanism. For this reason Aristotle, who was more concerned with the medical branch of science, left Athens. He resided for some time near Troy, where he made both political and biological investigations, taught for a while in Mytilene, and in 342 B.C. was called to the court of Philip of Macedonia to instruct Alexander. After six years with Alexander, Aristotle returned to Athens to found a school of his own, the Lyceum. For twelve years he lectured on philosophy (logic, epistemology, and metaphysics), rhetoric, politics, and ethics. He did his lecturing in the Peripatos, a covered walk—hence his school of philosophy was called "Peripatetic." Both he and his students were involved in a wide variety of research projects. When Alexander died in 323 B.C., Aristotle turned over the direction of the Lyceum to Theophrastus and fled Athens for fear that he would be subject to reprisals by the anti-Macedonian faction which had seized power. He died a year later in Chalcis on the island of Euboea.

In his intellectual work, it should be remembered, Aristotle never ceased altogether being a Platonist. What distinguished these two philosophers most from each other was their method and outlook.

. . . Where Plato is rationalistic, dogmatic, and contemptuous of the world of the senses, Aristotle is empirical, cautious, and anxious to consult all relevant facts and opinions before making up his mind. This seems to have been a temperamental difference between the two philosophers, but it is an important one. The history of human knowledge since their time has shown decisively that *a priori* dogmatizing gives no lasting results in the search for truth, and that cautious empiricism does in the end give genuine insight into the nature of things. That Aristotle failed to get nearer the truth than he did must be put down to the victory of his Platonic training over his scientific spirit.

Associated with this difference in intellectual attitude is a difference of approach and emphasis. Roughly speaking, Plato tried to deduce the nature of the universe from what he thought to be the nature of human knowledge. Aristotle started with the facts of nature as he saw them, and reduced them to a system. This contrast is oversimplified, but it brings out an important difference between them. Unfortunately, as we shall see, Aristotle's view of human knowledge was not entirely consistent. He inherited too much from Plato to enable him to view knowledge as just one more aspect of nature.

Plato had believed that only those things that were universal, permanent and changeless, could be genuine objects of knowledge. What was particular, mutable, and contingent might be the object of mere belief or guesswork but it could not, properly speaking, be known. Aristotle was sufficiently influenced by Plato to agree with this view. But as we shall see, he interpreted it in his own way. In particular, he rejects the Platonic theory of forms. At some places in his writings, indeed, he seems inclined to allow some value to the theory. But in general he rejects it decisively. His criticisms are scattered through his writings and are nowhere neatly and clearly summarized. Some of his points are trivial and some are very difficult to understand. The most important of them amount to the following:

1. Plato nowhere explained the relation of forms to the concrete individual things of the sensible world. He used merely metaphorical terms like "participation" (*methexis*) and "imitation" (*mimesis*) to describe this relationship. These do not explain in any way how form and thing are connected. They are, as Aristotle himself says, "mere empty phrases and poetic metaphors."

2. The hypothesis of the existence of forms does not account for the multiplicity of things in the world, nor for the coming into existence of these things or the ways in which they change. In short, the theory adds nothing to our knowledge.

3. The theory is, in any case, open to serious logical objections. Aristotle details these. They all stem from trying to separate the essential characters of things from the things themselves.

It has sometimes been suggested that many of Aristotle's criticisms of Plato are unfair and that the theory he attacked is only a caricature of Plato's real views. This may be so. But Aristotle was a pupil of Plato for many years and we may reasonably suppose him to have been better acquainted with Plato's meaning than any scholar of today. The upshot of his critique is this: Plato was correct in supposing that the only possible objects of genuine knowledge must be general or universal. But these objects cannot exist apart from the concrete individual things or facts in which they are found in human experience. . . .[2]

[2] Reprinted with permission of The Macmillan Company from "Aristotle" in *A Critical History of Western Philosophy* by D. J. O'Connor, p. 47. Copyright © 1964 by The Free Press of Glencoe, a Division of The Macmillan Company.

Because Aristotle believed that the objects of knowledge were universals,[3] he was as concerned with language and definition as Plato had been. From this initial preoccupation Aristotle developed formal logic (the science of deductive proof), an epistemology (theory of knowledge), and a metaphysics (theory of being). In the first area, logic, he made what many consider his greatest contribution. His invention of logic reveals that he was the first to be aware of the two thought processes of abstraction and proof.

Abstraction is the art of perceiving a common quality or qualities in different things and forming a general idea therefrom. We abstract, for instance, when we see churches, ranch houses and skyscrapers as buildings; when we see cartwheels, automobile tires and hula hoops as circles; when we see cows, cats and dogs as animals.

Proof is the art of arguing from premises to a conclusion in such a way that no flaws can be picked in any step of the argument. . . . But in order to have premises to start with, [the Greeks] invoked another mental process called induction. Whereas abstraction reveals a common denominator in *diverse* things—for instance, cats and dogs are both animals—induction reveals it in the *same class* of things. From our observation of dogs, we make the induction that *all dogs bark*; or from our observation of Doberman pinschers, we induce that *all Doberman pinschers are dogs*. Using the information in these two premises, we can, by a reasoning process known as deduction, prove that *all Doberman pinschers bark*. This inescapable conclusion, or theorem, can also have a corollary, a statement that necessarily follows from it. A corollary in this case would be: *My neighbor's Doberman pinscher barks.*

[3] In Plato's philosophy the words "Form" or "Idea" are used, whereas in Aristotelian philosophy the word "universal" is employed. "Form" and "Idea," on the one hand, and "universal," on the other, have much in common but are not identical. This distinction will be discussed at greater length later in the chapter.

The Greeks devised still another technique for achieving a proof, the method which we call by its Latin term *reductio ad absurdum* (reduction to the absurd). Through this we prove the validity of a premise by deliberately assuming the opposite to be true and then demonstrating that this opposite premise cannot stand up. Suppose that Mr. Smith, the neighbor who owns the Doberman pinscher, sets out to examine a complaint that his dog barks constantly. He starts with two premises: that *all dogs are animals* and that *all animals must eat and sleep*. From these he deduces the conclusion that *all dogs must eat and sleep*. He then sets up two more premises: that *some dogs bark constantly* (the reverse of what he wishes to prove) and that *dogs that bark constantly cannot eat or sleep*. From this latter set of premises he deduces that *some dog does not eat or sleep*. This conclusion, however, is absurd since it contradicts the earlier one that *all dogs must eat and sleep*. Smith then reexamines all four premises. The only questionable one is that *some dog barks constantly*. Since it led him to an absurd conclusion it must be false, and the opposite of it— that *no dog barks constantly*—must be true. He has thus proved—to his own satisfaction if not to his sleepless neighbor's—what he initially set out to prove.

As may be seen from Smith's mental journey, the principles of Greek proof are really no more than a formalization of the thought processes which we use when trying to present an orderly argument. . . .[4]

The principles which inform these thought processes are designated as the basic postulates of logic—the law of identity (*A* is *A*), the law of contradiction (*A* cannot both be *B* and not be *B*),[5] and the law of excluded middle (*A* either is or is not *B*). While all human beings reason with this set of intuitively accepted postulates, it was Aristotle who first became fully aware of them. Once this awareness had developed, he worked out a theory of knowledge; from this he was able, for the first time, to make explicit the rules of logic.

EPISTEMOLOGY AND LOGIC
Barbara Jancar[6]

Aristotle, like many of his fellow Greeks, firmly believed in man's capacity to know. For him it may be said that the central fact in the universe was that man was able to know and understand the universe in which he found himself. As the function of a knife was to cut, the function of man was to know. The world would have existed if man had not been born into it, but it would not have been *known* to exist. Thus, man and man's knowledge were the focus of Aristotle's philosophy.

It is not at all obvious that man can know the world about him. Plato believed the world of phenomena was unknowable. In modern times, since Descartes first made that puzzling statement, "I think, therefore I am," in the seventeenth century, there has been a growing distrust in man's abilities to know anything at all. Science has revealed the existence of tiny particles which are invisible to the naked eye. Some of them cannot be seen by any means. Only their paths can be traced. Psychology has shown us that man's outlook on the world is conditioned by his environment and upbringing, and that it is entirely subjective. It would seem as if we were in a world which was forever out of our reach.

[4] Reprinted by permission of *Time-Life Books* from the *Life* Science Library volume, *Mathematics*. © 1965 Time Inc.

[5] This is frequently referred to as the law of non-contradiction.

[6] From *Review Notes and Study Guide to the Philosophy of Aristotle* by Barbara Jancar, pp. 22–26. Copyright © 1964 by Simon & Schuster, Inc. Reprinted by permission of Simon & Schuster, Inc.

Aristotle held that there was nothing unnatural or even supernatural in man's ability to know. Man was a rational animal as a bird was a winged animal. It was no more surprising that a man should know than that a bird should fly. As birds fly in formations which are suited to their function of flying, so man lives in cities which are suited to his function of knowing. Knowing requires communication and communication requires language. Society provides the necessary condition for man's knowing, namely, the possibility of communication through language.

In Aristotle's view to be able to say exactly what something is, is *to know*. It does not mean "to reason." We reason about something before we know what it is. Once we can say what a thing is, there is no longer any need to discuss it. It is no coincidence that the Greek words for "to know" and "to see" are closely related. "I have seen" in Greek is the same thing as "I know." Knowing is seeing things as they are. When our newspapers talk about "clarifying" a situation, meaning by this that they want to enable us to understand it better, Aristotle would have understood just what they mean.

"*To know*" means to be able to see something so that you can say exactly what it is. Unfortunately, however, it is not easy to say precisely what something is. If we want to say what the maple standing just outside the front door of our house is, we can say what all maples are, and make a few statements about how this tree is different from other maples we have seen. Yet we have not said exactly what this particular maple *is*. We have only been talking in generalities. Life deals with individual concrete things, but reason deals with universal concepts. How can you bridge the gap between the two?

Plato tried to bridge the gap by his dialectic method of discussion. He believed that if you talk round a subject long enough, and look at it from every angle, suddenly the intrinsic characteristic, i.e., general meaning, of that subject will shine through. You will "know" what justice is, for example. Aristotle thought this method a good one in matters which did not concern things which "were always or for the most part" in a particular way. Plato's method was good for ethics, for instance, but Aristotle did not feel it satisfied the requirements of science, or rather theoretical science, such as physics or mathematics.

Aristotle called the method he invented analytics; we call it logic. Analysis means "breaking up." The analytic is the breaking up of an argument into its individual terms and the examination of what those terms mean. Analysis is thus not a science in its own right or a particular method of approach. It is a process common to all the sciences. It is the basis of scientific investigation, because it answers most closely the requirements of the process of thought. We reason by the addition and subtraction of terms in a thought sequence.

The process of analysis falls into two parts. There is first the process of discovery and then the process of demonstration. During the process of discovery we conduct an empirical investigation of the subject matter. We collect data and material necessary for the final proof. Reason enters into this first process insofar as we choose that material which is relevant to our subject. But it is when we come to the proof that the correctness of our thought sequence becomes vitally important. How to determine whether the thought sequence is a good one or a poor one? Aristotle's answer was the syllogism.

Aristotle's definition of a syllogism is as follows. "A syllogism is a formulation of words in which, when certain assumptions are made, something other than what has been assumed necessarily follows from the fact that the assumptions are such." An example of the simplest kind of syllogism is this: when A equals B, and B equals C, then A equals C. There are others which are much more complex. The advantage of the syllogism is that it expresses the relation of the terms with which we reason to one another without referring to any subject matter. A, B, and C can be anything. No matter what they represent, the thought sequence will be a good one, as long as you keep A, B, and C in their proper place.

The value of Aristotle's invention cannot be over-emphasized. By using the variables, A, B, and C, he broke up the process of thought into its several parts. The danger lies in the fact that it is possible to reason from false premises to a logically correct conclusion. Right thinking can become independent of what is thought.

In the use of the syllogism, however, it is impossible to let the variables stand. There comes a time when they have to represent something, if the thought process is to be meaningful. In the *Categories,* Aristotle analyzes the nature of individual terms, which can be put in place of the variables, A, B, and C, and their relation to one another. First, he discusses things that can be said "without combination." He examines single words or words in pairs that do not form a sentence. The fundamental term is substance, the individual object which alone can be the subject of definition, for example, man. All

the other terms depend on substance and are attributed to substance. There are nine of them: quantity (how many men); quality (what kind of men); relation (like, unlike); place (where); date (time); position (standing, sitting, etc.); state (armed, dressed, etc.); action (heating); and passivity (being heated). Second, he takes up terms and their contraries. In Aristotle's opinion, contraries are necessary in any account of change. There are four classes: correlatives (as in the concept of half or double, the other part of half an apple is "opposed to the first part"); opposites (good and bad, black and white); contraries (this means a positive state and its absence or privation, for example, sight and blindness, hearing and deafness); and finally affirmative and negative (true and false, "is" and "is not"). Toward the end of the *Categories* he defines those terms which identify change: generation (birth); destruction (death); increase (growth); diminution (growing smaller); alteration (as when something cold becomes hot); and change of place (walking, etc.). In *On Interpretation* Aristotle analyzes pairs of terms which can be put together to form sentences, which are made up of subject (man) and predicate (runs). There are four kinds of basic sentences: 1) a man runs; 2) a man does not run; 3) a not-man runs; and 4) a not-man does not run. Aristotle develops from these four basic kinds of sentences all the other more complex forms. Finally, in the *Prior Analytics* Aristotle takes up the combination of terms in groups of threes: two propositions or premises, and a conclusion. This is the syllogism.

To show the relation of terms in a syllogism it is not enough to know what your terms are. They have to have something in common one with the other which will serve as the basis of your picking those particular terms in the first place. You cannot reason without some common ground of argument. Earlier, we showed that Aristotle held there were three kinds of syllogism: the scientific syllogism, the syllogism based on opinion and conversation, and the syllogism which is not a syllogism. In general, the kind of syllogism or argument you have depends on the principles you choose as the basis of your argument.

In the *Posterior Analytics* Aristotle shows there are five subjects with which science is concerned: 1) what a name refers to, for example, what does the word "table" refer to; 2) whether this particular thing, like a table, exists; 3) what it is, i.e., its definition; 4) what are its basic properties. A table has legs and a top, for example. 5) Why it is. Now we know what a thing is when we can say why it is. It is the purpose of science to show the connection between an object and its cause. To show the connection between the "that" and the "why" is what Aristotle calls demonstration. Every scientific inquiry begins at stage 2, for we usually know what a word refers to, otherwise we would not use that word. And we usually know that the object is, otherwise we would not choose to find out "what it is." This means that we start with a number of observed facts, as the subject matter of our inquiry. The most significant fact of all the observed facts (i.e., the fact which all the other facts have in common) determines what kind of inquiry we have. For example, in physics we start with the most significant fact that the world is in motion. In psychology we start with the fact that man has something which makes him alive. In metaphysics we start with the fact that things are. Thus, every science

has its principle distinctive fact which sets it apart from all the other sciences. Every science has its own subject matter. Part of a scientific inquiry consists in classifying particular facts under the chief fact with which they are most closely associated.

In any thought process the only way we can reason with the facts we have on hand is, as we have said, to find their common ground. This common ground Aristotle calls *archai* or first principles. *Arche* is the Greek word not only for "principle" but also, and more commonly, for "rule" or "command." An *arche* of any science is the principle which controls and regulates the facts of that science. We might almost call an *arche* a law. As every science has its own subject matter, so every science has its own *archai* or laws. For example, Newton's laws of motion control the various phenomena associated with mechanical motion. The law of gravity controls all instances of things falling towards the earth.

What distinguishes scientific principles from principles based on opinion and conversation is that they are based on *experience*. Aristotle tells us that the fact that scientific principles are based on experience makes them true and certain. These principles are not something that are the result of reasoning. They are determined by a process of induction and intuitive perception. This means that first we look at a sufficient number of individual facts. We see what these facts have in common and wherein they differ. After looking long enough we become aware of the law that governs all those facts. For example, Newton had seen falling objects all his life. After a sufficient length of time he suddenly *knew* why those objects fell as they did. He had perceived the law of gravity. It is necessary to realize that Aristotle was very insistent on the importance of observation. His *Politics* begins: "Observation shows us." Science is true because it is based on objective experience. It is rooted in the nature of reality. If a first principle does not answer to the nature of reality, it is not a first principle. We must observe once more, perceive more accurately, and test our observation. This is the basis of all scientific experiment.

Once you have grasped the principle which governs your facts, it is a simple step to the definition of the particular subject matter you have chosen. Aristotle's favorite example of demonstration is the reason for the eclipse of the moon. First, we see there is no light on the moon. By seeing an eclipse often enough, we hit upon the universal truth that whatever has something between it and its source of light, loses its light. We then think, the moon has the earth between it and the sun. Therefore, the moon has no light. We have reasoned from the particular fact to the universal truth or first principle and *back again* to the fact. The scientific syllogism or demonstration consists in reasoning from the first principle back to the fact. Once we know the why, the what is nothing but a restatement of the why. The eclipse of the moon is its loss of light due to the earth's coming between it and its source of light, the sun.

As stated earlier, some syllogisms are not based on principles derived from experience but upon the structure of thought. For this reason, Aristotle tells us, they cannot be true and certain. For our thoughts sometimes can be true and sometimes not. Metaphysical and ethical syllogisms are based on such principles. Ethics especially is rooted in what is thought. Its foundation is opinion. When Aristotle defines happiness, for example,

he says we have to begin with the views that have generally been held about happiness. Since Aristotle is aware that reasoning based on what people *think* is liable to error, it is not strange that he considers tradition so important. What most people have thought over a long period of time is less likely to be wrong than what some person thinks up on the spur of the moment. There is wisdom in the accumulated thought and mythology of the ages. In accepting opinions as the basis of argument, Aristotle is careful to say which opinions he thinks are most foolproof. First, he accepts the opinions of the "many" either as expressed in tradition or as expressed collectively, for example, in an assembly of citizens. Second, he accepts the opinions of the "wise," of those men who have spent their lives dealing with difficult problems and solving some of them. Third, when he rejects the opinions of the "wise" in general, he will turn to the opinions of those few who are respected as the "wisest among the wise."

Finally, there are types of reasoning which neither follow the rules of right thinking nor are rooted in principles which can be shown to be based on either experience or opinion. Such are the syllogisms of the Sophists whom Aristotle makes the target of his book refuting their methods, the *Sophistic Elenchi*.

So familiar are Aristotle's concepts of induction, first principles, category, demonstration, syllogisms, and definition that it is hard for us to look back to a time when the implications of the interrelation of language and thought were not well understood. Aristotle's analysis of language as an instrument whereby men could arrive at an accurate understanding of observable facts opened the door to the development of science. His classification of the sciences according to subject method and first principles made scientific inquiry possible.

Aristotle's logic was closely related not only to his epistemology but also to his metaphysics and natural philosophy.

NATURAL PHILOSOPHY AND METAPHYSICS
A. H. Armstrong[7]

We have seen that Aristotle had come to the conclusion that Plato's attempt to solve the problem of true knowledge by postulating a world of transcendent separate Forms as its objects was a mistaken one and that reality of which we can have certain knowledge must be looked for in the world in which we find ourselves, the world revealed to us by our senses. The individual concrete entities of this world, Aristotle maintains against the Platonists, are real and scientifically knowable. Aristotle is of course too reasonable and too deeply influenced by Plato to say that these are the only real beings. He admits, as we shall see, the existence of immaterial entities perceptible by the reason alone and transcending and separate from the visible universe, but only so far as they seem to him necessary to explain that universe or to explain the workings of our own minds. And, of course, he admits the existence of universals of all sorts, but not as separate substantial realities, only as imminent and inseparable characteristics of the substances which we perceive.

[7] A. H. Armstrong, *An Introduction to Ancient Philosophy*, 3d ed. (London: Methuen and Co. Ltd., 1957), pp. 77–90. Reprinted by permission of Associated Book Publishers Ltd.

This acceptance of the individual beings of the sense-world as real and as the objects of true and accurate, that is scientific, knowledge, sets Aristotle a formidable problem to solve. He continues Platonist enough to be quite clear that the realities which are the objects of true knowledge must be stable, permanent and unchanging and not a mere flux of appearances. Yet the world revealed by the senses is one of unceasing change, in which things grow and decay and are perpetually transformed one into the other. It was this character of the sense-world which had made Plato look for reality elsewhere, and the questions which Aristotle had to answer when he rejected Plato's solution were first precisely what were the stable and unchanging realities which exist in this world of change, and then precisely how could one reality of this kind change into another, as the things revealed by our senses appear to do. It was, as far as we can tell, more by trying to answer these questions than by any other line of approach that Aristotle arrived at the great basic conceptions of his philosophical system, Substance, Form and Matter, Act and Potency.[8]

A substance for Aristotle is simply a real thing, a thing which actually exists. It is the thing as a whole, including its dimensions, qualities, relations, etc., which can only be separated from it by a process of mental abstraction but cannot actually exist apart from it. That is what Aristotle means when he says that substance is the primary category, which all the others presuppose. And it follows that a substance for Aristotle is always an individual thing, never a universal like a Platonic Form.

[8] Act and Potency are frequently referred to as Actuality and Potentiality. [Ed.]

But then the question arises; what is it in the individual substantial realities revealed to us by our senses which makes them substantial realities, and what is it which enables them to change? It is substance which is being in the strict and proper sense, the permanent and unchanging object of our thought; and yet individual substantial realities do change. Aristotle's solution of this problem is to be found in his analysis of the concrete substantial reality into Form and Matter, and in his doctrine of Potential and Actual being. The form of a thing is that which makes it what it is. A substantial reality cannot for Aristotle just vaguely, indefinitely, or abstractly "be." It must be something, some one thing definite and distinguishable. The form is just this definite, delimiting reality of things, the precise "thisness" or "thatness" of them which corresponds to their exact scientific definition in our minds. Aristotle is always very much concerned with this aspect of the form, as the unchanging reality with which the scientific definition of the thing must correspond if it is to be a true definition. For this reason he maintains the curious and difficult doctrine that, although individual things are the only things that exist yet the form in each individual thing is not a unique individual form but the form of the species, the narrowest class which can be scientifically defined. The forms of individuals are only numerically distinct, otherwise identical. In the case of concrete beings in the visible world which are compounded of form and matter, the matter is the principle of their individuality; though it is difficult to understand how this can be, for "matter" to Aristotle, as we shall see, is purely negative and has no proper characteristics of its own. And in the case of pure forms,

immaterial substances which are form uncompounded with matter, Aristotle gives no clue to the reason or nature of their individuality. . . .

The form of a substantial concrete material reality can for Aristotle never actually exist in separation from its matter. The two are only distinguishable by a process of mental analysis. They are not two things which are compounded mechanically or chemically to make another complete thing. The technical terms used by modern Aristotelians are particularly unfortunate here. "Form" and "Matter" suggest something like a jelly-shape or a children's seaside bucket into which some solid stuff is packed and then turned out with a definite external appearance. "The imposition of form on matter" suggests it even more definitely. Nothing of course could be further from what Aristotle means. The form is the intimate inward structure, the "thingness" of the thing; the matter is just the possibility of being that or another thing which is made actual for the time being by the reception of a particular form. If we were to speak of Pattern and Possibility instead of Form and Matter, though they would not translate accurately the Greek words Aristotle uses, they would perhaps convey a more accurate impression to modern minds—and would have more of the witch-doctor's-patter impressiveness of modern philosophical jargon. The purely-intellectual and non-physical character of the analysis which distinguishes Form and Matter, the fact that you can only separate them in your mind and not in reality, appears even more clearly in the analysis Aristotle makes when he is considering the actual process of change more closely. In this a third term appears, Privation, which means the fact of not being that which is going to be the result of change. A thing is what it is, by reason of its own substantial form; it is not some other definite thing into which it may change, by reason of its privation of the other form; it has the possibility of being what it is or another thing by reason of its matter.

Matter then is simply the element of possibility, of changeableness in things. Form is the stable, permanent, knowable, scientifically definable element in things. Matter is that element, itself undetermined but capable of successive determinations, which makes changes possible. Of course the possibilities of change in a thing are limited, because the matter which received the final form which made the thing what it is was already informed in a certain way. The matter which receives the form of "table" for instance is not just "matter" but "wood," that is matter which has already received (to simplify the process) the forms of the elements involved in the constitution of wood and the form of wood itself, and this to some extent determines and limits future developments. But if we pursue our mental analysis far enough we shall get down to something which Aristotle never actually mentions by name but to which he often clearly refers, the Prima Materia or "first matter" . . . , which has no form at all and is simply a bare, undefined and unlimited possibility of becoming. It never of course actually exists by itself. Matter without form can by its very definition never have any actual existence. Form on the other hand can exist without matter, as it does in the eternal substances, purely immaterial intellects, which form the highest ranks in Aristotle's hierarchy of realities.

From what I have just said about Matter it should already be fairly clear how Aris-

totle explains change. Everything in the material world actually is something and has in it the possibility of becoming other things. This is one of the most fundamental of Aristotle's doctrines, that of actual and potential being. It seems to us the merest common sense to say that a thing can be one thing actually and all sorts of other things potentially, but it took a very long development of Greek thought before Aristotle arrived at his simple-seeming doctrine, and it was not until he arrived at it that it was really possible to explain reasonably how a thing could be at the same time fully real and capable of change. . . . This doctrine of Act and Potency is perhaps the most important in Aristotle's system of thought, and is capable of very wide application, e.g., in ethics and psychology. We can now see the doctrine of Matter and Form as a special application of the doctrine of Act and Potency to real but changeable beings in the material world. The form is the thing's actuality, the matter which has not yet received a particular form is that thing potentially. For Aristotle Act always precedes Potency. The cause of a potential being coming into existence is always another being already existing in act. In this Aristotle is true both to the spirit of Plato and the dictates of common sense. A possibility of being a man which as yet is actually non-existent cannot, so to speak, lift itself into existence by the scruff of its own as yet only potential neck. There must be a father, in whom the form of man is already actualized, to beget and so start off the process of coming-to-be. The actual of course need not always precede the potential in time. But wherever a potentiality is coming to be actual there is always an actual being existing in full actuality from the beginning of the process which can be recognized as its cause. So behind the world of changing and moving things which we perceive by our senses there exist eternally one or more pure actualities, with no potentiality in them at all, substantial forms without matter which will never pass away because they have never come to be.

We are here on the threshold of Aristotle's theology[9]; but before we go on to discuss it we must spend a little more time on his philosophy of nature, keeping close to the fundamental theme of changeable reality.

The first topic that suggests itself is Aristotle's analysis of the different kinds of change and movement. The most important distinction which he makes is that between change involving the dissolution of one substantial thing and the coming-into-being of another, which he prefers not to call change at all but rather destruction and generation, and all other kinds of change (including local motion). This distinction is parallel to the distinction of Substance and Accidents, which is not really quite as important, I think, in Aristotelian philosophy as later theological controversies may suggest; it is in fact sometimes rather difficult to decide whether a particular quality or characteristic is part of the essential make-up of a thing, an indispensable element in its definition, an inseparable property or "proprium" of substance, or whether it is an accidental property, which can change, appear or disappear without affecting the substance. Yet a broad commonsense distinction can and must be made between properties essential to a substance and qualities which can vary and be there or

not there without affecting the essential nature of the thing they qualify. Platinum-blondeness is fortunately not an essential part of the definition of "woman."

Aristotle, then, makes clear the distinction between substantial transformation (destruction-generation) and change, which does not involve transformation of substance. It should be noted that for Aristotle destruction and generation are an inseparable pair. If one thing comes to be, it is out of the matter of something which has passed away. The sum of nature remains constant and the life of the sublunary world is made up of endless cycles of coming to be and passing away determined ultimately by the movement of the sun in the ecliptic.[10] The other kinds of change which Aristotle recognizes may be roughly summed up as those of quality, quantity, and position. Change of quantity is a specialized kind of motion in space, expansion over a larger space or contraction into a smaller one. Local motion, change of position, like all change is the actualization of a potentiality, the potentiality of being somewhere else. Therefore, like all other actualizations of potentiality it requires a cause already in act. A thing cannot move itself, like Plato's Soul, or be assumed to be in eternal uncaused motion like Democritus's atoms. This is a principle of very great importance in Aristotle's philosophy of nature and theology.

Like Plato, Aristotle is never satisfied to know simply how a thing happens, he wants to know why as well, and is convinced that things in general happen for some purpose. But he is more interested than Plato in the "how" as well as in the "why" of things. And he classifies the

9 More frequently this aspect of Aristotle's philosophy is referred to as metaphysics or First Philosophy. [Ed.]

10 The annual path of the sun in the heavens. [Ed.]

"how and why" of things under four heads. These are the famous "Four Causes," the four reasons which explain the fact that a particular thing has come to be, and is this definite thing and not another. They are: (i) the material cause, the matter out of which the thing is made; (ii) the efficient cause, the actually existing being necessary to initiate and sometimes to carry through the process of coming into being of a material thing; (iii) the formal cause, the form of the thing which as already explained gives it its definite being, makes it this thing and not another; (iv) the final cause, the end or purpose for which the thing comes into being. Of all of them the "efficient cause," the mover or initiator of the process of change, and perhaps the "final cause," the reason for the thing's existence, are the only ones which correspond at all to what we mean by a cause, and for this reason the translation "four *causes*" is rather misleading. They are rather the four Reasons Why the thing exists and is what it is.

The formal and final causes are generally identified by Aristotle. This means that the end or purpose for which a thing exists is to realize its form as perfectly as possible, to be as good a specimen of man, horse, tree, table, etc., as conditions will permit. In the case of natural (as distinct from manufactured) objects, too, the efficient cause is in a sense identical with the formal and final. For the principle that generates a plant or animal is normally another individual of the same species—spontaneous generation is a curious exception to this rule—and the form in individuals of the same species, though numerically distinct, is in all other ways identical.

The final cause is in a way the most important and interesting of all for Aris-

totle, for like Plato he is a thorough-going teleologist[11] and believes that everything exists for an end, and a good end, a principle which he applies vigorously throughout his biology, trying to show the purpose of every organ and distinctive feature of the animals which he studies. For Aristotle, however, unlike Plato, the purposefulness of things is imminent, inside them, though ultimately directed, as we shall see, towards a transcendent end. It is a natural impulse which drives everything to try to realize its form as perfectly as possible, thus imitating the divine perfection, and to take its place in the universal order. But he simply takes this natural inward impulse towards perfection and order for granted, and never seems to see that it must involve a directing intelligence, as well as a final perfection to aim at. In the same way he never tries to explain why the universe is an ordered universe at all. He has rejected Plato's conception of a ruling and ordering Mind as too mythical and has nothing to put in its place except the thoroughly unsatisfactory conception of an unconscious natural drive or tendency towards perfection and order. . . .

So far everything which we have discussed except the actual doctrine of Substance falls according to Aristotle within the bounds of that division of philosophy called Physics or philosophy of nature. In order to understand more precisely where Aristotle draws the boundary between this and First Philosophy or Theology (Metaphysics) it will be helpful to give a short sketch of the universe as Aristotle conceived it. It is a tidy and compact sort of

---

[11] The teleologist holds that everything in the universe has a purpose immanent in it and toward which it works, sometimes consciously, sometimes unconsciously. [Ed.]

universe, even more tidy and compact than Plato's, eternal and all-embracing, with nothing outside it, spherical in shape and with no void, no entirely unoccupied space, within or without. It is a hierarchically ordered universe in which every change and movement (with the restrictions noted above) has its cause and purpose, subordinated in its turn to a higher cause and purpose until we come to the highest of all. It is of course like almost all Greek pictures of the universe geocentric, with the spherical earth in the middle, immediately surrounded by the sublunary atmosphere, beyond which comes the largest and most important part of the cosmos, the system of the divine spheres of the heavenly bodies. Aristotle's universe is a stiffened and elaborated version of Plato's visible universe, very much affected as regards the spheres of the stars by the latest astronomical theories and calculations worked out by Eudoxus and Aristotle's own friend Callippus.

The central region inside the sphere of the moon, which includes the earth, is the region of change and decay, of the coming-to-be and passing-away of individual substances. That which is eternal and unchanging in it is the persistence of the species, of which there are a fixed and limited number. All things in it are made of the four elements, the first forms received by primal matter, earth, water, fire and air, which have each their natural motion in a straight line, the first two downwards to the centre, the second two upward to the circumference. It is the eccentric movement of the sun in the ecliptic which prevents them from ever separating out completely into their natural places and so making the existence of individual substances impossible. This oblique motion of the sun, which brings it

in regular succession nearer to and further from the earth, is the ultimate efficient cause of all coming-to-be and passing-away of individual substances by the increase and decrease of heat which it causes, for heat to Aristotle is the most essential factor in generation. The sun then is the highest cause in the ordered hierarchy of causes operating to produce the endless succession of generation and destruction of individuals which makes up the life of the sublunary world. But it is very far from being the highest cause in the universe. The cause of its motion is the tremendous machinery of the celestial spheres.

To give anything like a complete account of this would be impossible within the scope of this book, but something must be said about it if we are to understand the picture of the universe which was in most men's minds from the time of Aristotle until well after the time of Copernicus. For Aristotle, as for Plato, the sphere is the most perfect of figures and the rotation of a sphere the most perfect of motions, since it is self-contained and not directed to a goal outside itself like motion in a straight line. For him, therefore, as well as for Plato, the universe is a sphere in which the heavenly bodies rotate. The system of the celestial spheres, however, does not derive from Plato directly but from the observations of the great contemporary astronomers Eudoxus and Callippus. These, by a most brilliant piece of mathematical ingenuity, had succeeded in expressing the observed and apparently irregular motions of the sun, moon and planets as compound motions made up of the regular rotations of series of concentric spheres, rotating at different speeds and in different directions, each with its poles fixed in the surface of the larger one immediately outside it. On the basis of these calculations Aristotle built up a most elaborate mechanical explanation of the observed movements of all the heavenly bodies, which supposes them to be carried round by a nest of concentric spheres in contact, moving in different directions and at varying speeds. These spheres are material, made of a mysterious, translucent, bright, incorruptible substance, capable of no change (in our sense) or growth, but only of rotatory motion, the Aether, Quintessence or Fifth Element. They have to be in contact because there is no void in Aristotle's universe and also in order that they may impart motion to each other, for Aristotle holds that motion can be transmitted only by contact between the mover and that which is moved. In order to give a satisfactory mechanical explanation of the observed movements in accordance with these ideas, Aristotle finds it necessary to suppose the existence of fifty-five aethereal spheres. The smallest and innermost is the last sphere of the system of the moon, which encloses our atmosphere. The largest and outermost, whose motion supplies the main driving-force to the whole of the rest of the cosmic machine, is the sphere of the fixed stars. . . . All the inner spheres are required to explain the apparently irregular motions of planets, sun and moon (Plato had already protested indignantly that it was an insult to those divine and celestial beings, the planets, to suppose that their movements were really as disorderly as they looked and as their name of *planets*, "wanderers," implied).

We have then in Aristotle's universe an inner world of change and succession of individual things, of coming-to-be and passing-away in an endless circular process allowing for individual variations within a fixed framework of causality; the causes are arranged in hierarchical order, culminating in the eternal movement of the sun in the ecliptic which co-operates with all other causes of generation and destruction ("Man begets man, but so does the sun"). Through this motion of the sun the relatively small inner world of generation and destruction is linked to the far vaster region of the Spheres beyond the moon, which are eternal and indestructible, and in which there is no coming-to-be and passing-away but only perpetual motion in a circle. Both regions, outer and inner, fall within the scope of Philosophy of Nature; Aristotle defines Nature as a principle of movement or change within things themselves, and all things which are actuated by such an immanent (though not self-caused) principle of movement or change are to be studied by Philosophy of Nature or Physics. It is only when we ask: is there some more ultimate principle of movement or change? What is it that makes the spheres go round? that we pass on to Theology or First Philosophy.

The subject of First Philosophy, Theology, or as we call it Metaphysics, is reality or being as such. The primary kind of reality, that on which all others depend and which shows most fully the nature of being is, of course, Substance. It is therefore Substance which Metaphysics studies, and in acquiring a proper and complete knowledge of Substance it necessarily acquires a knowledge also of those less perfect forms of reality which cannot exist except in dependence upon Substance. It therefore is the business of Metaphysics to give an account of the distinction between Substance and Accidents, Form and Matter, Actuality and Potency, and to explain the precise meaning of these terms. Furthermore there are different grades of Substance. Besides the separate substantial individual beings which are subject to change, with which we have been mainly concerned . . . and which are studied by Philosophy of Nature, there are, Aristotle says, separate substances which are free from change, pure actualities with no potency in them at all. These are the highest class of substantial being, the most completely real things that exist. It is therefore on them that Metaphysics concentrates, because by studying being at its most perfect and complete it obtains the fullest possible knowledge of being as such. It is therefore First Philosophy because it studies the primary forms of being and Theology because these primary beings are divine.

How does Aristotle demonstrate that unmoved and unchanging substantial reality exists? Like [most] Greek philosophers . . . he believes most firmly in the everlastingness of the universe. He has no conception of eternity (in the Christian sense) and therefore holds that time must be everlasting, as otherwise there would be a time before time was and a time after it ceased, which is contradictory and absurd. But if time, then change, for time is only the "number" or measure of change. Now the only kind of absolutely continuous change, the only kind therefore which can be everlasting, is circular motion (motion being change of place). Therefore the circular motion of the spheres must be everlasting, without beginning or end. But motion is the actualization of a potency, and requires something already actual to produce it; and the something actual which produces the ultimate circular motion must be itself pure actuality, eternal, without movement or change, that is without potency, or we shall require a further actuality to actuate it and so on; we shall

go back in an infinite regress, and there will be no real causation at all because there will be no First Cause. So the first everlasting circular motion must be produced by the everlasting actuation of its potency by an Unmoved Mover, an eternal substance, purely actual, with no possibility of change or motion. This Unmoved Mover must be purely immaterial, since matter is potency. It must be capable of causing motion (which Plato's Forms, Aristotle says, were not); and it must ceaselessly exercise this power. It is a very important principle of Aristotle's philosophy that there are two stages of actuality, the first in which a thing possesses all its powers in full development but is not necessarily exercising them (like a man when he is asleep), and the second when it not only possesses the powers but is exercising them to the full (like the same man awake and going about his business). The Unmoved Mover must be necessarily and everlastingly in act in this second and fuller sense if it is to be the necessary cause of a continuous everlasting motion.

It is clear that this eternal, fully actual, everlastingly active, unchanging, immaterial object can only be one kind of thing, a Mind. Mind fulfils all the conditions and is in any case the only kind of immaterial substance left in Aristotle's system after the rejection of the Platonic Forms. But it must be a self-sufficient Mind, for if it needed any external object to be the object of its thought, it would have in it an element of incompleteness, of potentiality. Its thought must be intuitive, immanent, directed entirely to an object within itself. In fact, as it is pure Mind entirely active in a ceaseless single activity of thought, the only object which it can have is its own thinking. Its thought, then, is an eternal "thinking upon thinking." It would seem to be Aristotle's final conclusion that the Divine Mind has no knowledge of anything outside itself.

How, then, does this remote and self-contained being act as the universal first cause of motion? Not by any action on its part, for this would detract from its perfect self-sufficiency. <u>There is, therefore, according to Aristotle, only one way in which it can cause motion, and that is by being an object of love</u> or desire. The first heaven, the sphere of the fixed stars, which seems to be thought of as itself alive and intelligent, desires the absolute perfection of the Unmoved Mover and by reason of its desire imitates that perfection as best it can by moving everlastingly with the most perfect of all motions, that in a circle. And in so far as all movements and changes in the universe depend on this first movement, they are all ultimately caused by the desire inspired by the pure and perfect actuality of the Unmoved Mover, the Divine Mind or God; and it can be said in a sense that the striving towards the most perfect possible actuality, the most complete realization of form, which is for Aristotle the principle of all activity and actualization everywhere in the universe, is the expression of this desire for the perfection of God. . . .

. . . Aristotle's conception of God must seem to us highly unsatisfactory and inadequate. This Eternal Mind enclosed in a sterile self-sufficiency, everlastingly contemplating its own thinking, neither knowing nor willing the universe and only affecting it through the ceaseless rotation which desire for its unattainable perfection inspires in the First Heaven, is not at all like anything we mean by the word "God." It is simply the logical culmination of the hierarchy of substances and the ultimate explanation of motion and

change. But it is not a person or power exercising providence, ordering all things by its will. Still less is it a Creator or the inexpressible Absolute. Aristotle's thought is not really God-centred, but Cosmos-centred. It is the everlasting universe which is for him the Whole, the sum of being, the ultimate Reality. The First Mover or God is a part of that whole, not Absolute Being but the Supreme Being.

For Aristotle, theoretical science comprised the subjects of epistemology, metaphysics, natural philosophy (physics, biology, and astronomy), and mathematics. These sciences deal with the problem of being as it is related to matter and form. There are, however, other branches of knowledge, and these Aristotle designated as the practical sciences. In his opinion they could never become completely "scientific" because their subject matter consisted of the *different* forms of human conduct and social institutions. In spite of the limitations placed on these sciences, Aristotle brought to ethics and politics his brilliant capacity for definition.

ETHICS AND POLITICS
Herschel Baker[12]

The object of ethics . . . , as well as the object of good living, must be *eudaimonia*—an untranslatable word that <u>means some sort of happiness or</u> . . . well-being. It is the satisfaction resulting from moral conduct, "an activity of the soul in accordance with perfect virtue." In explaining the nature (or *physis*) of moral conduct, Aristotle never departs, as Plato often tends to, from the secular, common-sense

[12] Reprinted by permission of the publishers from Herschel Baker, *The Image of Man.* Cambridge, Mass.: Harvard University Press. Copyright 1947 by the President and Fellows of Harvard College. Footnotes have been omitted.

attitude that morality is a matter of daily living. Virtue is, therefore, not a transcendental Ideal, not a set of deific and superimposed restrictions, not Kantian duty, not arbitrary Blue Laws; it is nothing more than the proper functioning of reason, man's unique and highest faculty of soul; it is a final good that is an end, and not a means to an end. If man possessed only the sensitive soul, then sensation would be the entelechy of his nature; but because he enjoys the active intellect, reason is his entelechy, and rational conduct is virtuous conduct.[13]

Aristotle is not seduced by an ethics of impracticable elevation. Man is not purely rational: he is a mixed animal with a nutritive and a sensitive soul beneath his rational soul, and their functions cannot legitimately be ignored or denied. If a hand is amputated, its function of grasping is vitiated, and it is actually no longer a hand. Likewise, if a man drastically suppresses any natural function, he is no longer a complete man. Our natural—human, all too human—characteristics have been studiously abused by many eminent men, but not by Aristotle. His view is naturalistic. Man's functions, from nutrition and reproduction to conceptual thought, are all organic; and as a complex organism he should attempt to synthesize virtuously (i.e. rationally) all the complex functions of his nature. He possesses passions, "feelings that are accompanied by pleasure or pain"; faculties by which he satisfies his desires; and states of character, "the things in virtue of which we stand well or badly with reference to the passions"; and these multiple parts have to be adjusted into a well-functioning whole.

[13] The conduct of an animal is nonmoral, no matter with what human terms we burden it; because an animal lacks reason, morality is impossible for it.

As a Greek and a rationalist, Aristotle distinguishes degrees of moral excellence. Like Plato, he has a special regard for a life of pure thought, and this he calls dianoetic or intellectual virtue. Such virtue transcends the sphere of practical morality to soar into an almost Platonic realm of pure intellection; the speculative reason deals only with conceptual formal knowledge, and its truth is absolute because the object of its speculation never changes. On the other hand, practical or calculative reason, expressed by the twelve moral virtues, concerns the "variable" objects of sense and is therefore deliberative and, in a sense, expedient for good conduct.

> And let it be assumed that there are two parts which grasp a rational principle—one by which we contemplate the kind of things whose originative causes are invariable, and one by which we contemplate variable things; for where objects differ in kind the part of the soul answering to each of the two is different in kind, since it is in virtue of a certain likeness and kinship with their objects that they have the knowledge they have.

The functions of the highest or speculative intellect are scientific knowledge, intuitive reason (*nous*), and philosophic wisdom (*sophia*). Science, whose objects are constant, starts with the known, and either inductively or syllogistically proceeds ever upwards to those conceptual abstractions that both embrace and transcend the data of sense. It leads to that knowledge which Socrates, more emotionally and less schematically, had worshipped with a kind of religious fervor. But because some things are incapable of demonstration, we often use as a spring-board to higher intellection the truths revealed to us by intuitive reason. It puts us in "the states of mind by which we have truth and are never deceived about things invariable or even variable."[14] But the apex of man's intellection, and "plainly the most finished of the forms of knowledge," is philosophic wisdom, which synthesizes intuition and scientific knowledge. This, for Aristotle as for Plato, is the attribute of the true philosopher who transcends practicality.

> This is why we say Anaxagoras, Thales, and men like them have philosophic but not practical wisdom, when we see them ignorant of what is to their own advantage, and why we say that they know things that are remarkable, admirable, difficult, and divine, but useless; viz. because it is not human goods that they seek.

This kind of wisdom, Aristotle is quick to add, is not for the common man.

> Practical wisdom on the other hand is concerned with things human and things about which it is possible to deliberate; for we say this is above all the work of the man of practical wisdom, to deliberate well, but no one deliberates about things invariable, nor about things which have not an end, and that a good that can be brought about by action.

Here Aristotle appears at his most characteristic best, in framing an ethics for practical morality that may achieve goods brought about by action. His is the most urbane kind of humanism, one that candidly names as its object an attainable good. "The man who is without qualification good at deliberating is the man who is capable of aiming in accordance with calculation at the best for man of things attainable by action." Such a man attains the good by relying on those ethical or moral virtues which serve a constabulary purpose of harmonizing, not eradicating, the functions of the lower levels of soul under the control of reason. By exercising our moral virtues we achieve the highly practical goal of good behavior, or, in Aristotle's characteristically civic view, social conduct.

The best life for the average man, therefore, lies in blending dianoetic and moral virtue, in being a rational creature as well as a responsible member of a good society. He who lives (if such be possible) only on the nutritive level cannot be happy, for he ignores his higher functions of sensation and intellection. Happiness can mean nothing other than the most nearly complete functioning of the soul in its highest capacity: it is the just and orderly composition of those activities—and how often Aristotle uses this word—that "give life its character."[15] Moral virtue involves, then, the rational discipline of passion. The functions of our lower souls are to be regulated, but not . . . suppressed. Even though the mass of mankind, Aristotle candidly admits, prefers a "life suitable to beasts" to one of rational equilibrium, any one, through training and habit, can achieve rational, and therefore virtuous conduct without resorting to a vicious asceticism. . . . So long as each [part of the soul] fulfills its proper function, virtue and well-being result.

---

14 . . . Some of the obvious functions of practical reason are art and practical wisdom (phronesis), because they are subject to that kind of intellection that accepts, rejects, and balances.

15 . . . Aristotle charges Socrates with positing a priori a transcendental "knowledge" as the referent of all particular virtues—this in spite of his ostensibly inductive dialectic. Aristotle is more pragmatic in maintaining that practice or habit, inculcated by unremitting self-discipline, is the only weapon against dangerously passionate action. Ethics, Aristotle the philologist points out . . . , is cognate with ethos (habit). Education and training are the surest guides to good conduct, for they buttress and enforce the dictates of reason.

The verbalization of this characteristic Greek attitude is Aristotle's doctrine of the mean. By it, conflicting parts are reconciled into a harmonious whole; moderation is a virtue, excess is a vice. The wise man will determine his own mean, for no *a priori* norms, Pythagorean numerology, or superimposed Platonic Forms can achieve a balanced life for all men. To find the ethical mean between sensual bestiality and ascetic theorizing is difficult: "*that* is not for everyone, nor is it easy: wherefore goodness is both rare and laudable and noble." The most that Aristotle will commend, by way of moral precept, is what he calls "insight." Arising from the exercise of virtue and tending towards future virtue, it is the acquired judgment, tact, and good sense that makes morality essentially human. It is the last attainment of the wise man who is also, and inevitably, the good man. To feel the passions "at the right times, with reference to the right objects, towards the right people, with the right motive, and in the right way, is what is both intermediate and best, and this is characteristic of virtue." And thus Aristotle prepares for his celebrated pronouncement: virtue "is a state of character concerned with choice, lying in a mean, i.e. the mean relative to us, this being determined by a rational principle, and that principle by which the man of practical wisdom would determine it."[16] Man's reason permits rational choice, and his distinction lies in his ability to choose rationally with respect to the well-being of his whole complex nature.

Humanism has never been argued more soundly, or stated more appealingly.

The famous list of moral virtues exemplifying the mean—and how many dreary imitations it has spawned—has been vastly influential with later moralists, perhaps because it is so precise about matters usually treated with imprecision. If Aristotle's analysis appears clinical, at least it avoids Plato's error of melting all virtues into one nebulous, transcendental, undefinable, and virtually unattainable master-virtue. Relating to conduct and motive and dependent on deliberation and choice, the twelve moral virtues comprise the modes of a good man's activity. Courage and temperance, the custodians of the irrational parts of the soul, characterize the citizen-soldier and the man who with self-respect can indulge his appetites for food and drink and sexual intercourse. In liberality and magnificence Aristotle urges especial moderation, partly, no doubt, as a social corrective for the Athenian *nouveaux riches*. The remaining eight moral virtues are similarly concerned with man in a given social or cultural pattern. Honor and ambition are proper to the affable, solvent, and patriotic citizen who takes a proper pleasure in making his way in the world. Good temper enables one to succumb to anger "at the right things and with right people, and, further, as he ought, when he ought, and as long as he ought." Friendliness, truthfulness, and wit are all clearly social virtues. Shame, hardly a virtue at all, is encountered properly only in young people "because they live by feeling and therefore commit many errors." And justice, the last of all and the sum total of all the others, is the "complete" virtue because he who "possesses it can exercise his virtue not only in himself but towards his neighbor also."

---

[16] . . . Some passions (e.g. spite, shamelessness, envy) and some actions (e.g. adultery, theft, murder) patently do not admit of a mean. "For all these things and such like things imply by their names that they are themselves bad, and not the excess or deficiencies of them."

The difference between Aristotle the realist and Plato the visionary absolutist is nowhere more obvious than in their approach to politics. Plato, as we have seen, allowed his quest of the absolute to lead him into political despotism; Aristotle, with much more experience in the world of men and certainly with a more basic humanistic comprehension of man, made his political theory consonant with his ethics. Because his approach to both politics and ethics was practical rather than theoretical, he was willing to forego absolutes. Instead of seeking them, he said, we must be content with conclusions that are only approximately true, and workable. Plato, however, never forgot his moral shock of the democracy that had dispossessed his powerful relatives, and in his old age he found a sort of vicarious revenge in theoretically legislating democracy out of existence. But Aristotle, in shaping his views about man as a political animal, proceeded to scrutinize, with characteristic and painful thoroughness, man's political activity. He studied and wrote analyses of one hundred fifty-eight Hellenic constitutions, evaluated them carefully, and framed his conclusions on the basis of ample factual data. Note the famous, dispassionate opening:

> Every state is a community of some kind, and every community is established with a view to some good; for mankind always act in order to obtain that which they think good. But, if all communities aim at some good, the state or political community, which is highest of all, and which embraces all the rest, aims at good in a greater degree than any other, and at the highest good.

Aristotle has little respect either for the communism of the *Republic* or the oligarchy of the *Laws,* for both are impracti-

cable in details and, if practiced, would lead to ruinous dissension. Indeed, any state which is excessively one thing or another tends to deteriorate: monarchy becomes despotism, aristocracy becomes oligarchy, timocracy becomes democracy. There is imbalance, and hence a lessening of the general good, both in oligarchy and extreme democracy. "Whenever men rule by reason of their wealth, whether they be few or many, that is an oligarchy, and where the poor rule, that is a democracy." Aristotle is likewise skeptical of an aristocracy. . . . It too often happens that a noble stock degenerates "towards the insane type of character, like the descendants of Alcibiades or of the elder Dionysius."

In short, there is no absolutely preferable type of constitution; therefore in his government as in his ethics men should strive for a balanced mixture of various elements. In all states there are rich and poor and merely well-to-do, and since the latter are a majority the constitution should be built around the mean which they represent: "the middle class is least likely to shrink from rule, or to be over-ambitious for it; both of which are injuries to the state." Without mentioning his old master by name, Aristotle seems to have him in mind when he describes the pernicious effects of Plato's oligarchic despotism:

> Again, those who have too much of the goods of fortune, strength, wealth, friends, and the like, are neither willing nor able to submit to authority. The evil begins at home; for when they are boys, by reason of the luxury in which they are brought up, they never learn, even at school, the habit of obedience. On the other hand, the very poor, who are in the opposite extreme, are too degraded. So that the one class cannot obey, and can only rule

despotically; the other knows not how to command and must be ruled like slaves. Thus arises a city, not of freemen, but of masters and slaves, the one despising, the other envying; and nothing can be more fatal to friendship and good fellowship in states than this.

It follows, then, that "a city ought to be composed, as far as possible, of equals and similars; and these are generally the middle classes." Aristotle does not fear to extend his humanistic regard for man to the realm of politics; indeed, it is in communal life that man, who is by nature a political animal, finds his necessary fulfillment, for "the end of the state is the good life." When a good life is made politically secure for a majority of the citizens, the best state exists. This means that the most acceptable form of political organization will combine timocracy and democracy: "the mean condition of states is clearly best, for no other is free from faction; and where the middle class is large, there are least likely to be factions and dissensions." When every man, "whoever he is, can act best and live happily" then the state is good.

Thus Aristotle's thinking shapes towards its majestic end. In the vast sweep of activity that toils ever upward, through the interaction of form and matter, man marks merely a stage. A complex organism in a universe ineffably purposeful, it is his function to accommodate and harmonize all the stresses of his divided nature. Neither in nutrition nor sensation does he achieve his entelechy, but in reason. Because he must adjust himself to the moderate and temperate activity necessary to society (for he is a social creature), he employs his practical reason, exemplified by the moral virtues; but his highest func-

tion, speculative intellection, operates in the realm of pure conceptual thought. Aristotle, like Plato in the *Phaedo,* reveals a professional bias for the *bios theoretikos,* the life of theoretical speculation by which man approaches God's function of thinking on thinking, and with which he moves deifically in the realm of invariables.[17] But such a life, Aristotle has the common sense to realize, "would be too high for man." Happiness, clearly, is an activity that is good in itself, and not one that points to an ulterior good. It is, in short, activity in accordance with virtue, both moral and intellectual; and virtue means the highest coördination of all the disparate functions of man *qua* man.

Aristotle, no less than Socrates and Plato, found permanence and reality in conceptual knowledge. And as a rationalist in the great tradition, he marks the most systematic reaction against Democritean materialism, for, in spite of his insistence on the ontological significance of particulars, his teleology demands the greatest possible reverence for mind. Reason (*nous*) is for him, as for his illustrious predecessors, the governing permanence of the cosmos. His universe is through and through rational. Becausee Aristotle places man in his proper context at the middle of the *scala naturae,* he is able to formulate an ethics that requires not only the fullest exploitation of man's reason but also the gratification of those lower faculties without which he would cease to be man, and become something else. . . .

According to Aristotle, one of the most im-

[17] Such pure speculation, it would appear, involves mathematics, metaphysics, and perhaps natural philosophy. . . . The *Ethica Eudemia* more summarily calls it . . . "the contemplation and service of God."

portant means of promoting a life of virtue and happiness, as well as the kind of political order which he envisioned, was education.

> . . . For the exercise of any faculty or art a previous training and habituation are required; clearly therefore for the practice of virtue. And since the whole city has one end, it is manifest that education should be one and the same for all, and that it should be public, and not private—not as at present, when every one looks after his own children separately, and gives them separate instruction of the sort which he thinks best; the training in things which are of common interest should be the same for all. Neither must we suppose that any one of the citizens belongs to himself, for they all belong to the state, and are each of them a part of the state, and the care of each part is inseparable from the care of the whole.[18]

Aristotle's interest in education was also manifested in his work on rhetoric, an art closely related to public life, morality, and educational instruction—and one which belongs, like ethics and politics, to the practical sciences. Rhetoric deals with man as the sole animal endowed with speech, a faculty which makes him the only ethical animal, the only one which can express pain and pleasure through definitions of what is good and harmful.

As we have seen, rhetoric played a very basic role in the educational system of ancient Greece. Education began to assume a standard form during the Hellenistic Age. The elementary stage of education included instruction in reading, writing, and arithmetic, while secondary education comprised the study of grammar, Greek literature, numbers, Euclidian geometry, astronomy, and the theory of music. At the advanced or higher stage of education, emphasis was put on philosophy and above all on rhetoric. In all of these courses . . .

reading was done aloud, so that there was no borderline between the written and the spoken word; the result was that the categories of eloquence were imposed on every form of mental activity—on poetry, history and even . . . philosophy. Hellenistic culture was above all things a rhetorical culture, and its typical literary form was the public lecture.[19]

Rhetoric also was the medium through which the basic concepts of legal and political science were transmitted to students of law and public life. The art of rhetoric as it was taught in Hellenistic schools was greatly influenced by the work of Aristotle.

As with every other subject matter to which he addressed himself, Aristotle abstracted the methods of rhetoric and systematized its content. He did so by organizing the material of which rhetoric was composed into categories representing the essential qualities or functions of any speech. In other words, he delineated those elements which contribute to persuasion in any situation. These were proofs, style, and arrangement.

The methodical ideas which he introduced into the proofs were of epoch-making importance: (1) Every speech must be so constructed as to prove a point. (2) Every speech must play on the emotions of the audience. (3) The speaker's own character should appear in a good light. Into the construction of the speech Aristotle introduced the processes of induction and deduction to create what is called a rhetorical argument, a form of argument which is independent of subject matter. Both rhetorical deduction and induction are based on probability and are, therefore, simply an elaboration and systematization of the methods developed by the Sophists in the law courts during the fifth century B.C. According to Aristotle, rhetorical proofs by deduction are not to be confused with scientific deductive proofs, for they are proofs derived from what is true for the most part.

---

[18]Aristotle, *Politics,* in *The Basic Works of Aristotle,* trans. Benjamin Jowett (New York: Random House, Inc., 1941), p. 1305 [Book VIII, Chapter 1, 1337 a 19–30].

[19] H. J. Marrou, *A History of Education in Antiquity,* trans. George Lamb (London: Sheed and Ward, 1956), p. 195.

Good men do not commit murder;
Socrates is a good man;
therefore, Socrates did not commit murder.

Proofs by induction are based on examples used as analogies.

> We must prepare for war against the king of Persia and not let him subdue Egypt. For Darius of old did not cross the Aegean until he had seized Egypt; but once he had seized it, he did cross. If therefore the present king seizes Egypt, he also will cross, and therefore we must not let him.[20]

The second element in rhetorical proof is putting the audience into a certain mood. In other words, the orator must so construct and so deliver his speech that he can manipulate the emotions of his audience. Finally, the orator must speak in a way that gives the impression that he has "good sense, good moral character, and goodwill."[21]

In the matter of style or diction Aristotle went a long way toward fixing the qualities which a good speech or piece of prose should have. Among these were clarity, ornateness (provided in large part by the use of metaphors), and appropriateness. In addition, he arranged the speech into an introduction, statement (or narration), proof, and epilogue. It is to all of these characteristics of prose composition that we give the name "classical."

With the works of Aristotle the culmination of classical Greek intellectual development had been reached. What the Greeks subsequently accomplished in the Hellenistic Age, which began in the late fourth century B.C., was an outgrowth of an entirely different social, political, and psychological environment.

---

[20] Aristotle, *Rhetoric,* in *The Basic Works of Aristotle,* trans. by W. Rhys Roberts (New York: Random House, Inc., 1941), p. 1412 [Book II, Chapter 20, 1393 a 30–1393 b 1].

[21] Aristotle, *Rhetoric,* p. 1380 [Book II, Chapter 1, 1378 a 5].

CHAPTER 12

THE TWILIGHT AND DIFFUSION OF HELLENISM:
Philosophy, Science, and Religion in the Hellenistic Age

When Aristotle died, the city-state had already ceased to hold a place of first-rate importance in the political development of European society, which was destined henceforth to govern itself in larger units and to pursue other ideals. The city-state gave place to the world-wide empire, and the political ideals of the compact and self-centered urban community had to be reconstructed to fit the ideal of a universal community as broad as humanity itself. In one form or another the conception of a single humanity governed political philosophy for upwards of fifteen hundred years, until the appearance of modern nationalism, and so ingrained itself in the consciousness of western Europe that even national sentiment could not displace it.

G. H. Sabine and S. B. Smith, "Introduction" to Marcus Tullius Cicero,
On the Commonwealth

Epicureans and Stoics alike addressed themselves to the task of redressing the imbalance between little man and huge world, of restoring dignity to little man by arming him with *autarky* or self-sufficiency. Each school had its own physics and its own logic, as it behooved philosophical schools to have; but in both, these were mainly in the nature of scaffolding to support their main objective, which was ethics. . . .

To endow man with autarky in the face of a world which threatens to overwhelm him, either the world must be shown to be less important than it seems, or man more important. The first of these strategies is the way of Epicureanism, the second of Stoicism. . . .

Moses Hadas, Essential Works of Stoicism

The *Elements* [of Euclid] contains 13 books, or chapters, which describe and prove a good part of all that the human race knows, even now, about lines, points, circles and the elementary solid shapes. All this information Euclid deduced, by the most mind-sharpening logic, from just 10 simple premises—five postulates and five axioms. . . . Out of these premises Euclid constructed not only the geometry normally taught today in high school but also a great deal of other mathematics. . . .

After Euclid, mathematicians could only go up—out of the realms normally thought of as Greek geometry into the rarefied atmosphere of what is popularly known as higher mathematics. Inspired by the *Elements*, the two most gifted mathematicians of the next century were to originate as many new results and generate as many useful

264

formulas as all the pre-Euclidean Greeks put together. One was Apollonius, whose discoveries about the so-called conic sections later contributed importantly to astronomy, to the military science of ballistics and finally to modern rocketry. The other was Archimedes, whose brilliance at mathematics was matched by a genius for mechanics which made him the father of practical engineering.

David Bergamini and the Editors of Life, Mathematics

The world in which Aristotle brought Greek rationalist philosophy to its culmination was not moving toward the form of political life—the classical Greek polis—which he had praised so highly in his *Politics*. Under the influence of the empires established by Philip of Macedon and Alexander, the social and political life of all the lands bordering on the eastern Mediterranean was transformed.

HELLENISTIC CULTURE
Chester G. Starr[1]

Alexander left as his heirs a half-wit half-brother and a posthumous son, born to his new Persian wife, Roxane. Both were soon swept aside, along with his mother Olympias and all other members of Philip's house; for Alexander's marshals and satraps showed themselves to be extremely ambitious and also extremely able. Since the great bulk of his realm had long been united in the Persian empire, there was no reason why it should not have continued to enjoy political unity, save that the rival generals balked each other of securing over-all mastery. The most notable, Antigonus the One-Eyed (*c.* 382–01) and his brilliant but erratic son Demetrius the Taker of Cities (336–283), came close to downing the others but met final defeat

[1] From *A History of the Ancient World* by Chester G. Starr, pp. 403–410, 413–422, 430–431. Copyright © 1965 by Oxford University Press, Inc. Reprinted by permission.

at the battle of Ipsus in 301, in which Antigonus was killed. By this time the division of the Hellenistic world into several great monarchies was well advanced, though one of the victors at Ipsus, Seleucus (*c.* 358–280), who held the territory from Syria to India, continued to seek the mirage of universal rule until his murder in 280.

The Hellenistic state-system which emerged during the wars of Alexander's successors was as complicated as that of modern Europe. Beside a host of minor kingdoms, independent city-states, and leagues of city-states stood three major powers. The longest enduring of these was that of the Ptolemies in Egypt, which included throughout most of the third century Cyrene, south Syria and Palestine, Cyprus, the south coast of Asia Minor, and many of the Aegean islands. The Seleucid dynasty was the most important in many respects, for it held the great bridge of land from inland Asia Minor through Syria and Mesopotamia to Iran. The territory Alexander had won in India was yielded by Seleucus for 500 elephants, which helped him to win the battle of Ipsus. The other eastern provinces fell away in the next century through the rise of a native dynasty, the Parthians in Iran from 247 on and through a revolt of the Greek settlers in Bactria, who maintained their independence into the middle of the second century.

The third major line was that of the

Antigonids in Macedonia, founded by Antigonus Gonatas (c. 320–239), the grandson of Antigonus the One-Eyed. The Antigonids also generally exercised suzerainty over Greece, but the homeland of Hellenic civilization was far from exhausted. Although Athens and Sparta now rarely played active roles, the Aetolian league in western Greece and the Achaean league in the Peloponnesus grew steadily stronger as the greatest federal structures of antiquity. Rhodes, Byzantium, and other commercially important city-states continued to be free; and minor kingdoms, such as the Bosporus in the modern Crimea, Pergamum and Bithynia in western Asia Minor, and the Nabataeans in northwest Arabia, also had a place in Hellenistic political and economic activity.

Superficially the political history of the Hellenistic world is one of tremendous complexity and incessant wars. The greater monarchies were not firmly united territorial states, as the Greek city-states had been; rather, they were held together by the political and military abilities of the kings of the three major lines. This situation in itself led to wars to secure the necessary prestige for survival.

Under the surface there were more fundamental conflicts among the monarchies, for example, the need to keep lines open to the Aegean so as to secure Greek mercenaries, colonists, and administrators; and the competitive struggle to control the Mediterranean ends of the great trade routes. The Ptolemies and the Seleucids, thus, waged a series of Syrian wars for mastery of the coast of Syria and Palestine.

Throughout the third century the Ptolemies generally held the upper hand, not so much because their armies were efficient as because they were masters of the sea and had tremendous financial resources through their exploitation of Egypt. Yet the Hellenistic statesmen understood fairly well the principle of the balance of power, and so other major and minor states tended to unite against any dynasty which seemed overly powerful. Treaties of alliance, of dynastic marriage, and of financial subvention succeeded one another in the ever shifting lines of diplomatic activity much as in eighteenth-century Europe. In such a system warfare was not pushed to the bitter end of wiping out rival states, and for a time in the third century its practice became more humane as kings sought to make use of, rather than exterminate, the cities they conquered and as holy places secured formal grants of immunity from the horrors of war.

Quite apart from the contentions of the kings themselves, other forces tended to pull the Hellenistic world apart. The Greek cities of the Aegean world sought to free themselves from royal yokes; and the Iranian east, at the other geographical extreme, never reconciled itself to Hellenic mastery. Everywhere, but especially in Egypt, the natives murmured; both by land and by sea, where Rhodes sought desperately to check piracy, security was difficult to maintain. By 200 B.C. the Hellenistic monarchies had battled each other to a standstill. The way thus was open for Parthia from the east and for Rome from the west to be called in by dissatisfied elements and to absorb ever larger parts of the Near East.

Despite its political divisions the Hellenistic world formed a social, economic, and cultural unit which at times was called the *oikoumene,* or "inhabited world." Even politically its institutions had a common stamp, in which were blended Near Eastern and Greek elements. The greater kings, who had won and held their realms by the sword and by cunning, were as absolute monarchs as any Sargon or Thut-

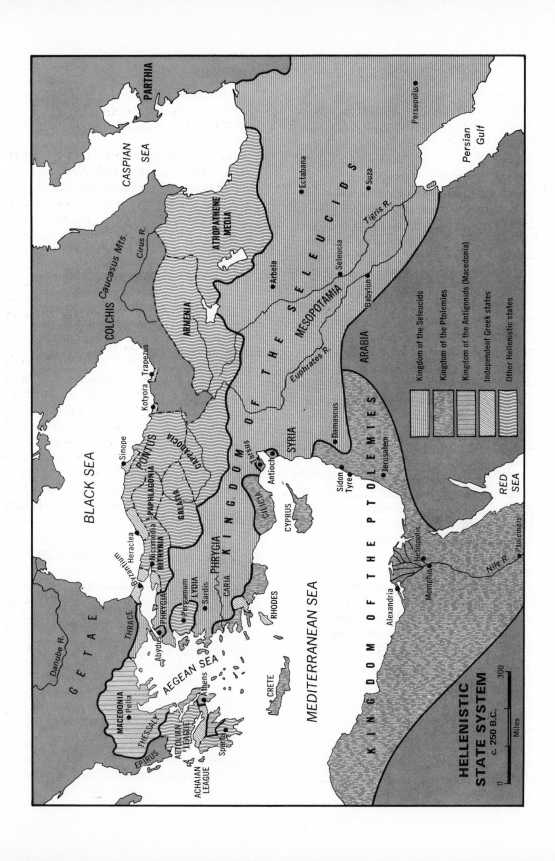

HELLENISTIC STATE SYSTEM
c. 250 B.C.

Miles
0   300

Kingdom of the Seleucids
Kingdom of the Ptolemies
Kingdom of the Antigonids (Macedonia)
Independent Greek states
Other Hellenistic states

PARTHIA

CASPIAN SEA

Caucasus Mts.

COLCHIS

Cirus R.

ATROPATHENE MEDIA

ARMENIA

Persepolis

Persian Gulf

Ectabana

Tigris R.

Suza

Arbela

Seleucia

MESOPOTAMIA

Babylon

Euphrates R.

ARABIA

K I N G D O M   O F   T H E   S E L E U C I D S

Trapezus

Kotyora

Sinope

PONTUS

PAPHLAGONIA

CAPPADOCIA

GALATIA

Damascus

SYRIA

Tarsus

Antioch

CILICIA

Jerusalem

Sidon

Tyre

CYPRUS

RED SEA

BLACK SEA

Nicomedia

Heraclea

Byzantium

BITHYNIA

PHRYGIA

PHRYGIA

LYDIA

Sardis

CARIA

Pergamum

Abydus

RHODES

K I N G D O M   O F   T H E   P T O L E M I E S

Heliopolis

Memphis

Alexandria

Nile R.

Ptolemais

Danube R.

G E T A E

THRACE

MACEDONIA

Pella

THESSALY

AETOLIAN LEAGUE

EPIRUS

ACHAIAN LEAGUE

Athens

Sparta

AEGEAN SEA

CRETE

MEDITERRANEAN SEA

mose; indeed, they were less confined by the prescriptions of ancestral tradition inasmuch as they had entered the Near East from the outside. Native aristocracies disappeared or were shoved to one side; but no Greek aristocracy came in with the kings to serve as checks.

To help them in keeping their vast realms together the kings had three main programs, spiritual, administrative, and military. Spiritually the monarchs could not build upon any sense of patriotism, nor did they venture to follow Alexander's rather bold schemes for uniting natives and Greeks. In all cases, accordingly, they relied principally upon the positive support of Greeks, though natives who became Hellenized found the way open to royal favor; but in their effort to create a more general spiritual bond several royal lines, including the Ptolemies and Seleucids, came to deify their rulers as earthly benefactors and saviors. The ancient Near Eastern political ideal of kingship by divine right thus rose above the Greek ideal of the free citizen and passed into the stream of western civilization. Some Greek philosophers went so far as to justify royal absolutism in theoretical terms.

While local structures of government largely remained as they had been before, a developed bureaucracy was swiftly created as a second bond in each of the new states. The Greeks thus brought Hellenic rational calculation into the traditional society of the Near East. This administration used the Greek language, calendar, and principles of law; state finances were conducted with coinage on the Attic standard. Only in Egypt was a Phoenician standard employed, in order to isolate its internal economic system from the outside world. The kings were much interested in economic development, as we shall see below; and state control of commerce and industry went far beyond the relatively free principles prevalent in earlier Greek times.

Militarily the Hellenistic state-system rested upon Greeks and Macedonians. Each of Alexander's successors had cajoled into his own service as many of Alexander's veterans as he could. Thereafter the rulers sought to build up dependable forces of Greco-Macedonian background. In Egypt military colonies were dotted over the land; the Seleucid kings relied more upon settled clumps of soldiers who could be summoned in war; both sought to keep open avenues by which they might recruit mercenaries in the Aegean world. Natives could be used very rarely both because of language problems and also from the fear that they might revolt. During the Syrian war Ptolemy IV turned in desperation to native Egyptians and trained them in the Greek fashion (217 B.C.), only to suffer serious internal disturbances thereafter. In military and political respects the Hellenistic world was administered in a Greek manner, though under the control of absolute monarchs; and in both respects organization was more skilled and professional than ever before.

Beside the kings, the administrators, and the soldiers stood a host of other Greeks in most of the Hellenistic states, who set the cultural tone of the world and dominated its social and economic system. These Greeks came largely of their own accord as traders, artisans, scholars, and others to seek the economic advantages of the new, "colonial" world; but the kings welcomed them enthusiastically.

The Seleucid line particularly sought to build up a solid Greek framework in its far-flung domains and performed yeoman service in establishing Greek cities, either old settlements which were reorganized under Greek control or entirely new centers such as the capitals of Antioch and Seleucia-on-the-Orontes. In Asia Minor some 80 colonies were founded by rulers of various houses, and a dense network of Greek cities was built up in Syria. Both areas thenceforth had a Greek veneer down to Arab days; but other cities appeared in profusion as far as Bactria and India. The Ptolemies were more loath to upset the patterns of life they had inherited, and in Egypt only three Greek cities existed: the great capital of Alexandria, a façade for the country; the old Greek trading colony of Naucratis; and one city up-country at Ptolemais. In Egypt, accordingly, the Greeks lived in more scattered fashion but grouped themselves in religious, social, and educational units based on the local *gymnasia*.

The Greek cities of the Hellenistic world were at least as important as the kings and long outlasted the major monarchies. To the kings the loyalty of the cities was vital, for they were the economic centers and provided significant revenues to the royal exchequers. The local leading classes were heavily burdened to meet the king's demands and also to keep up the physical elegance of the urban centers. Nonetheless most citizens were deeply attached to their communities and preserved earlier Hellenic political attitudes at least on the local level. From the kings, in return for their support, they expected protection from outside foes and also assistance in maintaining their locally privileged position; when the Hellenistic monarchs eventually failed them in these respects, the Greeks turned to Parthia and to Rome.

Socially and economically Hellenic elements formed a dominant level over great masses of natives. In Alexandria, Antioch, and the great Babylonian center of Seleucia-on-the-Tigris alike, groups of relatively few Greeks constituted an upper crust much as did the English masters of Bombay, Singapore, or Hong Kong in the nineteenth century. Culturally . . . these Greeks clung to their ancestral inheritance, though they were willing to admit wealthier natives to their ranks so long as these men Hellenized themselves.

During the century following Alexander's death the Hellenistic world appeared remarkably prosperous. Alexander had put into circulation the great masses of silver and gold stored in Persian treasuries, so that prices rose considerably down to 270. The demand both for Greek emigrants and for Greek products, however, relieved for most of this period the serious stresses that had afflicted the fourth-century Aegean world. Abroad, the new Hellenistic cities were burgeoning in their first decades. Caravan and local trade supported many inland cities; Alexandria, Seleucia-on-the-Orontes, and other ports grew rapidly. Rhodes became a main clearing house for Mediterranean trade, which spread out northward via Byzantium and Cyzicus into the Black Sea and westward via Corinth to Sicily and southern Italy.

Within the Hellenistic heartland, which extended from Sicily to Mesopotamia and from the Black Sea to southern Egypt, the conduct of trade became ever more professional. Ships grew larger; harbors, such as the famous port of Alexandria with its lighthouse (*pharos*) nearly 400 feet high, were systematized; banking became more widespread. Items of trade included slaves from backward areas; Attic pottery, which was exported for a time more widely than ever before, such luxuries as incense, perfume, glass, art objects, and jewels made or processed largely in Syrian and Egyptian workshops; metals, wood, papyrus; and great quantities of wine and olive oil, largely of Aegean origin, and wheat from the Black Sea, Egypt, and Sicily. Rhodian jars which served as shipping containers for these latter bulk items turn up in numbers all the way from the Carpathian mountains of central Europe to Carthage and Susa.

Exploration and trade moved even farther afield to distant corners of Eurasia. In the west the daring Pytheas of Massilia just before 300 circumnavigated Britain, where he observed the long summer days and heard of a distant island called Thule (Iceland or Norway); Carthaginian adventurers reached the Cape Verde islands. In the east Patrocles, a Seleucid official, explored the Caspian about 285, and an ambassador of Seleucus I, Megasthenes, wrote a treatise on India. Trade in spices, jewels, and other luxuries grew between India and the west, partly overland through Afghanistan, partly by sea up the Persian Gulf (through the intermediaries of the Gerrhaeans) and around Arabia to the Nabataeans and to Egypt. The polyglot nature of this trade is suggested by a surviving contract drawn up on the Somali coast by a Carthaginian, a Massiliote, and a Spartan. Overland trade to China, though never more than a trickle, began in the second century B.C.

A notable characteristic of Hellenistic economic activity was the large part played in it by state machinery, especially in Egypt. The Ptolemies of Egypt inherited a centralized system of government, which went back to the days of the pharaohs. As far as possible they maintained this structure but animated it by dextrous application of Greek rationalism and bookkeeping so as to increase and garner the production of the peasants. The roads were improved; new crops and animals were introduced; the use of iron tools became common for the first time.

But all was regulated by the Ptolemies for their own benefit. In each village a secretary made an elaborate census of land, animals, property, and persons, which was consolidated on the nome registers and forwarded to the central administration at Alexandria. Each year peasants were directed what to produce and were issued seed grain for that purpose; at harvest time a marvelously elaborated system watched to ensure that they turned over their due rents and taxes. From tax receipts it has been calculated that no less than 218 taxes were imposed; and for each receipt the taxpayer had to pay a small sum in addition. Monopolies processed and sold oil, salt, wine, beer, and other staples at great profit, which was protected by high customs duties. The peasants had also to yield their own labor to keep up the canals and roads and to move the state-owned grain to Alexandria, where it was sold abroad to secure the revenues with which the Ptolemies assured their pre-eminent international position. No ancient structure ever surpassed the skill and complexity of this machinery.

From about 250 onward prices rose again in the Hellenistic world as international stresses and inflation grew more prominent, and by the end of the third century the great economic expansion of the Hellenistic world had drawn to a close. The Ptolemies could not heal the division between the exploiting bureaucracy and the peasants. The former learned how to defraud the king despite elaborate checks;

the latter reacted to their terrific pressure by dragging their feet and at times by scattered strikes. In Greece the conflict of rich and poor again became intense in the later decades of the third century. Overseas migration was no longer so feasible as earlier, and the countryside continued to be absorbed into great estates. Open civil war broke out sporadically, as in Sparta.

Politically the kings wore themselves out in incessant, inconclusive wars. The over-all pattern of Hellenistic history was one of ever greater splintering, as Alexander's unified empire yielded to the great monarchies and these in turn lost outlying districts. Between the international disintegration and the growth of internal dissidence the Hellenistic powers became too weak to maintain themselves against attacks by less civilized but more firmly united states from the outside.

Nonetheless the conquests of Alexander had been one of the greatest turning points in ancient history. The remarkable vitality of Greek civilization, which had earlier led the Greeks to throw out scattered colonies all over the western Mediterranean and Black seas, had reached such a level that under Alexander the Greeks and Macedonians overthrew the native political system of the Near East itself. In this tremendous expansion Greek intellectual and artistic leaders were inspired to a new wave of cultural achievements which had great effects on neighboring peoples from Rome to India. The Greeks, moreover, had set themselves so firmly in social and cultural mastery of the Near East that Hellenistic civilization survived the terrific political and economic unrest which beset the last two centuries B.C. . . .

When Alexander's conquests threw Greeks and Near Easterners into close and continuing contact, each side represented a quite different system of thought and art. True, all parts of the ancient world shared many fundamental qualities of religious, social, and economic organization; moreover, Greek development had been indebted to Near Eastern models since Neolithic times. Yet the existence of fundamental differences in outlook between conquerors and conquered was obvious to both.

The Hellenistic world, which thus represented a meeting of two major civilizations, affords interesting parallels to the modern contact between European and Asiatic cultures. In many subtle ways the conquering Greeks and Macedonians were affected by their entry into the Near East. They had, for instance, a broader geographical outlook and far more wealth than in the days of Pericles; and they were now under the political domination of absolute monarchs. But the Greeks borrowed directly from their subjects only to a very limited degree.

Hellenistic civilization was not a fusion of two different outlooks; rather it adhered to the Greek way of life, especially as this had been developed in the fourth century B.C. The values of Hellenistic culture, however, came to be expressed in a more urbane, polished, and superficial fashion. The leading thinkers of the Hellenistic age may be termed cosmopolitan, specialized, and professionalized. Often they were erudite to the point that only the intelligentsia of the age could follow contemporary poetic or philosophic utterances; for popular and intellectual levels tended to grow apart. Both levels, nonetheless, shared a greater interest in the individual human being and in the natural world enfolding him, and tended to speak in more emotional and realistic terms than had been true in Hellenic times.

As a consequence the bright and gay ideas of the Greeks were more widely attractive than had ever been true before, and the Mediterranean world began to come together as one unified cultural sphere. . . . At this point the Hellenistic bloom itself must be considered down to about 200 B.C., though to round out developments in literature, the arts, philosophy, and science we must at points go on into the second century.

The royal courts of the Hellenistic world were important forces in many aspects of art and poetry, but the main vehicles of Hellenistic culture were the Greek cities and schools. Wherever it was possible to do so, Greeks lived in cities or, at the least, formed separately administered corporations, called *politeumata*, in native communities. The cities were organized in the Greek fashion with council and assembly but at times had a royal governor in residence; they were commonly laid out on the Hippodamian plan, with central *agora*, rectangular street grid, temples, and walls. One excavated example, Dura-Europos on the Euphrates, maintained its Greek quality on down into Parthian and Roman times, though only 20 to 40 Macedonian families then persisted to form the upper crust.

The natives formed almost all the farming population and must normally have furnished the bulk of the city inhabitants. Yet this proletariat does not often appear in our sources; what we can see, rather, is the governing level, that class which exhibited Greek polish. Through its classical background this group inherited a fundamentally aristocratic spirit, but in many aspects of its life it showed a more bourgeois flavor than ever occurred anywhere

else in the ancient world. Economically men sought to live off inherited capital, which was invested in land, in shops and stores, and in slaves to provide the labor and day-to-day management. Socially the leading circles were selfish, materialistic, and firmly intent upon maintaining their privileged position. Individual families now lived more for their own pleasure, as against the claims of the clans, and limited the numbers of their children at least in the upper levels; women, too, were more emancipated in the Hellenistic world than in earlier Greek society. Since the city-dwellers were usually subject to the wills of monarchs, political interests tended to sink in significance as against economic outlets for their energy.

Nonetheless the Greek upper crust was of great social importance, as noted [previously], and remained strongly attached to its local cities. Physically it sought to beautify the cities with fountains, statues, *gymnasia,* and the like; culturally it supported the writing of local chronicles and poetic treatments of the origins of the cities.

Generally the local upper classes did not themselves travel widely, but they were continuously affected by ideas which seeped in via books and the more mobile elements of this wide world. Among the latter were doctors, artists, professional athletes, philosophers, and the international guilds of "Dionysiac artists," that is, repertory companies which moved all over the Hellenistic world under royal guarantees of immunity. Through patronage of these elements and through the school system the Greeks maintained Hellenistic civilization and did more than any other element to set its standards.

Primary schools had been known in the Greek world since at least the sixth century B.C., and the sophists had done much to make more advanced education a conscious subject. Now an integrated system of education became widespread, for schooling had two vital functions: to ensure that the young learned the Greek culture of their forebears and to meet the cultural needs of a more fluid, individualistic world.

Literacy seems to have been more common among rich and poor Greeks alike than ever before, but only the sons—and sometimes the daughters—of the governing classes could hope to go through a full course of instruction. Education was almost wholly private, though endowments were occasionally made and public supervision was frequent on the top level, that of the *gymnasium*.

From the age of 7 to 14 children learned to read, to write, and to count; physical education (in the form of individual competition rather than team sports) was a very important element. Instruction on the primary level was largely through rote memorization and endless repetition, and failure to do well resulted in physical punishment. Ancient educators showed little interest in child psychology, and teachers were a very poorly paid, almost menial element of society.

Those students who could afford to go beyond primary instruction studied from the ages of 14 to 18 under the *grammatikos*. Here they read and memorized Homer, Euripides, Menander, and other authors; learned grammar and composed moral essays; and studied geometry, the theory of music, and kindred subjects. The capstone was the *gymnasium,* where the future leaders of the cities, called "ephebes," spent a year or two in learning some military skills and maturing their sense of Hellenic solidarity. Even in Egypt, where the Greeks of the countryside could not live in cities, the *gymnasium* was a widespread focal point for the maintenance of ancestral moral values.

Hellenistic education was clearly designed to inculcate the fundamental virtues and skills of a governing class. Much of it was conducted in oral terms, both because books were scarce and because leaders needed the tool of rhetoric. Athletics were also fostered, though in an ever decreasing degree, as a means of promoting individual self-confidence and bearing. Vocational skills as such played no part; ethical training was, on the other hand, heavily emphasized. Above all this educational system was designed to produce deep acquaintance with inherited standards rather than to lead the young toward questioning experiment. For the most part the children who entered the Hellenistic schools were Greek by birth, but the more open-minded and wealthy natives could send their children through the same process of education, to wind up as new members of the Hellenized level.

Those able men who wished to become specialists went on after their formal education to study with leading philosophers, rhetoricians, doctors, and the like. Medicine was centered mainly at Cos and Cnidus; philosophy and rhetoric were largely studied at Athens and Rhodes. For many subjects the most attractive center was bustling Alexandria, full of opportunities. In this city flourished the greatest research institute of the Hellenistic age, the famous Museum, where scholars and scientists could hope to gain the financial support of the Ptolemies, and to use the botanical garden, zoo, and the great libraries of Alexandria. There were 2 libraries, called the Great and the Smaller; the former, begun by the Peripatetic Demetrius of Phalerum about 295, numbered 400,000 volumes in the third century. Libraries also existed in Pergamum and other cities, for Hellenistic learning was not focused exclusively in any one center.

Hellenistic civilization was not only widely based but also covered more varied fields than had ever before been cultivated. One important area of study, the results of which had much to do with shaping our own classical inheritance, was that of literary scholarship. Since the days of the Athenian tyrant Pisistratus, men had tried to establish the proper text of Homer, and Hellanicus had begun to coordinate earlier Greek chronology. Now, scholars became far more methodical, more numerous, and more influential; in the usual fashion of professionals they also engaged in amusingly bitter controversies with each other. Much of Hellenistic scholarship revolved about the great Homeric epics. The *Iliad* and *Odyssey* were divided into the 24 books which have been standard ever since, and successive critical editions of the *Iliad* by Zenodotus, Aristophanes, and Aristarchus, all librarians of the Great Library, were issued at Alexandria in the third and second centuries. The last editor, Aristarchus (*c.* 217–145), made a careful study of Homeric language and usage to determine the proper readings in disputed passages. Other men wrote commentaries and assembled antiquarian lore; one such work, analyzing the list of Trojan heroes comprised in 60 lines of the *Iliad*, ran to 30 books. Similar editing and commentary was devoted to Pindar, Hesiod, and other poets. Lists of the major works within each literary form were drawn up for the benefit of educators and the reading public; and those plays and orations not on the lists began to disappear from circulation.

Out of this study emerged a great mass

of bibliographical work, as by Callimachus of Cyrene (*c.* 305–240); definitive studies of Greek chronology by Eratosthenes of Cyrene (*c.* 275–194) and Apollodorus of Athens (to 119 B.C.); treatments of punctuation; and the first Greek grammars. The work of Aristophanes of Byzantium (*c.* 257–180) on *Analogy* defined the Greek declensions; Aristarchus isolated the eight parts of speech; and the latter's pupil, Dionysius of Alexandria, called "the Thracian," wrote the first extant grammar.

The products of the many Hellenistic scholars illustrate the backward-looking quality of its civilization, but their effect for the future was more than that of simply consolidating the achievements of earlier Greek culture. In their labors they created a basically rational and critical approach which was to underlie Christian scholarship and Biblical study throughout the Middle Ages and which was in modern times to spur the development of history and other humanistic subjects.

Not all writers, moreover, were content to comment upon the past; the era from Alexander through the third century B.C. witnessed one of the most remarkable outbursts of Greek letters. After the hiatus of the fourth century poetry again became a significant subject. Poets often took as their subject obscure mythological legends, especially of the unhappy love of mortal beings or a mortal woman and a god. These authors, who are commonly called "Alexandrian," sought avidly to strike out on new paths and to dazzle their cosmopolitan audiences by virtuosity and polish, though they could rarely speak deeply from the heart. Most commonly their product was learned and complicated in references, and was couched in hexameter or elegiac meter; prominent were the narrative *epyllion* and the terse *epigram*.

One of the most famous poets was Callimachus, whose *Aitia* (or "Causes") was a narrative elegy of the poet's inquiry of the Muses about early myths; other products of his pen were satirical *Iambi,* hexameter and elegiac *Hymns,* epigrams, and lyric poems. His bitter opponent, Apollonius Rhodius (born at Alexandria *c.* 295), was librarian of the Great Library until his retreat to Rhodes; Appolonius wrote a major epic, the *Argonautica,* about Jason's search for the Golden Fleece. This work was unusual in the normally cold pattern of Hellenistic literature in that the figure of Medea was sympathetically and romantically developed.

The third great poet of the third century, Theocritus of Syracuse (*c.* 310–250), was attracted to Cos and then to Alexandria. While he wrote *epyllia,* he was most famous for his *Idylls* or celebrations of pastoral life, which merged realism and romanticism and were written in a literary Doric hexameter. Other men versified discussions of the heavenly bodies and of weather signals, as in the *Phaenomena* of Aratus of Soli (*c.* 315–240); or treated of snakebites and their remedies and of poisons, as in the *Theriaca* and *Alexipharmaca* of Nicander of Colophon (second century); Lycophron (perhaps also second century) described the prophecies of the Trojan Cassandra in his *Alexandra,* which he filled with obscure references and words never found elsewhere. Perhaps the most appealing works of the age are its brilliantly polished, terse epigrams, which were eventually collected in anthologies. One of the most poignant, yet restrained, of these is by Callimachus:

They told me, Heraclitus, they told me you
    were dead,
They brought me bitter news to hear and
    bitter tears to shed.
I wept, as I remembered, how often you and I

Had tired the sun with talking and sent him
    down the sky.

And now that thou art lying, my dear old
    Carian guest,
A handful of grey ashes, long long ago at rest,
Still are thy pleasant voices, thy nightingales,
    awake,
For Death, he taketh all away, but them he
    cannot take.[2]

Besides the learned poetry there flourished a great variety of popular poetry, including ballads and realistic skits dealing with brothel-keepers, unruly schoolboys and the seamy side of life, as in the *Mimes* of Herodas (third century). Rising above this ephemeral work was the New Comedy at Athens, the greatest figure of which was Menander (342–291). Menander, who was a contemporary of the philosophers Zeno and Epicurus, sensitively observed the dissolution of old ways and beliefs about him and turned his observation into more than 100 comedies. These comedies of manners had love plots involving prostitutes, and parents and children at odds; the life they portrayed was materialistic, even brutal. Yet Menander had a sympathetic, keen-sighted view of the world; and many of his brilliant lines became famous quotations. St. Paul cited two of his observations, including "Evil communications corrupt good manners"; and one famous passage sums up his view of life[3]:

Think of this lifetime as a festival
Or visit to a strange city, full of noises,
Buying and selling, thieving, dicing stalls,

[2] *Greek Anthology* 7.80; tr. William Cory, *Ionica* (London: George Allen, 1905), p. 7.

[3] Paul, I Corinthians 15:32–3. Gilbert Murray, *New Chapters in the History of Greek Literature,* II (Oxford: Oxford University Press, 1929), p. 10.

And joy-parks. If you leave it early, friend,
Why, think you have gone to find a better
inn;
You have paid your fare and leave no enemies.

Very little Hellenistic literature survived intact to enter directly into the main
stream of western literary inheritance,
for not one work was adjudged by later
ages to be a real masterpiece on the plane
of the epic, dramatic, historical, or rhetorical achievements of earlier centuries.
Much of Hellenistic prose and poetry was

Hermes, by Praxiteles (?), c. 330–320 B.C. The relaxed attitude of this sculpture of the son of Zeus
with the infant Dionysus is in contrast to the pos-
ture of the Kouros (see pp. 119 and 125). The
Hermes group represents what critics generally
regard as a deficiency in several of the Hellenistic
pieces—affectation. The stylized pose and lyrical
yet artificial setting indicate a weakened artistic
commitment to the natural portrayal of the body.
(Royal Greek Embassy)

marked by jargon, obscure references, and a style which departed from the classic Attic models. Much, too, was superficial, for the age as a whole lacked deeply rooted standards. Yet, besides its weaknesses, Hellenistic literature also reveals the interest of its authors and readers in the romantic, the realistic, and the individual human being; these forces led to the beginnings of biography and romance.

So far as we can discern, this work was entirely Greek, both in language and in attitudes. Its polished urbanity and skillful technique made it, nonetheless, deeply attractive to men of Near Eastern background, such as cultivated Jews, and also to the Romans. Through translation and adaptation by Roman authors, indeed, Hellenistic poetry has had a wide influence on modern poetry, particularly in respect to meter and the use of mythological conceits.

The same qualities that stamped the literature of the era are also visually evident in its art and architecture. While the *polis*, the Olympian cults, and the aristocratic outlook—all creative forces in earlier art—were losing their powers of inspiration, the Hellenistic world yet inherited esthetic forms and a spirit from the fourth century which supported its own arts in new triumphs. The Hellenistic

The Victory of Samothrace ("Winged Victory"), early second century B.C. The goddess Victory (Nike) is represented here still partially airborne as she alights on the prow of a ship. The artist has captured the effect of the headwind for the entire statue, particularly the folds of the drapery, conveys an impression of movement against a powerful outside force. This is one of the earliest and most impressive examples of animation. (Archives Photographiques)

world, moreover, was relatively wealthy and had an abundance of patrons in the form of the absolute monarchs, the wealthier citizens, and the cities. The result was a vast volume of art and architecture that was technically competent, often emotional, and superficially attractive to neighbors of the Hellenistic world.

The creation of many new cities, supported by the wealth of the Near East, gave rise to a great volume of building. About the market places colonnaded porticoes called *stoas* were erected; one of the best known, which has recently been reconstructed, was that commissioned by Attalus II of Pergamum at Athens (*c.* 150 B.C.). The other civic buildings and port structures were built in a flamboyant style, richly decorated with a free use of color, and at times several stories high.

Sculptors took their line of departure from the naturalistic, emotional approach, which had evolved in the fourth century, especially in the workshop of Lysippus. His famous depiction of Alexander encouraged a more realistic, yet romantic treatment of portraiture, some of the masterpieces of which are the tiny portraits of the Hellenistic kings on coins. Beside royal representations stood symbols of the cities. One influential model of this type was the *Tyche* (or Fortune) of Antioch, a female seated on a mountain with turreted crown and the personified river god Orontes below, by the chief pupil of Lysippus,

Aphrodite of Melos (Venus de Milo), c. 100 B.C. This famous statue of the goddess Aphrodite shows an important characteristic of Greek sculpture: contra-posta (counter-poise). That is, instead of being erect and linear, the body is turned. The different positioning of the limbs creates a more natural, yet aesthetically harmonious effect. (Roger Jean Segalat)

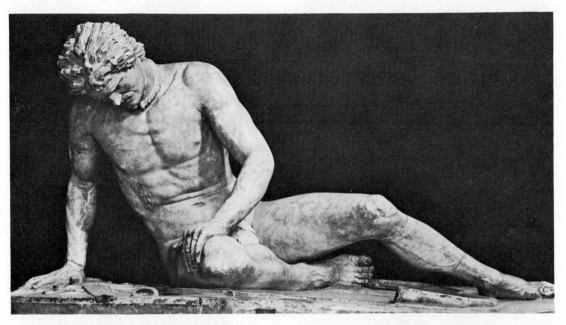

Dying Gaul (Roman copy after bronze original), c. 230–220 B.C. The pathos of the *Dying Niobid* (p. 147) is here conveyed more realistically. The Gaul struggles with pride and defiance against man's ultimate enemy—death. Though in anguish, he does not abandon his dignity and sense of self-worth. Death is portrayed as a concrete physical process, both attracting and repelling the viewer. (Alinari)

Veiled Dancer (said to be from Alexandria), c. 200 B.C. The *Veiled Dancer,* a bronze statuette eight and one-half inches high, is typical of works created for private collectors. The amazing feature of this sculpture is that when viewed from a variety of angles it gives a vivid impression of sequential movement. (Collection of Walter C. Baker)

Eutychides. Religious sculpture tended to be conventional, but two works in this field may be singled out. One was the bronze Colossus of Rhodes, representing the local patron deity Helios (the sun); created by Chares of Lindus, it fell in the earthquake of 225 some 60 years after its erection. The other was the statue of the god Sarapis, made by Bryaxis, which was the canonical representation of this new Greco-Egyptian deity.

Two of the major artistic centers were Rhodes and Alexandria; besides these appeared later a very influential style at Pergamum. In the late third and the second centuries the kings of Pergamum celebrated their victories over the barbarian Celts or Gauls, who invaded Asia Minor in 278, by erecting monuments at Athens and at Pergamum. The Great Altar of Pergamum, depicting the battle of Giants and Olympian gods as a symbol of the Pergamene defense of civilization against barbarism, reflected at once realism in its details and a highly emotional treatment of the conflict. Through the political and intellectual connections of Pergamum with Rome in the second century this style

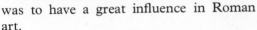

was to have a great influence in Roman art.

A great deal of Hellenistic art was modeled on a smaller scale for a citizen market. The beauty of the female body was now displayed in partly clad or nude forms, such as the Aphrodite of Melos and other statues, which were later copied en masse for the Roman market. These were, in part, designed for public display; but private homes could have small bronze and marble figurines. Some of these represented in brutal reality old fishermen and market women; others were purely decorative renditions of satyrs and the like. Those inhabitants of the cities who were too poor to afford bronze or marble could buy terra-cotta figurines, made at Tanagra (in Boeotia), Myrina (in Asia Minor), and many other places.

Wealthy burghers also adorned their homes with mosaic floors and painted walls; and gold jewelry and gems were made on a scale previously unknown in the Greek world. Poorer citizens could buy glass gems and gold-appearing bronzes; before the end of the Hellenistic age the blowing of glass had been invented for goblets, vases, and other objects. For all levels, from kings to simple folk, the Hellenistic arts provided graceful, polished products, even though the spirit animating this work rarely rose above a rather superficial blend of the romantic and the realistic, and reflected more the ephemeral and decorative interests of the age than the timeless, ideal quality of classic Greece. . . .

The Hellenistic world is an intriguing

one both in the complexity of its political organization and in the new flavor of its widely spread culture. This civilization was fundamentally Greek. Literary works were produced in Greek, albeit in the standardized *koine* dialect as a rule, and drew almost exclusively from Greek forms, poetic styles, and concepts. Art and architecture were Greek in idiom; so too was philosophy. Only in the sciences can indebtedness to Near Eastern knowledge be clearly established.

The Greeks of the Hellenistic world were influenced by the new environment, but that influence was displayed more in the scale and lavishness of products and in the tone of the era than in direct borrowings or cultural amalgamations. Even in the field of religion the Greeks continued to worship their old gods, though at times in a new spirit. The one cult of Near Eastern background which gained some Greek support, that of Sarapis and Isis, was cast in a Hellenized form by Ptolemy I.

Frequently, as one looks at the religious, philosophic, and political patterns of this age, one feels that the Hellenistic era stood as a preparation for greater changes to come in the Roman period. Its own attainments have rarely received high praise. In contrast to the great triumphs of archaic and classical Greece the works of the post-Alexandrian era appear, on the one side, pedantic and professionalized; on the other, overly romantic, emotional, and purely decorative. The audience of the age,

The Laocoön Group, first century B.C. An emotional force different from that of the *Niobid* and *Dying Gaul* is apparent here. A sense of the dramatic is evident in the artist's depiction of the death of Laocoön and his sons. The exaggerated dynamism of the group is characteristic of the sculpture of the Hellenistic era. (Hirmer)

which helped to set its tone, consisted not only of kings and their courts but also of a rather smug, conservative leading class in the cities.

Yet the products of the era were widely attractive at the time. Although there was no real integration of Greek and Near Eastern cultures into one new outlook, Hellenistic poets, artists, and thinkers created a remarkably pleasant and deeply influential set of patterns. This outlook was spread over a wider area than had been true of Greek culture down to Alexander; for many leaders were cosmopolitan and mobile, and natives were accepted if they became Hellenized. . . .

If one notices the dates of the greater Hellenistic thinkers and artists, it is quickly obvious that almost all of them flourished before 200 B.C. In every aspect the greatest bloom occurred in the century following Alexander's death; then the Hellenistic world declined politically, economically, and culturally. The student of this age must always keep in mind that it represented a thin, though powerful governing layer of Greeks (and some Hellenized natives) on top of a great mass of subjects.

Nonetheless the Greek element was tenacious and maintained itself under Parthian and Roman rule. In doing so it preserved and consolidated earlier Greek achievements; and after a long period of chaos Greek civilization was to revive in the peace and prosperity that eventually

Three Graces, Pompeii, early first century A.D. Some of the art works considered thus far are praiseworthy, others are vulnerable to criticism, yet all of the art of antiquity shares an unfortunate susceptibility to physical decay. The *Three Graces* is a case in point. (Alinari)

resulted from the Roman conquest of the Mediterranean basin.

During the Hellenistic Age the philosophical traditions established by Plato and Aristotle continued to attract adherents. Significant changes, however, were made in their original doctrines. In the Academy, for example, the Platonic theory of the Forms was given up and in the Lyceum Aristotle's successors seem to have become proponents of the Atomic theory.

Not unexpectedly the rationalism of Plato and Aristotle did not have any widespread appeal in this era, though the new philosophies to one degree or another drew upon their thought. What the individual—in this case, the intellectual —needed was not abstract knowledge but an ethic to replace that which had been provided by, and enforced in, the small polis-community. Though the polis still existed as a political unit, it no longer fulfilled its former moral function. The fourth- and third-century philosophies of Skepticism, Epicureanism, and Stoicism all arose to meet the needs created by the new cultural environment. All in one way or another were concerned with the good life, with the happiness of man and the conduct that would lead to happiness. They all, therefore, traced their descent to the hedonism implicit in the thought of Socrates. All had as their watchword self-sufficiency through self-control.

Hellenistic Philosophy
D. W. Hamlyn[4]

Before turning to the Stoic, Epicurean, and Skeptic schools, it will be well to note the existence before the death of Aristotle

[4] Reprinted with permission of The Macmillan Company from "Greek Philosophy After Aristotle," by D. W. Hamlyn in *A Critical History of Western Philosophy*, ed. by D. J. O'Connor, pp. 63–74. Copyright © 1964 by The Free Press of Glencoe, a Division of The Macmillan Company.

of movements that were influential in determining some trends in post-Aristotelian thought. The Cynics, originated by Diogenes (although the ancient world gave the credit to Plato's rival Antisthenes), and the Cyrenaics, originated by Aristippus, both thought of themselves as followers of Socrates. They both eschewed theory of every sort and stressed practice, the one proclaiming the virtues of austerity and self-sufficiency, the other those of pleasure. The Cynics made claims for the dignity of man independently of his ties to social conventions and laws (Diogenes was notorious for flouting even the most obvious conventions), and this led to a belief that men were citizens of the world, a belief that was to be emphasized strongly by the Stoics. As opposed to Diogenes, and despite what might be expected from his proclaimed views, Aristippus seems to have practiced and preached a sober way of life. He thought the pursuit of pleasure would lead to wisdom, and indeed be the only thing that could lead to it. Nevertheless (and in this respect he differed from Epicurus), he maintained that it was the pleasure of the moment that was to be pursued, pleasure that was not just the absence of pain. The wise man will practice virtue because and only because it will produce real pleasure. Diogenes Laertius quotes a saying of Aristippus to the effect that the advantage of philosophy lies in the fact that if all the laws were done away with "we should go on living in just the same way." However difficult it is to square such a dictum with the overt aims of the school, it is clear that the pursuit of pleasure was meant to lead to the observance of a definite morality. . . .

So much, then, for the movements that influenced one or another of the main schools which started around 300 B.C. The

Skeptics, originated by Pyrrho, did not, in all probability, constitute a formal school at first; but one arose later. The Stoa and the Epicurean school were teaching schools from the beginning, and Epicurus' school (known as the Garden because of its location, just as the Stoa received its name from its location) formed some kind of society for life. The Stoa was in many ways in direct contrast with Epicurus and was probably founded in conscious opposition to him.

EPICUREANISM

Epicurus claimed to be salf-taught, and he was certainly critical and even abusive toward those philosophers from whom he might have been expected to have derived something (he even denied the existence of Leucippus, the father of Greek Atomism). He lived an austere life and showed great fortitude during his last very painful illness. The society which he founded in Athens seems to have lived frugally, and there was in it a great stress on friendship. (Indeed, it has been suggested that the Epicurean society was the prototype of the later Christian society.) . . . Although Epicurus was a prolific writer, little of his work has survived, and apart from fragments, we are almost entirely indebted to the three letters and the maxims included in Diogenes Laertius' biography. . . . Epicurus' philosophy . . . , like that of other contemporary philosophers, was meant to teach wisdom, and the metaphysical view that he provided of the world, the gods, and the human soul was meant to be put to that end. Epicurus was attempting to provide a new kind of remedy for people's ills by giving a new view of the world. The new view was meant to show that there was no reason to worry about things, and thus the goal of all wisdom was *ataraxia*, or freedom from care. In a parallel way, the Skeptics taught that the only correct attitude to the world and its problems was indifference, whereas the Stoics provided a new conception of man's place in the universe with the same aim as that of Epicurus. The latter's recipe for men's ills can be summed up in the "quadrupal remedy" given by Philodemus: The gods have no concern with us, death is nothing to us, pleasure is easy to obtain, pain does not last long. But the only way to show this was to produce a metaphysical view of the world from which such conclusions could be derived. Hence Epicurus' system is a good example of a deductive metaphysics.

Epicurus had no interest in or knowledge of logic, but he prefaced his system with what he called *Canonice*—a theory of knowledge and methodology. In this he insisted upon the fact that all knowledge rests upon sensations (in common with other Greek philosophers, he failed to distinguish between sensation and perception). Sensations are the result of contact with a sense organ on the part of "*eidola*" —i.e., films of atoms given off by objects. Sensation is thus immediate and admits of no check (a fact on which he insisted). Hence it is useless to look for any other source of knowledge. He seems to have held that in some sense every sensation is true (although this has recently been disputed); but by this he seems to have meant that no sensation is corrigible in itself. Even delusions and dreams are "true" in the sense that a man cannot be mistaken as to what they are *of*. Hence sensations were for Epicurus rather like the sense data which some modern philosophers have invoked; and also like some modern philosophers Epicurus thought that the primary use of words should correspond to these sensations. Nevertheless, he did hold that it was possible to distinguish between veridical [truthful] and nonveridical presentations or appearances of objects, and indeed that we do in fact make mistakes in perception. He believed in fact that objects seen at close quarters produce clear and distinct presentations on which science must rely.

Knowledge, therefore, cannot consist only of sensations, even if it rests upon them. Epicurus makes clear that it also involves "preconceptions," a preconception being a sort of abstract idea built up in experience and stored in the mind in such a way as to be applicable to the objects of perception. Thus, on his view, perceiving consists both in the receiving of a sensation and its falling under a concept. Error arises in consequence from wrong expectations with regard to sensations. . . . Knowledge, then, depends upon sensations and "preconceptions," and although our sources sometimes mention feelings as a criterion of truth, it is clear that feelings were the concern of ethics and had nothing to do with the Epicurean theory of knowledge.

Because some things—for example, the stars—cannot be closely inspected, perception of them can never, in Epicurus' view, be clear and distinct; hence it is necessary for us to make inferences as to their nature and behavior from what we *can* closely inspect. But Epicurus is strangely tolerant about what he was prepared to count as a good inference in this respect. In the letter to Pythocles, and again in Lucretius, one finds catalogues of celestial phenomena with a variety of alternative explanations for each. Any hypothesis that seemed to be consistent with the phenomena was held to be possible, and Epicurus showed no inclination to speculate

further. He clearly had no conception of any canons of scientific inference or inquiry, and thought that all that mattered was that a hypothesis should be consistent with sensation.

Epicurus' tolerance with regard to detailed astronomical phenomena did not extend to his metaphysical principles. This has semed puzzling to some people, but it is less puzzling when the difference between his views on metaphysics and his views on science is seen. It is clear that his metaphysical system depended upon a series of primary truths, for which he attempts to provide some rational justification. These truths are probably twelve in number. . . .

Epicurus started from the common pre-Socratic tenet that nothing comes into being out of nothing or disappears into nothing; but he supports this dogma with arguments to the effect that otherwise there would be no specific causal history for each thing. In other words, anything could have come about in any way whatever, and also, if things went out of existence everything would have perished long ago. A further corollary of this is that the sum total of things is constant. Next, he states that everything consists of bodies and the void (the existence of bodies is obvious, and the void, he thinks, is necessary for motion). Some bodies are compounds, some indivisible elements—i.e., the atoms. The latter are infinite in number, and the void is infinite in extent. The atoms are in continual motion, falling with equal velocity through the void. . . .

The atoms vary in size, although they are never visible and never infinitely small. To prove the last point Epicurus introduces a curious argument to the effect that just as there is a *minimum visibile* in the case of perceptible things, so, by analogy, must there be limits to the divisibility of atoms even in principle. That is to say, the atoms are composed of minimal parts that are not capable of independent existence, and such parts are not capable of being divided even in principle, let alone in fact! The atoms also vary in shape, but not with infinite variety, for the shape of an atom depends upon the structure of the minimal parts. The third property of the atoms, that of weight, has already been remarked upon. It is responsible for the motion of the atoms but not for the velocity of that motion. Atoms possess no other properties, and all the other properties that ordinary things possess are secondary, produced by atoms in forming compounds. In this connection, Epicurus distinguishes between those properties which are permanent and those which are mere accidents. . . .

When the atoms collide they set up semistable systems within which the individual atoms rebound off each other, so setting up a state of vibration. . . . The compounds formed by such systems vary according to the density of the atoms—for example, in gases the atoms are dispersed, while in solids they are closely packed. It follows from this view that the identity of any object is given, not by the constituent parts (for these may change—atoms may leave the system and others may arrive), but by the *system* as a whole. Groups of objects form higher-order systems, the highest being a world, of which Epicurus thinks that there are an infinite number. Between the worlds, where the density of the atoms is least, are the gods, who preserve their identity, not because they are gods, but because, as systems of atoms themselves, they are least subject to buffeting there. They function only as patterns to which men may look. The worlds

themselves are always liable to perish, and new ones are liable to come into existence.

The grandeur of this scheme of things is obvious. Everything comes about as a result of mechanical forces. There is no providence, nor is there fate in any sense that implies retribution for men's sins. In this way, Epicurus provides a general remedy for the fears of men. There is nothing to fear, he holds, for both we ourselves and the gods are part of the nature of things; we come into being and die, and that is all there is to it.

This conclusion is reinforced by his account of the soul. He maintains that it is a complex of atoms like everything else, but in this case of very fine atoms which permeate the body and are held together by it. The main constituents of the soul are "particles resembling breath and heat." . . . Sense perception comes about when *eidola* (simulacra or images) come from things in succession and affect the sense organs and thereby the part of the soul that is in them. Epicurus gives a complicated account of the different forms of perception and the illusions to which we may be subject, but there is no space to discuss this account here. He maintains also that on occasion, individual simulacra may affect our minds without there being a succession of them to affect the sense organs, and this he adduces to explain figments of the imagination, dreams, and even visions of the gods. Nevertheless, the soul, being composed of atoms, is dispersed with the body when we die. Hence there is no possibility of life after death. Death, says Epicurus, is nothing to us; for after death there is no "us." Hence there is nothing in death to fear. This is the second aspect of his remedy for men's fears.

Epicurus' system of ethics is typical of

those of the time, in that it is naturalistic in the special sense that he thought he could indicate what men ought to do by appealing to a view of nature in general and of human nature in particular. The idea is that if it can be discovered what it is natural to do, then what one *ought* to do is thereby discovered. One feature of this belief is that the philosopher concerned is liable to write into his account of what is natural something of the ethical ideal that he wishes to advocate. That is to say, at a crucial stage in the account of what is natural, ethical notions are slipped in, whether intentionally or not.

Epicurus maintains that "pleasure is the beginning and end of the blessed life." This means that the attainment of pleasure is at least a necessary condition of the good life. This is true, as Epicurus stresses, even of the pleasures of the stomach. But is the attainment of pleasure a sufficient condition of the good life? The limit of pleasure, Epicurus thinks, is to be found in complete absence of pain, and it arises both from the satisfaction of desire and from the equilibrium subsequently attained. Because pleasure is a natural phenomenon it is in man's power to attain that limit; but it must be noted that pain must sometimes be endured in order for greater pleasure to result. For this reason, Epicurus says that the wise man will be happy even on the rack (although this view is given no other justification).

But at this point Epicurus begins to adjudicate on what sort of pleasure is to be pursued. He is not content merely to say that, the pursuit and attainment of pleasure being natural, the good life consists in its pursuit. For, apart from the general invalidity of the move from statements about what is natural to statements about what one ought to do, the view that we should pursue pleasure in general *because* it is natural would lead to ethical views other than those which Epicurus wishes to maintain. In other words, the attainment of pleasure is not in itself a sufficient condition of the good life. Not any pleasure is to be pursued. Epicurus maintains that pleasures may be natural and necessary, natural and not necessary, or neither natural nor necessary. The last kind of pleasure is to be eschewed and the first made the primary object of one's aims. Thus, although Epicurus has started from the premise that pleasure is a natural phenomenon, at the crucial point where the supposed ethical consequences are drawn, not all pleasures are allowed to be natural. It is clear that this last use of the word "natural" is at least partly normative, so that to say that Epicurus deduces what men ought to do from an account of human nature is not strictly true. To say that certain pleasures are natural is to say that they are at least permissible, not that it is human nature to pursue them.

It follows that the good life is not any life according to any view of nature, but the life according to the view that incorporates in its conception of what is natural the end to be sought. Epicurus' conception of the good life is a life of friendship without fear of what lies beyond. Nevertheless, in putting forward his view of morality, Epicurus was bold enough to set it against any conventional morality. One of his sayings is "I spit upon what is noble (i.e., what men call noble) and upon those who vainly admire it when it does not produce any pleasure." Whether or not pleasure is a sufficient condition of the good life, it is certainly for him a necessary condition. In a similar way he maintained that there is no such thing as absolute justice which has value apart from its conduciveness to the production of pleasure. Justice is the result of a sort of social contract, to which men adhere for the sake of expediency.

The Epicurean view of morality is not of the sort that is likely to have far-reaching social effects, and it is clear that, unlike Stoicism, Epicureanism had no widespread influence. It was a view meant to provide guidance and comfort for the individual or the group of individuals bound together by ties of friendship. The metaphysical view of nature, which is the essence of Epicureanism, was an austere one that possessed a certain grandeur, but not one that could provide an acceptable view of the world to ordinary men. In its approach to social affairs it was too negative. Nevertheless, it stands as a clear-cut example of a deductive metaphysical system with very explicit ends. The same will be seen to be true of Stoicism, to which it may be opposed. But the Stoa provided a conception of man's place in nature such that it was eventually capable of acceptance as a philosophical basis for Roman humanism.

STOICISM

The Stoa was founded in Athens, perhaps in conscious opposition to Epicurus, about 300 B.C., by Zeno of Citium; the most important figure was Chrysippus, who became known as the "second founder" of the Stoa. . . .

. . . Stoicism was a compromise between Naturalism in a radical sense and Cynicism; it was, in effect, a Cynicism made to fit a certain view of the world. This accounts for the fact that it embraced certain Cynic doctrines—for example, the man is a citizen of the world and that the law established by the wise man is universal, for all men. These aspects of Stoi-

cism in particular were passed into Roman thought and culture, and the school existed as some sort of entity until the death of the emperor Marcus Aurelius at the end of the second century A.D.

In their teaching, the Stoics divided philophy into logic, physics, and ethics, each of which was thought of as interdependent with the others (a fact which they liked to illustrate by means of picturesque analogies). For them logic was a part of philosophy, not, as for Aristotle, merely an instrument for it. Their season for this belief was that the wise man must know the principles of argument—i.e., he must know what reason is. Hence the Stoics were interested in logic as giving the principles of argument leading to conviction; they were not concerned with demonstration. The aim of logic, that is, is not to enable one to demonstrate necessary truths but to teach one how to be reasonable. . . .

The Stoic physics was a direct antithesis of Epicurean physics. In particular it maintained that the world was a rational entity, and that it was to be thought of as a continuum rather than as a jumble of atoms. . . .

It is form which makes the world rational, and as the world consists essentially of the interaction between matter and form, it is thus rational throughout. Form was given many titles—for example, God and intelligence, but especially "the seminal reasons or principles" which act as the soul of the world (*pneuma*). The world was thus looked upon as living and organic, not merely mechanical. Indeed, the whole point of the Stoic view of the world was to exhibit it as living and intelligent. The Stoics were rather ambivalent as to whether God was the creator of the world or the rational principle or soul of that world, and there were definite complications as to what happened at the periodic conflagration of the world which they believed to take place. If the world was destroyed and God was the soul of the world, what happened to God? Chrysippus took the view that at this time everything became soul, but in the context it is difficult to see exactly what this means, or how it helps. Nevertheless, the rational nature of the world meant that there was room for providence, and a Stoic notion which became more prominent with the later Stoic Poseidonius was that of cosmic sympathy, an acting together of all the forces in the world. . . .

In the details of their world-picture, the Stoics were reactionary; for they identified reason with fire and in general harked back to Heraclitus, whom they interpreted according to their wishes. Hence the emphasis on the periodic conflagration of the world, out of which a new world was thought to be born. God survives this, the whole process being a victory for God in that everything becomes soul (soul being, of course, fire)—a victory of form over matter. They did, nevertheless, attempt to explain individual phenomena in an interesting way, in terms of continuous processes. Thus, they thought that vision was brought about, not by the impinging of atoms on the sense organs as Epicurus thought, but by the movement of a continuous medium which extends from the object of vision to the eye. . . . The antithesis between their approach to physics and that of Epicurus—the antithesis between continuity and atomicity—has its parallel in modern physical theory in the antithesis between field theories and particle theories. The Stoics thought of the individual soul as corporeal because it acts and is acted upon. It functions as the unifying principle of living creatures—animals as

opposed to plants, on the one hand, and sticks and stones, on the other. It is to the physical body what the world soul is to the world, but *qua* individual soul it is perishable (although the souls of the good may survive until the conflagration). The Stoic psychology was extremely intellectual. According to it, the faculties are set under the controlling reason, and most aspects of the soul, including the passions, are therefore connected with kinds of judgment. Here again the effort to stress the rationality of everything becomes evident. Stoic physics is, in fact, the story of the working out of the principles of right reason in the world at large. It remains to be seen how this affects the individual, how it provides a way of life.

The Stoic conception of the ideal life was the life which is in accordance with nature, and regardless of whether this means human nature or nature as a whole, it does involve a life in accordance with reason, since nature itself was thought to be rational. The first instinct of man, the Stoics held, is self-preservation (not, as Epicurus said, pleasure); but with the acquisition of reason, man aims at reason. In consequence, the supremely wise man will aim only at that which is consistent with reason. For him only what is ideal will be good and only what is vile will be bad. . . . Everything else will be indifferent. It is somewhat difficult to see why if only what is ideal is good, only what is vile is bad. Certainly the one does not follow from the other. But this extreme view was one inherited from the Cynics, and it was perhaps taken over without much question. However that may be, the Stoics thought that virtue can be acquired, since, being a province of reason, it is a form of knowledge, and once attained it is never lost. This sense of virtue, however, is complete virtue, the possession of all the virtues; and at this level, all goods are equal and similarly all ends. For either you have virtue or you do not; there is no value in mere improvement.

This extreme view, inherited from Cynicism, was now given a naturalistic justification, in the view that such a life is according to nature. But even if it be maintained that nature as a whole is completely rational in some sense, it does not seem obvious that human nature is always rational, to say the least. The consequence is that there tended, in Stoic thought, to be a compromise between what was held appropriate to the wise man and what was held appropriate to the ordinary man. Hence it was maintained that among the things that were originally called "indifferent," some are preferable to others, perhaps because they were thought to be useful for the fulfillment of human nature in the ordinary sense. Thus Stoicism always tended toward a compromise between the extreme views inherited from Cynicism and their view of nature. . . . Nevertheless, there was, in the early period at any rate, a harking after the cult of the supremely wise man as well as an ethical view appropriate to ordinary mortals, and in consequence there was produced a sort of double moral standard. This can be most clearly seen in their account of duties.

"Duty" is not quite the right word to use in this connection (Latin "*officia*"), for the notion is more closely connected with what is fitting. Nevertheless, it is perhaps the nearest that the Greeks got toward the notion of moral obligation. In general, an action was thought to be fitting when it was in accord with nature, but ordinary duties (*officia media*) may be distinguished from the perfect duties (*officia perfecta*), which are appropriate to the wise man in as much as they are in accordance with complete virtue. The point seems to be that the completely virtuous wise man, who lives in accordance with nature as a whole, and not merely in accordance with human nature as, at best, ordinary men do, does not have to ask on each occasion whether his action is good—i.e., whether it is justifiable in terms of some principle. The ordinary man may live in accordance with moral principles but without the knowledge and insight that the wise man possesses; and in consequence he will not have complete virtue. The ordinary man is good in so far as he does what is fitting, but only in so far as this, and not to the extent that he has what Kant[5] called "a good will." To perform a perfect duty, therefore, it is necessary not only to do what is fitting but to do it with a good will; that is to say, what is fitting must be done *because* it is so, and that it is so can be seen only by one with insight into the ends of life. The wise man who has this insight will be completely virtuous, and whatever he decides to do will be right by definition, even if, for example, it means committing suicide.

Emotions were thought to be irrational movements of the soul, which are contrary to its nature in the sense that they are contrary to reason. Nevertheless, something cannot have an emotion unless it is the sort of thing that can be rational. In this context, the Stoics tended to run together different things—desires, emotions, feelings, etc.—but there is much in their general point of view that rationality and the emotions are connected. Because of this connection an emotion involves some notion of the immediate end to be pursued

[5] Immanuel Kant (1724–1804) was a German philosopher. [Ed.]

(for instance, greed is the supposition that money is good) and thus *a fortiori* some form of judgment. Emotions, then, are judgments opposed to those arrived at by reason in their erroneous conception of the end to be pursued, and as such they are to be eschewed. This results in the Stoic ideal of "*apatheia*"—freedom from passions. Only by such freedom from passions can the wise man be completely rational, completely free from making irrational judgments about things.

The Stoic views on politics are corollaries of all that has been discussed already, and are once again antithetical to those of Epicurus. Society, the Stoics held, is a natural phenomenon based on natural fellow-feeling, and justice is a natural virtue, being to society what cosmic sympathy is to the universe at large. . . . Generally speaking, in politics as elsewhere Stoicism was a compromise between Cynicism and the facts (or theories) of nature. In Stoic views on politics we meet with emphasis upon the royalty of the wise man, although with it goes the realization that existing states are by no means perfect. Nevertheless, the Cynic views on cosmopoly were given even greater emphasis by the Stoics, since it was argued that man, *qua* man, was part of nature, and as such could be viewed as subject to universal, and not merely local, law; hence he could be viewed as a citizen of the world. By the same token, the view that justice was a feature of nature led to the notion of natural law, and this became of importance when the Romans identified the *ius gentium,* the common law of nations, with the natural law. It was the Stoics too who handed down the notion of natural law and natural rights to the Middle Ages and later times.

All in all, the Stoic metaphysics pre-sented a view of the world entirely different from that of Epicurus, and in the attempt to show that the universe was a rational being writ large, the Stoics provided a picture of man's place in that universe as able to be in community with it. As a faith, this could well provide consolation, and indeed it did so for many people in the early Roman Empire. . . .

Like Epicureanism, Stoicism is of interest by virtue of providing a model of a metaphysical theory of a deductive sort, which sets out a picture of the world and seeks to derive conclusions from it. The specific arguments used, where there are any, are of less importance than the general outline of the theory. This is true of much of the post-Aristotelian Greek philosophy, but it is less true of those who must be considered next. For . . . the Skeptics . . . were critical in approach, and thus for them arguments were of great importance.

SKEPTICISM

Pyrrho, who founded the Greek Skeptic school, produced no overall picture of the world, and he was himself probably unsystematic. As the school grew, system grew too, and it came to be realized how little of a positive nature a Skeptic may say, if consistency is demanded. It was because this conclusion was reached that Hegel[6] rightly looked at the Greek Skeptics as the *truly* skeptical philosophers, and perhaps the only ones. . . .

Pyrrho is perhaps the only certain case of a Greek philosopher who was at all influenced by oriental thought; he traveled to India and talked there with the "Magi and Gymnosophists." He was reported to have been consistent in applying his phi-

[6] Georg Wilhelm Friedrich Hegel (1770–1831) was a German philosopher. [Ed.]

losophy to his daily life, with the result that he feared "neither wagons, precipices, nor dogs"! In much of this he copied Socrates, as he saw him, and he was anxious, like the Stoics and Epicureans, to provide the recipe for the attainment of human happiness. To this end, he thought, we should consider (1) what things are like, (2) what attitude we should take toward things, and (3) what we should do about our attitude. His answer was that it is clear that sense experience is contradictory in what it tells us of the world. Hence, we should accept appearances, but suspend judgment about their causes. For it is speculation about these that produces anxiety. The goal of this refusal to speculate is freedom from fear, and its positive result, silence. It is clear that here also the recipe is designed to cure a disease caused by a rival philosophy; it consists in the refusal to be dogmatic. . . .

It seems, therefore, that the Skeptics attempted to solve the problems that confronted Epicurus and the Stoa also, not by constructing a rival theory about the world, but by trying to show that any such theory involved inconsistencies. They were thus genuinely antimetaphysical in their aspirations, whatever their results. . . . They had, in a sense, no positive philosophy at all; they were merely critical. Their approach was intended to be therapeutic in the sense that as a result of it a man might give up the attempt to speculate or philosophize at all and content himself with the acceptance of what things appear to be.

During the Hellenistic Age science followed the same line of development as philosophy: first a burst of creativity and then stagnation. Again like philosophy, which was concerned with the practical ways of leading a good life, science was preoccupied with the practical and empirical. Thus, in both Greek philosophy and science the practical for the first time took precedence over the abstract.

HELLENISTIC SCIENCE AND MATHEMATICS
J. D. Bernal [7]

. . . The great contribution of Greek science to the science of later times was for the most part derived from the work in the early Hellenistic or the Alexandrian period (330–200 B.C.) and largely at Alexandria itself, the most important Greek city of the new empire of the successors of Alexander —the Ptolemies. Greek science was brought into direct contact with the problems as well as the technique and science of the old Asian cultures, not only those of Egypt and Mesopotamia but also to a certain extent those of India. And now, for the first time in human history, there was a deliberate and conscious attempt to organize and subsidize science. The Museum at Alexandria was the first State-supported research institute, and although its artistic, literary, and even philosophic production was negligible apart from its preservation of ancient texts, it contributed more to science than any single institution had done before and possibly has done since. The scientific work of the Museum, taken together with that of its ex-members and correspondents in the rest of the classical world such as Archimedes, was far more specialized than any other had ever before been or was to be for another 2,000 years. It reflected the isolation of the Greek citizen to an even greater degree. The

[7] Reprinted by permission of the publishers from *Science in History* by J. D. Bernal. Copyright © 1965, 1957, 1954 by J. D. Bernal. Published by Hawthorn Books, Inc., 70 Fifth Avenue, New York, New York.

scientific world was now large enough to provide a small, appreciative, and understanding *élite* for works of astronomy and mathematics so specialized that even the average educated citizen could not read them, and at which the lower orders looked with awe mixed with suspicion. This enabled the scientists to venture into complex and refined arguments, and by mutual criticism to make enormous and rapid advances. At the same time these advances were very insecure. The whole scientific effort depended on the patronage of an enlightened State. When that went the edifice of learning largely collapsed and, because it had no living roots outside the big cities, was largely forgotten, though it left a few vitally important writings to be brought to light again in the Renaissance.

The main trends of work in the early days of Alexandrian science followed those of Aristotle and his school. The Museum might indeed be considered as the Egyptian branch of the Lyceum, which, as it was better endowed, in a few years came to overshadow the earlier foundation. Strato, *c.* 270 B.C., the most generally competent of the Hellenistic scientists, taught both at Alexandria and Athens and was the last important head of the Lyceum.

The scope of research at both institutions did not, however, embrace the whole of Aristotle's vast programme. His own biological and sociological interests were not developed further except by his immediate successor, Theophrastus, who did for botany what Aristotle had done for zoology and who began a descriptive mineralogy which, though crude, was not substantially improved for 2,000 years. It was especially physics in its *astronomical, optical,* and *mechanical* branches that was

intensively studied. Instead of Aristotle's preoccupation with *logic* there was a rapid development of *mathematics* along Platonic lines. This was primarily concerned with the inherent beauty of ideal forms and the need to impress them on the merely observable world. Nevertheless it could be, and was, used on a lower plane to provide more exact astronomical descriptions and to reduce mechanics, pneumatics, and hydrostatics to exact sciences.

With ideal conditions for work, improved instruments, and scope for experiments, the cruder intuitions of Plato and Aristotle were soon left behind. Teleology, the doctrine of natural places and final causes, was abandoned, so was the Aristotelian theory of motion which made a vacuum impossible. Much of the atomic theory of Democritus, which the Athenian philosophers had so sternly expelled, was readmitted. To a great extent the first stage of the destruction of the philosophy which the Middle Ages believed to be that of the Ancients had been accomplished by the beginning of the third century B.C. Boyle[8] would have found himself in complete agreement with the views of Strato. But he was never to learn them. Except in mathematics the advanced thought of Hellenistic times was largely lost. The reason for this . . . was the effective isolation—social and ideological—of the scientists of Alexandria, Athens, and Syracuse. They were no longer philosophers. Strato, according to Cicero, "abandoned ethics, which is the most necessary part of philosophy, and devoted himself to the investigation of Nature." They therefore drifted out of the main current of interest, which in those times of crises and deca-

---

[8] Robert Boyle (1627–1691) was an English scientist who is generally referred to as the "father of chemistry." [Ed.]

dence turned inward on the inner world of the individual. Their advanced views were not propagated and, except in astronomy, where they were still needed for the more limited tasks of the time, particularly astrology, they were forgotten while the more common-sense and unscientific views of Plato and Aristotle were carefully preserved.

The mathematical and physical sciences were pursued in the Hellenistic world with two ends in view, the academic and the practical. The academic, which was of course the higher, was centred on mathematics and led to an extension and systematization of one branch—geometry. Numerical calculations were considered definitely inferior and were disguised as geometry when needed. But here solid and admirable results were obtained. Archimedes applied and improved these methods of Eudoxus to determine the value of π to five places—the practical squaring of the circle—and to find the formulae for the volumes and surfaces of spheres, cylinders, and more complex bodies. This was the effective beginning of the infinitesimal calculus which was to revolutionize physics in the hands of Newton. There was a great study of higher curves for the purpose of solving the classical and useless problems of trisecting an angle and doubling a cube. Of far greater ultimate significance was the elaboration by Apollonius of Perga, c. 220 B.C., of the studies of the conic sections—ellipse, parabola, and hyperbola—discovered by Menaechmos in c. 350 B.C. His work was so complete that it could be taken up unchanged by Kepler and Newton nearly 2,000 years later for deriving the properties of planetary orbits.

Even more important than their separate achievemnts was the systematization of mathematics achieved in Hellenistic times. Logical linking of theorems was known before—indeed Aristotle's logic is a copy in words of the geometrical procedure of proof. It was, however, not until Euclid (c. 300 B.C.) that a large part of mathematical knowledge was built together in one single edifice of deduction from axioms. The value of this for mathematics was considerable, as shown by the fact that Euclid is still in one form or another the basis of geometrical teaching. Its value in physical science is more doubtful, emphasizing as it did the superiority of proof over discovery and of deductive logic based on self-evident principles over inductive logic based on observations and experiments. The success of geometry held back the development of algebra, as did the very primitive Greek number notation. A partial exception is the work of Diophantus, c. A.D. 250, on equations. This work, which comes late, shows internal evidence of the influence of contemporary Babylonian-Chaldean mathematics.

The study of astronomy lay midway between the theoretical and practical. According to Plato it was the study of an ideal world in the sky, suited to the dignity of the gods that lived there. Any deviations which could be observed in the real sky were to be ignored or explained away. On the other hand the implied importance of the skies required that the position of the stars, and particularly of the planets, should be accurately known, and known in advance, if there was to be any hope of dodging the predictions of astrology. As a result of these two tendencies, Hellenistic astronomy—the only part of Greek science to come down to us without a break—was largely engaged in trying to make ever more complicated schemes fit the observations without violating the canons of simplicity and beauty. This pursuit encouraged the development both of mathematics and physical observation. It may be said that astronomy, almost up to our own time, was the grindstone on which all the tools of science were sharpened.

The mathematical basis of astronomy was the spheres of Eudoxus, but for actual working out it was easier to consider planetary motion in the flat and to save the appearances by introducing "wheels within wheels." This was done by the greatest observational astronomer of antiquity, Hipparchus (190–120 B.C.), who invented most of the instruments used for the next 2,000 years and compiled the first star catalogue. His planetary system, though more accurate, was far more complicated than that of Eudoxus and removed its last shred of mechanical plausibility. In the form in which it was presented by Ptolemy (A.D. 90–168) 200 years later it was to be the standard astronomy till the Renaissance. It was accepted because it removed all the difficulties from earth to heaven, where, after all, there is no reason to expect that vulgar mechanics would hold. Further, as it was made to measure—epicycles being added as required—it gave tolerably accurate predictions.

The alternative tradition, that it was the earth that turned, put forward by Ecphantus in the fourth, or perhaps by Hicetas in the fifth century B.C., had never been lost. It was powerfully supported by Heraclides of Pontus (c. 370 B.C.), who adopted the system of a revolving earth still in the centre of the universe round which the moon and sun turned, but with the planets turning round the sun and not the earth. This system, which completely describes what is observed, was later to be that of Tycho Brahe.[9] The final logical

⁹ Tycho Brahe (1546–1601), a Danish astronomer, was a major figure in the second scientific revolution. [Ed.]

step was taken by Aristarchus of Samos (310–230 B.C.), who dared to put the sun and not the earth in the centre of the universe. This system, however, despite the eminence of its propounder, won scant acceptance largely because it was thought to be impious, philosophically absurd, and violated everyday experience. It remained, however, a persistent heresy transmitted by the Arabs, revived by Copernicus, and justified dynamically by Galileo, Kepler, and Newton.

The development of astronomy made a metrical and scientific geography possible for the first time. The problem of constructing a *map* is one of relating the astronomic positions on a sphere, the imaginary parallels of latitude and meridians (midday lines) with the positions of towns, rivers, and coasts, as reported by travellers and officials. This is equivalent to measuring the *size of the earth*, which was first achieved by Eratosthenes of Cyrene (275–194 B.C.), a director of the Museum. The value he found for the circumference—24,700 miles—is only 250 miles wrong, and was not improved on till the eighteenth century. The conquests of Alexander had greatly enlarged the boundaries of the world known to the Greeks, but there they stopped—there was no economic drive to further exploration east or west, apart from a few lone voyagers like Pytheas of Marseilles (c. 330 B.C.), until the time of the Renaissance. The lack of interest in ocean voyages made it unnecessary to develop an accurate navigational astronomy, for coastal voyages could well enough be made with a very elementary knowledge of the stars.

Optics was also a minor appendage of astronomy. The Ancients never achieved a lens—their glass was too full of flaws and crystal was too rare. Their catoptrics—the study of reflections in mirrors—was developed to the extent of arranging illusions and burning mirrors, but had no serious use. On the other hand their dioptrics—the measurement of angle by sights—was used in accurate surveying. In spite of this they never seem to have realized true perspectives, which had to wait till the Renaissance.

It was in mechanics that the Hellenistic age furnished its greatest contribution to physical science. The first impetus probably came from the technical side. Greek workmanship, particularly in metals, had reached a high level before Alexander. Transplanted to countries such as Egypt and Syria, with far greater resources at their command, it could be used to effect radical improvements in all machinery, especially those of irrigation, weight shifting, shipbuilding, and military engines. We know that a great crop of apparently new devices appeared around the third century B.C., but their origin is still obscure. They may well have come from the discovery by invaders of traditionally developed machinery of local craftsmen, afterwards written up and further developed by literate Greek technicians. The mutual stimulation of accurate workmanship and precise calculation was to be observed again in the Renaissance. The compound pulley and the windlass may have come from sailing-ships, and gearing from irrigation works; but the screw seems a somewhat sophisticated invention. Some mathematician may have had a hand in it. On the demands of their royal patrons, philosophers were by then prepared to debase themselves by considering the mathematical design of machinery. Certainly all the legends of Archimedes' war machines must have some foundation, though Plutarch says of him, "He looked upon the work of an engineer and everything that ministers to the needs of life

as ignoble and vulgar." Archimedes (287-212 B.C.) was one of the greatest figures in Greek mathematics and mechanics, and the last of the really original Greek scientists. He was a relation of Hiero II, the last tyrant of Syracuse, and took a large part in the defence of that city against the Romans. He was killed, while working out a problem, by a Roman soldier who either did not know or did not care what he was doing. Though he was very much in the tradition of *pure* Greek science, we know from the chance discovery of his work on *method* that he actually used mechanical models *to arrive at* mathematical results, though afterwards he discarded them *in the proof*. For the most part his work was not followed up in classical times. It was only fully appreciated in the Renaissance. The first edition of Archimedes' works appeared in 1543, the same year as the *de Revolutionibus* of Copernicus and the *Fabrica* of Vesalius, and had an effect comparable with them.

In his *elements of mechanics* Archimedes gave a full and quantitative account of the working of the simple machines and laid the foundations of the science of *statics*, a characteristically Greek analysis of the conditions under which forces would exactly balance. He was also the founder of *hydrostatics*, the laws of floating bodies, which was to have two important uses. One was for the determination of the densities of bodies by weighing them in water; this, because it could be used for the testing of precious metals, was taken up at once and never lost. The other, the estimation of the burden of a ship, was well enough known by tradition to shipbuilders and was not calculated till the late seventeenth century.

One radically new branch of mechanics was pneumatics—the study and use of air movements. Here Ctesibius (*c.* 250 B.C.)

and Hero (c. A.D. 100) provided many ingenious tricks working by compressed air, mostly for use in temples. Hero even constructed a rudimentary steam-engine working on a jet reaction principle. A more practical development was that of pumps. In this the technical proficiency of the metal-workers produced double-acting force-pumps as good as anything that existed before the present century and cheap enough to be used even in remote Britain. Another pneumatical device was the water-driven wind organ with stops, operated by keys just as our own organs and pianos are.

The mechanical knowledge and attainments of the Hellenistic period were in themselves quite sufficient to have produced the major mechanisms that gave rise to the Industrial Revolution—multiple drive textile machinery and the steam-engine—but they stopped short of this point. It is true they lacked the prime material of that period—cheap cast iron—but they possessed all the means to make it, power-driven bellows were well within their scope. The decisive reason was the lack of motive. The market for large-scale manufactured goods did not exist. The rich could afford hand-made goods, the poor and the slaves could not afford to buy anything they could do without.

The mathematical-mechanical character of the science of the Greeks, together with their unwillingness to concern themselves with anything that would dirty their hands, prevented them from making any serious progress in chemistry, though the beginnings of alchemy and the key chemical process of distillation may date back to early Alexandrian times. Whether alchemy and with it scientific chemistry originated in Alexandria is still an open question. The first reliable writings, such as those of Zosymus of Panopolis and Mary the Jewess, come very late in the fourth and fifth centuries A.D. Any theory they had may have been affected by the influence of Chinese alchemy. The technical achievements of Hellenistic chemistry, on which the whole of modern chemistry rests, was due to improvements in glass blowing, needed for the still (ambix), and in the preparation of pure materials.

Little need be said about the achievements of the Hellenistic scientists, other than doctors, outside the field of the physical sciences. The impetus given by Aristotle to a complete study of all aspects of the universe did not last more than a generation. Only a few significant advances were made in the study of animals and plants though a beginning was made on books on practical agriculture.

It was in medicine, even more than in astronomy, that the social conditions of Hellenistic and Roman times favoured a continuity of tradition and even a limited advance. The rulers and the wealthy citizens could not do without doctors. Indeed the increasingly unhealthy life they led made them more and more dependent on them. The Museum encouraged much research in anatomy and physiology.

Herophilus of Chalcedon (fl. 300 B.C.) was a great anatomist and physiologist basing himself on observation and experiment. He was the first to understand the working of nerves and the clinical use of the pulse, and distinguished the functions of the sensory and motor nerves. Erasistratus (280 B.C.) went further and noted the significance of the convolutions of the human brain. Although most of the finest work of the early Alexandrian period has been lost in the original, the essence of it was passed on in the tradition and was incorporated in the vast production of the last of the great classical doctors, Galen (A.D. 130–200). He was born in Pergamum in Asia Minor, but after training there and at Alexandria ended by taking a very lucrative practice in Rome. He in turn became the fount of Arabic and medieval medicine and anatomical knowledge, and acquired a reverence and authority as great in his field as that of Aristotle. The doctors of later times, impressed by his range of knowledge and experimental skill, hesitated to pit their own observations against his. Indeed, the Galenic system was a skilful blend of older philosophic ideas, like the doctrine of the three spirits or souls, with acute but often delusive anatomical observations, largely because he was limited to dissecting animals. Galenical physiology, with its ebbing and flowing of spirits and blood in arteries and nerves, with the heart as the origin of heat and the lungs as cooling fans, still indeed lives in popular language. It was as much the basis of human belief about the little world of man—the microcosm—for over 1,000 years as Aristotle's cosmology was about the great world of the heavens. . . .

During the third century B.C., Greek creativity declined at an ever increasing pace. At the same time, however, the Greeks made the new Mediterranean power, Rome, their intellectual captive. Through Rome (and later through Christianity) the Greek heritage came to occupy a permanent place in the civilization of the West.

When people talk about our "heritage from Greece and Rome" they mean many things—literary, esthetic, institutional—from the Apollo Belvedere and the Corinthian column to natural law. But the core of this heritage is a set of ideas worked out by Greek poets, statesmen, and philosophers who prized moderation and the

". . . ordered life, and justice, and the long
Still grasp of law not changing with the strong
Man's pleasure."

The good life, these Greeks held, consists in an all-round personal development, in which every citizen best attains his own good by co-operation with his fellow citizens in the city-state. And at the same time that they were developing this secular ideal of conduct, these Greeks were developing a secular conception of nature as an orderly and regular process capable of being understood by men.

The chief weakness of this Greek ideal, from our modern view, hardly occurred to the Classical mind. That mind was too much accommodated to the institution of slavery, and too sure of there being radical differences in human capacity, to feel, as we today feel, that the restriction of the working out of this ideal to a small elite was unduly exclusive. What did occur to the Classical mind were, first, the problem of validating the ideal, of showing that the values experienced were really and objectively what the poets and the philosophers experienced them to be; and, second (and much later), the problem of adjusting these values, which were based on a city-state culture, to the vastly different social environment of the Roman Empire. Now, after twenty centuries, our modern society is passing through a strikingly similar period of intellectual crisis, world war, and cultural dissolution. Greek philosophy therefore has a special relevance for modern men. Both the questions that plagued the Greeks and the answers they gave as they sought to defend their cultural ideal have survived to this day.

Philosophy, then, was born out of the struggle to show how knowledge, and especially a knowledge of values, was possible. The earliest Greek scientists had been overconfident and facile. They had assumed that underlying the visible changes in nature there is a material stuff in process. The problem, they conceived, was simply to ascertain the nature of this material (was it water or air or fire?) and the stages through which it passes as it progresses (evaporation, silting up, and so on). It gradually became clear, however, that the assumptions on which this procedure rested were not unambiguous. What does it mean to say that something endures through change? What is the relation between the one real stuff and its many appearances? Since the various answers suggested contradicted each other, there came to be a widespread scep-

Left, *Aphrodite* (terra-cotta), c. fourth–third century B.C. (Metropolitan Museum of Art, Rogers Fund, 1923)

Right, bronze statuette, Edgar Degas, nineteenth century. "We are all Greeks," wrote Shelley in the preface to his play *Hellas*. His meaning is apparent when one compares the terra-cotta Aphrodite with Degas' statuette. The graceful bronze has its antecedent in the Aphrodite by an unknown Greek artist. Shelley, it appears, was correct when he further claimed that "Our laws, our literature, our religion, our arts, have their roots in Greece." (Metropolitan Museum of Art, Bequest of Mrs. H. O. Havemeyer, 1929)

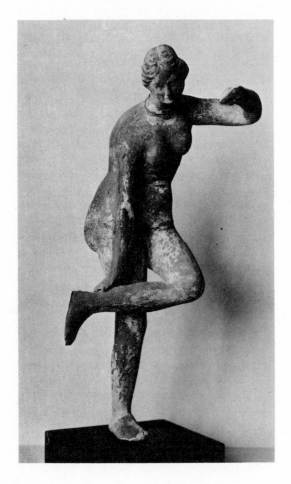

ticism about the power of reason as an instrument. And if one could not trust reason, what *could* one trust?

Meanwhile a parallel development was occurring in Greek thought about conduct. A new type of man had emerged from the changed economic and social conditions that had overthrown the old feudal nobility. The new-rich of the industrial age repudiated the old chivalric ideal of honor and loyalty, and "passion" became an excuse that justified every excess. Natural science had its repercussions on this situation. In a purely natural process what place was there for man as a moral being?

All of these currents of thought and feeling came to a focus during the prolonged world war that occurred in the last quarter of the fifth century, and as a result of the political and economic dislocations which that exhausting struggle brought in its train. Zeus had been dethroned and whirlwind was king.

Left, *Kore*, c. 530 B.C. (Greek National Tourist Office)
Right, *Mademoiselle Pogany III*, Constantin Brancusi, 1931. The works of Brancusi are solid and self-contained. Often identified with the movement in art known as constructivism (developed by the Russian Vladimir Tatlin), Brancusi wished to exploit the inherent character of the material with which he worked. Both the Greek sculptor of the head of the Kore and Brancusi wished to provide a sense of fluidity and implied movement in their works. (Philadelphia Museum of Art)

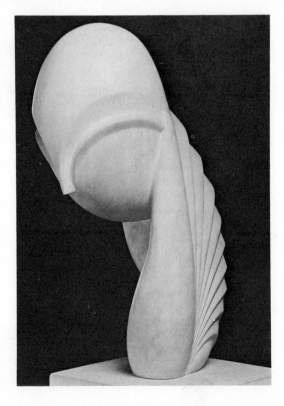

The central philosophical question, accordingly, was how to rehabilitate the old belief in the existence of an objective public truth cognizable by reason. To do this it was necessary to resolve those paradoxes about change, about the one and the many, and about appearance and reality that had led to the Sophists' scepticism. Two major solutions were worked out, each of which achieved a substantial endurance in the Classical period

Right, *Temple on the Island of Delos*. (Royal Greek Embassy)
Below, *Temple of Apollo,* an example of pop art by Roy Lichtenstein, 1964. The reference to Greek form and structure is apparent when one compares it with the ruins of the temple on the Island of Delos. (Collection of Mr. and Mrs. Robert Rowan, Courtesy Leo Castelli Gallery)

and has been a recurring influence on subsequent thought in the West. One of these solutions was Atomism, according to which the universe is a purposeless congeries of small material particles differing only quantitatively. The other was the theory of forms, first stated by Plato and subsequently modified by Aristotle. As Plato conceived them, forms were supra-sensible entities whose relation to the particulars of sense was incapable of clear formulation. Aristotle sought to avoid this difficulty by introducing the concept of individual substance, which he held to be an amalgam of form and matter, of achievement and possibility. Despite great differences in emphasis, both versions of the theory of forms held the universe to be a purposive system, and both insisted on the importance and reality of qualitative differences.

All of these philosophers also sought to provide a new rationale (long-range happiness) to replace the exploded religious myths which had once provided a sanction for socially oriented conduct. Unfortunately, in the time of troubles following the dissolution of Alexander's abortive empire, men began to abandon hope for an active life of all-round development and public achievement, and to fall back on negative ideals of apathy and passivity. Though the emergence of the Roman imperium for a time halted the collapse of Classical culture and enabled the Stoics to develop a social theory which wove together strands from both the old and the new points of view, it too met with disaster. As the barbarian hordes overran the ordered life of the West, the old Classical poise and self-assurance vanished and men came more and more to lean on a greater-than-man.

But though this Greek belief in self-sufficiency thus disappeared for centuries, it proved astonishingly resilient. It was revived about five centuries ago, and even in the complex, interdependent societies of the twentieth century it remains an ideal that haunts the West. And, while our modern emphasis is less on contemplation as an end in itself than on knowledge as an instrument for changing the world, our notion of the universe is essentially secular and natural like the Greeks.' The idea of science and the idea of man are our greatest heritage from Greece and Rome.

SUGGESTIONS FOR FURTHER READING

The following select bibliography is intended for the student who wishes to follow up points raised by his reading. It does not include all of the works cited in the text. Therefore students should also consult the footnotes. Much more comprehensive bibliographies are included in the general historical works cited below. Books available in paperback are marked with an asterisk.

Reference Works
The American Historical Association Guide to Historical Literature. New York, The Macmillan Company, 1961.
Cary, Max, *The Geographic Background of Greek and Roman History*. Oxford, Clarendon Press, 1949.
————, and others, *The Oxford Classical Dictionary*. Oxford, Clarendon Press, 1949.
Edwards, Paul, ed., *The Encyclopedia of Philosophy*. New York, The Macmillan Company and The Free Press, 1967.
Platnauer, M., ed., *Fifty Years of Classical Scholarship*. New York, Oxford University Press, 1954.
Sills, David L., ed., *International Encyclopedia of the Social Sciences*. New York, The Macmillan Company, 1968.
van der Heyden, A. A. M., and H. H. Scullard, *Atlas of the Classical World*. London, Nelson Publishing Company, 1959.

General Works
Adkins, Arthur W. H., *Merit and Responsibility: A Study in Greek Values*. Oxford, Clarendon Press, 1960.
Andrewes, Antony, *The Greeks*. New York, Alfred A. Knopf, 1967.
Bonner, R. J., and G. Smith, *The Administration of Justice from Homer to Aristotle* (2 Vols.). Chicago, University of Chicago Press, 1930–1938.
*Bowra, C. M., *The Greek Experience*. Cleveland, World Publishing Company, 1957.
*Burn, A. R., *The Pelican History of Greece*. Baltimore, Penguin Books Inc., 1965.
Bury, J. B., *History of Greece,* 3d ed. rev. by R. Meiggs. New York, The Macmillan Company, 1951.

The Cambridge Ancient History, Vols. III–VII. New York, Cambridge University Press, 1923–1939. A new edition is now in preparation.

*Dickinson, G. Lowes, *The Greek View of Life.* Ann Arbor, University of Michigan Press, 1958.

*Dodds, E. R., *The Greeks and the Irrational.* Berkeley and Los Angeles, University of California Press, 1951.

*Ehrenberg, Victor, *The Greek State,* rev. ed. New York, Barnes & Noble, 1969.

*Finley, John H., Jr., *Four Stages of Greek Thought.* Stanford, Calif., Stanford University Press, 1966.

*Finley, M. I., *The Ancient Greeks: An Introduction to Their Life and Thought.* New York, Viking Press, 1963.

*Forrest, W. G., *The Emergence of Greek Democracy.* New York, McGraw-Hill Book Company, 1966.

Glotz, Gustave, *The Greek City and Its Institutions,* trans. by N. Mallinson. New York: Barnes & Noble, 1965.

Greene, W. C., *Moira: Fate, Good, and Evil in Greek Thought.* Cambridge, Mass., Harvard University Press, 1944.

Hammond, N. G. L., *History of Greece to 322 B.C.,* 2d ed. Oxford, Clarendon Press, 1962.

Heichelheim, F. W., *An Economic History of the Ancient World* (3 Vols.). New York, Humanities Press, 1964–1966.

Jaeger, Werner, *Paideia: The Ideals of Greek Culture,* trans. from the second German edition by Gilbert Highet (3 Vols.). New York, Oxford University Press, 1939–1945.

Jones, J. W., *The Law and Legal Theory of the Greeks.* New York, Oxford University Press, 1956.

*Kitto, H. D. F., *The Greeks.* Baltimore, Penguin Books Inc., 1951.

*Lloyd-Jones, H., ed., *The Greek World.* Baltimore, Penguin Books Inc., 1961.

Onians, Richard Broxton, *The Origins of European Thought about the Body, the Mind, the Soul, the World, Time, and Fate.* New York, Cambridge University Press, 1954.

*Snell, Bruno, *The Discovery of the Mind: The Greek Origins of European Thought,* trans. by T. G. Rosenmeyer. Cambridge, Mass., Harvard University Press, 1953.

Voegelin, Eric, *Order and History.* New Orleans, Louisiana State University Press, 1956–1957.

Mycenaean Greece, The Dark Ages, and Homer
*Finley, M. I., *The World of Odysseus.* New York, Viking Press, 1954.

Gordon, C. H., *The Common Background of Greek and Hebrew Civilizations.* London, Collins, 1962.

Kirk, Geoffrey S., ed., *The Language and Background of Homer: Some Recent Studies and Controversies.* New York, Barnes & Noble, 1964.

Mylonas, G. E., *Mycenae and the Mycenaean Age.* Princeton, N.J., Princeton University Press, 1966.

*Page, Denys, *History and the Homeric Iliad.* Berkeley, University of California Press, 1959.

*Samuel, Alan E., *Mycenaeans in History.* Englewood Cliffs, N.J., Prentice-Hall, 1965.

Starr, Chester G., *The Origins of Greek Civilization, 1100–650 B.C.* New York, Alfred A. Knopf, 1961.

Greek Religion

*Grant, Michael, *Myths of the Greeks and Romans.* New York, World Publishing Company, 1965.

*Guthrie, W. K. C., *The Greeks and Their Gods.* Boston, Beacon Press, 1968.

*Nilsson, Martin P., *A History of Greek Religion,* 2d ed., trans. by F. J. Fielden. New York, Oxford University Press, 1949.

*Oswalt, Sabine G., *Concise Encyclopedia of Greek and Roman Mythology.* Chicago, Follett Publishing Company, 1969.

*Rose, H. J., *Handbook of Greek Mythology,* 6th ed. New York, Dutton, 1960.

*———, *Religion in Greece and Rome.* London, Hutchinson and Company, 1946.

Archaic Age

*Andrewes, Antony, *The Greek Tyrants.* London, Hutchinson, 1966.

Burn, A. R., *The Lyric Age of Greece.* New York, St. Martin's, 1961.

———, *The World of Hesiod.* New York, E. P. Dutton & Co., 1937.

Ehrenberg, Victor, *From Solon to Socrates: Greek Civilization During the Sixth and Fifth Centuries.* New York, Barnes & Noble, 1968.

Woodhouse, W. J., *Solon the Liberator.* New York, Oxford University Press, 1938.

Greek Science

*Claggett, Marshall, *Greek Science in Antiquity.* London, Abelard-Schuman Ltd., 1957.

*Cornford, F. M., *Before and After Socrates.* New York, Cambridge University Press, 1932.

*———, *Principium Sapientiae: A Study of the Origins of Greek Philosophical Thought.* New York, Cambridge University Press, 1952.

*Farrington, B., *Greek Science.* Baltimore, Penguin Books Inc., 1953.

*Kirk, Geoffrey, *The Pre-Socratic Philosophers: A Critical History with a Collection of Texts.* New York, Cambridge University Press, 1957.

*Sambursky, S., *The Physical World of the Greeks*. New York, Humanities Press, 1956.

Greek Art
*Boardman, John, *Greek Art*. New York, Frederick A. Praeger, 1964.
*Bowra, Sir Cecil M., *Ancient Greek Literature*. New York, Oxford University Press, 1960.
Lesky, A., *A History of Greek Literature,* English translation of the 2d ed. by James Willis and Cornelius De Heer. New York, Crowell, 1966.
Marinatos, S., *Crete and Mycenae*. New York, Abrams, 1960.
Matz, F., *The Art of Crete and Early Greece*. New York, Crown, 1962.
Oates, W. J., ed., *From Sophocles to Picasso: The Present-Day Vitality of the Classical Tradition*. Bloomington, Indiana University Press, 1962.
Strong, Donald, *The Classical World*. New York, McGraw-Hill Book Company, 1965.

Fifth-Century Greece
Most of the general histories cited in the opening section of the bibliography treat this period in some detail.
Burns, A. R., *Pericles and Athens*. New York, Collier Books, 1962.
———, *Persia and the Greeks*. New York, St. Martin's, 1962.
*Ehrenberg, Victor, *From Solon to Socrates: Greek History and Civilization During the Sixth and Fifth Centuries*. New York, Barnes & Noble, 1968.
*Finley, John H., Jr., *Thucydides*. Ann Arbor, University of Michigan Press, 1963.
Hignett, C., *The Athenian Constitution*. New York, Oxford University Press, 1952.
Jones, A. H. M., *Athenian Democracy*. New York, Norton, 1965.
*Michell, H., *Sparta*. New York, Cambridge University Press, 1952.
*Zimmern, A. E., *The Greek Commonwealth*. New York, Oxford University Press, 1961.

The Hellenistic Age
Bury, J. B. and others, *The Hellenistic Age*. New York, Cambridge University Press, 1925.
Cary, Max, *A History of the Greek World from 323 to 146 B.C.* New York, Barnes & Noble, 1959.
Griffith, G. T., ed., *Alexander the Great: The Main Problems*. New York, Barnes & Noble, 1966.
Rostovtzeff, M., *Social and Economic History of the Hellenistic World*. New York, Oxford University Press, 1941.
Snyder, J. W., *Alexander the Great*. New York, Twayne, 1966.

*Tarn, W. W., *Hellenistic Civilization,* 3d ed. (rev. with G. T. Griffith). London, E. Arnold & Co., 1952.

Greek Philosophy

Bailey, Cyril, *The Greek Atomists and Epicurus.* New York, Russell & Russell, 1964.

*Cornford, F. M., *Before and After Socrates.* New York, Cambridge University Press, 1932.

———, *Principium Sapientiae: A Study of the Origins of Greek Philosophical Thought.* New York, Cambridge University Press, 1952.

*DeWitt, Norman Wentworth, *Epicurus and His Philosophy.* Minneapolis, University of Minnesota Press, 1954.

Farrington, Benjamin, *The Faith of Epicurus.* New York, Basic Books, 1967.

Festugière, André Marie Jean, *Epicurus and His Gods.* Cambridge, Mass., Harvard University Press, 1956.

*Grene, Marjorie, *A Portrait of Aristotle.* Chicago, University of Chicago Press, 1963.

*Grube, G. M. A., *Plato's Thought.* Boston, Beacon Press, 1958.

Guthrie, W. K. C., *A History of Greek Philosophy* (3 Vols.). New York, Cambridge University Press, 1962–1969.

*———, *The Greek Philosophers: From Thales to Aristotle.* London, Methuen and Company, 1950.

*Jaeger, Werner, *Aristotle,* 2d ed. Oxford, Clarendon Press, 1948.

*Kirk, Geoffrey S. and J. E. Raven, *The Pre-Socratic Philosophers: A Critical History with a Collection of Texts.* New York, Cambridge University Press, 1957.

Mure, G. R. G., *Aristotle.* New York, Oxford University Press, 1964.

*Randall, John Herman, Jr., *Aristotle.* New York, Columbia University Press, 1960.

*Raven, J. E., *Plato's Thought in the Making.* New York, Cambridge University Press, 1964.

*Ross, W. D., *Aristotle,* 5th ed. New York, Barnes & Noble, 1960.

Shorey, Paul, *Platonism Ancient and Modern.* Berkeley, University of California Press, 1938.

*———, *What Plato Said.* Chicago, University of Chicago Press, 1933.

*Taylor, A. E., *Plato: The Man and His Work.* New York, Dial Press, 1936.

———, *Socrates.* New York, Doubleday, 1952.

Wenley, Robert M., *Stoicism and Its Influence.* Boston, Cooper Square, 1930.

Zeller, Eduard, *Stoics, Epicureans and Sceptics,* rev. ed. New York, Russell & Russell, 1962 (originally published in 1880).